THE MUNDAS AND THEIR COUNTRY

THE MUNDAS AND
THEIR COUNTRY

SARAT CHANDRA ROY, M. A., B. L.

ASIA PUBLISHING HOUSE

NEW YORK

DS
432
M8
R6
1970

SBN 210.33988.8

PRINTED IN INDIA

BY N. M. PARWAL AT BINANI PRINTERS, 38, STRAND ROAD.
CALCUTTA - 1 AND BY R. BHATTACHARYA AT THE PRINTMAN (INDIA),
101 BAITHAKKHANA ROAD, CALCUTTA - 9 AND PUBLISHED BY P.S.
JAYASINGHE, ASIA PUBLISHING HOUSE, INC. AT 118E 59th STREET,
NEW YORK, NY 10022

FOREWORD

SARAT CHANDRA ROY was born on November 4, 1871, and died at Ranchi on April 30, 1942. He received his education in Calcutta and obtained his M.A. degree in English in 1893 from the General Assembly Institution. After taking his B.L. degree in 1895, he started practice in Alipore, 24 Parganas, in 1897. The next year he moved over to Ranchi where he was able to build up a successful legal career.

The Munda people were at that time passing through severe hardships on account of heavy encroachments into their customary rights over land. This led Sarat Chandra Roy to champion their cause and become deeply interested in the history of their land system as well as in their customary social and religious practices and beliefs. The result of his studies appeared in 1912 in the shape of a monograph entitled *The Mundas and Their Country*. Its publication immediately attracted the attention of anthropologists all over the world.

The distinctive feature of the book lay in the combination which Roy had been able to achieve between pure ethnography and history. The book has, moreover, been regarded as authoritative in the High Courts of Judicature in Calcutta and Patna in so far as the rights of the Munda tribe are concerned.

Unfortunately, *The Mundas and Their Country* has not been available in the market for a very long time, although it has always been regarded as a classic in Indian ethnography. I am thankful to Asia Publishing House for making it available to the reading public.

15 February 1968   NIRMAL KUMAR BOSE
37A, Bosepara Lane
Calcutta-3

PREFACE

THE object of this book is to supply the want of a history and ethnography of one of the most interesting of Chotānāgpūr tribes. A history of the Mūndās is practically a history of the district they inhabit. Unfortunately, however, it is only from the beginning of British rule that we have perfectly reliable materials for a history of the people and their country. Of the importance of that history, Colonel Dalton in his *Descriptive Ethnology of Bengal* writes :

It cannot but be of moment to Indian statesmen and administrators to have, when dealing with such a people, a clear understanding of the nature of our relations with them, since they and the officers of the British Government first met, to possess an account sufficiently in detail of the circumstances under which they have been found so frequently in an attitude of hostility to a Government that certainly has no prejudices against them, but on the contrary is inclined to treat them with favour bordering on partiality.

If the political history of the Mundas and their country is of such interest to the statesman and the administrator, the ethnography of the people is of no less interest to the anthropologist and the sociologist.

I am painfully conscious that the present account is exceedingly imperfect. The greater portion of this book originally appeared as magazine articles written in the intervals of business. This will partly account for some of the many defects which will doubtless be noticed in the book. If, however, the information conveyed in these pages is found to be of any practical use and serves to attract more competent workers to the field, it will not have been written in vain.

My most grateful acknowledgements are due to Mr. E.A. Gait, I.C.S., C.I.E., not only for the Introduction he has so kindly written for the book but also for having kindly looked through the book as it was passing through the press and making several valuable suggestions for its improvement. To the Rev. Father J. Hoffmann, an acknowledged authority on the Mundas, I am indebted for much valuable advice and for the trouble he very kindly took in revising the proof-sheets of the chapters on Ethnography (Chap. VI) and Land Tenures (App. III). My sincere thanks are due to Mr. T. S. Macpherson, M.A., I.C.S., for some valuable suggestions, and to Mr. J. Reid, I.C.S., late Settlement Officer of Chotanagpur, for having kindly supplied me with the statistics for my chapter on Land Tenures. I am under great obligation to Mr. H. J. McIntosh, I. C. S., Commissioner of the Chotanagpur Division, Mr. D. H. Kingsford, I.C.S., Judicial Commissioner of Chotanagpur, and Mr. W. B. Thomson, I.C.S., Deputy Commissioner of Ranchi (on leave), for having kindly permitted me access to several old records in their respective offices. To the Rev. Dr. A. Nottrott, D. D., of the Chotanagpur German Mission, the Rev. Father Van Hoeck, S. J., of the Chotanagpur Catholic Mission, and the Rev. H. Whitley, B.A., of the Ranchi Anglican Mission, I gratefully acknowledge my indebtedness for several items of information regarding their respective missions. I am further indebted to these three reverend gentlemen as also to some Indian friends for most of the illustrations of the book.

Ranchi
March 14, 1912   S. C. R.

CONTENTS

INTRODUCTION

BABU Sarat Chandra Roy has asked me to write an introduction to his book on the Mundas, and I comply with much pleasure. The author is one of the few persons, other than missionaries, who can speak the language of the Mundas ; and he is well acquainted with their manners and customs. When I was Commissioner of Chotanagpur, the settlement of the Munda country was drawing to a close, and I had to decide, on appeal, numerous disputes connected with their peculiar land tenures. The majority of these disputes were between the Mundas and alien landlords on their creatures. In almost all these cases, the author appeared as the sturdy champion of the Mundas. In this country, which contains so many primitive tribes, possessing peculiar rites and customs of the greatest anthropological interest, it has long been a reproach to educated Indians that the task of collecting information regarding them has been left almost entirely to Europeans. It is, therefore, all the more satisfactory that Babu Sarat Chandra Roy should have devoted his leisure to a study of the Munda tribe.

In the earlier portion of his book, the author makes some speculations regarding the original abode and wanderings of the Mundas before they reached their present home in the Chotanagpur plateau ; but it is not until comparatively recent times that we have any real information regarding them. They were then already settled in Chotanagpur. The whole country was parcelled out into groups of villages or *pattis*. Each village was occupied by the descendants of the family by whom the land was originally cleared ; and their rights in it were unquestioned. The headman of a *patti* or group of villages was known as the *Manki*. The Mundas already acknowledged the supremacy of a Raja ; but their allegiance sat very lightly on their shoulders. They were liable to military service in time of war and furnished the Raja with limited supplies for his household and court. The holders of each village also paid him a small quit-rent, which was fixed in perpetuity and was collected on his behalf by the *Manki*. The troubles of the Mundas began when their Raja was converted to Hinduism and gradually brought in from Bihar a crowd of hangers-on of all kinds, whose services he rewarded, or whose goods he paid for, by the transfer of his rights over various villages. The new landlords set themselves to exact as much as possible from the villagers, and to oust from their lands and replace by low-caste cultivators from Bihar those who resisted their demands. This struggle between the aboriginal cultivators on the one side and the alien landlords and their creatures on the other has continued unceasingly. The story is well told in the following pages of the oppressions to which the Mundas were subjected, of their periodic savage risings, and of the measures which have been taken in recent times to allay their discontent and preserve to those Mundas who still possess them the rights in their land which they have claimed with such unwearied pertinacity.

An interesting account is given of the growth of Christian missions in Chotanagpur ; and it is shown how much the Mundas are indebted for their escape from utter ruin to the education and support given them by the missionaries. There is no doubt that the great success of the Christian Missions in obtaining converts is due largely to the secular benefits which the Mundas thus obtain. This is freely admitted by the missionaries themselves.[1] The total number of Christians in the Ranchi District has risen from 36,000 in 1881 to 177,000 in 1911. More than one-eighth of the inhabitants are Christians.

But to most readers the chapter on Ethnography will prove to be the most interesting part of the book. This chapter contains a full account of the daily life of the Mundas, their dress, agriculture, tribal organization, social and religious ceremonies, folklore and songs. It has evidently been written in the light of a close personal knowledge of the people and a deep and sympathetic insight into their feelings, mentality and views of life. One curious feature of their social system, which they share with many other

[1] See, for instance, the Report quoted on page 198

primitive tribes, is the fact that the boys and girls of the village sleep in separate dormitories and not in the houses of their parents. The greatest freedom is allowed between the sexes prior to marriage, but afterwards immorality is very unusual.

The physical affinities and origin of the Mundas are problems which have often been discussed. Their language, with the kindred dialects spoken by the Santals, Hos and other tribes inhabiting the Chotanagpur plateau, has been shown by Pater Schmidt to form a sub-family of the family called by him the Austro-Asiatic, which includes also Mon Khmer, Wa, Palaung, Nicobarese, Khasi and the aboriginal languages of Malacca. There is another family which he calls the Austronesian, including Indonesian, Melanesian and Polynesian. These two families again are grouped into one great family which he calls the Austric.

In the western part of the Chotanagpur plateau there are various tribes, such as the Oraons, who speak Dravidian languages. To the south of it languages of that family are almost universally prevalent, though they have receded somewhat before Aryan forms of speech in the open country on the west of the Peninsula. No connection between the Dravidian and any other linguistic family has yet been proved, but it has been suggested that it is allied to the languages of Australia. North of the Chotanagpur plateau, Aryan languages are spoken everywhere, except in Baluchistan, where the Brahuis have a Dravidian dialect, and in the Himalayan region and parts of Assam, where Tibeto-Burman dialects are current.

There are indications that Munda languages were formerly spoken in the Gangetic valley. The 'Pronominalized Himalayan Group' of Tibeto-Burman languages bear traces of having originally belonged to that family. There are striking points of agreement between the Munda languages and Kanauri, which is spoken in the neighbourhood of Simla.

Anthropometry has shown that there is no recognizable distinction in respect of physical type between the speakers of the Munda and those of the Dravidian languages. This type is commonly, though somewhat inconveniently, known by the philological term 'Dravidian'[2]. Its main characteristics are a broad nose, a long head, plentiful and sometimes curly (but not woolly) hair, a black or nearly black skin and a rather low stature. There is a Negrito element in the south of India, but it is much smaller than has sometimes been supposed. It has been modified by contact with other races, and the distinctive woolly hair of the Andamanese is practically never seen.[3] There is on the West Coast an intermixture of some short-headed race, possibly Mongolian, which may have found its way thither by sea, or along the coast. Except where it has been influenced by immigration from the north-west or north-east in comparatively recent times, the general uniformity of physical type throughout India seems to show that the speakers, both of the Munda and of the Dravidian languages, must have been settled there for countless ages, during which inter-marriages and climatic influences and environment gradually destroyed the former racial distinctions and evolved a uniform type.

Dr. Grierson opines that the so-called Dravidian ethnic type may be really that of the Mundas and should be called the Munda type. His suggestion is that the Dravidian type was dissimilar, that (exactly as happened in the case of the Aryans) they inter-married with Mundas, and their children gradually gained the Munda ethnic type, while they (again exactly like the Aryans) retained their own language. This would account, he says, for the Brahuis who speak a Dravidian language, having nothing 'Dravidian' (or 'Munda') in their physical appearance. The Brahuis are, of course, a mixed race, mainly Iranian in type, but if the so-called 'Dravidian' ethnic type were really 'Dravidian' we should expect some signs of it still to be found among the Brahuis. But there are none.

I venture to think that one difficulty in the way of the above

---

[2] Dravida, like Arya, was originally a racial designation, but it was annexed by Bishop Caldwell as the name of a linguistic family,

[3] Thurston says : I have only seen one individual with woolly hair, and he was of mixed Tamil and African parentage.—"Castes and Tribes of Southern India".—App. I

hypothesis is that there are no traces of the Munda languages anywhere in the south of India. They have been displaced by Aryan languages in the north of India, but this is because the Aryans had a superior civilization, whereas there is nothing to show that the original Dravidian speakers were superior to the Munda speakers. And even if they were, one would have expected, if there had even been Munda speakers there, to find small islands of Munda speech in the hilly tracts of Southern India which are even more inaccessible than those of Chotanagpur where Munda languages still hold their own, or traces of their influence on the Dravidian dialect similar to those left by them on certain Himalayan dialects of the Tibeto-Burman family. Moreover, as no connection has yet been proved between the Dravidian languages and those of any other family, it would seem more reasonable to suppose that they had their origin in Southern India than that they came in from elsewhere. And it seems less improbable that the original type of the people who gave their language to the small Brahui tribe should have disappeared than that of the great mass of Dravidian speakers in the south of India should have done so.

An earlier generation of ethnologists was impressed by the fact that the Mongolian and Dravidian races both differed markedly from the Aryan in certain respects, and especially in the shape of their noses, which are broad and bridgeless. They inferred from the existence of these common points of difference that the races in question sprang from the same stock, and that the Drāvidians had a northern origin. They further recognized the distinction between the Munda and Dravidian languages and observed that, while the former resemble those of the Mon Khmer group, whose Austric affinities were not then known, the latter claim Brahui as an undoubted member of their family. On this basis the theory was evolved that the Munda speakers entered India from the north-east and the Dravidian speakers from the north-west. This theory has recently been reasserted by Mr. A. H. Keane. There is, however, very little solid foundation for it. The points of difference between the physical type of the Mongolians and the so-called Dravidians are greater than the points of resemblance. In spite of their broad noses, the Dravidians are not flat-faced like the Mongolians who have remarkably prominent cheek bones ; their heads are long, while those of the Mongolians are broad ; they are much more hairy ; their colour is black not yellow ; their frames are less sturdy, and though short they are not squat ; lastly, their eyes are full and round, and have not the narrow sloping lids which give to the Mongolian eye such a peculiar appearance. On the other hand, the 'Dravidian' type resembles very closely that of many of the other tribes whose languages belong to the Austro-Asiatic family. There is no trace of any linguistic affinities between the languages of aboriginal India and those spoken north of the Himalayas, such as have been shown to exist between the Munda languages and those of Australia and the intervening islands. Various 'Dravidian' customs have their counterpart in the same region. Everything points to a connection with the races to the south and east rather than with those to the north. Geologists tell us that the Indian peninsula was formerly cut off from the north of Asia by sea, while a land connection existed on the one side with Madagascar and on the other with the Malay Archipelago ; and although there is nothing to show that India was then inhabited, we know that it was so in palaeolithic times, when communications were probably still easier with the countries to the south-east and south-west than with those beyond the Himalayas.[4]

In the absence of any evidence of subsequent, but pre-Aryan, immigration, it is not unreasonable to suppose that the present inhabitants are, in the main, the descendants of the people who made the celts, which are found in large numbers in many parts of the country, and who erected the dolmens and kistvaens so frequently seen in the uplands of the Deccan and Southern India. Mr. Thurston tells us that the hill Kurumbas of the Palmanair plateau erect dolmens to this day. To the suggestion that the

---

[4] Topinard mentions that in the west of Africa about Madagascar there are black tribes with smooth hair who may be a survival of some non-Negro race.—"Anthropology, 1894."

existence of a Dravidian form of speech in Baluchistan is a proof that the Dravidians entered India by that route, it may be replied that it can equally well be explained on the hypothesis that a tribe of Dravidian speakers migrated thither from the south. It is not unlikely that, at the time when Northern India was inhabited by speakers of Munda languages, Baluchistan, Sind and Bombay, like the South of India, were occupied by speakers of Dravidian languages.

Calcutta
29th December, 1911   E. A. GAIT

CHAPTER I

THE ORIGIN OF THE KOL TRIBES, AND SOURCES OF ANCIENT MUNDARI HISTORY

Look back, who list, unto the former ages,
And call to count what is of them become.—Spenser

The Ruins of Time

In India, we have vast fields for historical research as yet lying unexplored or but partially explored. The early history of the so-called Kolarian aborigines of India is one of those obscure tracts that have hardly yet been rescued from the darkness of oblivion. A thick curtain of mystery hangs over the antiquities of these prehistoric tribes. Of their real origin and their primitive abode, we are in utter darkness,—of their successive migrations in ancient times through different parts of India, we have no written records to enlighten us, and of the various vicissitudes of fortune they underwent in the dim dark ages of antiquity, our present knowledge is next to nothing. And yet these are the peoples whose remote ancestors were once masters of Indian soil,—whose doings and sufferings, whose joys and sorrows, once made up the history of the Indian Peninsula. The historian of India generally dismisses from consideration these and other aboriginal tribes as "an unclaimed ignoble horde who occupy the background of Indian History as the jungle once covered the land to prepare the soil for better forms of life".[1] A total absence of historical traditions regarding the antiquities of these tribes is tacitly assumed to exist by writers on Indian History. Not even a chapter of decent length is allotted to these peoples in any standard work on the history of India. And thus the story of their past has hitherto remained practically untold.

Patient inquiry, however, will reveal that some of these tribes still retain ancient traditions that may shed some light on their past history. These materials with which the story of their past might be partially rebuilt, are, day after day slowly but steadily slipping out of our hands. With the lapse of time and the progress

---

[1] Hunter's *Annals of Rural Bengal*, p. 110.

of civilisation amongst these tribes, they appear every day to have
been paying less and less heed to the traditions handed down by
their ancestors.   And thus it has come to pass that at the present
moment a few stray old persons here and there remain the sole
custodians of these heirlooms of their past. And the time may not
be far off when this valuable traditionary lore, now in a rapid
course of detrition and decay, may be lost to posterity beyond
all chance of recovery.

  It is high time, then, that antiquarian investigators should turn
their attention to the quasi-historical traditions of these interesting tribes,—and, with the aid of such traditions, seek to trace
back their early history so far as is still possible. It is indeed a
matter of regret that no Indian scholars have yet thought fit to
devote that time and attention to the subject which it undoubtedly
deserves.   In fact, the subject is so vast and spreads out into so many
ramifications that it would require the patient and persevering
collaboration of a whole society of investigators to remove the dense
mass of mists that has gathered around it, and open out to us
'that new world which is the old'. All the success that solitary
inquirers may hope to attain is at best to uplift the corners of the
misty veil and take an imperfect peep into a limited portion of this
dark domain of mystery and oblivion.

  The so-called Kolarian aborigines of India count more than a
dozen tribes amongst their number. We shall here attempt, with
the help of such feeble lights as we may lay hold on, to trace the
traditional history of one important section of the Kols—the
Munda tribe now inhabiting the highlands of Chota Nagpur.

  Dark brown—almost black—in colour, short in stature[2] but
sturdy in his limbs, with irregular features, scanty beard, thick lips,
broad nose, a low facial angle, with a head long or doliko-cephalic
like that of the average Dravidian's, the Munda is a typical representative of the great Kol race.

  The lamp of inquiry has hardly yet been lighted to illumine the
dark caverns and hidden recesses of ancient Mundari history.
And in the misty mazes of Munda antiquities, the first historical
inquirers will now and again have to grope their difficult and often
doubtful way through bye-paths of surmise and inference.   Crude
and conjectural as our account of the successive migrations of the
Mundas may appear to be, our only excuse for placing it before the

  [2] The average height of an adult Munda male is 5 ft. 6 in.

public is that it may excite and perhaps assist inquiry, and invite worthier workers to the rich field of Kolarian antiquities. Ours will be but a feeble attempt to trace the bare outlines of a difficult and comprehensive subject. And it will be for more assiduous and leisured inquirers to fill up the details, and perhaps to alter the outlines themselves in the light of further research and fresh information.

As regards the remote past, Mundari History, if history it can be called, hardly passes beyond the region of mythical legends. And even such myths and legends as have been handed down to the Mundas by their remote ancestors do not appear to carry us back to a period anterior to the Aryan occupation of Hindusthan. In the pre-Aryan era of Mundari History, we have not even the rush-light of a myth to guide us. The scanty traditions of the tribe open their blurred and dusty pages at a comparatively later chapter of Mundari History.

On the name or geographical situation of their original home, the traditions and legends of the Mundas do not appear to throw any light. It has indeed been sometimes supposed that *Ekasipidi Tirasibadi*, the land of eighty-one up-lands and eighty-three elevated rice-fields, celebrated in the Mundari legend of Lutkum Hadam and Lutkum Budia[3], was the original seat of the tribe. But this supposition will hardly bear scrutiny. The name alone seems to suggest that the legend cannot date back to a period prior to the colonisation of Northern India by the Aryan Hindus. Notwithstanding the professed antiquity of the legend, the hybrid name *Ekasipidi Tirasibadi* points to a previous contact with the Sanskrit-speaking Hindus and an acquaintance with their language. The Hindu Numerals *Ekasi and Tirasih* have no place in the vocabulary of the Mundas who use *upun-hisi-mid* and *upun-hisi-api* respectively for eighty-one and eighty-three. And it does not appear at all likely that the conservative Mundas would profane the sacred cradle of the tribe by sacrilegiously transforming its name into a mongrel form even for the sake of euphony. And *Ekasipidi Tirasibadi*, even if such a place had any local existence at all, must have been situated within the confines of Hindustan, and not improbably within Chota Nagpur itself. In fact, Colonel Dalton proposed to identify the place with a village still known as *Ekasi* and situated in the Borway Pargana of the Ranchi District.[4]

[2] Vide *Appendix*. [4] Vide Dalton's *Ethnology of Bengal*, p. 221.

The tradition still extant among the Mundas of a sanguinary struggle in the uplands of Chota Nagpur between themselves and their kinsmen the Asura tribe who had occupied the country before them, would appear to lend support to this suggestion. If, then, this identification of *Ekasipidi Tirasibadi* be correct,— and none other has been or can probably be suggested,—it is clear that that place could not have been the cradle of the tribe,— for, the traditions of the Mundas speak of their previous residence in other parts of India before they finally entered Chota Nagpur.

Seya Sandi Bir[5], the vast desolate forest,—which a second Mundari tradition names as the original home of the tribe, is much less capable of identification, and it will probably ever remain a *tera incognita* to us.

The Munda Cosmogonic legend[6] which names Ajabgarh as the place which was first raised out of the Primeval Ocean and where the first parents of the Mundas are said to have been created by Sing Bonga—the Sun-God or Supreme Deity of the Mundas,— is evidently a later invention, or rather a confusion of two distinct traditions regarding two distinct epochs widely distant from each other in point of time. The origin of the cosmogonic part of the tradition would seem to have been borrowed much later from the Hindus who appear to have been acquainted with the geological truth of the Age of Fishes having been followed in the order of creation successively by the Age of Reptiles, the Age of Mammals, and the Age of Man. For, the statement in the Hindu *Puranas* of the *Matsya Avatara* of Vishnu in the first age, the *Kurma Avatara* in the second age, the *Varaha Avatara* in the third age, and the *Nrishinha Avatara* in the fourth age,—is in all probability an allegorical exposition of the scientific knowledge of creation possessed by the ancient Hindus. Modern geologists tell us that animals allied to the crab were abundant in the Primary Epoch, and the tortoise was born and reptiles predominated in the Triassic period of the Secondary Epoch. But it was not till the Pliocene, or, at the earliest, the Miocene[7] period of the Tertiary Epoch that we have any positive evidence of the existence on earth of any being resembling man. And the Ajabgarh of Munda tradition,

---

[5] The words *Seya* and *Sandi* would seem to be obsolete Mundari words.

[6] Vide *Appendix*.

[7] The chipped flint implements discovered at Pay Courney in the Upper Miocene strata and at Thenay in the Lower Miocene, have been pronounced by

which, as we shall see later on, is identical with the modern District of Azimgarh in the *United Provinces* was not in existence till post-Tertiary times[8] when we find man widely diffused over the earth,—though in a condition of primitive savagery, chipping his rude stone celts and scrapers, flakes and arrow-heads.

Other legends of Munda mythology and Munda folklore bearing

A HO (SINGBHUM)

some authorities to be of human origin.—Vide Samual Laing's *Human origins*, Ch.X.

   [8] According to geologists, the only parts of India which were in existence in the Primary Epoch were the Punjab, Bhotan, the country round about the Aravallis Bundelkhand, Chota Nagpur, parts of Bengal, of Burma and of Kashmir.

on the point, are generally so grotesque and absurd, and the kernel of historic truth in them, if any, is so tightly pressed down under the thick shell of fiction that they can give us no clue whatsoever to the original habitat of the tribe. And the site of the original home of the Mundas will perhaps ever remain hidden from view in the mist of ages. Whether the Mundas immigrated into India from the now-submerged hypothetical continent of Lemuria which has been supposed to have once connected India with Madagascar and Africa, or whether they entered India from the

KOROWAH

north-east as has been sometimes supposed[9],—or whether they originated from a mixture of colonists from Eastern Tibet of Western Chinacross the Himalayas with the Australo. Dravidians to the south of that range[10], or whether indeed they are genuine autochthones of Indian soil as the Mundas and their congeners

BHUMIJ MUNDAS (SINGBHUM)

[9] See Hewitt in the *Journal of the Royal Asiatic Society*, 1888 and 1889.
[10] See "On some Traces of Kol-Mon-Anam in the Eastern Naga Hills," by S. E. Peal—*Asiatic Society's Journal, Bengal*, vol. LXV, Pt. III. pp. 20 etc.

in India assert,—we have, in the present state of our knowledge, hardly any materials to ascertain.

All that the patient linguistic researches of distinguished European Philologists have succeeded in discovering, is that a wide belt of territory extending over various parts of India, Further India and Cochin China, the Malay Peninsula, the Nicobars, the Phillipines, the Malacca Islands, and Australia, is to this day inhabited by rude tribes speaking dialects that bear unmistakable affinities with one another. Points of similarity in vocabulary, in details of grammatical forms, and in principles of language-building, appear to establish a close connection between the Kolarian Mundari, Santali, Bhumij, Ho, Birhor, Koda, Turi, Asuri, Korwa, Kurku, Kharia, Juang, Savara and Gadaba dialects of India, on the one hand, and, on the other, the Sakei and Semang dialects of the Malay Peninsula, the Anamese, Bersisi, and Mon-Khmer languages including Khasi,the dialects of the aborigines of the Malacca Isles, the Dippil, Turubul, Kamilaroy, Wodi-wodi, Kingki, Wailwun, Toungurong and other dialects of the Australian tribes,—and the Car-Nicober, Chowra, Teressa, Central, Southern and Shompen dialects of the Nicoberese language. The so-called Kolarian tribes of India, the Khasis of the Khasi hills, the Sakei and Semang tribes of the Malay Peninsula, the Mon-Khmers of Further-India including the Anamese of Cochin China, the rude Nicobarese, the aborigines of the Malacca and the Phillipines, and several wild tribes in southern and western Australia,—all speak allied dialects which seem to point to an intimate racial contact in the past, if not to a common origin.

Philology, however, seeks to explain this remarkable similarity of the languages of so many lands in a different way. It contents itself with the supposition that at some distant age, all these countries were inhabited by an old race since extinct, whose language alone now survives as the common substratum underlying all the so-called Kolarian forms of speech.[11] But with due respect to the eminent Philologists and Ethnologists who have started this theory, we must confess that it does not carry conviction to our minds. We do not know of another instance in the history of the world in which a widely-diffused race which was powerful enough to

[11] Vide, Dr. Grierson's *Linguistic Survey of India*, Vol. IV, p. 5.

impose its own language on a number of other peoples, has been utterly effaced from the face of the globe. Nor is such a whole-sale extinction of a race of men at all probable. If we were permit-ted to hazard a conjecture at variance with the opinions of these eminent servants, we would suggest that most[12] of these tribes now speaking languages allied to Mundari are perhaps descended from one and the same original people, and that these common forefathers of the various rude tribes named above, were perhaps the earliest inhabitants of India. And we might further suggest that this primitive stock from which we have supposed the Mundas and other allied tribes in and outside India to have been descen-ded, had their original abode in the hilly regions extending from the Aravalli mountains and proceeding eastwards along the Vin-dhyan and Kaimur ranges as far as the modern state of Surguja and the South Eastern districts of Chota Nagpur. It is in these parts of India that remains of the most ancient human settlements have been discovered. Traces of the Stone Age have been found as far east as in the modern Districts of Singbhum and Manbhum and in the south-eastern parts of the Ranchi District. Quart-zite axes and spearheads have been discovered in the Jheria coal-fields in Manbhum[13] and also near the village of Gopinathpur[14] 11 miles to the south-west of Beharinath Hill in the District of Manbhum. In the year 1868, Captain Beechang, commander of a company of the 10th Madras N. I. on his march from Ranchi to Chaibassa for the purpose of quelling some disturbances in the tributary state of Keonjhar, lighted upon a number of chert flakes and knives at Chaibassa and also at Chuckerdhurpur—a place about 16 miles from Chaibassa.[15] Mr. Ball not only discovered similar flakes in many parts of Singbhum but discovered a beauti-fully made celt at the foot of a small hill near the village of Buradih,

[12] We say "most" because it is not unlikely that a few of these tribes may not improbably have adopted the language of superior alien tribe. Thus, it has been supposed that the Semangs of the Malay Peninsula, though now speaking a dialect akin to Mundari, were Negritos in origin but abandoned their original speech and adopted their present dialect. To come nearer home, we find that a large number of Dravidian Uraons round about the town of Ranchi, have long aban-doned their own language for that of their Kolarian Munda neighbours.

[13] Vide, *Proceedings of the Asiatic Society of Bengal*, 1865, p. 127.

[14] Vide, *Proceedings of the Asiatic Society of Bengal*, 1867, p. 143.

[15] Vide *Proceedings, Asiatic Society, Bengal*, 1868, p. 177.

south-east of Gamaria, in the eastern pargana of Tamar in the District of Ranchi.[16]

When these hilly regions no longer furnished space enough for their multiplying progeny, adventurous bands would naturally leave the original cradle and march off to the north and north-west and settle down in the fertile tracts along the mighty rivers of Northern India. In the hilly fastnesses that separate the Vindhyas on the south and the Gangetic plains on the north, there have been discovered numerous rude caves with occasional rude attempts at ornamentation that bear evident traces of having been once used as human dwellings. And around these dwellings, large quantities of stone implements have been discovered. And even to this day may be found in the hills and jungles to the east and south of the Azimgarh District a scattered population of Cheros, Seoris, Kols and Kharwars. A few families of Korwas too are met with in the jungles in the southern parts of the Mirzapur District. "The wild country now known as Saktisgarh, a *tappa* of the ancient Parganah of Kantit, was once a Kol demesne, and was frequently called by their name *Kolana*."[17] The Santal-Kharwar tradition of their ancient residence in Khairagarh[18] possibly refers to the parganah of that name in the adjoining District of Allahabad. The stone implements that have been unearthed in the District of Ghazipur, south of the Azimgarh District point to a period when the district, in the words of Mr. Carleylle, was "a wilderness, inhabited by rude pre-historic wandering aboriginal tribes".[19] Along with these stone implements, Mr. Carleylle discovered two very strange things—"one, a large poison-fang of a snake, and the other the long sharp saw-edged fin-bone of some fish of the kind called *Tengra*". And as to these, Mr. Carleylle remarks,—"I have no doubt they were used by the aborigines of the Stone-Age to tip their arrows with".

Nor is it in the Districts of Mirzapur and Ghazipur alone that

[16] Vide *Pr.*, *A.S.B.*, 1870, p. 268. This is described by Mr. Ball as the best formed celt weapon till then obtained in South-West Bengal.

[17] Aitkinson's *Statistical Account of the N. W. P.*, Vol. XIV, part I, p. 117.

[18] Some authorities such as Colonel Dalton [*Ethnology of Bengal*, p. 211] would identify the Khairagarh of Santal tradition with a place of that name in the District of Hazaribagh. The Bir-Hors also name Khairagarh as one of their ancient seats.

[19] Cunningham's *Archaeological Reports*, Vol. XXII by Carlleylle, P. 102.

such ancient stone implements have been met with. Throughout the southern borders of the Gangetic valley as well as in modern Bundelkhand and Rewa, ancient stone weapons and flint chips have been discovered. In an article in the Journal of the Calcutta Branch of the Asiatic Society for the year 1894, Mr. John Cockburn writes :

"All along the Gangetic valley, in the wilder alluvian fringing the Vindhians and Kymores and as far south of these hills as I have been, in Sirgoojah and Rewah, the soil teems with fragmentary of ancient stone weapons. I have picked up as many as fifty perfect chert knives and two broken celts in a cotton field within 500 yards of my bunglow at Banda.[20]

Thus, we have grounds for inferring that the Mundas and other Kolarian tribes originally lived in the hilly regions along the Aravalli and Vindhyan ranges and gradually spread further to the north and occupied the valleys of the mighty rivers of Northern India. Subsequent admixture with some Dravidian tribes of the south hailing from across the Vindhyas may have contributed in assimilating their physical characteristics—the shape of the skull, the dimensions of the nose, cheek bones, orbits, forehead and zygomatic arches, the breadth of the pelvis, the colour and texture of the hair, and so forth, with those of the Dravidians proper,—the ancestors of the tribes who speak the Tamil, Telugu, Malayalam, Canarese, Kurukh (Uraon) and other allied languages. The isolated tribe of Brahuis who now live in the mountainous regions in Eastern and Central Beluchistan and the neighbouring Districts of Sind speak a language akin to the Dravidian languages of Southern India, and may be supposed to represent the unabsorbed remnants of the first migration of the Dravidians of the south to Northern India, while the other allied tribes who joined them in this northward journey would seem to have been absorbed in the great Kol race. Such an intermingling of races, as ethnologists testify, has been steadily at work since neolithic times, and to

---

[20] Vide *Journal of the Asiatic Society of Bengal*, Vol. L XIII, Part III, p. 27 Mr. Cockburn found forty-three stone hammers, flakes, spalls, &c. in some deep ravines cut through a Neolithic burial-ground near the village of Kon in South Mirzapur and two flint implements at Barkacha, 5 miles south of the town of Mirzapur. "So numerous are waste flint chips in this locality (properly called spalls)", says Mr. Cockburn, "that I collected several hundred-weights . . . . The site, however, is Neolithic rather than palaeolithic."

this process of miscegenation we owe the blurring of all primeval types. When, subsequently, the Aryans began to pour into India through the north-western passes,[21] some of the congeners of the Mundas unable to resist the on-set of the invaders would naturally emigrate eastwards and passing through Pragjyotisha or ancient Assam would gradually follow a southerly direction. One band, the ancestors of the Khasis, settled in Central Assam. A second band, the progenitors of the Mons or Telangs of Pegu established themselves in the country fertilised by the Irawady.[22] Other branches of the Kol race moved on further to the south and settled in the several countries now known as the Malay Peninsula, the Phillipines and the Nicobar Islands. Some other tribes, again, proceeded probably in their rude canoes further to the south-east as far as to Australia. Rude stone implements and celts, such as are met with in India, have been found in Pegu and many other countries whither the kinsmen of the Mundas migrated in those prehistoric times. And these would seem to lend support to the supposition we have ventured to put forward.

Among the Kolarian tribes who were left behind in the rude fastnesses of their original home along the Vindhyan Range were perhaps the Juangs who now dwell in the inaccessible hills of Keonjhar, Dhekanal, and a few other tributary mahals of Orissa, whither they appear to have been pushed forward by successive waves of immigration. Their primitive habits as well as their traditions[23] would seem to favour such a conjecture.

[21] There appear to have been two successive Aryan migrations into India from the north-west by two different routes.

[22] The termination di or ti some European scholars would identify with the Mundari and Santal word da meaning 'water'.

[23] In Notes of a forest race called Puttoas or Juangs by E.A. Samuells, Esq. B. C. S. in the Proceedings of the Asiatic Society of Bengal, for the year 1856 (pp. 290—300) we are told that the Juangs have a tradition that they have always occupied the land they now live in. Their only religious festival, we are told, consists of sacrifices and libations offered to the manes of their deceased in the month of Baisakh and their religious homage is confined to the nameless spirits inhabiting the woods and mountains. They know no Munda or secular head nor Pahan of village priest, and no distinction of rank is observed, one and all calling themselves 'Pudhan' the title which their neighbours the Uriyas give to the headman of a village. Moreover, as Colonel Dalton points out they still employ some genuine Kolarian words, e. g. 'gone' for 'tooth' & 'lerang' for 'moon' which have dropped out of the other Kol dialects, (except Kharia) in which terms of Sanskrit derivation have been substituted for them. [Dalton's Ethnology of Bengal, p. 152.]

However hazardous it may be to point our finger definitely at any particular locality as having been the original home of the Mundas it seems pretty certain that they were one of the non-Hindu peoples whom the Aryan immigrants found in occupation of the country when they first set their foot on Indian soil. The traditions of the Mundas themselves concur with various statements in the ancient Sanskrit works in suggesting that the Mundas and other cognate tribes occupied Northern India before the forefathers of the Aryan Hindus entered the country.[24] The woods and valleys by the side of the ancient Drisadwati and Saraswati rivers appear to have rung with the Bacchanalian songs or *durangs* of the Mundas and other allied tribes long before the venerable Arya Rishis of old chanted their sonorous Vedic hymns on their sacred banks.

Colonel Dalton tells us that the Juangs have a tradition of a Bora Raja, probably some allusion to the *Baraha avatar* of Vishnu, having had a fort in the heart of the country now occupied by Juangs, the remains of which are still in existence, and it is said that the Juangs are a remnant of his people. In the conjecture we have made above, we have the support of Colonel Dalton, who says, referring to the stone implements occasionally found in the hilly tract occupied by the Juangs, 'it is not improbable that they are the direct descendants of those ancient stone cutters and that we have in the Juangs representatives of the stone age *in situ.*,'—Dalton's *Ethnology*, p. 153. When Colonel Dalton visited Keonjhar in 1866, the Juang women who appeared before him had no clothing on, but wore girdles of beads "from which small curtains of leaves decended before and behind" as in the accompanying illustration.

[24] The passages in the *Vishnu Purana* (1, 5, 28—32), which describe the Asuras as the first born of Brahman, from whose thigh they sprang, and the similar statement in the Mahabharata (Santi Parva 84) that the Asuras were the elder brothers of the Gods,—and the further statement in the Taittiriya Upanishad (V1.2) that the earth formerly belonged to the Asuras while the gods had only as much as a man can see while sitting, have been supposed by Muir and other Orientalists as referring to the former occupation of the country by the black aborigines. And the German Orientalist Weber (Ind. stud 1. 18., 11, 243) pointed out that the Devas and Asuras of ancient Sanskrit literature referred to the two broad divisions of Indian population, the fair skinned sacrificing Aryans and the godless black aborigines. Later authorities, however, seem to identify the Asuras, in some at least of the many passages in the earliest Sanskrit literature in which the name occurs, with the ancestors of the modern Parsis, the worshippers of Zu Ahuras. But there can be no doubt that the term Asura has also been employed in ancient Sanskrit literature with reference to the black aborigines of the soil. And we may point out the very significant fact that one of the Kolarian tribes in Chota Nagpur is even to this day known as the Asuras (otherwise called Agorias).

Many are the hymns in the *Rigveda* in which we hear the fair skinned Aryan warriors invoking the aid of their bright and beneficent gods against these and other black races who long and strenuously fought—but fought in vain—to stem the tide of Aryan progress into the country. For the aborigines with their black skin (*twacham Krishnam*),[25] fierce eyes (*ghora chakshas*),[26] deformed nose (*visipra*)[27] and imperfect speech (*mridhravach*)[28] the proud Aryans knew no better appellations than 'Dasas'[29] and Dasyus[30] slaves and robbers[31].

Nor is later Sanskrit literature less sparing of similar contemptuous epithets towards these natives of the soil—the prehistoric population of India. In the great Sanskrit Epics of Valmiki and Vedavyasa, the aborigines are denominated as monsters, monkeys and bears.

Some ancient Sanskrit writers, indeed, either in pursuance of some *a priori* theories of their own or perhaps from motives of policy sought to assign what looks like a fictitious origin to the aboriginal population of India. Thus, in the oft-quoted tenth chapter of the *Manu Sanhita* (X. 4), we are told—"Three castes, the Brahman, the Kshatriya, and the Vaisya, are twice-born; the fourth, the Sudra, is once born; and there is no fifth." And as a necessary corollary, all other castes and tribes are derived from a series of complicated crosses between members of the four so-called original castes. And the tribes which by loss of sacred rites became outcastes from the pale of the recognized castes and sub-castes are the Dasyus.[32] Again, in the *Aitareya Brahmana*[33] and a few of the

---

[25] *Rig Veda*, 1, 130, 8. [26] *R. V.* VII, 104, 2.

[27] *R. V.*, V. 45,6. [28] *R. V.*, 1. 74, 2; V. 32, 8; VIII, 6, 3.

[29] *Rig Veda*. 1. 32, II, 1. 104, 2, II, 11, .II 4; 20., & 7 VI. 20, 10, VI, 25, 2, etc.

[30] *R. V.* 1. 33, 4; 1. 3-18, 1. 51, 5. 11. 20, 18; 11, 11, 19, 11, 13, 9, 111, 9, 34, VI, 1-, 12, V. 31, 7; VI.-1, 4, etc.

[31] Among other epithets applied in the *Rig Veda* to the aboriginal population of India may be mentioned the following:—*Krishna-garbha*, 'black born, the dusky brood', 1. 101, 1 ; *anasa* 'noseless', V. 29 10; *Sisnadeva* 'lascivious'. VII, 21,5 *X*,99 3; *Simyu* 'destroyer', 1. 100, 18 and VII. 18, 5 *Kravyada* 'eater of raw 'flesh', *X*. 87. 2, *Kimidina* 'treacherous and malevolent being', *X*, 87, 24; *Yatudhana*, 'explained as *Rakshas* by Sayana, *X*, 87,5 and 15, and 1, 35, 10; *ayajwana* 'non-sacrificer' 1. 103, 6, and 1. 121, 13, and 1 33, 5 and 6: *abratam* 'riteless', 1. 33, 5 *muradeva* 'worshipper of mad gods',VII. 104, 54 *bramhadvisa* 'hater of Brahmanas' III. 31, 17.

[32] Vide, Manu, *X*. 4,5 and Kulluka's commentary thereon.

[33] *Aitareya Brahmana*, VII, 18.

Puranas, most of the Dasyu tribes are said to have been descended from the cursed younger sons of the sage Viswamitra, the great rival of Vasistha. In the *Mahavarata*[34] the supposed degradation from the rank of Kshatriyas to that of Sudras, of a number of Non-Aryan tribes is attributed to their 'seeing no Brahmans'.

Another ancient Sanskrit work[35] gives still another fabulous account of the Kols—the generic name for the Mundas and other Kolarian tribes. It tells us that Raja Bena having been tainted with sin, the Rishis went to remonstrate with him. The Raja with a wave of his hand beckoned the Rishis to depart. Thereupon the sage Angira cursed him, and, as a result of the curse, the offending right hand of the Raja was immediately converted into a churning stick. And from this arm sprang a man short in stature, black as the crow, with short arms, high cheek bones, small legs and flat nose, red eyes and tawny hair. This man became Nishada. When the Rishis began to churn the left hand of Bena, three more men came out of the arm the *Mushahantara,* the Kolla and the Villa,—the first ancestors of the Mushahars, the Kols and the Bhils of our own days.

"प्रथमो मुषहन्तारं द्वितीय कोल्लमेव च
तृतीयो भिल्ल संख्यातमित्यैते च उदाहृताः ।[36]

The untenability of most of these theories is too obvious to call for any serious discussion. If any refutation were necessary their mutual contradictions might be referred to as sufficient for the purpose.

Amid all these fanciful theories and legendary inventions, however, the one fact which stands out clear in the pages of ancient Sanskrit writers is that from the earliest Vedic times down to the dawn of the *Aitihasik* period,—as the period of the great Sanskrit Epics has been called,—the black aborigines were often the greatest opponents of the Aryan Hindus. Beyond this broad fact,

---

[34] *Mahabharata,* Anusasana Parva, verses 2103, etc.

[35] Cf. *Bhagabat Purana,* Bk. IV. Ch. XIV. See also *Vishnu Purana,* Bk 1, and *Padma Purana,* Bhukhanda.

[36] This *sloka* and the story were cited by a writer in the *Calcutta Review* Vol. LXIX p. 349; but we have not found out the last portion of the story nor the *Sloka in the Bhagabat Purana* to which the writer in the *Calcutta Review* attributes the passage. The *Bramha Vaivarta Purana* ascribes the origin of the Kols to a Tivara mother. In the *Parasara Sanhita,* the Bhillas and Pulindas are said to have been born of a Tivara father by a Brahmana woman.

the authors of Hindu sacred writings tell us but little about these interesting tribes.

When we pass on from the region of mythical legends and unauthenticated traditions to what may be called the semi-historical region we are on ground more tangible, though not infrequently slippery, if not miry.

The historical consciousness of races as of individuals is a plant of slow growth. The historical memory of unlettered tribes is necessarily short and faulty. Young races, like young children, possess a short memory. The present fills their mental horizon,— the enjoyments and sorrows, the hopes and anxieties of the hour absorb all their attention, and they have neither the capacity nor the leisure to look before or behind. And the Mundas could have been no exception to the rule. It was only when more settled conditions of tribal life allowed them time to think, that their traditions must have taken their rise. And in that wide interval of time, how many an important event of the past must have been entirely forgotten, how many but dimly remembered, and what a considerable part must imagination have played in shaping, modifying and at times transforming the original traditions!

As for contemporary records, ancient Sanskrit literature rarely makes more than passing references to the aborigines of India —references that occur mainly in connection with the accounts of the victorious progress of Aryan arms into the country. Occasionally indeed we hear of the humiliation of Aryan prowess at the hands of the hated Dasyus. Thus, in the Saptasati of the Chandi Patha of the *Markandeya Purana*,[37] we hear of some pigeating[38] warriors of an unclean tribe defeating the Aryan king Suratha of the Chaitra race—a contemporary of the second Manu Svarocisa. This however was but a temporary defeat for the Aryan prince. Deprived of his dominions, Suratha retired to a hermitage and was there instructed by a Rishi to worship the goddess Sakti. And, by the favour of the goddess, he was before long restored to his kingdom. And Suratha is said to have been reborn after his death as the Eighth Manu Savarni.

[37] *Chandi;*—LXXVII, 3—11.

[38] The epithet कोलाविध्वंसिन: slayers of pigs, i.e. Pig-eaters, in this passage has been supposed by Herr Jelinghans and others to refer to the Kols or Kolarian tribes, so called from their habit of eating pigs which are considered unclean by the Hindus.

2

Again, in the Anusasana Parva of the *Mahabharata*, we have a story as to how the gods were conquered by the Asuras or Danavas, whereupon the gods applied to the Rishi Agastya for protection, and Agastya expelled the Danavas from heaven and earth, and made them fly to the south.[39]

Similarly, the Asura Bali,[40] son of Virochana, we are told, conquered Indra, the chief of the gods, and, for a while, enjoyed 'the three worlds'. But he was not destined to enjoy this proud position for any length of time. For, Vishnu, at the supplication of Indra and the other gods, assumed the form of a dwarf, and for the benefit of the gods, by a trick occupied the whole earth and removed Bali to Patala or the nether regions.[41]

Beyond such meagre incidental references, ancient Sanskrit writers disdain to take any notice of the despised aborigines.

> What wrongs the oppressor suffered, these we know.
> These have found piteous voice in song and prose.
> But for the oppressed, their darkness and their woe,
> Their grinding centuries,—what Muse had those ?

And even such scanty references as we meet with in early Sanskrit literature, are so vague and general as often to leave much room for conjecture regarding the identity of the different races therein mentioned.

Still less illuminating are the ancient foreign writers on India. One wades in vain through the accounts of the Greek writers on India in the pre-Christian era in search of any indubitable reference to the Mundas or their past geographical location. The Marundai or Mandi of Pliny[42] and the Marundai of Ptolemy have indeed been supposed by Colonel Wilford and a few other antiquarian scholars to refer to the Mundas of Chota Nagpur, but this identification, though very probable, is not altogether free from doubt.

[39] Muir's *Sanskrit Texts*, Vol., II. p. 166. It is, however, doubtful whether the Asuras spoken of here and in the next paragraph refer to the aborigines or to the worshippers of Zu Ahuras.

[40] The name *Balia* is a common enough name among the Mundas.

[41] See *Mahabharata*, Santi Parva; *Vishnu Purana*, II., 1 & c., *Bhagabata Purana*, VII, 5.

[42] Pliny lived in the 1st century, A. D. From Pliny's account, it would seem that the Mandi lived near Benares. 'In the interior behind the Palibothri', says he, 'are the Monedas and the Suari among whom is Mt. Maleas.' Nat.H. vol. VI. 83.

Nor do the Chinese travellers[43] of the opening centuries of the Christian era throw any light on the Munda people as they then existed, or the particular part of India they then occupied, though many other races and most other parts of India are favoured with notices from the lucid pen of Fa Hian[44], Hiuen Tsang[45] and some subsequent pilgrims[46] from the Celestial Empire.

As for distinctive architectural remains, the Mundas have none to boast of, unless the rude stone-memorials they put up on the mortal remains of their dead be classed as such. Nor have their ancestors left anything in the way of inscriptions. For, as may be expected, they were utter strangers to the art of writing or even to hieroglyphics—the first step to the more developed art. And Epigraphy as a source of ancient history is of no avail in the case of the Mundas. The science of Numismatics, too, affords no help to the student of Munda antiquities,—for, coins of any sort, the Mundas do not appear to have ever minted.

It is then to the traditions of the Mundas themselves with such side-lights as ancient Sanskrit writings may shed upon them, that we must look for the early history of this people. Occasional references to similar traditions of other allied tribes may perhaps prove of some help by way of corroboration or correction. Archaeology, too, will, now and then, come to our aid. However meagre these few available sources of ancient Mundari history, if we can only get at the right clues we may perhaps succeed in making a near approach to historic truth. In the chapters that follow we shall attempt to construct the barest outlines of that history with such materials as we have been able to gather.

[43] The first Chinese historian Sumas-Chie, who completed his great work about 100 B. C., and has a good deal to say about India, did not visit the country.

[44] Fa Hian is believed to have begun his travels in 399 A. D. His work is styled Fo Kwoki or Record of Buddhistic Kingdoms.

[45] Hiuen Tsang began his travels about 629 A. D. He is believed to have learned the Sanskrit language.

[46] Fa-Hian and Hiuen-Tsang were followed by a host of Chinese pilgrims to India. Many of them left records of their visits.

CHAPTER II

THE TRADITIONAL HISTORY OF THE MUNDAS

[FROM THE RIG-VEDIC[1] PERIOD TO THE SIXTH CENTURY, B.C.]

THE slender stock of traditions that the Mundas of Chota Nagpur still possess must necessarily, as we have seen in the last chapter, form our main guide in any attempt at constructing a narrative of their remote past. True, tradition is not always a safe or reliable guide. It is apt, on the one hand, to forget facts, and, on the other, to invent fictions. But the records of tradition in the case of the Mundas may, as we have seen, be partially tested and at times supplemented, by other evidence,— the evidence of similar traditions of allied tribes, the occasional evidence of contemporary Sanskrit literature, the evidence of language, and occasionally perhaps the evidence of Archaeology. And thus although 'History', in the sense of a narrative of facts based on authentic contemporary records and capable of precise

---

[1] European Orientalists differ in their opinions as to the antiquity of the Rig-Vedic Epoch. Ducker places the date of the Aryan immigration into India at about 2,000 B.C., and that of the earlier hymns of the Rig-Veda in the sixteenth century B.C. Haug places the date of the older Rig-Vedic hymns between 2,400 and 2,000 B.C., while Max Muller considers them to have been composed between 1200 and 1000 B.C. According to the more recent theory of Prof. Jacobi of Bonn, the Rig-Vedic period goes back to at least 4000 B.C. There appear to be good grounds, however, for supposing that these hymns date back to a much earlier period. As Count Bjornstjema (*Theogony of the Hindus*, p. 134) points out: "The Bactrian document called Dabistan (found in Kashmir and brought to Europe by Sir William Jones) gives an entire register of Kings, namely, of Mahabadernes, whose first link reigned in Bactria 5,600 years before Alexander's expedition to India." And it is now generally admitted that these Bactrian Kings were Hindus. Thus the Aryans in India must have been a highly civilised people about 6,000 B.C., and the antiquity of the Vedas must go back to a much earlier date. (Vide H. B. Sarda's *Hindu Superiority*, p. 8.). In an article on the 'Indian Ancestry of the Western World' in the *Indian Review* for April, 1908, the Hon. Alex. Del Mar has adduced convincing evidence to show that ancient Egypt, Phoenicia, Chaldea, Syria, Greece and Italy are all indebted to ancient India for their civilisation.

chronological arrangement, we can hardly have any in the
case of the ancient Mundas, we can at any rate possess what we
have called their Traditional History.

The earliest glimpses we catch of the ancient Mundas in the
light of tradition, reveal them as leading a pastoral existence
in the mountain fastnesses and sunny valleys of Northern India.
The traditions of the Mundas as well as of some other Kolarian
tribes point with one concurrent voice to those regions as their
earliest-remembered home.   And these traditions receive further
confirmation from the traditions of their quondam opponents,—
the Hindus.   Such a tradition we have in the Hindu legend which
relates how Yayati[2], an ancestor of Jarasandha made a division of
his empire among his five sons, and in the tenth generation from
Turvasu, four brothers, Pandya, Kerala, Kola, and Chola divided
India amongst themselves.[3]   Northern India, it is said, was allotted
to Kola, whose descendants are the Kols—the generic name applied
to the Mundas and other allied tribes.[4]   And eminent antiquarians
like Colonel Wilford[5] and Sir George Campbell[6] have even gone the
length of supposing that Kolara or the land of the Kols, was the
name by which India was known to the ancient world. This
theory however, has been since controverted, and the text of the
younger Plutarch's work on 'Rivers' on which the theory is based,
has been since impugned by competent classical scholars as an
incorrect reading.[7]

Whatever may have been the ancient name of India before the
Aryan Hindus found their way into the country, Hindu legends
concur with the traditions of the Mundas themselves in locating this
people and other Kolarian tribes in north-western India, when the
worshippers of Brahma stepped on the threshold of the country.
The Asuras, a small Kolarian tribe of Chota Nagpur and near

---

[2] Even in the *Rig Veda* we hear of a Yayati, a Son of Nahusa, one of the great
progenitors of the human race.

[3] Cf. *Harivansa* XXX, verses, 1616, etc., XXXII, 1836, etc. and also *Vayu
Purana*.

[4] Vide *Asiatic Researches*, Vol. IX, pp. 91-92.

[5] Vide *Asiatic Society's Journal* (Beng.), XX, pp. 227-28, 'A Comparative
Essay on the Ancient Geography of India', By Colonel Wilford.

[6] Vide *A.S.J.* (Beng.), XXXV, Supplement to Part II, pp. 27-28, on the Ethnology of India, By Justice Campbell.

[7] Vide Gustave Oppert's *Original Inhabitants of Bharatbarsa*, pp. 128-32.

kinsmen of the Mundas, specifically name the Chaulagir and the Mainagir as the localities in which they dwelt of old. And there can be little difficulty in identifying the Dhaulagir and the Mainagir of the Asura tradition respectively with the Dhabalgiri in the Himalayas and the Mainak-Mountains—the Sewalik range of modern times.[8] Many a sanguinary battle must have been fought, many a Munda patriot must have laid down their lives to repel the invasion of their birth-right by the new-comers. But unfortunately the Mundas of those days had no bards to celebrate their victories or bewail their defeats. And lost for ever is the memory of most of those mighty Munda warriors of old who fought and bled, struggled and fell—un-named, un-honoured and un-sung by posterity.

> The mighty clamours, wars, and world-noised deeds
> Are silent now in dust,
> Gone like a tremble of the huddling reeds
> Beneath some sudden gust.

Only a stray tradition of the Mundas vaguely speaks of a bloody warfare waged in the Land of the Five Rivers by their ancestors against the invading Hindu intruders.[9]

More instructive is the *Rig Veda Sanhita*, that invaluable record bequeathed to posterity by the proud Aryan victors. This priceless volume tells us of numerous conflicts between the invading Arya warriors and the despised Dasyus. The names of a number of Dasyu warriors and their Aryan opponents have been preserved in the pages of that invaluable work. And among these names of hostile Dasyu leaders we find not a few bearing a close resemblance to names still in use among the Mundas of our own days. For

---

[8] Vide *Asiatic Society's Journal*, Bengal, Vol. L. VII, Part 1., p. 7, 'Notes on some Colarian Tribes' by W. H. P. Driver.

[9] Vide *Appendix*. In the 18th hymn of the 7th Book of the *Rig Ved* we read of a terrible battle on the banks of the Saraswati in which the Aryan Hero Sudas, king of the Tritsus, fought against the several Non-Aryan tribes mentioned generally as the Simyus (destroyers) and particularly by names, such as the Pakthas, the Bhalanas, the Alinas, the Sivas, the Vishanins, the Ajas, the Sigrus, the Yakshu. (These names are sometimes explained as referring to the various ministers at religious rites). In verse 19, the Yamuna and the Tritsus are said to have aided Sudas in this battle. And in the concluding verse of the hymn, the seven flowing Rivers (of the Punjab) are said to have glorified Indra. Can this be the battle referred to in the Mundari tradition?

want of any evidence to the contrary, we may perhaps take some of them to refer to the ancestors of the Mundas.[10]

Thus, we read of a Dasa named Sambara, son of Kulitara, and head of a hundred cities, who is said to have been hurled down from a lofty hill by Indra for the benefit of the Aryan hero Atithigva of the Kuru race.[11] And the name Sambara looks like a Sans-kritized transformation of the name Sumber—a name still in use among the Mundas of Chota Nagpur. The handless Kunaru[12] who is said to have been crushed by Indra, would seem to be a namesake of Kuar Munda of our own days. The Rig-Vedic name of the Dasyu Ahisuva[13] who shared the same fate with Aurnavabha and others would appear to be a Hinduized form of the name Asiba met with among the Mundas of the Ranchi District. The name of the Asura Bala[14] who used to 'keep the cows of the Aryans im-prisoned,' and was rent by Indra aided by the Angirasas, may be recognised in the modern name of Balia Munda. Karanju and Parnaya[15] who are both said to have been slain by the Aryan hero Atithigva in battle are perhaps represented by Kalang and Parna or perhaps Parhau Munda of our own times. The name Karanjua too is not unknown among the Mundas. The names of Kuyava,[16] the black-skinned opponent of the young and brilliant Kutsa, son of Arjuni, is perhaps a transformation of the Munda name Kuba. In the name of the Dasyu chief Vangrida[17] who is said to have been blockaded by the Aryan hero Rijiswan, we may perhaps trace the modern Munda name of Bangra. The name of the Dasyu Danu[18] who is said to have been defeated by Indra, is still borne by some Mundas of the present day. And analogous names, such as Dana, Danu and Dandu are also met with among modern Mundas. The Dasyu Byansa[19] who is said to have been

[10] In some passages of the *Rig-Veda*, these aboriginal people are called *Muras* explained as 'foolish ones', a term which reminds one of the name *Mura* applied to the Mundas in the Manbhum District and in the adjoining eastern parts of the Ranchi District.

[11] *Rig-Veda*, 1. 51, 6; 1, 130, 7; ll, 24, 2; IV, 130, 13, etc.; VI, 18.8; VI 26,5, VI; 43, 1; VI 47,21 & 22; VII 18.20. In some of the passages he is also called variously Atithivaga, Divodasa, and Prastoka. [12] *Rig Veda*, III, 32,8.

[13] *Rig-Veda*, VIII, 32,26, VIII, 32,2 & 26; VIII, 66,2.

[14] *Rig-Veda*, II, 11,20. [15] *Rig Veda*, I, 53,8; X, 48,8.

[16] *Rig-Veda*, VII, 19,2; I, 104,3. [17] *Rig Veda*, I. 537.,

[18] *Rig-Veda*, I, 51,5,11, 14,5; VI. 18,8; VIII, 32,2; X, 99,11; X, 138,3.

[19] *Rig-Veda*, I. 101,2.

struck down by Indra is perhaps the same as our Biyan Munda.
The name of the Asura Ongha who was worsted in a battle against
the Aryan King Sudasa[20] will be recognised in that of Onga Munda
of our days. A few other names of Rig-Vedic Dasyus such as
Dasoni (II, 20,8), Asna (VI, 4, 3), Tarukshu (VIII, 46,32),
Namuchi (V, 39,7; VII, 19,5) and Chamuri (II, 15,9; VII, 19,4;
VI 18, 8; VI, 20, 13) bear resemblances more or less close to
modern Munda names.[21]　And we must recollect that the Aryans
naturally softened down and modified the barbarian names into
Sanskritic forms so as to make them fit into their own sacred
hymns. These references then may, not unreasonably, be taken
to corroborate the traditions current among several Kolarian
tribes as to their ancient residence in the north-west of India.

And now arises the question, which particular part of north-
western India was occupied by the Mundas in those prehistoric
days? Mention has already been made of a Mundari tradition
which speaks of a deadly struggle in the remote past between the
Mundas and the Aryan invaders, in the Punjab. A second traditionary legend of the Mundas mentions Ajamgarh as the cradle
of the race. Now General Cunningham tells us that the hill
districts between the Beas[22] river in the Punjab and the river
Tons[23] were in ancient times known as the Kuninda-Des, Kulinda-
Des, or Kaulinda—the land of the Kulindas. And the name
Kulinda it seems probable enough, was one of the names applied to
the Kolarian aborigines by the Aryans of old.[24] The Kunets,
probably a race of mixed descent, who now form much more than
half the population of the Kulu district in the western part of this

---

[20] *Rig-Veda*, I. 63,7.

[21] The names of some of the Rig-Vedic *Asuras* (which term though originally
meaning *gods* came gradually to be applied to aerial demons and goblins) would
appear to bear some resemblance to personal names among some of the Kol
tribes,—but this resemblance in the case of the Rig Vedic *Asuras*, unlike the
resemblance in the case of the Rig-Vedic Dasyus, is probably purely
accidental.

[22] The ancient Vipasa of the Hindus, and the Hyphasis of the Greeks.

[23] The Hindu Tamasa in Oudh. It flows through Azimgarh and falls into
the Ganges. The banks of this river are associated with the early life of the great
Sanskrit poet Valmiki.

[24] In the *Parasar Sanhita*, Kuninda is used as the name of a tribe, and Kauninda
as that of their country. As a substitute for *Kuninda* the Markandeya Puran
uses Kaulinda. In the Vishnu Puran we have *Kulinda* for *Kuninda*.

tract, have been supposed by General Cunningham to have derived their origin from the Kulindas, and to be connected with the Mundas of Chota Nagpur. Thus writes the former Director-General of Archaeological Survey of India:

All the ancient remains within the present area of Kunet occupation are assigned to a people who are variously called Mowa- or Mons, and all agree that these were the Kunets themselves. The fact is that Mon is simply their Tibetan name while Kuninda or Kunet is their Indian name.[25]

Again, with respect to the name Mon, which is given to the Kunets and Khasas by the Tibetans, it does not appear to be a Tibetan word, as it is used by the Kunets thesmselves to designate the ancient possessors of the hills, whom they acknowledge to have been their own ancestors. I think it is therefore very probable that the Mons of the Cis-Himalaya may be connected with the Mundas of Eastern India.[26]

Although the Kunets now speak a corrupt dialect of Hindi, their present language, it is said, still retains traces of their original Kolarian language. General Cunningham cites the Kuneti words *dak* or *dhungu* for a stone and *di* for water, as corresponding respectively to the Mundari words *diri* and *da* and the Korku words *dega* and *da* or *di*.

In this ancient Kulinda-Desa, then, the ancestors of the Mundas and other Kolarian tribes appear to have dwelt when the Aryans first appeared on the scene. The mention of mountains in connection with the Dasyus in several passages of the *Rig-Veda*, would seem to indicate their partiality for mountainous regions and their former residence in the hilly tracts of North-Western India. We have already mentioned the tradition still extant among the Kolarian tribe of Asuras of their former residence in Dhaulagir and Mainagir. The tradition of the Mundas as well as of the Santals that they formerly lived in the vicinity of Marang Buru, the great mountain, would seem to lend further support to this view. Now, indeed, wherever the Mundas settle they select some high mountain or hill in the neighbourhood on which to locate the Marang Buru Bonga—the God of the High Mountain.[27]

[25] Cunningham's *Arch. Rep.*, Vol. XIV, p. 127.   [26] *Ibid.*, p. 128.
[27] Thus the Santals now call the Paresnath Hill their Marang Buru.

Another tradition which Mr. Garrick,[28] who was Assistant to Sir Alexander Cunningham, came across in Behar, would seem to afford further confirmation to these traditions. It relates that in the Satya Yuga or the Golden Age—the earliest epoch of Hindu Chronology, the Savaras were predominant in Northern India. And the name Savara, as General Cunningham points out, in early times covered all the different divisions of the Kols.[29] The dominion of the Savaras or Suirs, as Mr. Garrick tells us, extended in ancient times as far as the present districts of Azimgarh and Ghazipore. And traces of ancient Savara supremacy are to be found in several places in these parts of the country.[30] Thus about six miles to the south-west from the present town of Ghazipur there is an extensive mound of ruins with several smaller mounds round about, which is believed to mark the site of an ancient town of the Savaras or Suirs and is still called Suirika Raj. About

[28] Vide Arch. Rep., Vol. XIX, by Garrick, pp. 40-42.

[29] Cunningham, Vol. XVII, p. 139.

[30] The colloquial Bengali expression Saper mantar, Cunningham considers to be a corruption of Savar Mantra, an unintelligible jargon such as are used by the Savaras or Kols. In proof of the statement that the general name 'Savara' included all the different Kolarian tribes, the following facts may be mentioned. The Kolarian Santals, as we know, are called Savaras by the Male Paharias (vide Cunng. XVLL, p. 125). The Parna-Savaras named by Baraha-Mihira (about 550 A.D.) has been supposed to refer to the leaf-clad Juangs, another Kolarian tribe. The Kolarian Bendkars who now live about the Thakurani Hill on the boundary-line between Singbhoom and the tributary state of Keonjhar described themselves as Savaras in the Census of 1872. Even now, the name Savara is borne by the southernmost branch of the Kol race living in the two northernmost districts of Madras and the neighbouring districts of Orissa and the Central Provinces. The Savaras and Pulindas are almost always mentioned together in ancient Sanskrit literature, and it is probable enough that these were two names for the same race. It has been sometimes supposed that a tribe of the name of Savaras, in later times, expelled the Cheros from Shahabad, and established themselves in what is now the Bhojpore Perganah, and were, in their turn, expelled either by Raja Bhoja or by the Pramar Rajputs of Dharnagar. But we have no reliable information about this supposed tribe of Savaras who must not be confounded with the ancient Savaras we have been speaking of. Not a single remnant of this supposed Savara conquerors of the Cheros is to be found in Shahabad at present, the name of Savara as that of a particular tribe being unknown in the district, although the Kolarian Mushaharas still form a small proportion of the population. On the other hand, a number of Cheros still live in the Shahabad district and point to a later Chero predominance. According to another tradition, it was a tribe of the name of the Hurihobans, and not the Savaras, who expelled the great body of the Cheros from Shahabad.

twenty-five miles west-south-west from the town of Ghazipore there is a very large and high mound of ruins called Masaondih nearly a mile to the north of a village of the name of Joharganj.[31] And Masaondih is said to have been anciently called Dhanawar. Mr. Carlleyle excavated this mound of ruins to a considerable depth, and, as he himself says, "found it a regular historical epitome ranging from recent times back to the Stone Age". Stone implements and other pre-historic remains, but not a single article of metal, were found in the earliest stratum which Mr. Carlleyle reached.[32]

The last traditional king of the Savaras is said to have belonged to the Treta-yuga, the second age of Hindu Chronology. And the same tradition goes on to relate that the Bhrigu, the Raghu and the Naga races combined to rob the Savaras of their kingdom which then passed to the Bhrigu-vansa.[33] And this tradition seems to have the support of the *Rig Veda* itself. In the *Rig Veda* we read of the race of Bhrigus as having established Agni or Fire among mankind.[34] And it is Agni who is said to have "struck down the noseless (*anasan*) Dasyus with his weapon and overthrown the imperfect speakers (*mridhrabacha*) in their homes."[35] But the overthrow of the great Kol race could not have been effected at once. For a time, the Mundas and other allied tribes appear to have waged wars on equal terms with their Aryan opponents.[36] In those days of their glory, these Kolarian tribes were not, as their degenerate descendants are represented in later Sanskrit writings to have been, a despicable horde maintaining their rude anarchic existence without order, without civilisation and without arts of any sort whatever. The scanty glimpses of light afforded

[31] The word *johar* in Mundari and in Santali means 'salutation'.

[32] Cunningham's *Arch. Rep.*, XXII, pp. 97-101.

[33] *Arch. Rep.*, Cunningham, XIX, pp. 40-42. According to Hewitt the Bhrigus of India are identical in race with the Bruges of Thrace and the Phrygians of Asia Minor and they made the household fire their chief god, and introduced the patriarchal age which superseded the matriarchal rule of village mothers. *Vide* Hewitt's *Primitive Traditional History*, Vol. 1,p. 219.

[34] *Rig Veda* I, 60, I; I, 56, 6; I, 143, 4; I, 58, 6.

[35] *Rig Veda*, VI, 29, 10; See also I, 59, 6, & V, 2, 1—The description of Agni in these verses, Muir tells us, "applies not to the sacrificial fire but to the fire that clears the jungles as the new settlers advance into the country."

[36] Thus in the *Rig Veda*, III, 30, 17 a hymn attributed to the Rishi Viswamitra, we read—"Root up the race of Rakshas, O Indra, Rend it in front and crush it in the middle. How long hast thou behaved as one who wavers? Cast thy hot dart on him who hates devotion (*Brahmadwisha*)."

by the *Rig Veda* into the then state of the Kol tribes reveal a degree
of progress in arts and civilisation that must have taken the Kols
a considerable time to work out. Several of these tribes appear to
have already passed from the primitive hunting stage and the
succeeding stage of nomad farmers to that of founders of permanent
villages.[37] Tribal organisation does not appear to have been
altogether unknown. Thus we hear of the hundred ancient cities
of the Dasyu leader Sambara,[38] the hundred cities of Vangrira[39]
and the ninety-nine cities of the Dasyu leader Pipru.[40] In several
other passages of the *Rig Veda* we hear of the strongbuilt cities of
aborigines.[41] In the eighth verse of the eighteenth hymn of
the Sixth Book we read of the castles of Chamuri, Dhuni, Sambara
Pipru, and Sushna. These castles have been sometimes supposed to
refer to 'the brilliant battlemented cloud-castles so often visible
in the Indian sky', and the Asuras to 'the demons of drought'.[42]
Though this may perhaps be true of some, it is certainly not so
with regard to all. Thus, in the ninth verse of the forty-fifth hymn
in the sixth book of the *Rig Veda*, castles built by the hand of man
are distinctly spoken of. "Lord of Strength, Caster of the stone,
destroy the firm forts built by men, and foil their arts, unbending
God;"[43] and in the third verse of the 103rd hymn of the first
Book, and the 6th verse of the 12th hymn of the 3rd Book, we hear
of 'the forts which the Dasas held'. And by no stretch of imagination can these Dasas be identified with the supposed demons of
drought.[44] The reference in the *Rig Veda*, II, 20, 8, to the iron

---

[37] The Mundari name for a village, *hatu* (Santali, *atu*) does not appear to have
been derived from any Sanskritic dialect and goes to show that the Munda is
not indebted to any alien influences in conceiving the idea of establishing villages.
The village organisation of the Mundas under a headman appears to have impressed the Aryans, for it is they who first applied the name *Munda* (literailly,
head) to this people. How far the Aryan Hindus were indebted to these democratic aboriginal Mundas for their ideas of village organisation it is now difficult to
ascertain.

[38] *Rig Veda*, II, 14, 6. [39] *Rig Veda*, I, 53, 9. [40] *Rig Veda*, I, 174, 8.
[41] Vide *Rig Veda*, VI, 61, 4; I, 174, 8; II, 63, 7.

[42] Muir's *Sanskrit Texts*., Vol. II, p. 379. [43] Griffith's Translation.

[44] In much later times, in the Epic Period, the days of the *Mahabharata*, we read
of the Daitya Maya building a palace for the Pandavas. And the historian of
Ancient India in the *Historians' History of the World* remarks: "It was from the
natives that the Aryans learnt the art of building in stone, they themselves like
other Indo-Europeans understanding only how to build in wood and piles, or
dwelling in caves."

cities of the Dasyus may indeed be metaphorical, and perhaps alludes to the great strength of their fortifications.

The wealth of the Dasas or aboriginal tribes is not overlooked by the sacred singers of the *Rig Veda*. The wealth of the Dasa Kuyava is envied by Kutsa Angirasa, the composer of the 104th hymn of the First Book of the *Rig Veda*. "He who hath only wish for his possession casts on himself, casts foam amid the waters. Both wives of Kuyava in milk have bathed them. May they be drowned within the depth of Sipha."[45] And the interpretation of this passage is thus given by Ludwig,—"While the poor Aryan who can only wish for the wealth which he does not possess has not even ordinary water to wash himself in, the wives of the enemy in the insolent pride of their riches, bathe in milk." In the second verse of the twenty-fourth hymn of the Second Book, we read of the strong-holds of Sambara within the mountain, stored with wealth. As is only natural, a great portion of this wealth consisted of herds of animals, for the Kols appear to have been a pastoral race in those days. The notions of the family and of the State appear to have been already developed. In some passages of the *Rig Veda*, we find indications that the institution of individual marriage had already been established amongst these aboriginal inhabitants of Ancient India and that the matriarchal age had been already succeeded by the patriarchal. Thus, for example, the Dasa chief Sambara is described as the son of his father, Kulitara. The two wives of Kuyava, as we have seen, are distinctly spoken of. As for their notions of the state, these Dasa tribes would appear to have evolved common-wealths of their own, with some Dasa chief at the head of each city or group of cities. We read of groups of cities varying from seven to one-hundred, and each group ruled over by one of these tribal chiefs. The arts of war and peace were not unknown. Stone and flint weapons were used in warfare and implements of the same materials appear to have been utilised for house-hold purposes.

Such were the peoples whom the vigorous Aryan race from the colder regions of the north encountered in India and with whom

[45] Griffith's translation.—Sayana's explanation of this passage is as follows: "The Asura, or demon, Kuyava, who knows the wealth of others, carries it away of himself, and being present on the water he carries off the water with the foam. In this water which has been carried away Kuyava's wives bathe."

they now engaged in a life-and-death struggle for supremacy. Herdsmen and farmers by occupation, these aborigines of the soil could build houses for themselves, erect castles of stone, make flint weapons fitted for all uses, and understood the benefits of law and order. Then, as now, the Kols appear to have taken the utmost delight in drinking and in singing. The Mundas, to this day, sing a song bewailing those good old days which are not to return again :

Sato jugu Kale jugu, Sato jugu taikena,
Sato jugu Kale jugu, Kali jugu hijulena.
Sato jugu taikena ilige-ko nukena,
Kale jugu tebalena, rengetako goetana.
Neaiting sanaiya, ilige-ko nukena,
Chakating moninga, rengeteko goetana.

TRANSLATION.

Then was the Satyug,—now the Iron Age.
   O gone the Golden Age of old !
Then reign'd the Satyug,—now the reign of Kal,
   On Earth hath come with woes untold.
Men in that blessed ancient Age of Gold,
   Had naught to do but drink their ale.
Now that the cursed Kali reigns supreme
   Dire death from hunger doth prevail.
Oh ! for the days when men no cares did know,
   But drank their fill of home-brewed ale.
Woe to this age when men on earth below,
   Do daily die of famine fell ![46]

In the end however the fair-complexioned new-comers proved too strong for the black-skinned aborigines. And the sun of Kol prosperity sank below the horizon. The Aryans, who first established themselves on the banks of the Indus and its tributaries in the Rig Vedic period, gradually pushed their way up to the valley of the Ganges and by the period of the great Epics, became supreme all over the tract from the banks of the Indus and its tributaries on the west to the banks of the Kausiki and the Ganges on the east and

[46] This is a free translation of the Mundari song.

south-east and from the Himalayas on the north up to the banks of the Jumna to the south. Different branches of them established separate kingdoms of their own. The Kauravas held sway around Indraprastha, about two miles south of modern Delhi. The Panchalas established themselves round about Kanyakubja or modern Kanauj, and at a later date advanced up to the banks of the Charmanvati, the modern river Chambal. The Kosalas were supreme in the tract between the Ganges and the Ganduck. The Kasis established themselves around Baranasi, our modern Benares. The Videhas settled in the tract between the river Ganduck on the west and the Kuasiki or Kusi on the east.

Gradually pushed eastward by the advancing tide of Aryan conquest, the Mundas appear to have come up as far as the present district of Azimgarh, and here they must have dwelt unmolested for some time. For it is Azimgarh that forms the starting point of their historical traditions. The most exhaustive of these traditions begins with their ancient residence in Azimgarh.[47] The present district of Azimgarh is included in the Benares Division of the North-western Provinces, and is bounded on the north by the river Gogra and by the Fyzabad District in Oudh and the District of Goruckpur, on the south by the Ghazipur and Juanpur districts, on the east by the Balia and Ghazipur Districts, and on the west by the Juanpur, Sultanpur and Fyzabad districts. But, according to local tradition, the Azimgarh District was in ancient times included in the kingdom of Ayodhya, and "most of the traditions of the district", as we learn from the *Statistical Account of the North-Western Provinces*, "refer to the Rajbhars and Suiris as the former occupants of the soil".[48] We have already pointed out that General Cunningham has identified the Suiris or Suirs of tradition with the Savaras of ancient Sanskrit literature, and the name *Savara* as that distinguished archaeologist proves by a lengthy discussion, was in all probability a generic name for the different divisions of the Kols, including the Kurkus and the Bhils in the west, and the Santals and the Bhuinyas, the Mundas and the Hos, the Bhumijes and the Juangs in the east.[49] Thus the tradition of the Mundas themselves finds unexpected

[47] *Vide* an article on 'Munda Cosmogony and traditional History' by the present writer in *The Indian World* for December, 1907.

[48] Aitkinson's *Statistical Account of N. W. P. of India*, Vol. XIII, p. 131.

[49] *Arch. Rep*, Vol., XVII, 139.

support from the traditions preserved by the Hindus of the Azimgarh District, and we may therefore safely accept the Mundari tradition of their former residence in Azimgarh as correct. Nor will it perhaps be unreasonable to suppose that the name Azimgarh or Azabgarh, as the Mundas call it, owes its origin to its original inhabitants, the Kols. The name Azim, Ajam, or Ajab is clearly not of Hindu origin. Nor is this name, as it might appear at first sight to be, of Mahomedan origin,—for Mahomet was not born till ages after the foundation of Azimgarh, and the countrymen of Mahomet were utter strangers to India when Azamgarh was peopled by the Kols. Among the Mundas, on the other hand, the name Asiba or Asba is still met with as a proper name of persons, and Azimgarh or Azabgarh[50] was not improbably the place where Asiba or Asba Munda had his fort.[51] About twenty-four miles east of the present town of Azimgarh, at a place called Ghosi, are still pointed out the remains of a large mudfort which local legends attribute to the Asurs.[52] And *Asura*, as we have seen, was at one time a generic name for the Kolarian aborigines and is at the present moment borne by one of those

[50] It may also be noted that in Mundari the word *Ajom* means 'to feed'. The word *Garh* though generally supposed to be a corruption of Sanskrit *griha* meaning 'house', may not improbably owe its origin to the Mundari word *gara* (Santali *garha*) meaning a pool of water or a water-channel, and may have reference to the ditches or water-channels with which the Non-Aryan *Garhs* or 'forts' used to be protected on all sides.

[51] Other places which might at first sight appear to have equal claims with Azimgarh to be considered as identical with the Ajabgarh of Munda tradition are : (i) Ajabgarha in Rajputana. Geologists assert that "either during the new Pliocene or perhaps the Post-Pliocene or the early part of the recent period, not only the desert, but also the flat intermontane plains of Rajputana were an actual sea, or formed part of the ocean, but was dotted over, here and there, with a sort of archipelago of mountainous islands occurring at long intervals, and that this sea gradually dried up, partly by the silting up of rivers, partly by the formation of sandy dunes and great drifts of sand at their mouths and partly by volcanic forces" (Cunningham, *Arch. Rep.*, Vol. V, 146). But as according to popular tradition this place was founded by Somasi, a son of Karna Pal, a Tomar Raja of Delhi (circa 12th or 13th century), its identification with the Ajabgarh of Munda tradition would seem to be untenable. (*Vide* Cunningham, Vol. XVI, p. 154). (ii) Ajegarh or Ajaygarh in Bundelkhand. Though this is an old city, its claim to identity with the Ajabgarh of Munda tradition is not sustainable as the ancient name of this city appears to have been Jaynagara, (Vide Aitkinson's *Stt. Acct.*, Vol. I, p. 264).

[52] Aitkinson's *Statistical Account*, XIII, p. 131.

tribes now dwelling in Chota Nagpur. In the Azimgarh District, there still exist traces of a large excavation which seems to have once connected the Koonwar and the Munghi rivers, and is still known by the name of Assooraeen.[53]

Before the time when the famous king Rama Chandra reigned in Ayodhya, the Mundas appear to have left Azimgarh.[54] For local traditions tell us that in the time of Ram Chandra[55] it was only the Raj-Bhars who were living in Azimgarh, and the Savaras or Asurs are heard of no more.[56] And we may very well imagine, the freedom-loving Mundas to have left the country when the Aryans became supreme in the tract.[57] The ancient kingdom of Ayodhya, as we learn from the Ramayana, was founded by Ikshaku from whom Ram Chandra traced his descent. Prof. Heeren certainly did not err on the side of over-calculation when he remarked of ancient Ayodhya, "We do not, perhaps, assume too much when...we venture to place its origin from 1500 to 2000 years before the Christian Era."[58] Thus in accordance with the testimony of the traditions noticed above, we may take it that the Mundas migrated from Azimgarh more than three thousand years ago.

From Azimgarh, so runs the Munda tradition, the Mundas migrated successively to Kalangjar, Garh Chitra, Garh Nagarwar, Garh Daharwar, Garh Pali, Garh Pipra, Mandar Pahar, Bijna-

---

[53] Settlement Report of Dt. Azimgarh (1837), in the *Journal of the Asiatic Society of Bengal*, Vol. VIII, p. 77, at p. 90.

[54] It is in the time of the sunborn King Ikshaku that according to Hindu tradition there had been a great deluge. And the Mundas too, speak of a great deluge before they left Azimgarh.

[55] The celebrated Rama Chandra is sometimes said to have been born in the seventeenth century before Christ. Prof. Heeren places him in the 37th generation and Sir William Jones in his article "on the Chronology of the Hindus" (*Asiatic Researches*, Vol. II.) places Ram Chandra in the fifty-sixth generation, from Ikshaku.

[56] Vide, *Calcutta Review*, Vol. LXIX, p. 350.

[57] The name *Kikata* in verse 14 of hymn 53 of the third *Mandala* of the Rig Veda, ("Among the Kikatas, what do thy cattle? They pour no milky draught, they heat no cauldron.") has been sometimes supposed to refer to the aborigines then living in modern Behar, and to include the Mundas and several other Kolarian tribes. But as R.T.H. Griffith remarks (Foot note to p. 374 of Griffith's Edition of the *Rig Veda* Vol. I), probably the verse referred to the then Non-Aryan inhabitants of Kosala or Oudh.

[58] Heeren's *Historical Researches*, Vol. II, p. 207.

3

garh, Hardinagar, Laknourgarh, Nandangarh, Rijgarh and Ruidasgarh, and thence across Burmughat to Omedanda in Jharkhand Chota Nagpur.

If we follow the order indicated in this tradition, the Mundas would appear to have migrated from Northern India southwards to modern Bundelkhand and Central India, thence across Eastern Rajputana back again to North-Western India and thence through modern Rohilkhund and Oudh to Behar and finally to Chota Nagpur. Though this circuitous route may appear strange and perplexing to us, and though perhaps we may be inclined to suppose that they should have proceeded from Bundelkhand direct to Behar and thence to Chota Nagpur it will be wiser to follow the rule laid down by the German philosopher Schlegel with regard to the investigation of ancient history. Says he,

Historical tradition must never be abandoned in the philosophy of history, otherwise we lose all firm ground and footing. But historical tradition ever so accurately conceived and carefully sifted doth not always, especially in the early and primitive ages, bring with it a full and demonstrative certainty. In such cases we have nothing to do but to record, as it is given, the best and safest testimony which tradition, so far as we have it, can afford, supposing even that some things in that testimony may appear strange, obscure, and even enigmatical; and perhaps a comparison with some other part of historical science or, if I may so speak, stream of tradition, will unexpectedly lead to the solution of the difficulty.[59] Again the same learned author of the "Philosophy of History" says :

I have laid it down as an invariable maxim constantly to follow historical tradition and to hold fast by that clue, even when many things in the testimony and declarations of tradition appear strange and almost inexplicable, or at best, enigmatical, for so soon as in the investigations of ancient history we let slip that thread of Ariadne we can find no outlet from the labyrinth of fanciful theories and the chaos of clashing opinions.[60]

In the present account, therefore, we can do no better than trace the course of the successive migrations of the Mundas in the order in which their own traditions recount them.

[59] Schlegel's *Philosophy of History*. (Translated by J. B. Robertson, p. 71).
[60] Schlegel's *Philosophy of History*, p. 81.

From Azimgarh, Mundari tradition tells us, the remote fore-fathers of the Mundas proceeded to Kalangjargarh. Kalangjar or Kalinjar, is, as we know, a famous place in the Banda District in modern Bundelkhund. It is situated on the river Tons or Tamasa, and is 90 miles to the west-south-west of Allahabad and sixty miles to the north-west of Rewa. As to its remote antiquity we have ample testimony in ancient Sanskrit literature. Kalinjar is, as Wilson tells us, mentioned in the Vedas as one of the *tapas-thans*, or 'spots adapted to practices of austere devotion'. In the *Mahabharata*, great religious merit is attached to ablutions in the lake of the gods in Kalinjar.[61] In the *Padma Purana*, Kalin-jara is mentioned as one of the nine *ukhalas* or holy places in Northern India. Many and varied are the vicissitudes of fortune that Kalinjar has seen.[62] Towards the beginning of the Christian Era, Kalinjar was occupied by the Kulachari princes of Chedi. And under the celebrated Gupta Kings who established their suzerainty all over the country between the Jumna and the Nerbu-dda, Kalinjar rose to be the capital of Chedi.[63] We next hear of Kalinjar as one of the chief cities of the Chandela Rajputs.[64] It was during the reign of the Chandela Raja Gauda Deva that Mahmud of Ghazni besieged the fortress Kalinjar in 1023 A. D. After the Chandels, the Khangars established themselves in the land; and they, in their turn, were expelled by the Bundellas about the fourteenth century. It was with the greatest difficulty that Sher Shah could capture the fortress in 1545. The Marhattas next appeared on the scene and established their supremacy in the country. And last of all, a British force under Colonel Martindell besieged it and was repulsed in 1812; but at length the Raja surrendered the fortress to the British Lion and accepted in exhange an estate of equal value in the plains.

[61] *Vanaparba*, 85th Canto—Sloka 56.

[62] The statement in the Ferista that Kalinjar was founded by Kedar Raja, a contemporary of Mahomet (7th Century) is certainly erroneous, for the place is repeatedly mentioned by name in ancient Hindu mythology.

[63] The Naga Kings of Bundelkhund, numerous coins of which dynasty have been discovered in Narwar and Bundelkhand, appear to have ruled Bundel-khand under the suzerainty of the Guptas of Magadha.

[64] The chandels would however appear to have been originally aboriginal Bhars who gradually get themselves admitted first as *Kayaths* and next as chhatris. Vide *Indian Antiquary*, Vol. I, p. 265.

History has, however, omitted to record the name of the peoples
who occupied it before the Aryan Hindus heard of its existence.
But the unequivocal tradition of the Mundas points out this place
of hoary antiquity as having been founded by their own ancestors
by making clearances in the then primeval forest. The name
Kalangjar[65] perhaps owes its origin to some ancient Munda
patriarch of the name of Kalang— a name still found among the
Chota Nagpur Mundas,—and the Mundari expression *Jara Ma*,
the act of clearing a virgin forest by cutting down the trees and
burning them. The Hindu derivation of the name *Kalangjara*
from Siva himself who as Kala, time, causes all things to decay
(*jar*) would appear to be rather far-fetched.[66] On the other hand,
in Hindu mythology this place is said to have successively borne
the distinctive Hindu names of Ratankot, Mahadgiri, and Pingala
in the Satya, Treta and Dwapara Yugas respectively.

There is a farther fact which would seem to lend support to the
Munda tradition of their having once lived in these parts. From
references in ancient Sanskrit literature, it would appear that
these parts, were in ancient times known as Pulinda-desa the land
of the Pulindas. And the Pulindas (Pulindai of Ptolemy and
Molendae of Pliny), like the name *Savara*, appears to have been
used by ancient Sanskrit writers as a generic name for the Kol
tribes.[67] In fact, the two names *Pulinda* and *Satara* are often
found in juxtaposition in ancient Sanskrit writings.[68] Aryan

---

[65] We meet with the expression *Jara ma* in the name of the Munda folktale of
Kula ad jara ma harama kahini, the legend of the tiger and the old man clearing
the forest.

[66] Vana Parba, *Mahabharata*.

[67] Wilson in his translation of the *Vishnu Purana*, (p. 186, footnote) in explaining
the Topographical lists prepared by himself from the *Mahabharata* (Bhisma Parva,
II, 343), says "Pulindas is applied to any wild or barbarous tribe, those here
named are some of the people of the deserts along the Indus; but Pulindas are
met with in many other positions, especially in the mountain and forests of Central
India, the haunts of the Bhils and Gonds. So Ptolemy places the Pulindas along
the banks of the Narmada to the frontiers of Larice the Late hur of the Hindus,
Khandesh and part of Guzerat."

[68] Vide *Aitareya Brahmana*, VII, 18.

In the Katha Sarith Sagara composed by the Kashmiri poet Soma Deva in the
12th century (from the prose-tales of the Brihat Katha of Gunadhaya (6th century)
who was probably a contemporary of Varaha-mihir and Amar Sinha), the terms
'Pulinda' and 'Savara' are used indifferently with reference to Vindhya-ketu,
a Bhil King. And the Bhils appear to have been a branch of the great Kol race.

expeditions against Pulinda-desa are described in the *Mahabharata*. Local tradition asserts that before the time of Raja Virat who

BIRSA MUNDA

ruled in these parts, the District of Banda was inhabited by the Kols. And even to this day, in the valleys that separate the Banda District from the State of Rewa and other tributary states, there are "vast jungles with hardly any cultivation, where villages consist of scattered huts, inhabited by half-savage Kols, and where wild animals remain almost undisturbed".[69]

[69] Aitkinson's *Sttl. Account of N.W.P.*, Vol. I, p. 49 I.

How long the Mundas and their kinsmen hid themselves in the
jungly and rocky fastness of the Kaimurs and subsequently in
the hilly regions of the ancient Pulinda-desa, it can by no means
be definitely ascertained.   But they must have spent a rude dreary
existence in these fastnesses for a considerable length of time.   And
in that wide space of time, they probably unlearnt some of the
peaceful arts of civilisation that they had acquired in their pre-
Aryan days of peace and prosperity.   In their constant struggle
with the adverse forces of the physical and animal world, it is
no wonder that they would have slipt down the few rungs of the
ladder of civilisation that they had climbed up in happier
days.

The next place after Kalinjar that Mundari tradition fixes as
the abode of the Mundas is Garh-Chitr.   And this place is in
all probability no other than the celebrated place of pilgrimage
known as Chitrakut or Chitrakot in parganah Tarawan and
Tahsil Karwi of the Banda District in Bundelkhand.   The student
of ancient Sanskrit literature is aware that this place rose to great
sanctity in the Treta Yuga.   It was then that the celebrated Ram
Chandra of Ayodhya visited it during his exile and the hermits
living around Chitrakuta piteously complained to him of the
harassment to which the *Anarya* savages so frequently subjected
them.

रक्षांसि पुरुषादानि नानारूपानि राघव ।
वसन्त्यस्मिन् महारण्ये व्यालाश्च रुधिराशना: ॥
उत्साद्य तापसान् सर्व्वान् जनस्थाननिबासिन: ।
भ्रान्ति चास्मिन् महारण्येतान् निवारय राघव ॥[70]

"Men-devouring Rakshasas of various shapes, and wild beasts,
(or serpents) which feed on blood, dwell in this vast forest. They
harass the devotees who reside in the settlements and slay them in
the forest. Repress them, Raghava."[71]   And the Rishis go on
to describe these black denizens of the woods as 'Shapeless and
ill-looking   monsters';—*anarya*   wretches,   'wicked   monsters',
'uttering frightful sounds'.[72]   And Rama is warned that "it is

[70] *Ramayana*, III, I, 14 etc.   [71] Translation by Muir.

[72] In the *Ramayana*, III, 28,18, Khara, one of the Rakshasa Chiefs describes his
people as of fearful swiftness (See T. S. 74) unyielding in battle (See T. S. 74)
in colour like a dark black cloud (See T. S. 74)

not expedient for him to tarry alone with his spouse in the neighbourhood of these cruel Rakshasas, for though he is indeed able
to destroy them, he should not be too confident, for they are a
treacherous race".   Here perhaps is a reference to the ancestors
of the Mundas and other cognate tribes.   And the famous Chitrakuta not improbably owes its name to its original occupants, the
Mundas.   These people call the *titir* or partridge by the name,
Chitri, and though the name Chitrakuta is sometimes said to be
derived from the Sanskrit word *Chitra* (painting), from the various
hues of its rocks, the derivation from the Mundari word *Chitri* or
partridge which in company with other birds haunt the hill is
not unlikely.   Around this hill Chitrakuta:—

Auspicious hill, where all day long,
The lapwing's cry, the Koil's song,
Make all who listen gay,—
Where all is fresh and fair to see,
Where elephants and deer roam free,[73]—

the ancestors of the Mundas appear to have dwelt in the Treta-
Yuga of Hindu chronology.   Their kinsmen the Korkus, moved
down farther south, and to this day they occupy the Satpura,
Maikul and Mahadeo Hills in the Central Provinces.   The Korwas
of Sirguja and the western parts of the Ranchi District, another
allied tribe, still speak of the Mahadeo Hills as their old home.[74]
And the state of Baghelakhand or Rewa on the adjoining east of
Bundelkhand still contains a considerable population of Kol Muasis.
Nor is the name *Savara* unknown in these parts.   A large old village of the name of Saurai, 27 miles to the west of Shagarh and 9
miles to the north of Madanpore contains several families of Kols,
and "must have derived its name from the Sauras or Savaras".[75]

In this wide tract of forest country which, as we have already
seen, was known in ancient Sanskrit literature as the Pulinda-desa,
the Mundas and other Kol tribes, thus appear to have ensconced
themselves to seek immunity from alien control.   And eminently
fitted indeed was the country where 'hill peeps o'er hill and Alps

[73] Griffith's Translation of the *Ramayana*.
[74] Vide article on "The Korkus" by W. H. P. Driver, in the *Asiatic Society's
Journal*, Bengal, Vol. LXL, p. 128.
[75] Cunningham's, *Arch. Rep.*, Vol. XXI, p. 170.

on Alps arise', to afford a safe refuge against hostile attacks.   On the west rolled the mighty Chambal, 'the paramount lord of the floods of Central India', as it has been called.   On the south and the south-east, the Vindhya range stretched across the peninsula like a gigantic 'adamantine barrier'.   On the north, rolled the sacred Jumna with vast jungles on her southern banks.   In these hilly regions, as we have seen, a few tribes, allied to the Mundas, linger on in communes of the primitive type, even to this day.

By the time the Gonds appeared in Central India, the Mundas had probably left these parts.   For, in the famous Gond song of Lingawad about the creation of the World and the Gond people, we find mention of the Korkus or Kurkus and the Bhils, but not of the Mundas.[76]

During their long residence in the tract of country between the Chambal on the west and the Tons on the east, the Mundas appear to have lived in comparative immunity from hostile attacks. Occasionally, it appears, the mighty Aryan princes of the north, in their ambitious conquering expeditions (*digvijayam*) throughout the then accessible Bharatavarsa, assailed them in their forest homes.   But the conquerors hardly left behind them any permanent traces of their vain-glorious triumphs.

At length, however, the Mundas set out once again on their dismal wanderings.   In that Dark Age of the History of Aboriginal India, successive tides of Aryan conquest appear to have been followed by confused waves of migration among the aboriginal population.   Whether it was the aggressions of the rising kingdom of Chedi on their west, or the incursions of aboriginal tribes from the south or elsewhere it is hardly possible at this distance of time to ascertain.   But Munda tradition represents this people as tracing their steps backwards to the north-west[77] till they entered

[76] Vide '*Papers Relating to the Aboriginal Tribes of the Central Provinces left in Mss. by the late Rev. Stephen Hislop,*' Edited by R. (afterwards Sir Richard) Temple, C. S. I. (*Vide* lines 55 & c. of the Song of Lingawad).

[77] The two distinct classes of sepulchral mounds found in Northern India probably belong respectively to two Epochs—the Pre-Aryan and the Post-Aryan, in which we have supposed the Kolarian aborigines to have immigrated into and dwelt in those parts.   These two classes of sepulchral mounds, as Z. A. Ragozin (Vedic India, p. 287) points out, "represent two stages of culture since in some only flint implements and the roughest of pottery are found, while others contain iron weapons, gold and copper ornaments".   The former, we may very well infer, belong to the period when the Mundas and their conquerors lived in Northern

the country between the Pariparta mountains of the Pathar Range of our days on the east, and the parallel range known as the Karkotaka, the Karkota Range of our maps on the west. Here appears to have been located the Garh Nagarwar[78] of Munda tradition, which may not improbably be identified with the ancient town of Nagar, or Nagara. The modern fortified town of Nagar and the adjoining site of the ancient city of Nagara lies to the east of the Karkota range, about 15 miles to the South West of Uniyara and is now included within the territory of the Raja of Uniyara, a tributary of the Maharaja of Jeypore. Local traditions name Rajah Macchakanda son of Mandhata[79] as the founder of the ancient city of Nagara. It is here that the Asura, Kal by name, whom Krishna himself pursued in vain, is said to have been killed by Raja Macchakanda at the instigation of Krishna. And tradition adds that the tribesmen of Kal soon had their revenge when, being invited to the marriage of the daughter of Macchakanda, they devoured all the provisions the Raja had in store, and, next, all the inhabitants of Nagara, and finally destroyed the city of Nagar itself by raining down ashes upon it. The site of the ancient city of Nagar forms a conspicuous elevated tract of ground, comprising an area of nearly four square miles, composed of extensive lofty mounds or *tilas* forming long ridges, which are strewn with fragments of ancient bricks of large size, and covered with trees and jungle. It rises out of a flat, almost treeless plain, and it is situated about 4 or 5 miles to the east of the nearest part of the Karkota range of hills.[80] Not improbably the traditions of the Asura Kal may refer to some Kol

India before the Aryans entered the country and pushed them to the south. The latter class of sepulchral mounds, it appears, belong to the period we are now describing when the Mundas and some other Kol tribes once more returned to Northern India and learnt the use of gold and copper from their Aryan neighbours.

[78] One or two of the men from whom I heard the Mundari tradition, give the name of Garh Nagarwar twice in the enumeration of the places successively occupied by the Mundas. The second Garh Nagar unless it be a mere repetition may perhaps be identified with the modern State of Nagodh in Bundelkhand, between the State of Rewa on the east and that of Panna on the west. The modern fort of Nagodh stands on the Aramn, a tributary of the Tons, at an elevation of 1099 feet above the level of the sea.

Vide Atkinson's *Statistical Account*, Vol. I, p. 552.

[79] Colonel Tod thinks Mandhata belonged to the Pramara tribe.

[80] Cunningham, *Arch. Rep.*, (by Carleylle), Vol. VI, p. 162.

leader who was killed by the king of the place. And the Kols probably wreaked their vengeance by destroying the ancient city and establishing themselves on its ruins.[81] The human bones discovered underneath the numerous *tilas* or mounds of earth, may be the mortal remains of the ancestors of the Mundas and their congeners who here buried their dead and erected these mounds to mark their *smasan* or burial places.

Garh Daharwar, which is mentioned in Mundari tradition along with Garh Nagarwar as one of the places where the ancestors of the Mundas lived in the past, is in all probability the ancient Dhand, the deserted *khera* or site of which city is now pointed out some twelve miles to the south-west of Nagara. The present inhabitants of Nagara believe that the old Khera or city of Nagara extended all the way to Dhand,[82] and fragments of old bricks may still be found that way. Ghar is the name of the modern village situated partly on the ancient *khera* or site of Dhand.[83] As a further item of evidence in support of the identification of the ancient Dhand with the Garh Daharwar of Munda tradition, may perhaps be mentioned the discovery by Cunningham of several flakes of quartzite, and two rude implements of the same material, "the work", as Mr. Carleylle says, "of the ancient stone-chipping aborigines".

From here the Mundas appear to have moved farther north and to have settled at a place which their tradition names as Bijnagarh. And this would seem to be a variant of the name of the modern Bianagarh or Biana, a place on the left bank of the Gambir river, about 50 miles[84] to the south-west of Agra. This place, as General Cunningham tells us, "is situated at the foot of a south-eastern salient angle of a massive and precipitous range of granite hills constituting simply one immense elevated granite table-land".[85] Hindu tradition attributes the foundation of the place to Banasur, who is said to have been the son of a Raja Bal or Bali[86] of the

[81] The supposition that the legend may refer to some sudden catastrophe such as earthquake or volcanic convulsion, is uncalled for.

[82] Cunningham, *Arch Rep.*, Vol. VI., p. 195.

[83] Cunningham, *Arch. Rep.*, Vol., IV, p. 160.

[84] About 65 miles by the road.

[85] Cunningham, *Arch. Rep.*, Vol., VI, p. 40.

[86] Compare the name *Balia* which is a common enough name among the Mundas.

Asura race. The great strength of Banasur is allegorically described
in the legend which represents him to have been gifted with a
thousand arms, all of which except four were cut off in battle by
the Sudarsana Chakra or discus of Krishna. In ancient times,
the country around Biana was included in the land of the Yadavas
or Surasenas who had then their capital at Mathura. Even so
late as in the time of Alexander's invasion, this teritory of the
Surasenas was but partially cleared, as is indicated by the names
of the different forests into which it was divided, namely, Mahavana,
Madhuvana, Khadiravana, Talavana, Vrindavana, and Piluvana.
Besides these Mahavanas or great forests, there were in this tract
a number of Upavanas or lesser forests. A forest covered tract
like this would naturally prove welcome to the Mundas. Remnants
of burial stones and cairns similar to those still used by the Mundas
have been discovered at various places in this ancient land of the
Surasenas. At Satmas, about 16 miles south of Fatehpur
Sikri, in a cleft between two hills, there are numerous cairns, of
which Carleylle writes :

I counted nearly thirty cairns on the slope of the hill,
which appeared to me on examination, to be really ancient,
and built for sepulchral purposes, besides others on the
ridge of the hill which had a more modern appearance,
and which latter may have been constructed by cattle-herds
as *amiras* or elevated seats to sit on while watching their cattle
grazing on the hill sides. With regard to those of the cairns
which I distinguished from the rest as being really old, as indicated above, I found reason from personal examination, to consider
them to be the work of aborigines."[87]

Again, Mr. Carleylle discovered some sepulchral cairns on
the ridge of a hill at a little distance to the north-east of
Khera, a village 4 miles to the west of Fatehpur Sikri.[88]

---

[87] Cunningham's *Arch. Rep.*, Vol. VI (by Carleylle), p. 33. Of the three different
forms of cairns the round topped, the flat-topped, and the cormlech cairns, which
General Cunningham examined after clearing out the earth and small stones,
he found, "in some cases, mostly in the round-topped cairns and cromlechs, a
few small fragile fragments of bones *in situ*,..." Among the Mundas, both processes
of interment have been in vogue.

[88] Cunningham's *Arch. Rep.*, Vol. VI, p. 13.

About 10 miles to the south-west of Fatehpur Sikri and about a mile and a third to the south-west of the present town of Rup-bas, near the south bank of the Banganga river, at an ancient deserted site, Mr. Carleylle found numerous small stones standing erect on the ground, some of which appeared to him as if they had once formed portions of stone circles, and he also found "certain solitary erect slabs of stone of which the width across horizontally was generally equal to and sometimes a little greater than their vertical height above ground, and which latter stones might possibly originally have formed the ride-stones of cromlechs".[89] To these proofs of the previous residence of Kolarian aborigines in these parts of India, one more may be added. At a distance of about ten and a half miles to the south-west of Agra, there exists a village still known as Kolara situated on the left bank of an ancient deserted bed of the river Jumna.[90] And it is perhaps not unreasonable to suppose that the place owes its name to its former Kol residents.[91]

How long the Mundas dwelt in these jungle-covered regions, it is now impossible to determine. But we hear of a people named *Mundas* as taking part in the great Kuru-Panchala War on the historic field of Kurukshetra[92] in which, as in the Trojan War—[93]

"Whole tribes and nations ranged on either side."

[89] Cunningham, *Arch. Rep.*, Vol. VI, p. 17.

[90] Cunningham, *Arch. Rep.*, Vol. IV, p. 97.

[91] We learn from Aitkinson's *Statistical Account of the N. W. P.*, Vol .VIII, part I, p. 153, that according to the traditions of the district of Mutra a race called the Kalars were the original occupants of the country.

[92] The whole region of Kurukshetra or Samanta Panchaka, from the Sarasvati on the south to the Drisadvati on the north, was divided into seven *banas* or forests, viz., Prithu-ban, Kam-ban, Aditi-ban, Sit-ban, Phalaki-ban, Vyas-ban. In this circuit or chakra of Kurukshetra, we meet with at least two distinctively Kol names of places. The one is Kol or Kul (since Hinduized into Kultaran Tirth) and the other is Kora (meaning 'son' in Mundari) now changed into Kamya Tirth (vide, Cunningham's *Arch. Rep.*, Vol. XIV, p. 100).

[93] In comparing the Mahabharata War to the Trojan War in respect of the variety of peoples taking part in it, we do not forget the immense superiority of the Kurukshetra War and the *Mahabharata*, over the *Iliad* and the war it celebrates Whereas the subject matter of the *Iliad*, as Herbert Spencer (*Auto biography*, Vol. I, p. 262) remarks, "appeals continually to brutal passions and the instincts of the savage", as regards the *Mahabharata*, it has been truly observed by Prof. Monier Williams (*Epic Poetry of India*) that "a deep religious meaning appears to underlie all the narrative". As has been further remarked by Prof. M. Williams

In the account of the Great War in the *Mahabharata*[94] we hear Sanjaya in describing the arrangement of the Kaurava army name the Mundas with the Karushas, the Vikanjas, and the Kentibrishas, as forming the left wing commanded by Vrihadvala. Again, we hear the great Aryan warrior Satyaki comparing the Mundas to the Danavas or Demons when he boasts :

मुण्डानेतान् हनिष्यामि दानवानिव वासव: ।

"I shall kill these Mundas even as Indra killed the Danavas."[95] And it does not appear unreasonable to suppose that the ancestors of the present tribe of Mundas are referred to in passages like this.

It was but natural that the Mundas would range themselves on the side of the Kurus against the army led by Krishna, the great national foe of the aborigines. For it is Krishna who slew the Asuras Pitha and Mura and the Rakhasa Ogha, who attacked Nirmochana and slew numbers of other Asuras, who destroyed Putana and Sakuni—the daughter of the Daitya Bali, and who caused Jarasandha to be slain.[96]

"The diction of the Indian Epic is more polished, regular and cultivated, and the language altogether in a more advanced state of development than that of Homer." The superiority of the Indian Epic over the Greek, in respect of description of scenery and domestic life and manners, has also been very rightly pointed out by Prof. Monier Williams. And the learned Professor further points out: 'The battlefields of the Ramayana and the Mahabharata are not made barbarous by wanton cruelties, and the descriptions of Ayodhya and Lanka imply far greater luxury and refinement than those of Sparta and Troy."

[94] *Mahabharata*, Drona Parva, 117, 23. The comparison of the Mundas to the Danavas would seem to indicate that the reference was to an aboriginal people of the name of Mundas. That some aboriginal tribes actually took part in the battle of Kurukshetra is evident from many passages of the great Epic.

[95] *Mahabharata*, Bhisma-Badha Parva, 117, 23. See also 117, 25.

[96] It is perhaps to the great Kurukshetra War in which near relatives fought amongst themselves that the following ancient Mundari song of a great war refers :

JADUR

Sasang hatu nale sasanghatu!
Bindabor nagar nale Bindabor nagar!
Sasang haturenko tupuingtana!
Bindabor nagar-renko mapakana!
Hagaea hagaeako tupuingtana!
Kumaya gereako mapatana!
Ichabasarteko tupuingtana!
Murudba kapiteko mapatana!

After the memorable defeat of the Kauravas, their allies, the Mundas, naturally left the country. From here they appear to have proceeded in a north-easterly direction through North Pan-

Translation

The village of Sasang, oh !—the village of Sasang !
The town of Bindabor, oh !—the town of Bindabor !
The men of Sasang do their arrows shoot !
And they of Bindabor do their axes wield [are cutting down men with
their axes]
There brothers and cousins at their own kinsmen shoot !
Nephews and cousins to pieces one another hack !
Thick fly their arrows like icha flowers bright !
Like murud flowers gay their battle-axes strike !

The word *Sasang* in Mundari means *turmeric*, and *Sasanghatu* would be identical with *Haldinagar*, a place in which the Mundas dwelt for a time. There is a place named, Hardi, on the Majhora River, [*vide* Cunningham *Statistical Account*, XII, page 191], another in the Bareilly District of the Rohilkhand Division (Aitkinson's *Sttl. Account*, Vol. IV, page 762) and the town of Jasso, 10 miles to the South-west of Nagodh was also called Hardi in former days. (Vide Cunningham, *Stt. Acc.* XI, p. 99). Later on, we have sought to identify this Haldinagar with village Hardi in the Monghyr District in Behar, but the name may not improbably have been borne by some other place near Kurukshetra. It is also sometimes called aldi-ban. The contest referred to in the above song between maternal uncle (Kumaya) and his nephews (Gereako) may perhaps apply to Salya, king of Madra who was the maternal uncle of Nakul and Sahadeva, two of the Pandavas. As an ally of the Kauravas Salya sided with the enemies of his nephews. Satyaki, with his one अक्षौहिणी (21870 elephants, 921870 chariots, 65610 cavalry, 109350 infantry) belonged originally to Mathura and sided with the Pandavas. Brindaban was on the outskirts of Mathura. The five Pandava brothers were cousins of Duryodhan and his brothers, and were uterine brothers of Karna who sided with Duryodhan. This great war between the Pandavas and the Kauravas, as it has been truly observed by the author of 'Hindu Superiority' was the turning-point in the history of Ancient India. "This momentous event decided the future of ancient India, as it closed the long chapter of Hindu growth and Hindu greatness."—H. B. Sarda's *Hindu Superiority*, p. 2. We cannot agree with those European orientalists and their Indian followers who suppose the events narrated in the *Mahabharata* to have taken place before those narrated in the *Ramayana*. The whole body of ancient Sanskrit literature and the age-long traditions of the Hindus,—not to speak of the difference in the style of composition of the two Epics and the reference in the Mahabharata to the incidents narrated in the Ramayana,—would all seem to lead to the opposite conclusion.

chala or modern Rohilkhand into the Kosala country —the Modern Oudh.[97]

In western Rohilkhand about 8 miles north of Bijnour[98] there is still a large old town known by the name of Mundawar, Mundor or Madipur (the Mo-ti-pu-lo of Hwen Tsang), where numerous small mounds and other signs of antiquity are still met with. This place appears to have obtained its name of Mundawar after the days of the *Ramayana*, for in that Epic the place is called Pralamba, And it is not unlikely that the name Mundawar was applied to it some time after the battle of Kurukshetra when the Mundas fixed their residence here.

From North Panchala, the Mundas appear to have entered the ancient country of Kosala. It is known, that after Vrihadbala[99] the then King, fell fighting on the field of Kurukshera, his kingdom

---

[97] The Bhars who lived in the valley of the Ganges and Doab once more rose to power on the extinction of the Hindu Empire after the Great War. The Mundas and other Kol tribes naturally passed on to the north of the country occupied by the Bhar tribe. Could the ancestors of the Bhars have belonged to the great Kol race ? The name "Bhar" might perhaps have been transformed from the word "Horo" the national name of the Kols. The transition from the "H" sound to the "bh" sound is not uncommon, thus we have भण from हुण भल from हकल etc., and so on. We may state that Messrs. Sherring ct Elliot (*Chronicles of Unao*) considered the Bhars and Cherus to be identical in race. And the Cherus are considered to have originally been a branch of the Kols.

[98] Tradition ascribed the foundation of Bijnour, now the chief town of the Bijnour District in the Rohilkhand Division, to King Ben, the mythical ancestor of the Kolarian aborigines, and the claim of Bijnour to identity with the Bijnagarh of Mundari tradition in preference to Biana Garh, are not unworthy of consideration. There is a castle mound at Budaun named Binawar in memory of Raja Ben. The appellation Ben-Bans is still borne by "several aboriginal tribes dwelling in or near the Vindhyas in the North-western Provinces" (Aitkinson's *Stt. Acc.* Vol. V, p. 342). The Bhils are mentioned by name as one of the tribes descended from King Ben.

[99] The date of Vrihadbala's death is sometimes given by European Orientalists as B. C. 1426. He is said to have been killed in battle by Abhimanyu, son of Arjun. According to orthodox Hindu opinion (Vide "On the Chronology of the Hindus" by Sir Wm. Jones, in *Asiatic Researches*, II. See also *Aitihasic Nirikhshan* by Pandit Lekh Ram, pp. 23—25) the battle of Kurukshetra took place at the junction of the Treta and Kali-yugas (the Brazen and Earthen ages) (31000 B. C.). But European orientalists appear to go to the other extreme. Thus, Prof. Macdonnel (*History of Sanskrit Literature*, p. 285) says "the historical germ of the great Epic is to be traced to a very early period, which cannot well be later than the tenth century, B. C."

lay prostrate and his capital Ayodhya lay deserted until the time of Vikramaditya[100] in the first century of the Christian Era. The greater part of the country relapsed into dense jungle. Immense forests like the Gandharva-ban and the Banaudha covered extensive tracts of the ancient Kosala country. And in this dark age of Hindu history, the aborigines whom the first invasion of the Aryans drove into the mountainous and jungly regions to the south, once more reappeared on the scenes of their former glory. If we trace the history of this dark period from the traditions of the country and the traces of aboriginal supremacy that survive to this day in the names of places and in architectural and other ruins, it will appear that wave after wave of aboriginal invasion passed over North-Western India, and that the Mundas and Cherus were gradually pushed forward to the east by the Bhars, and the Bhars, in their turn, by the Tharus.

The Modern districts of Basti and Gorakhpur appear to have formed the north-eastern corner of the ancient kingdom of Kosala. And in these districts we find the Mundas and their congeners the Cherus dwelling for a time. The Mundas still preserve the memory of their former residence in this part of Kosala. For, the Laknour of Munda tradition would appear to be identical with Laknaura, a village some three-quarters of a mile north-east of the old site of Basti. Here and in its neighbourhood are to be seen decayed mounds and other ancient ruins still attributed to the aborigines, though generally to the last comers—the Tharus.[101] About a mile to the north-east of the town of Gorakhpur, at a village called Jallai, there is an ancient tank known as Asuran Ka Pokhara[102] which, tradition asserts, was excavated in a single night by an Asur Ka Raja from the south with the assistance of his Asura followers with a view to win the hand of Kaolpati, the daughter of Sripal, the Raja of the place. Over 4 miles and 8 miles respectively to the north-east of Gorakhpur, on the road to Pipraich, are two ancient ruins known as Baital-garh and Maola

---

[100] The Vikramaditya to whom the rebuilding of Ayodhya is ascribed has been identified by General Cunningham with a powerful prince of the name who, as we learn from Hwen Thsang, reigned at Srabasti about 78 A. D., the initial year of the Saka Era of Salivahana, vide Cunningham's *Arch., Rep.,* Vol. 1, p. 37.

[101] Atkinson's, *Stt. Acc.* Vol. VI, p. 751.

[102] Cunningham's *Arch. Rep.,* XXII, pp. 68-69.

Kol, which appear to have once belonged to the Kolarian aborigines.[103]

Again, on the present road from Basti to Gorakhpur, there is a place about 2 miles to the west of Katnya river, bearing the name of Mundera Parao which would seem to suggest a former connection with the Mundas. It was perhaps the rise of the Dom Katar Chiefs in what we now know as the Gorakhpur District that made the Kols move on further to the east.

In the modern district of Balia, south-east of Gorakhpur, there are numerous ruins of antiquity attributed to the aboriginal chiefs of the Cheru tribe who appear to have been the predominant tribe amongst the Kols of those days. The most remarkable amongst these ruins are those of Pakka Kot, near the Saraju. They consist, we are told, "of earthen embankments of considerable extent faced with brick-work; but beyond the tradition of their Cheru origin there is little apparently to be learnt about them".[104] Another ancient mound near village Bansdih in the Balia District is reputed to have been the site of the ancient fortress of a second Cheru Chief, Mahipa by name. A similar mound at Zirabasti, in pergana Balia, is said to enshrine the memory of a Cheru Chief Zira by name. At Karnal, a few miles to the west of Zirabasti, there is another mound of the same nature. And these are "a few of the many places where similar traditions survive".[105] The names Chai-Chera and Cherethi, both of them places to the west of the Ghagra river and of Chandpur, have been supposed to bear reference to the ancient occupation of this part of the country by the Cherus.[106] Chai or Chay, a name still preserved in the tradition of the Cherus and also of the Santals, was, as Carlleyle suggests, probably the denomination of a ruling clan amongst the Kols.[107]

Gradually, however, the Bhars appear to have established their supremacy over the entire country north of the Ganges as far as the Gandak to the east. And the Mundas and other Kolarian tribes with the Cherus at their head appear to have crossed the

[103] Atkinson's *Stt. Acc.* Vol. p. 757.

[104] Atkinson's *Stt. Acc. of the N. W. P.*—Vol. XIII, pt. III, p. 41.

[105] Atkinson's *Stt. Acc.* XII, pt. III. p. 41.

[106] Cunningham's *Arch. Rep.*, XXII, p. 75.

[107] It may not improbably refer to the Soi clan (kili) of the Mundas and of the Santals.

Gandak and passed on to Videha or Mithila, the northern part of modern Behar.

About ten miles to the east of the Gandak we may perhaps recognise the Nandangarh of Munda tradition in the ancient fort of Nandangarh which stands half a mile to the south-west of the present village Lauriya. Here may be seen extensive ancient remains which would seem to support this indentification. These remains consist of three rows of earthen barrows or conical mounds of earth, some of which have been extremely hardened, almost petrified,—by age.[108]

The remote antiquity of this place is borne out by the tradition which ascribes the fort of Nandangarh to Raja Uttanapada, king of Brahmavarta, or the Gangetic Doab, and son of Manu Swayambhuba, the first-created of Brahma and the progenitor of the human race, from whom Raja Vena, the reputed ancestor of the Kolarian aborigines, is said to have been the seventh in descent.[109]

About twenty miles [110] north-east of Nandangarh and adjacent to village Rampurwa is another and a larger village now known as Pipariya. This place may perhaps be identified with the Garh Pipar of Munda tradition.[111] Though situated almost on the frontier of Nepal, Pipariya is included in the present Champaran District. The place is now noted for one of the monoliths bearing an Edict inscription of king Asoka. This is called Bhim's Lat by the Tharus of the district, and tradition thus explains this name : Bhima Sena, brother of Yudhisthira, says Tradition, "was carrying two loads of earth in a banghy supported across his shoulder, and when he reached the spot, the pole broke and the loads of earth consequently fell down on the ground on either side, and thus formed the two mounds, while the broken pole stuck in the ground in the midst, and became petrified, and thus formed the broken

---

[108] Cunningham calls it Navandgarh, but the name is given as Nandangarh in the map published by the Calcutta topographical survey. Mr. Vincent A. Smith also spells the name as Nandangarh. Vide V. A. Smith's *Early History of India* (1st Edn.) p. 139 (foot note) ct p. 149 (foot note).

[109] Cunningham, Vol. XVI, p. 110.

[110] About 32 miles north of Betia.

[111] Cunningham, *Arch. Rep.*, Vol. XXII, p. 51.

There is also a village known as Pipra in the Bhagalpur District about 13 miles south of Pratabganj.—See Hunter's *Settlement Account of Bengal*, Vol. XIX, p. 95.

pillar which stands midway between the two mounds !"[112] It may not perhaps be unreasonable to suppose that the mounds were originally erected by one of the Kol tribes who occupied the country before the Tharus, and that King Asoka subsequently found it a suitable monument to inscribe his edicts upon. For, as a matter of fact, other pyramid shaped mounds have been discovered in these parts and tradition ascribes them to the Kols.

The Haldinagar of Munda tradition, unless it be the name of some place neat Kurukshetra, may probably be identified with village Hardi in the Madhepura Sub-division of the Monghyr District. It was here that the now-deified Lurik, a man of the Ahir or milkman class who is said to have eloped with one Chanddin, wife of one Seodhar, fought with and defeated the local chief and re-igned in his place for twelve years. At last, Lurik went back to re-visit his native place—Agori (now Rajauli) in Bihar.—His brother Semru who lived at a place called Pali, a few miles north of Raj-auli, had, in the meanwhile, "been killed by the Kols, and all his cattle and property had been plundered".[113] It is probably this tradition which is remembered by the Santals who still recount their fights with Lourik Sourik.

Thus in this ancient Videha or Mithila[114] country we find the Mundas located for some time. Traces of its former Kol occupa-tion are still to be met with in many parts of this ancient province. Thus, at a village called Digha Dabaoli, about 33 miles north of Chapra, two pyramid-shaped mounds are to this day pointed out as the work of the Cheru-Chai, that is, of the aboriginal Cherus— once the dominant tribe amongst the Kols who then occupied this part of the country.[115] Again, at a village called Cheran, 7 miles to the south-east of the town of Chapra, there are mounds of ruins of a very ancient city. Tradition ascribes the foundation of Cherun to the Cherus, or as the common people say Cheru-Chai.[116] On the north bank of the Ganges, nearly opposite to the north of the

---

[112] Vide *Journal of the Asiatic Society*, Bengal, Vol. XI, Part I, p. 141. "Behar Legends and Ballads".

[113] Cunningham's *Arch. Rep.*, VIII, p. 80.

[114] The ancient kingdom of Videha was bounded on the north by the Himalayas, on the south by the Ganges, on the east by the river Kausiki or Kusi, and on the west by the river Gandaki or Gandak.

[115] Cunningham's *Arch. Rep.*, Vol. XXII, pp. 73-74.

[116] Cunningham's *Arch. Rep.*, Vol. XXII, p. 75.

Karmanasha, there are the remains of a very ancient fort called Ambikot which, tradition says, once belonged to Cheruka Raj, though originally founded by Ambariksha Rishi. At Kasturia 16 miles to the east of Motihari there is a large mound of brick ruins which, according to tradition, was once the place of a Cheru Raja. "To the west of the mound there is a gigantic Pakur tree (*ficus glomerata*) under which is seated a female figure, which the people know as Durgabati Rani but which appears to be the Goddess Durga, as she holds the usual bow and arrows."[117] According to tradition, Durgabati Rani was the wife of one of the Cheru Rajas. One day, while seated under the Pakur tree, a Banjara robber attempted to take off her bracelets and other ornaments. But on her supplication to the Deity, she was forth-with turned into stone with all her ornaments.

At Sabhegarh, 18 miles north-west of Muzaffarpur,[118] there is a ruined fort about the middle of which there is a high mound which is locally reputed to have been the ancient residence of a Cheru Raja of the name of Sahe Deo.[119]

At Jouri Dih (the burnt mound) about 12 miles from Hajipur, and 23 miles from Muzaffarpur, there is an ancient mound. And the tradition goes that it was the site of a fort and a town of the Cheru Raj which was burnt down by the family of the last Raja of the fort when they wrongly apperhended that the Raja had been killed in battle with "an enemy from the west".[120]

The Mandar Pahar of Munda tradition is in all probability none other than the famous Mandara-giri of Sanskrit literature, the Mons Mallus or Maleus of Greek geographers. It is situated within the Banka Sub-division of Bhagalpur and is reputed to have served as the churning-rod with which the gods churned the ocean for *amrita* (divine ichor) with the help of the Assuras. Extensive runs scattered about the foot of the hills for over 2 miles, are still locally atributed to the Kol Rajas of old. Half way up the hill there is a colossal figure in a sitting posture measuring 52 feet 8 inches in height. In Dr. Buchanan's time (1810 A. D.) the image

[117] Cunningham's *Arch. Rep.*, Vol. XVI, pp. 26-27.

[118] Mr. John Cockburn found some flint implements at Muzaffarpur near the stone-dam over the Chunderparba river.—*Asiatic Society's Journal*, Calcutta, Vol. LXIII, Part III.

[119] Vide Cunningham's *Arch. Rep.*, Vol. XVI, pp. 30-32.

[120] Vide Cunningham's *Arch. Rep.*, Vol. XVI, Part II, pp. 84-86.

was called Madhukaitabh and attributed to the Kols of ancient times.[121] But by a versatility of the Hindu Religion", says Captain Sherwell, "it is in 1851, called Bhima Sena, although, still attributed to the Kol Rajas"[122] Near the foot of the hill is a large building of stone which attributed to Raja Kola or Chola, who is said to have flourished 22 centuries ago.[123]

The Chai Champa of Santal tradition is probably identical with Champa or Champapuri, near Bhagalpur,[124] once the capital of the ancient Anga kingdom of Lomapada of the *Ramayana* and of Karna of the *Mahabharata*. Chai, as we have seen, is a term frequently suffixed to the names of places occupied by the Cheru-Kol tribes. Again, the Khairagarh of Santal tradition may perhaps be identified with Kheri-garh or the Fort on the Hill at Kherhi, 10 miles south-west of Bhagalpur. Numerous ancient remains are to be found both on the hill and in the village below. The principal object of interest is the fort on the hill. "This is an irregular enclosure of rough large blocks of stones laid on each other without cement, occupying the whole of the tolerably level top of the east-most hill." Numerous low mounds exist at the foot of the hill, and also numerous others further west.

In ancient Buddhistic times, the political boundaries of Champa including Modagiri or Monghyr, Kankjol or Rajmahal, appear to

[121] Dr. Buchanan's *Bhagalpur*, p. 61. Here the Asura Madhukaitava is said to have been subdued by Vishnu.

[122] Captain W. S. Sherwell's "A short notice of an ancient colossal figure carved in granite on the Mandar Hill in the District of Bhagalpur". *Journal of the Asiatic Society of Bengal*, Vol. XX, p. 272.

[123] In Bk. VI, Canto 26, of the *Ramayana* Ravana is described as surveying the Vanar-army encamped is Lanka and his old minister Sarana described some of the chiefs among them (Dass' *Ancient Geography of India*, p. 51). Among these chiefs, we read of "Pramatha and his Hari tribes (who) dwelt on the Mandar Hills south of the Ganges." Dass' *Anc. Geog.*, p. 52. These Hari tribes may perhaps refer to the Santal, Munda, Ho and other Kolarian tribes who call themselves to this day the "Horo" tribes. And thus the evidence of the *Ramayana* may perhaps be adduced to support the tradition of the Mundas as to their former residence on and about the Mandar Hill. Though they did not perhaps dwell there at the time of Ram Chandra, we may take it that either at the time when this passage was actually composed or at some period before that of which the memory survived, the Mundas and other allied tribes had their residence in these parts.

[124] The name of Colgong or Koholgram, a village east of Bhagalpur, perhaps points to a former settlement of the Kols. It was on a hill about a mile from Colgong that, it is said, the Pauranic Rishi Durbasa had his hermitage.

have extended from Lakhiterai to Rajmahal on the Ganges, and from the Parasnath Hill along the Damuda river to Kalna on the Bhagirathi.[125] The vocabulary of the Mundas would seem to confirm the supposition we have made as to their having at one time resided in these parts. For, it must have been during their residence here that the Mundas incorporated in their vocabulary that large number of words, whose striking similarity to Maithili as well as to Bengali words would, at first sight, appear quite surprising.[126]

Thus, कोता or ओकोना for 'where', the vocative हे, दादा for 'an elder brother, ठोड़ for 'the beak of a bird', पूँथि for 'a book', डोङ्गा for 'a canoe or boar', दिशुम् for 'country', डेला for 'a clod of earth, डुड़ा for 'dust', टिप for 'drop', हारित for 'defeat', मानाति for 'obeying', गोठ for 'a flock of cattle', कोयासि for 'fog', वेश (genuine Mundari वृगिन) for 'good', कदल for 'plantain', आकदन्द for

---

[125] Champa was also the old name of Bhagalpur and its political boundaries "may be stated as extending from Lakhiterai to Rajmahal on the Ganges, and from the Parasnath Hill along the Damudar River to Kalna on the Bhagirathi". Cunningham's "Ancient *Geography of India*", p. 478. Colonel Dalton (*Ethnology of Bengal*, page 211) identifies Khairagarh and Chai Champa of Santal tradition with places in the Hazaribagh District. But it seems more probable that these names were given by the Santals to places in the Hazaribagh District after the names of their former homes in the north and west.   (At p. 219, however Colonel Dalton speaking of the Birhors, says that according to tradition they came to Hazaribagh District from Khairagarh (in the Kaimur hills).

[126] Can the *gopinis* with whom Krishna is said to have been on intimate terms be really 'cow-herds' called 'gupinis' in the Mundari language? Among Sanskrit words naturalised in Mundari may be mentioned :—दारु tree; सुनुम् oil, गिदि for गृबिनी (vulture), इदाँ(early) for इदानीं, सुनुम् for thread, तुल, to weigh, जलोम्, for net, सामड़ोम् (Sans. सुवर्णम्) for gold. Before the Aryans came into India, the Mundas and other Kol tribes do not appear to have been cultivators. If they knew agriculture, it must have been only a very rudimentary form of it. For, their words relating to agriculture appear to have been mainly borrowed from Sanskrit : E.g., सि, सिउ (Santali. सी) to plough (Sans. सि),—दावोम्(Snatali दावे), a sckle (sans, दावम्)—वुसु (Santali वुसुप), straw (Sans. वुसम्),—कासोम् (Santali कासकोम्) the cotton plant (Sans. कार्पासम्)—रोया, to plant (Sans. गपणम्) The fact that the Mundas use these and similar words (such as *achara*, to sow rice in low moist land previously ploughed and harrowed) (Santali *achra*) in common with a few other Kolarian tribes who separated from the Mundas before the latter came to Chhotanagpur, would go to show that the Mundas learnt the cultivation of paddy and other grains before their entry into Chota Nagpur.

strange, wonderful, वाका for 'the stork', वाकली for 'the bark of a tree' विषि for 'poison,' वुइनि for 'a younger sister', वाउ for 'a younger brother', चौदोर for 'a conveyance' (Bengali चतुर्दीला), दुलाड़, दुकु for 'pain or sorrow', तोवे for 'then', हसति for 'to bear', शिशिरदा for 'dew, सेवा for 'worship', सुकु for 'happiness', ठाउका for 'right' (ठीक), किरि for 'to buy' and आर्किरि for 'to sell', and numerous other words.

According to Chero tradition, some enemies from the west expelled them from Mithila.[127]

From Mithila, the Mundas, Cherus and other Kol tribes appear to have moved towards the south-east and entered Magadha or South-Bihar. Here we may recognise the Paligarh of Munda tradition in village Pali, 13 miles to the north-west of Gaya. Of Pali-garh, General Cunningham writes :

There are several mounds of ruins covered with broken bricks and stone figures and fragments of architecture. The largest mound which is called 'Gharh' or the 'Fort' is most probably the remins of a castle.[128]

Not far from Paligarh there still exist other ruins which tradition ascribes to the Kols. In the large village of Conch, 18 miles from Gaya, two ancient mounds are traditionally ascribed to the Kol Rajas of ancient times.[129] South of Conch there is a large village named Kabur with extensive mounds all around it and a large ancient mud fort adjoining the village. The people of the place attribute this fort to the Kol Rajas of old.[130]

The ancient village Chirkawan in the Gaya District which has a similar mud fort adjoining it and the village Cheon (pronounced Cheoa) not far off, appear to have derived their names from the Chai clan to whom we have already referred. And the same origin may perhaps be attributed to Chain, some distance to the

[127] According to the tradition among the Cheros they once lived in the Sub-Himalayan tract called Moreng whence they went to Kumaon and thence proceeded southwards and at length went to Bhojpur, where they reigned for seven generations.—Dt. Gazetteer of Palamau (1907), p. 19.

And, as we learn from Sir William Hunter, "It is probable that the Bengali province of Mithila included the whole of the country called Moreng"—Hunter Statistical Account, Vol. XIV, p. 103.

[128] Cunningham's *Arch. Rep.* Vol. XVI. p. 51.

[129] Cunningham's *Arch. Rep.* Vol. XIII, p. 61.

[130] Rough notes on some of the Antiquities in the Gaya District, by W. Peppe, Esqr., in the *Asiatic Society's Journal*, Calcutta, Vol. XXXV, Part 1, p. 49 at p. 53.

south-west of Cheon.[131] Here a number of large mounds with no figures or inscriptions on them, cover a large acreage. The ancient village of Deokilli at the foot of a cluster of hills about a mile to the south of Cheon, would seem to preserve the memory of one of the Kilis or Clans into which the Munda tribe was divided.

About 15 miles east of Gaya and about a mile to the south-east of Punawa, are two smalll isolated ranges of low hills, the valley between which still bears the name of Kol and the place itself Hasra.[132] "It appears", says Mr. Beglar, "that there was once a village named Hasra here, though now none exists. The entire space between the hills is thickly studded with remains".[133] We may also mention the rude stone circles near the foot of the Pret-sila at Budh-Gaya, which local tradition attributes to the Kols.

Scattered all along the boundary line between Bihar and Chota Nagpur, may be seen the characteristic mounds or sepulchral stones which testify to the former occupation of the country by the Mundas and their congeners. As we learn from a note by Mr. T. F. Peppe in the *Asiatic Society's Journal* (Bengal Branch), Part 1, p. 119:

> In the wilder parts of Bihar, in Parganas Japla, Balamja, Sirris, Kutumba and also in Sherghati, they (monumental stones) are often to be met with, and their being found scattered over the country leaves little doubt of their Kolarian origin, to which local tradition assigns them.

The Rijgarh of Munda tradition would appear to be identical with Rajgir[134] or Rajgriha, a former capital of Magadha. Mention is made in the *Mahabharata* of this place under the name of Girivraja as the ancient capital of Jarasandha. In Fa Hian's language, around this city "Five hills form a girdle like the walls of a town". And this would be just the sort of place that the Mundas, with their characteristic exclusiveness, would choose for their residence. When Fa Hian visited India at the close of the fourth century, he found Rajgir a deserted city. The memory of the Kolarian aborigines is perhaps preserved in the name of the Asura Cave or

---

[131] Compare the name of Chainpur in the District of Ranchi.

[132] The name *Hasra* is probably of Munda or Kol origin, as it appears to have been derived from Mundari *hasa*, earth, with the genetive sign *ra* suffixed.

[133] Cunnigham's *Arch. Rep.* Vol. VIII, pp. 123-24.

[134] Such instances of metathesis are not uncommon.

'place of the Asurs', mentioned by Hiuen Tsang as situated in Yastivana, and also in the cave behind Jarsandha's Baithak known as the Pippal Cave, whidh too is attributed to the Asuras.

By degrees, the Cheros apppear to have moved eastwards to Karusha-desa where they established themselves as rulers of the country and gradually became Hinduised. In this Karusha-desa, the modern Shahabad District, traces of Cheru occuption are present to this day. Almost all ancient buildings in the District are attributed to the Cheros, and to this day a number of Cheros may be found living in the hills to the south.

The Hinduised Chero Chiefs, with the zeal of proselytes, erected many temples in the country.[135] And as they began to form marital connections with high-caste Hindus they gradually cut themselves off from their congeners, the Mundas and other Kol tribes, who retained their impure habits and their primitive spirit-worship.[136] The superior pretensions of their cousins, the Cheros, naturally incensed the haughty Mundas who could ill brook to remain in the country any longer; and they appear to have marched up the Sone till they came in sight of Rohtasgarh, which has more than once proved an ever-ready asylum to troubled races, tribes and families.[137]

[135] The most famous of these are three shrines attributed to the Chero Raja Phul Chand or Pushpa Chandra who is said to have lived shortly before Vikrama-ditya. These are Deo Chandi at Barnarak, Deo Munga at Muga, and Deo Barsad at Markanda.—*Vide* Cunningham's *Arch. Rep.* Vol. XVI, pp. 59-60 and 64. Six miles to the north of Deo Markanda, in a large village called Karath, there is a high brick mound surmounted with a *lingam* which is known as Jageswar. The large fine tank near it is known as Cherwani Karwa after the name of the Cheru Raja who had it excavated—*Vide* Cunningham's *Ach. Rep.* Vol. XVI, p. 61.

[136] Wilford supposed that they accepted the religion of Buddha but were sub-sequently converted to Hinduism; and on the failure of the direct line from Jara-sandha, their prince might have succeeded to the sovereignty of the Gangetic Provinces. This prince, Major Wilford supposed, might be identical with Sanaka from whom Ajaka or Asoka was the 4th in succession. The last known incumbent of the Chero Raj appears to have been a prince of the name of Fudi Chandra, who, according to an inscription obtained in the beginning of the last century, reigned about the year 561 A. D.

[137] The Mundas and some other Kol tribes appear to have left behind them some traditions of their former occupation of the valley of the Sone. It is the primitive forests of Buxar (Byaghrasara), Arra (Aramnagar) and Saseram (Sahansarama) that harboured the monstrous Bakasura, the man-eating Hirimba, and the terrible Sahasra-bahu. It is to the Daitya Chief celebrated in the Puranas as Munda general of the forces of the two Daitya Princes Shambhu and Nishambhu, that

The name of Rohtasgarh conjures up a thousand memories in the mind of the student of Indian History. It has been from the earliest times the successive refuge of many a ruling tribe and many an exalted family in the days of their reverses. It was here that Rohitaswa, son of king Harishchandra, flying from the sacrificial knife of his father, sheltered himself; this was the sanctuary to which the descendants of the last Hindu Emperor of India finally betook themselves; this was the celebrated fort that afforded a safe asylum to the family of Prince Khuram (afterwards, Emperor Shah Jahan) when he rebelled against his father Jahangir; this was the sanctuary which, after the famous battle of Gherria, sheltered the family of Mir Kasim, the deposed Nawab of Bengal[138]; and lastly, it was here that only about half a century ago, a considerable number of Sepoy mutineers sought refuge from the avenging wrath of the British Lion. Against this bold rock-fortress successive wavers of conquest and migration have rolled from the north from before the dawn of history. And tribe after tribe, dynasty after dynasty, leader after leader, have appeared on this fortress-plateau and disappeared after a while like so many bubbles on the surface of the sea. But there, to this day, stands unchanged the stately rock-fortress of Rohtasgarh, as it has stood for ages—the silent witness of their successes and reverses, the dumb confidant of their hopes and fears,—serenely looking up to the blue sky above and overlooking the Kaimur plateau at its foot. And one may fancy this 'Queen-fortress of the Vindhyas' with her myriad memories dating back to a period anterior to the dawn of history, repeating to herself the words of the poet :

---

the temple and hill of Mundeswari in modern Shahabad owe their names. And this Munda had a brother of the name of Chanda, who is reputed to have ruled in Chainpur, formerly known as Chandapur after the name of its Daitya founder. "Beneath the crust of Mythology", it has been observed, "the story of the battle of the battle of Parbati as the protector of the Aryan invader, with the Daityas or the primeval princes of India, appears to have a foundation in fact". Vide *The Calcutta Review*, Vol. LXIX, p. 349.

[138] It was on the 2nd of August,1763, that Kasim Ali,the ex-Nawab of Bengal, was defeated on the plains of Gheriah. His family sheltered themselves in Rohtasgarh till the battle of Buxar in 1765, after which Rajah Shah Mull the Governor of Rohtasgarh, delivered the fortress to the British. The average height of Rohtas is 1,000 feet, and its area about 20 square miles. Here Raja Man Singh, the viceroy of Bengal and Bihar under the Emperor Akbar, built his favourite palace.

Race after race, man after man
Have dream'd that my secret was theirs,
Have thought that I lived but for them,
That they were my glory and joy.
They are dust, they are changed, they are gone,
—I remain.

This famous Rohtasgarh is without doubt the Ruidasgarh of
Munda tradition. How long the Mundas dwelt here, it is impossible now to determine; but even this strong fortress failed to
afford a lasting refuge to the tribe. The tradition of the Mundas as
well as of their companions and kinsmen the Santals, speak of a
struggle with another aboriginal tribe—the Kharwars—before they
left Rohtasgarh and retreated to the wilder recesses of the Vindhyas.
Munda as well as Santal traditions speak of a Kharwar chief named
Madho Das and his followers as having surprised them at dead of
night and driven them into the mountain fastnesses of the Binji
hills as the Vindhyas are called by these tribes. The reason for this
attack, it is asserted, was the refusal by the Mundas (or by the
Santals, according to Santal tradition)[139] to bestow the hand of
one of their girls on the son of Madho Das Kharwar. The traditions
of the Kharwars afford corroboration to this tradition of the Mundas
and the Santals. The Kharwars, too, assert that while migrating
south wards from Khayra-garh, they came upon the Kols, the
Cheros and Agorias or Asurs being specifically mentioned by name,
— and occupied the heights of the Kaimur range.[140]

Some of the Kol tribes such as the Korwas, the Asuras, the Birjias
and the Kisanrs, appear to have followed the course of the Koel[141]
till they reached the present Districts of Plamau[142] and Ranchi.
And even to this day these tribes coccupy the south-eastern parts
of the district of Palamau and the western parts of the Ranchi

[139] It is not unlikely that up till this period, the Santals and Mundas formed
one tribe.

[140] Vide an article on the Primitive Races of Shahabad, *Calcutta Review*, Vol.
LXX, p. 349 at p. 356.

[141] The Koel takes its rise in the Central plateau of the Ranchi District, and
passing through the District of Palamau, joins the Sone not far from Rohtas.

[142] The name *Palamau* seems to have been derived from the Kolarian word
'Pahal' meaning tooth, in reference to the rocks in the bed of the Auranga river
which look like so many jagged teeth when the river is in flood.   Vide District
Gazetteer of Palamau, pp. 1-2.

District. The Mundas and the Santals crossed the Sone and marched
on in a south-easterly direction along the borderland that separa-
tes the present district of Hazaribagh from the districts of Palamau
and Ranchi.   Not far from this border land is village Omedanda
which Munda tradition names as the first settlement of the Mundas
in 'Nagpur'—as they name the Ranchi District.

Now at length the Santals and the Mundas parted company.
The Santals left Nagpur (Chota Nagpur) crossed the Damodar
and settled down in Sikharbhum (the modern district of Hazaribagh), and later on, followed the course to the Damodar and passed
on to Manbhum and to the Santal Parganas.[143] Their kinsmen, the
Bhuiyas, appear to have preceded them along the same route and
then down the course of the Cossai river into what are now the
Manbhum and the Singbhum Districts.   The Mundas preferred
to stay on in the forest-covered regions of what is now the Ranchi
District:

> Where they saw before them rudely swell,
> Crag over crag and fell o'er fell.

In this new home of the Mundas, their kinsmen, the Asuras,
appear to have already preceded them and worked some of the
iron-ores which abounded in the country.   The Mundari legend
of Lutkum Haram and Lutkum Buria to which we have already
referred, appears to preserve the tradition of a sanguinary struggle
between the Mundas and the iron-smelting tribe of Asuras in
which the later were worsted.   And the Asuras appear to have
retreated to the remote western parts of the present district of
Ranchi and left the Mundas undisputed masters of the entire
country.   Here the Mundas found a land of primeval forests
abounding in live game and edible roots and fruits.   Here all
around them the scenery was picturesque and, in places, magni-

---

[143] According to Santal tradition, the Santals migrated from Hihiri Pipri to
Sasangbera, thence to Khojkaman, thence eastward through Sinpass and Bahipass
to Aere, and thence to Khande.   From Khande taking a north-easterly direction
they entered Chae, and turning south-eastward and passing the Chae and Champa
passes, they arrived at Champa with the sen rivers.   Thence passing through many
places, they came to Nagpur and thence removed to Sikhar, and finally to the
Santal Parganas; Vide Rev. L., V. Skrefrund's *Grammar of the Santali Language*,
pp. v-vi.   The coincidence of the greater portion of this tradition with that of the
Mundas is striking and can admit of but one explanation.

ficent, and the climate delightful. The valleys afforded lands suitable for cultivation and the forests afforded extensive pasturage for their cattle. No enemies would any longer dog their steps in these forest-clad highlands, no intruders would penetrate into these hilly fastnesses and forests to wrest their new-found home from them. Now at length they could count upon a long abiding truce to their interminable wanderings and an immunity from those ever-recurring hostilities to which they had so long been subjected.

And we may picture to ourselves the Mundas rejoicing at the thought of having at length discovered :

> Some boundless contiguity of shade
> Where rumour of oppression and deceit,
> Of unsuccessful or successful war,
> Might never reach them more.

CHAPTER III

THE EARLY HISTORY OF THE MUNDAS

> Man with man in communion mixing,
>   Taming the wild ones where he went,
> Into the peace of the homestead fixing
>   Lawless bosom and shifting tent.
>
> —*Schiller (Lytton's translation).*

WE have seen how the remote ancestors of the Mundas finally secluded themselves in the valleys and jungles of Chota Nagpur. Here, at length, their age long wanderings were followed by a long era of peace. Here, in the primeval forests of 'Jharkhand' or the 'forest country' as it appears to have been once called,—here, the first Munda immigrants made clearances in the jungles and established their primitive Kol villages, just as we see their latter-day descendants doing even in our own times in the south-eastern parts of the Ranchi District. And, in this way, in the heart of the deep dense forests where hitherto the rays of the sun had hardly penetrated, smiling villages grew up, and went on steadily multi-plying. Thus, by degrees the Mundas spread over the entire north-western parts of what forms the present district of Ranchi.

All through the long centuries of Hindu Rule in India, the Jhar-khand Mundas appear to have remained unmolested in their isolated mountain fastnesses. Walled off from the outside world by chains of wooded hills, they long remained in occupation of the north-western parts of what is now the Ranchi District. The long immunity from hostile disturbances which the Mundas now enjoyed enabled them to build up those social and administrative organisations which may still be seen in more or less mutilated forms in the southern and eastern Pargans as of the Ranchi District.

The idea of private property, as we have seen in the last chapter, had already been developed amongst the Mundas. Their cherished idea of ownership of land, however, was the archaic one of joint ownership by the family or by a group of agnatic families. The country they now entered was practically *res nullius*, and the Mundas occupied it and meant to keep it always for themselves. Each family made in the virgin forests its own clearances which came to be called the *Hatu*, later on known as the Khuntkatti-hatu, or the village of the family of the original settlers. The boundaries of the village were laid down by the *Pater familias*. And even to this day, the Mundas regard as sacred and inviolable these boundary-lines over which the boundary-gods (*Siman-bongako*) keep a vigilant watch.[1] The method by which these boundaries were laid down by the old Munda patriarchs was a very simple one. Huge bonfires were lit up at four corners of a selected tract and straight lines drawn across the tract from one point to the next, connecting the four bonfires. These lines formed the boundary-lines of the new village. And within the limits of the village thus demarcated, all the land, cultivable as well as waste, all the hills, jungles, and streams,—every thing above ground and underground, became the common property of the village-family. One or more bits of jungles were specifically reserved for the village-gods (*hatu bongako*) and called the Sarnas.[2] When the sons of the *Pater familias* came

[1] The recent disturbance of these boundary-gods by the *amins* of the Survey and Settlement were very distasteful to the Mundas, but prudential considerations made them submit to the inevitable. In the Kadleta festival the Bongas of *Chatursriman* (the four boundaries) are worshipped along with the spirits of *Garhas*, *Jharkas*, *Khunts* and *Piris*.

[2] From the village jungles, every member of the Khuntkatti group has the right to cut and take wood for domestic and agricultural purposes according to his necessities. The Parja Horoko alone have in some cases to ask the permission of the Khuntkattidars for the purpose, although even they were not required to do so in early times. In course of time, when the Khauntkatti family increased in numbers and the village-jungles shrank into smaller dimensions, rules grew up in some villages as to the mode and time of a general felling of timber and lopping off of branches. Generally, it is in the month of *Chait* or *Baisak* (March to May) before the rains set in, that in many villages the Munda and Pahan on a day appointed beforehand lead the villagers into the village-jungles and the necessary fuel and timber for the year is cut down by the villagers from a specified part of the jungle, leaving the other part or parts to be similarly dealt with by rotation in successive years. And the wood thus cut down is then taken home by the villagers according to their respective needs. By this prudent procedure, the village jungles can never be devastated. By the time the last division of the jungle is approached, the portion first attacked again develops into a suitable jungle, the new shoots having in the meanwhile developed into trees suitable for the axe. To this day, the Mundas follow this procedure, especially in the Bhuinhari Pattis where the

of age, they married girls of other villages; and on the father's death, the married sons often separated from one another and built separate houses for themselves in the same *Hatu*. And in this way, the original village-family would branch off into a number of separate families belonging to the same *Kili* or sept. On the death of the founder of the village, his eldest son would come to be the patriarchal head of the different branches of the family. The whole village acknowledged his chiefship in matters temporal as well as spiritual, for in those early days the functions of the Munda or secular head of the village and of the Pahan or the ecclesiastical head do not appear to have been separated. In course of time, men not belonging to the village-family appear to have been introduced. Relatives by marriage,—men of different *Kilis* or septs,—a son-in-law, for example,—would sometimes come and settle in the village. Again, a primitive agricultural tribe,—for such the Mundas appear to have been when they established themselves in Chota Nagpur,—would require the services of blacksmiths to make and mend their plough-shares, cowherds to tend their cattle, and weavers to weave their clothes. And for these and similar services men of inferior status, though originally belonging to the same race, appear to have been employed, and remunerated with plots of lands in the village. These outsiders were the *eta-haturenko* (literally, men of other villages) the *parja-horoko* of later times as contradistinguished from the *hatu-horoko* who were the Khuntkattidars—the descendants of the original village-family. These outsiders with the exception of such relatives of the Khuntkattidars as might have been admitted into the village-family by a ceremonial public adoption, had no right to the village-lands but could only enjoy the crops of such specific plots of land as might have been allotted to them by the Khuntkattidars for their maintenance. This village-system was the unit of ancient Munda polity, and whatever has been since evolved out of it partakes of the nature and characteristics of the original unit.

We should be greatly mistaken, however, if we suppose that any

---

jungles are more scanty than in the Khuntkatti Patties. This custom of periodical wood-cutting is also in vogue in most Uraon Villages in the Ranchi District, and was probably introduced by the Uraons, as the improvident Munda is not usually in the habit of taking any thought for the morrow, and if he followed his own natural bent, he would attack the nearest forest, and that whenever any necessity would arise.

superior rights of property were attached to the office of a Munda.
His position has been aptly described as that of a *primus inter pares*—
a chief among equals.   He had his share of the village-lands just
as the other members of the *Khuntkatti* group had.   Occasionally
perhaps the *pater familias* sought and obtained the assistance of the
brotherhood in the cultivation of his fields.   But such assistance,
when rendered, must have been reciprocated as much as was
possible consistently with the dignity of a Munda.   When, however,
any feuds broke out between one village-community and another,
all the adult members of each village-community were bound to
follow the lead of their Munda.   And it is said that even females
would gladly render military service to the community under the
leadership of their Munda on such occasions.   These services
by the different members of the brotherhood to the village community as a whole, would be rewarded with a share in the booty that
might be taken.

Over and above this village organisation, the Mundas, in course
of time, came to have a tribal organisation of their own.   Motives
similar to those that prompted them to hold together in villages
would appear to have led them gradually to organise larger unions
made up of groups of villages.   As time went on, the Munda saw
the necessity of making himself stronger so as to be able to effectually
protect his brotherhood against the aggressions of other village-
units that were growing apace all around.   And this led to the
wider organisation known as the *patti* system.   The villages by
batches generally of twelve—but sometimes more and sometimes
less—came to be grouped together as a *patti* with the strongest and
most influential amongst the headmen of these villages as the
Manki or *patti*-chief.   The remaining village-headmen swore
allegiance to the elected Manki.   Military service was the primary,
and, in the beginning, perhaps the sole condition.   But in course
of time, it was thought proper to symbolize the relationship.   Each
village-headman of the *patti* would make periodical presents to
the Manki of certain quantities of *mahua* (flowers of the *bassia
latifola*), *herua, barni, chop, Kapsa* (cotton) and similar other things.
But in course of time, the origin of these periodical presents was
lost sight of.   And what began as free gifts came to be regarded as
rightful dues.

But all the same, the Manki, like the Munda, was always looked
upon as a chief among equals—a leader and not a ruler.   Nor did

5

any superior rights of property appertain to the Mankiship. As with most Oriental institution, the offices of the Manki as well as of the Munda, gradually came to be hereditary. In the internal administration of each village, the Munda was assisted by the village-*Panch* or Council of village elders. The tribunal thus constituted, arbitrated in all disputes amongst the villagers *inter se*. Custom was the recognised law. And offences against the Code of Custom were punished with fines and in extreme cases with expulsion from the village-community. In disputes between village and village and in cases of unusual importance or tribal interest, the *Patti-Panch* presided over by the Manki, was called upon to adjudicate. And even now the village-*Panch* and the *Parha-Panch* or *Patti-Panch* play important parts in Munda village polity. "Sing-bonga (the Sun God) on high and the Panch on earth" (*Sirmare Sing-bonga otere Panch*)[3] is the orthodox formula for an oath amongst the Mundas to this day.

As for the pursuits of the Mundas in those early days, agriculture soon appears to have become their chief occupation. Besides this, iron-smelting, as their ancient legends tell us, was known to the people. Hunting, originally a necessary occupation, seems to have always remained a favourite pastime with the Mundas. Their love of drink appears to have been almost an inborn propensity with the tribe. According to their legends, the mysterious root used in the manufacture of *ili* or rice-beer was pointed out to their first parents by Singbonga Himself. Then, as now, the Munda, after a hard day's labour, knew no better occupation than drinking, dancing and singing up to a late hour of the night.

As for their religion, the Mundas do not appear to have ever been fetish-worshipers. For them, the earth is full of invisible spirits whose blessings they invoke and whose wrath they seek to avert by various sacrifices. Their principal Deity—*Sing-Bonga* (literally, the Sun God, and secondarily but in reality the Superme Deity)—is altogether a beneficent Deity, ever intent on doing good to mankind.

Cremation of the dead seems to have been in vogue from very early times. Only the bones of the deceased used to be interred in the family-*sasan* or burial ground.[4] And the village-*sasan*

---

[3] This is the opening sentence in the formula of worship in the *So-So* festival.

[4] ...Recently there appears to have been a tendency amongst some of the Sonepur Mundas towards giving up cremation altogether and burying their corpses in

with the rude stone-slabs (*sasan-diriko*) that guard the mortal remains of the ancestors (*haram-horoko*) of the village-family, is to this day, a favourite meeting-ground of the once almighty *Panch*, and there even to this day, on occasions of public importance :

> "Reveren'd sit,
> On polished stones, the elders in a ring."

Thus, these self-contained confederate republics, nestling among their spirit-haunted sai-groves, pursued the even tenour of their uneventful existence, knowing no enemy within or without save the wild beasts and reptiles of the surrounding forests.

A few centuries later, however, a Dravidian tribe, followed hard by pursuing enemies from the North, found their intrusive way into the jungle tracts which hitherto the Mundas had called all their own. These unwelcome intruders were the Kurukhs, better known to us as the Uraons.[5]

The ancient history of the Uraons is enveloped in still deeper darkness than even that of the Mundas. Students of Uraon antiquities have not yet succeeded in lifting even the fringes of the veil that hangs over the earlier chapters of Uraon history. Neither early Sanskrit literature nor foreign writers on ancient India have anything definite to say about them.[6]

---

imitation of the Munda converts to Christianity. But ordinarily burying is only provisional, for the bones are taken out of the provisional burial-place on the occasion of the annual feast called *Jang-topa*, and placed under stone-slabs in the family-*sasan*.

[5] ...The name *Kurukh* has been sometimes supposed to mean 'hill-men'. Colonel Dalton seems inclined to think that the name is derived from Konkan, the people of the Konkan being supposed to be identical with the *Kaunkanas* named in the topographical list given in the Vishnu Purana. The form *Kurukh* is supposed to be due to the Uraon's partiality for guttarals, and Konkan is supposed to have been the cradle of the race. (Vide Dalton's *Ethnology*, p. 245). More probable, however, appears to be the derivation of the name which I have heard some Uraons give. According to them the name *Kurukh* is a variant of Coorg where the Uraons formerly lived. Mr. Dhanmasi Panna of the Subordinate Executive Service, the first Uraon Graduate of the Calcutta University is one of the Uraons who gave me this derivation.

[6] Since writing the above I have come across a paper on the Uraons and Mundas, contributed by the Rev. Father F.A. Grignard, S. J. in the *Anthropos*, edited by the great Ethnologist Dr. Schmidt. Father Grignard has sought to prove the identity of the Uraons or Kurukhs with the Karushas of Sanskrit literature. He further maintains that the term *Rakshasa* as applied to the aborigines is nothing else than a wilful mispronunciation of the word Karusha. These opinions however

The Uraons claim their descent from Ravana, the legendary king of Lanka. Whatever may be the worth of this ambitious claim to renowned ancestry, it seems pretty certain that at some remote period in their history they had lived in Southern India.[7] Philologists trace in the language of the Canarese of the South a close resemblance to the Kurukh or Uraon tongue.

The legend which the Uraon Panch or Sankatolas recite at the *Palkhansna* or *Dant-katna* ceremony is but a sorry transformation of the Hindu story of Ramchandra, Sita and Hanuman. The story has been given at length in a paper by the late Rev. Father Dehon in the Memoirs of the Asiatic Society for Bengal.[8] A perusal of the legend leads one to suppose that the Uraons probably took part in the great struggle between the Aryans of the North and the aborigines of the South celebrated in the pages of the immortal epic of Valmiki.

Later, the Uraons appear to have proceeded up the Nerbudda till they reached the valley of the Sone. For a time, they appear to have lived in the country round about Aramnagar (Arra) and Byaghra-sara (Buxar), places one sometimes hears the Uraons naming as their ancient seats. Ultimately they took shelter in the Ruidas Hills. Here they seem to have dwelt much longer than did the Mundas and some other aboriginal tribes before them.

---

appear to be of very doubtful value. The Uraons do not ever appear to have played any important part in the Karusha country so as to give its name to the country. Whereas the derivation of the name *Karusha* from the Cherus who once held sway over that country would appear to be more likely. As for Father Grignard's theory of the Uraons having been the companions of the Mundas in all their migrations from the Aryan invasion of India's hills, it does not appear to be supported either by the traditions of the Mundas or of the Uraons. Some Uraons indeed appear to have adopted the Munda tradition of their migrations from Azimgarh through Hardi nagar, Pipragarh and other places to Ruidasgarh, just as they have adopted some other traditions and customs from the Mundas. Thus the Uraons have even invented a story according to which the first Raja of Chota Nagpur, Fani Mutuk Rai, was the grandson of Lakhan Bhagat, an Uraon. As soon as this future king of Chota Nagpur, it is said, saw the light at Sutiambe-Biarkho, his parents died, and a cobra protected the baby with his hood till he was picked up by an old Munda couple, and when this child came of age, he was elected as their Raja by the Mundas.

[7] For ought we know, Ravana might have been a Dravidian king to whom the *Kurukhs* (the ancestors of the Chota Nagpur Uraons) were subordinate. And Ravana's kingdom might have included a portion of Southern India.

[8] The Religion and Customs of the Uraons, *A. S. J.*, *Bengal*, Vol. 1, No. 9, pp. 125-32 (1906).

One of the Uraon folktales is but a reproduction of the Hindu Pouranik story of Rohitaswa, son of Raja Harischandra.[9]

In the end, the Uraons had to measure their strength against a more wily enemy[10] than any they had hitherto encountered. Taking advantage of the drunken revelry in which the Uraons were engaged in the *Khadi* or *Sarhul* festival, the enemy attacked them unawares and though at first repelled by the Amazonian Uraon women attired in masculine dress, they at length succeeded in capturing the Uraon citadel. Dislodged from the same strong-hold that once the Mundas had to surrender to the enemy under similar circumstances, the Uraons appear to have split up into two divisions. The smaller branch, the ancestors of the present Male tribe, proceeded up the Ganges and finally settled in the Rajmahal hills. The second division, by far the larger of the two, proceeded down the river Koel till they entered the country now known as Chota Nagpur. A number of Uraons, however, managed to stay on, and even to this day their descendants may be seen living in and about Rohtas.

Thus appeared the ancestors of the modern Uraons in Jharkhand, the forest country, already opened up for human habitation by their precursors, the Mundas. The new-comers appear to have felt the superiority of the Munda people, and from them they gradually adopted their village organisation with its Munda Khunt, and Pahan Khunt, the system of tribal government under *Pattis* or *Parhas*, and even some of their religious festivals.[11]

The Uraons appear to have carried with them to their new home a recollection of the title 'Raja' (king) in vogue amongst their erstwhile neighbours,—the Hindus. And thus the Parha chiefs among the Uraons or Kurukhs came to be known as 'Parha Rajas' instead of Mankis as among the Mundas.

It was probably at this period of the history of the Horo or Munda race, that one branch of them, more conservative perhaps

[9] Vide *Folktales of the Uraons*y Rev. Dr. Hahn.

[10] According to Father Grignard these were the Kouravas. But the Uraons themselves, as I have heard them recount the incident, name them as the Mlechas, an appellation given by the Hindus to allimpure tribes including the different aboriginal tribes.

[11] It is sometimes supposed that the Uraons came to Chota Nagpur much later, having been invited by the then Raja of Chota Nagpur to help him in suppressing the Mundas who had made him king and whom he gradually came to hate. This account does not appear to be quite unlikely.

than the rest, marched off southwards down the river Koel and at length found themselves in that part of the present district of Singbhum which is now known, after them, as the Kolhan. Not infrequently along the course of this route which we have supposed the Hos to have pursued,—in Parganas Panari, Nowagarh, Doisa, Bhour-Pahar and Basia,—through or near which the South Koel passes in her downward course to the present district of Singbhum, may yet be seen traces of their passing settlements in the characteristic Munda monumental and sepulchral stones they left behind them, in the Mundari names of a number of villages on both sides of the river, and in the sprinkling of Munda inhabitants still to be met with among large masses of Uraon and Kharia population in these parganas. The further we follow the downward course of the Koel towards Singbhoom, the greater becomes the proportion of the Munda population. Thus, in the southernmost *thana* of Basia, the Munda element preponderates, and in the next northern *thana* of Kolebira, the Munda element exceeds that of the *thanas* further to the north on the banks of the Koel. The number of villages along the valley of the Koel bearing names with distinctive Mundari endings, such as—hatu,—bera,—piri,—sereng,— gutu, —hutup, —hutu, —jang, —gara, —ba, —baru, —kel,— kera, —kela, —ora, —da, —dag, —dage,— daga, etc., may be safely taken to have been founded by these southward-bound Horoko or Hos. And we have also to add to these the many villages along the river with pure Mundari names, such as Meral, Sibil, Sim-hatu, Hesa, Silinga or Jilinga, Soso and a number of others.

Again, if we trace the history of particular villages in the valley of the Koel, we shall perhaps find material support to the theory we have ventured to put forward. Thus, village Palkot is said to have been derived from the Mundari words 'Pahal' and 'Kote', and it is said that the Mundas who once resided in the neighbourhood used to come to that village to have their *pahals* of ploughshares sharpened at the smithies of some Munda *lohars* or blacksmiths who once dwelt there. And even to this day you may see a few Munda families at Palkot living amongst a multitude of Kharia and Uraon neighbours. The present village of Basia is always called by the Mundas of the neighbourhood by the name of Ban Sing, the reputed Munda founder of the village. The village of Samtoli is said to have been originally known as Samutoli, from

Samu Munda who is said to have founded it. Instances like these might perhaps be considerably multiplied.

An additional circumstance which would appear to lend support to our supposition is that the Hos of Kolhan yet retain a tradition of their emigration from the country of the Mundas, but they preserve, so far as we have been able to ascertain, no tradition about the rise of the Nagbansi Raja . This is perhaps a clear indication that the Hos separated from the Mundas before the latter in their turn left the north-western parts of the present Ranchi District and made for the Central Plateau where they subsequently elected their first Raja. These emigrants into Singbhum, from Chota Nagpur 'proper' were the ancestors of the Hos, or Larka Kols, who still retain the national name. They appear to have broken up the earlier settlements of the Srawaks or Seraks in those parts.[12]

Actuated probably by considerations similar to those that influenced the Hos, small bands of Mundas appear to have crossed the long chain of hills that mark off the plateau from the country further West and passed into pargana Borway, in the present Ranchi District, and pargana Chechari in the Palamau District,[13] and into the tributary State of Sirguja.

Let us return once more to the main body of the Mundas. For them, too, their original settlements in the north-western parts of the present Ranchi District appear to have gradually lost much of their former attraction. The prolific Uraons who had come to live amongst them, multiplied so thick and fast, that the Mundas deemed it desirable to seek fresh fields and pastures new. And accordingly up they proceeded by slow stages along the valley of the North Koel and passed further East beyond the source of that river not far off from village Nagri. A Munda patriarch, Risa Munda by name, so runs the tradition, led the main body of the Mundas, 2,100 in number, and at length came up and halted on the site of the present village of Muruma, since famous for the great dancing festival or *jatra* held there every year. These 2,100 Mundas, it is said, included the 21 *Kilis* or clans into which the Mundas were then divided.[14]

---

[12] Vide *Proceedings of the Asiatic Society of Bengal*, 1865, p. 169.

[13] This seems also to be the opinion of the Rev. Father Dehon. Vide *Memoirs of the Asiatic Society of Bengal*, Vol. 1, No. 9, p. 123.

[14] The names of the 21 original *Kilis* appear to have been, *Kachua, Topno, Bhengra Sandigura, Dungdung, Lipi, Honre, Hau, Kandir, Kerketa, Barla, Tuti, Hemrom, Kongari*

On the way, a follower of Risa Munda, Korumba by name, settled in what is now known as village Korambe, so named after its original Munda founder. A second follower, Sutia by name, the ancestor of Madra Munda—the reputed foster-father of Fani Mukut Rai—founded a village which came to be called Sutiambe after him. These two places Sutiambe and Korambe are still mentioned by the Mundas of the central plateau to have been the cradle of the 'Konkpat' of 'Kompat' Mundas as they call themselves. From Sutiambe, it is said, the Mundas went to Pithouria, and from Pithouria later on to Chutia. The patriarch Chutu hadam[15] is the reputed founder of this suburban village of Chutia which is sometimes stated to have given the name of Chutia Nagpur or Chota Nagpur to the country.

In this way the central plateau of Chota Nagpur appears to have been gradually colonised by the Mundas.

The Munda tradition of a compact body of twenty-one thousand Horoko (Mundas) marching up from the north-west and settling in the central portion of the modern district of Ranchi, has to be taken with a large grain of salt. We are not to suppose that the journey was effected in a brief space of time, or even in one generation. No : it must have taken the Mundas a long—long—time and the journey must have been effected by several slow and succesive stages. We can picture to our imagination the toilsome marches and the long halts, the travel-worn Mundas with their anxious womenfolk and their wondering children panting for rest and peace, family after family settling down on the way, many a Munda man and woman losing their lives during the journey, and their sons and grandsons resuming the eastward journey after the older folks are laid in their desolate wayside graves. In this way in two generations or more, up rugged hills and down steep descents, through pathless jungles and along sandy river-beds, the Mundas at length reached the elevated central plateau of Chota Nagpur.

Sanga, Kujri or Kujur, Soi, Tiru, Tuyu, Orea and Purthi. Subsequently the number of Kilis seems to have been increased by sub-division or otherwise. Thus the Purthi Kili seems to have been since sub-divided into Engapurthi, Hasa Purthi and Chutu Purthi Kilis. Among the Mundas now residing in Pargana Tamar one meets with Kili names evidently coined later on under Hindu influence. Thus in villages Diuri, Punriditi, Raidi, Amlesa, Sutilong, Murridi, Nouidi and a few other villages we find Mundas of the Kamal gotra.

[15] Hadam is a Mundari word, meaning, an old man.

The route which these Mundas followed in this eastward journey may be traced almost step by step through the Mundari names of numerous villages from Lohurdagga to Muruma, the characteristic Munda burial stones all along the line that have to this day fairly withstood the ravages of time, and the sprinkling of Munda inhabitants amongst vast masses of Uraon population in those parts of the district. That the Mundas were the first to penetrate the intervening jungles and establish villages on their way to the East is abundantly in evidence—not only in the names of some villages along the route[16] but also from the fact that in not a few villages along this line although the bulk of the population consists of Uraons, the only Bhuinhars are the two or three Munda families still residing there.[17] And another fact not less significant than this is that in quite a number of Uraon villages along this track, the Pahan or village-priest is still a man of Munda extraction. And the reason the Uraons assign for this is that the Mundas were the first clearers of the jungles and, as such, the proper persons to propitiate the invisible gods or spirits of the localities.

In the meanwhile, the Uraons who had been left behind in the north-western parts of the district were fast multiplying. And with the increase in their number, the Uraons in course of time spread further and further beyond their original settlements till once more a large section of the tribe came to live amongst the Mundas. Here, then, in the country round about the present town of Ranchi, the Mundas and Uraons once more dwelt side by side for some length of time.

It was during this period of their joint residence in the Central Plateau that a momentous change was introduced in the simple polity of these races,—a change which though apparently considered harmless at the time was yet pregnant with consequences of a far-reaching character and destined eventually to revolutionise the entire country.

We have already described the *Patti* or *Parha* system in vogue among the primitive Mundas and subsequently adopted by the

---

[16] The origin of some names of places along this route are not obvious at first sight. But a little inquiry amply rewards the labours of the investigator. Thus Lohardugga, now a Uraon village is said to have derived its name from the Mundari words, *rohor* (dry) and (*da*) water, and it is said that a spring of water which frequently dried up gave the name to the place.

[17] For example, in villages Masiatu, Chapadi Bhaisadone, Sero, Khundiari, etc.

Uraons. The most influential of the patriarchal heads of villages, as we have seen, used to be chosen by the Mundas as their leaders or Mankis, and by the Uraons as their Parha-Rajas. As the late Mr. G. K. Webster, C.S., Quondam, Manager of the Chota Nagpur Estate wrote in his well-known *Report of the Government of Bengal*, dated the 8th April, 1875:

> This arrangement being found clumsy, one head Raja was chosen, whose descendants are now the possessors of the Chota Nagpur Estate.

The tradition of the Mundas and Uraons regarding this incident as well as the family traditions of the Maharajas, will not fit in with the theory of conquest now occasionally suggested. The story of the Romulas-Remus type which describes the birth in the woods of the first King Fani Mukut Rai, the immediate voluntary death of the mother on the sudden disappearance of her husband, the appearance of the great serpent Pundarika Nag,[18] guarding the deserted baby with its expanded hood, the adoption of the child by Madra Munda—the then Parha chief of Sutiambe,—would seem to contain a grain of truth in a bushel of fiction, and we shall briefly give the story here.

The tradition of the Chota Nagpur Raj family as to its origin takes us back to the Pauranik time when Raja Janmenjaya was seeking to destroy the entire race of serpents by the celebration of *Sarpa-yajna*. One of the serpents, Pundarika Nag by name, managed to make good his escape, and, having assumed a human form, travelled to Benares and there succeeded in winning the hand of Parvati, the daughter of a learned Brahman. Notwithstanding

---

[18] Can this story of Pundarika Nag have been subsequently suggested by the name of *Pandu bing* or the white snake which according to the Munda legend sheltered the child left in the woods by its mother and taken up by Madra Munda? The Nagbansi Rajas are considered by Col. Dalton to have been of Kol or Mundari extraction. But, says Father F.A. Grignard (*Anthropos*, Vol. IV). "They were a branch of the Chero family to which...Behar belonged in sovereignty when the whole population of that province was Kolarian, and which continued or resumed its power there, for many centuries after a good part of the population had immigrated. When the Chero princes were expelled, in A.D. 500, by the Savaras, some of them went to Palamau, where their descendents are still found. Is it not likely that other members of the same family, in search for something to replace their lost grandeur, should have fallen back on the Munda Settlement of Chutia Nagpur, hitherto neglected by them? Anyhow, the probable date of the establishment of the Nagbansi Raja of Chutia Nagpur corresponds with the date of the overthrow of the Chero power is Shahabad and Bihar."

his otherwise human appearance Pundarika could not, however, get rid of the serpent's forked tongue which, not long afterwards, attracted the notice of his wife. Parvati naturally became inquisitive about it, and asked her husband what this meant. Pundarika put off answering the inquiry to some future day. And to divert her mind from the subject, he took her on a pilgrimage to the holy temple of Jagannath at Puri. On their way back, they passed through Jharkhand, as Chota Nagpur was then called. The Mundas and Uraons had already occupied the country. Arriving near the hill of Sutiambe, Parvati was found to be in the throes of child-birth. And now once more she importuned her husband to tell her the secret of his forked tongue. The explanation could be put off no longer, and Pundarika now gave out his real history and forthwith disappeared in his proper form into a pool of water close by. Parvati in great agony of mind now began to curse her own womanly inquisitiveness, and immediately after the birth of the child, immolated herself on a funeral pyre as befitted a Sati. Just in the nick of time, there turned up a Sakaldwipi Brahman carrying an idol of *Surya-devata*, the sun god. The Brahman was thirsty, and placing his idol by the side of the pool he began to quench his thirst with the pool-water. How great was his wonder when, about to resume his journey, he found that the idol could not be moved! He was casting about for an explanation, when, to his astonishment, he noticed a huge cobra protecting a baby from the sun with its hood expanded over the baby's head. And now the snake revealed himself to the Brahman as Pundarika Nag, and narrated his strange history. The snake went on to prophesy that the child was destined to be the Raja of the country and that this Sakaldwipi Brahman would be his priest and the idol he now carried was to be the tutelary deity of the child's family.[19] This child, said Pundarika, was to be named Phani Mukuta Rai, and the country Nagpur. These revelations over, the snake once more returned to the pool and was seen no more. True to his promise, the Brahman now took up the infant in his arms and carried it to the house of a Munda who lived in a village close by. This Munda happened to be the Manki of the *Patti* in which the village was included, and was known as Madra Munda. Madra readily consented to be the foster-father of the

[19] It is indeed very significant that the Sun-god or *sing-Bonga* is the principal Deity of the Mundas.

forlorn baby.   And the Munda patriarch soon came to love this
baby as dearly as his own son of about the same age, and both the
children were brought up together.   When both the boys attained
the age of twelve, Madra tested their respective capabilities in
various ways and selected his adopted son to be his successor in
preference to the son of his loins.   And when all the Mankis or
Parha-chiefs assembled at Madra's instance to elect a head Manki,
it was unanimously agreed that Phani Mukut Rai should be their
leader, and he was accordingly proclaimed Raja of Nagpur
(Chota Nagpur).

The family chronicle of the Chota Nagpur Raj published in
Hindi verse agrees with the traditions of the Mundas themselves
in stating that they voluntarily superseded the son of their own
patriarch Madra Munda of Sutiambe in favour of Madra's foster-
son Phani Mukut, in consideration of the latter's superior
intelligence.   And Phani Mukut was by common consent elected
the Raja of the Mundas as well as of the Uraons.   As the family
chronicle of the Maharaja says :

अमित उराँओमुण्डा गाँओ गाँओ ठाँओ ठाँओ,
परहा प्रति रोहिदासहुते आयो जानिओ ।

And to this day the simple folk of Sutiambe point out the dilapi-
dated ruins of an ancient fort at the foot of a low hill named
Mundara-buru as having been the first royal palace of Chota
Nagpur.

Thus arose a Raja in the realm, and the 'Nagbansi' chief became
the chosen head of the population of the country.   As to the
approximate date of this fateful event, the present Maharaja Protap
Udainath Sahi Deo is, according to the family chronicle, sixty-first
in descent from Phani Mukut Rai.   If we allow on an average
25 years to the reign of each of these 61 princes, we have a total
period of 1525 years.   This will take us to the year A.D. 384. But
considering that even according to the family annals several of
the Rajas had very short reigns (for instance, the 43rd king Berat
Coran, 5 years, the 44th Pankeytoo Coran 11 years, the 52nd the
Sibnath Sahi 9 years, the 53rd Udainath Sahi 7 years, the 54th
Shambooder 5 years, the 55th Billoram 3 years, the 56th Mumnath,
14 years,) we may perhaps be justified in reducing the total period
of Nagbansi rule still further. The family chronicle indeed which

assigns as many as 94 years to Phani Mukut's reign, 55 years to the next king and similarly long periods to some others, fixes the inauguration of Phani Mukut at Sambat 121 or 64 A. D. But we can very well understand this liberal computation. It is from the Nagbansi family that the name of the country seems to have been changed into Nagpur.

But the change in the name of the country was as nothing compared with the more momentous changes that followed in the train of Kingship. In the beginning, it would seem, the original settlers or *Khuntkattidars* who thus submitted to the suzerainty of a Raja had only to give honorary attendance to him. "They constituted," says Colonel Dalton, "the militia of the state." "The remainder,"[20] adds the same authority, "supplied food and raiment." "Before the Hindu Jaigirdar first obtained a footing in the country," writes Mr. Webster, "there being no landlord, there could have been no *rent*." But this introduction of the alien Jagirdar and the consequent revolution in the simple polity of the Chota Nagpur village came about much later. That is another story, and we shall describe it more fully in the next chapter.

As time went on, the Mundas whom we had seen settle in the Central Plateau and in time elect their first Raja, bethought themselves of a fresh change of abode. The prolific Uraons living in their midst had by this time multiplied to an appalling extent. The Rajas too perhaps showed signs of lording it over the people. And the assumption of an aggressive policy by the newly made Raja would naturally send an irritable shiver through entire Mundadom. And what with the one circumstance and what with the other, the situation became extremely distasteful to the proud and conservative Mundas whose instincts were essentially democratic. The thorn they had themselves planted in their midst began to bleed them to desperation. And away they marched once more and crossed the Subarnarekha and the Kanchi and migrated further ahead to the jungles on the south and southeast of the central plateau, leaving the Uraons in occupation of what are now the parganas of Khukra and Udaipur.

The names of numerous villages within a few miles of Ranchi,— such as Ulatu, Edelatu, Bariatu, Mariatu, Merel, Madkam, Kudadih, Karsidag, Tatibera, Barudih, Tiril, Jilingsereng, Jaher, Soparom, Serengtoli, and a host of other villages ; the many

---

[20] That is to say, the *parja-horoko* or outsiders settled in the village.

characteristic Munda Sasan-diris or sepulchral stones, that have
survived centuries of change and decay all around; the existence of
a Pahan or priest of the Munda tribe amongst masses of Uraon
population[21]; the wholesale adoption of the Mundari language by
the Uraon population around the present town of Ranchi[22];—all
these bear unmistakable testimony to the former Munda
occupation of this part of the Plateau. Even Ranchi bears in the
very heart of the town, evidence of its former Munda occupation.
The name of Hind-piri, a principal quarter of Ranchi, though
commonly supposed to have something to do with the Hindus,
is in reality a Munda name. For it is nothing more than a corrupt
form of Ind-piri, the piri or upland on which the *Ind* festival of
the Mundas used to be held, and is, in fact, celebrated to this day.
The name of Ranchi itself is derived by the Mundas from the Mundari word 'aranchi' (Hindi, *Paina*) or short stick used in the Giving cattle. The origin of the name of Doranda, too, is traced by
the Mundas to two Mundari words *durang* (song) and *da* (water)
and a story is told how the Mundas who first came there stopped
by the stream-let that flows past the place and drank their fill
of its water (*da*)and rested there, singing songs (*durang*) and
dancing to their hearts' content.

According to Munda tradition, Raja Phani Mukut's foster-
brother of the Munda race had a son of the name of Setea. And
Setea had eight sons. Of these eight great-grandsons of Madra
Munda, the eldest went southwards and established a Khuntkatti
village which he named Khunti—the present head-quarters of
the Munda Sub-division of the Ranchi District[23].

The tradition further goes on to say that when the Mundas
first went to Khunti and its neighbourhood, they found that part
of the country in the occupation of the Asuras and the Tirkis. The
Asuras, it is said, were the raiyats (*parja-horoko*) and the Tirkis the
Bhuinhars of the land. The many worked-out iron-ores found in
this part of the country are attributed by local tradition to the

---

[21] As for instance, in villages Mahilong, Arra, Boram, Harhatu, Tatisiloi, Chatra,
Lalganj, Sugnu, Pertol, Khatanga,   Gari, Tiril, Jorar, Namkom, Kokor.

[22] The corrupt dialect of Mundari spoken by these Uraons round about Ranchi
is sometimes called Horolia Jagar or Munda-like speech. It is also known as
Kera Munda, from the fact that the past tense of verbs is formed by these Mundari-
speaking Uraons with the ending—kera, instead of—keda.

[23] More correctly speaking the original village of the name of Khunti stands
one mile to the north of the present sub-divisional headquarters.

Asuras, and heaps of bricks of very large dimensions occasionally unearthed in these parts are pointed out as having belonged to the buildings of the Tirkis, who, it is said, had their *garh* at Doisa. And the tradition goes on to relate how when the Mundas with their stalwart physique appeared in the country, the Tirkis and Asuras got terribly frightened. For, it is triumphantly asserted, that the Munda women of those times used to wear glittering jewellery weighing as much as ten seers each and the men could carry loads weighing as many maunds. And the Mundas to this day recite a couplet which describes how the Tirkis fled in troops when they saw the Nagpur Mundas (Naguri) approach with their many ornaments sparkling in the sun.

तिरकि   तिकि   तिकि   चि
नागुरि   जालाव   जिलिव ।

The Asuras went westwards to Basia Pargana and Nagra.[24]

Similarly, the second son of Setea, it is said, went eastwards to Tamar. And many a Munda followed his lead. To the east, the Mundas appear to have occupied the five parganas of Silli, Baranda, Rahe, Bundu, and Tamar, and thence several bands of them appear to have moved further eastwards beyond the Subarnarekha and at one time occupied the parganas of Jhalda, Bygonkudar, Bagmari, and Patkum. The numerous collections of distinctive Munda gravestones, the traditions still extant in those localities, the distinctive Mundari names of many places and hills in these Manbhum parganas, leave no room for doubt as to their former occupation by the Mundas. According to local tradition, the Kurmis expelled the Kols from these western parts of the Manbhum District.[25]

It was to these wilds of Panch Pargana, as they are now called, that the largest migration of the Mundas took place. These

[24] The Tirkis, whom it is difficult to identify and who are in all probability an imaginary tribe suggested by the huge bricks sometimes found underground in those parts, are said to have migrated to Vilayat (!) and are, says Munda tradition, the ancestors of the Sahebs (Europeans)! This tradition is apparently due to the natural habit of associating every thing great and extraordinary with the mighty peoples of Europe.

[25] Vide *Journal of the Asiatic Society of Bengal*, Vol. XLII, Pt. I, p. 116, "Rude Stone Monuments in Chutia Nagpur and other places."—By Col. E. F. Dalton, C.S.I.

parts appear to have then been outside the limits of Nagpur, and to have formed part of the dominions of the Raja of Mayurbhanj. And here for several centuries the Mundas lived in peace in villages and *pattis* organised on the model of those they had left behind them. With the lapse of time, however, some of the descendants of their elected chiefs or Mankis became ambitious of rising in the social scale, and of assuming greater powers. History repeated itself, and some of these elected chiefs gradually became Hinduised and formed marital connections with families long recognised as Hindu Rajputs and Kshatriyas. And they called themselves Rajas or Thakurs or Tikaits. The story goes that a clandestine intrigue of one of the Tamar chiefs with a Mayurbhanj lady of rank was punished by the Mayurbhanj Raja by presenting a poisoned shirt to the former who died on his arrival home with the shirt on, and the Mundas of the Panch Parganas, enraged at this deceitful conduct on the part of the Mayurbhanj Raja, indignantly threw up their allegiance to him, and went over to their old Raja of Chota Nagpur once more.

Of the many burial-places in the 'Latar Disum' or the Lower Country of the Panch Parganas, the one at village Chokahatu (literally, the place of mourning) between Bundu and Baranda is by far the largest. It covers almost seven acres of ground, and the number of stone slabs that stand out above ground exceed seven thousand. Many of these have an appearance of hoary antiquity. Many are now level with, and some even below, the surface. "Probably," says Colonel Dalton, "excavation would disclose an understratum of similar graves."[26] Not a few of these stone-slabs, as Colonel Dalton was told on the spot, were known to cover the ashes of several members of a family. Judging from the present population of Chokahatu and the villages which were originally colonised from Chokahatu—for, according to Munda custom Mundas of such villages alone would be permitted to bury the ashes of their dead in the burial-ground,—this vast number of sepulchral stones at Chokahatu is almost inexplicable. Such an extensive burial-place is not to be found in any other part where the Mundas have settled. May we not suppose that when the Mundas who had settled in the Manbhum Parganas already

[26]In Colonel Dalton's account of this burial-place (*Journal of the Asiatic Society of Bengal*, Vol. XLII, part I, p. 112) the number was given as 7,360. Residents of over 50 villages and hamlets now use this burial-ground.

named had been driven back by the Kurmi immigrants, these repulsed Mundas took their stand for some time in and around Chokahatu which is near the boundary-line between the Manbhum and Ranchi Districts ? After some length of time, their descendants, we may suppose, spread over the five Parganas and a number of them proceeded southwards and swelled the numbers of the Singbhum Mundas. And the majority of the Munda families now settled in the Sonepur and Siri Parganas appear to have immigrated from the Parganas further east. In this way, the majority of the Mundas once more secluded themselves away from all aliens in the rocky fastnesses and jungles, of Parganas Sonepur, Tamar, Bundu, and Siri, and founded new villages of the same primitive type that they had left behind them.

In course of time, these new villages too came to pay a certain nominal contribution called *chanda* or subscription to the Maharaja through their Mankis or *patti-chiefs*. Beyond this, the Mundas of the south and east had practically little or no concern with their feudal overlord—the Maharaja.

On rare occasions, when there was a big marriage in the Raja's family or enemies had to be repelled, these far-off Mundas appear to have been sent for. The following old song still sung by the Sonepur Mundas indicate how slender was the connection between these Mundas and their distant king in those days.

> *Okotepetana hale senhoratanko udubalepe,*
> *Aledole senotana isu sangin disumte.*
> *Ayumanale menaiatabu raja gomke,*
> *Atamatabirko paromte*
> *Kulabingmocha isu sangin disum*
> *Raja gomke johartale senotana.*

TRANSLATION

Say, whither travellers, whither, so,—
Do tell us where,—Oh where ye go.
To a far-off place we wend our way,
Where dwells our king as people say.
Across a deep dense forest drear,
Where serpents bite and tigers tear;—
We seek that distant region now,—
Before that king our heads to bow.

6

Far different was the tune to which the Mundas living nearer the Raja's seat had to sing. For, as time went on, their position turned from bad to worse. With the lapse of time, the growing demands of the Raja and more particularly of his underlings and jagirdars, necessitated further and still further encroachments upon their cherished rights. And then it was too late to mend matters. And there was nothing left for the Mundas but to repent their folly, and to exclaim with the poet :

The thornes we have reaped
Are of the tree we planted,—
They have torn us and we bleed.
We should have known what fruit
Would spring from such a tree.

CHAPTER IV

THE MEDIAEVAL PERIOD OF MUNDARI HISTORY

[FROM THE SIXTEENTH TO THE EIGHTEENTH CENTURY A.D.]

When the interest of State wrought the general woe,
The stranger a friend, and the native a foe.

Drennan

As the distinctive feature of the Second Epoch of Mundari history
is the breaking up of Munda democracy by the rise of a Raja,
the most remarkable features of the Third Epoch are the introduction of a horde of strangers into the country, the creation by the
Raja of a class of middlemen out of them, and the consequent
revolution in the communal system in the majority of Mundari
villages. In the Second Period, as we have seen, the Raja was
content with limited supplies for his household and his court from
the various villages, and with military services in time of need.
His position appears to have been no more than that of a feudal
overlord and leader of the people. Thus things went on till we come
down to the Third Epoch of which for the first time we possess
materials more tangible and reliable than mere traditions and con-
jectures. These materials consist of a few contemporary records
in Mahomedan chronicles. The late Professor Blochmann in
an article in the *Journal of the Asiatic Society of Bengal* for 1871,
gave extracts from two Persian works, the *Akbar namah* and the
Tuzuk-i-Jahangiri. These accounts tell us that Kokrah,[1] as Chota
Nagpur proper appears to have been called by the Mahomedan
writers, maintained its independence of Moslem suzerainty till
about the thirtieth year of the great Akbar's reign. In the year
A.D. 1585, Shabaz Khan Kambu, we are told, sent a detachment
thither and the then Raja was reduced to the position of a *Malgu-
zar* or tributary. In the reign of Jahangir, again, the Mahomedan

---

[1] Kokrah, or more correctly Khukra, is now the name of a Pargana or fiscal
division (in Mahomedan times) round about Ranchi. The name is probably
derived from the *Kurukhs* or Oraons who have formed the bulk of the population
of this Pargana ever since the Mundas migrated to the southern and eastern
parts of the plateau.

governors of Bihar, we are told, frequently sent detachments into Kokrah of which the then ruling chief was Durjan Sal. As the roads were fortified and the jungles impenetrable, the Mahomedan governors had hitherto been generally satisfied with a tribute of two or three diamonds. But now Ibrahim Khan Fathe-Jang, the then Governor of Bihar, under special instructions from Jahangir invaded Kokrah, defeated the Raja, deprived him of his family diamonds, and carried away 23 elephants to boot. This was about the year A.D. 1616.

From the chronicle of the Chota Nagpur Raj-family we learn that Durjan Sal, the 46th king, after he had been defeated, captured and taken to Delhi, was kept in duress in the Gwalior fort for a period of 12 years, at the end of which his success in distinguishing a real from a false diamond was rewarded with his release and restoration to his former dignity. Henceforth he was to pay an annual tribute of Rs. 6,000. The generous Durjan Sal further begged of the Emperor to release a number of other Rajas who had been his companions in prison, and his prayer was granted. Before this, village Khukra in Pargana Khukra was the head-quarters of the Raj-family. In the Ayeen Akbari, we find Chota Nagpur called Khokrah and included in the Subah of Bihar. Even to this day 52 *bagaichas* (gardens) and 53 *pokhras* (tanks) once belonging to the Raj-family are spoken of with admiration by the simple folk of the now obscure village of Khukra, and its neigh-bouring villages. By the time of Aurangzeb's occupation of the throne of Delhi, the Chota Nagpur Raja appears to have removed his seat to the present village of Doisa 40 miles to the south-west of Ranchi. Till then it would appear, the Rajas used to live in insignificant houses. It was some time after Raja Durjan Sal's return from Delhi, that the construction of the magnificent build-ings of which the ruins may still be seen, came to be taken in hand. The story goes that when the released Rajas whose liberation from prison had been procured by Raja Durjan Sal, came to Jhar-khand to pay their respects to their liberator, they were not a little surprised at finding him dwelling in a house not at all suited to his dignity. And, accordingly, on their return home, they sent down architects and masons, marble slabs and other materials from their own dominions for the construction of a suitable palace in the capital of their 'diamond king'. And thus came to be built the fine structure known as the *Nauratan*, the five-storied palace with its water-gate and *garh khai* arrangement, the court-house(Kutchery) and its beautiful marble flooring, the nice treasury-house with its winding alleys in which, it is said, the Raja and Rani used to play at hide-and-seek, and the awful prison-cell with its underground dungeons, —which made *Doisa-nagar* famous in its time.[2] From three[3] old inscriptions two on a temple of Jagarnath and the third on a temple of Kapilnathji we learn that the architectural activities at Doisa went on till at least the year 1767 of the Sambat Era corresponding to A.D. 1711. It was in the time of Durjan Sal's great grandsons Maharaja Ram Sahi Deo and Kuar Harinath Sahi Deo that several of the temples were built.

Besides Khukra and Doisa, villages Pithoria, Chutia, Palkot, and Bharno claim the honour of having at one time or other formed the seats of the Raj-family now established at Rantu.[4] None of those places, however, retain any important architectural remains of the ancient royal residence. The temple of Rama and Sita

[2] The Mahadeva Mandir (temple of Siva) with its mysterious traditions and the rest house of Jagarnath made of small red bricks appear to have been built at an earlier date. The rock-temple close by with its unsavoury associations appears to have been built later. The *Dhobi Math* appears to be of a still more recent date. The ruins of the *Panchmath* or the Five Abbeys are worthy of notice.

[3] The inscription on the front door of the Jagarnath temple shows that it was built in Sambat 1739 or A.D. 1683 by one Harinath the spiritual guide of the then Raja. It runs as follows :

सम्वत ग्रह गुण सिन्धुशशी, शुचि तृतीया रवि साथ
जगन्नाथ कहँ मन्दिर भूपति गुरु हरिनाथ ।

The second inscription is on the left hand side of the *veranda* and gives the same date. It reads :

अङ्ग्राग्नि मुनि शुभ्रांशा तृतीयायां शुचौ शिते
असौ कृष्णालयं चक्रे श्रीरघुनाथ सदगुरुः ।

The third inscription which is in the temple of Kapilnath—i.e. Srikrishna, gives its date as 1767 sambat or A.D. 1711. It is in Hindi and runs as follows:

सुनि रससिन्धु शशी समाजन, कार्त्तिक शुक्ल रविवार प्रमाण।
श्रीहरिनाथ देव क्रतराज, गोकुलनाथ सङ्ग विराज ।।

[4] From Doisa, the Raj family went to Palkote and thence in 1868 to Bharno and thence to Rantu.

at Chutia, close by the Ranchi railway station, is a comparatively recent structure. The inscription[5] on the northern wall of the temple shows that it was constructed by one Hari Brahmachari in the Sambat year 1742 corresponding to A.D. 1685 during the rule of Raja Raghu Nath, the fiftieth in descent from Phani Mutuk Rai.[6] That quaint little temple with its arched roofs and verandas and the underground stairs leading to the well, appears to be the only object of antiquarian interest within the municipal limits of the present town of Ranchi.

It was during the reign of Raja Raghunath Sahi that a number of other Hindu temples were erected in the country. The picturesque temple of Jagarnathpur, about six miles to the south-west of Ranchi, was built by Thakur Aini Sahi just six years later, in Sambat 1748 or A.D. 1691. This fort-like temple with its solid masonry work and towering steeple, stands queen–like on the top of a solitary hill as if presiding over the destinies of the plateau which it overlooks. The annual fair held at the foot of the hill on the occasion of the Rathajatra festival attracts thousands of men and women from all parts of the Chota Nagpur Division.

It was in Raja Raghu Nath's time that the stone-temple at village Borea about five miles to the north-east of Ranchi came to be constructed. The two inscriptions that may still be seen in that temple tell us that Luchmi Narain Tewary, an ancestor of the present Tewaries of Borea, had the foundation of this temple of Madan Mohan laid in the Sambat year 1722 (A. D. 1665) during the reign of Raja Raghu Nath and that the building was completed in Sambat 1739 (A.D. 1682) and cost the devout Tewary as much as rupees fourteen thousand and one.[7] The architect was a Hindu named Aniruddha.

Both these inscriptions and another in village Tilmi on a well in the fortress of the Nag-vansi Thakurs of that village, have been

---

[5] The Devnagari inscription runs as follows :

सम्वत् करयुगसिन्धु शशी अक्षयतृतीया चन्द ब्रह्मचारी हरि मठ किश्रो श्रीरघुनाथगरिन्ब ।

[6] It was Raja Madan Rai, the fourth in descent from Raja Fani Mukut, who is aid to have selected Chutia for his capital.

[7] Of the two inscriptions, the inscription on the wall of the temple, runs as follows :

described by Mr. Rakhal Das Haldar in an article in the Asiatic Society's Journal of the year 1871 (*A.S.J.* XL, p. 108). The Tilmi inscription is in Sanskrit and is dated Sambat 1794 (A. D. 1737) and runs as follows :

श्रिधि धर्म्मं जयाचन्द्र सम्वत्सर प्रमोदकः ।

माधवे मासि शुक्लेव तिथौ गुणभृगोःदितैः ।

प्रतिष्ठा दीर्घकपस्यात्करोत्साह श्रीत्रकवरः ।

धर्म्मार्थकाममोक्षाय विष्णवे प्रियते सदा ।

The very interesting Minute of April 1832, written by Mr. Thomason, Deputy Secretary to Government at the time of the Kol Insurrection of 1832, embodies the following synopsis, prepared by Rajah Sital Roy, showing the connection of the Mahomedan Sovereigns with Chota Nagpur.

१ श्रीराम सत्य ।

सम्वत सतरसइ वाइस ।

वैशाख सुदि दशमी रजनीश ॥

श्रीरघुनाथ नरेशबिराज ।

लक्ष्मीनारायण ईश्वर मठसाज ।

The second inscription on a black slate runs as follows :

श्रीमदनमोहन (नमस) ते

श्रस्ति श्री सम्वत १७२२ समय वैशाख सुदी दशमी १० (सीमा) रके श्रीश्री मदनमोहन क मटटदायादल ग्राउ सम्वत १७२५ समय सायन सुदी दशमी १० के दरयाजा श्रो कोटरी श्रो छायदेयाली का दावा देल तैयार भेल सम्वत १७३६ के ताकरलशीत भेल रुपैया हजार १४००१ चौद ईश्वर निमित्ते ये किछु लागल हय से सत्य हय ताकर हिन्दु भय मट दरयाज छारदेयाली टाहायाय से गाइकवकतपीयय ब्राह्मणमारलेकहत्या गुरुमारलेकहत्या ताक हय मुसलमान भय मठदरयाज छारदेयाली ढाहा याय तो शुयर खाय—श्राखन मारलक श्रो पीरक थारा शुयर कहरा डारलक दोषतेहि—मुसलमानक (हय) ते वारि लक्ष्मीनारायण भगवतइ विनति लिखाय राखल हय कारीगर श्रनिरुद्धक विनति सांच हय ।

He (Rajah Sital Roy) represented the country to have been first subdued, A. H. 952 (A. D. 1545), in the reign of Akbar Shah, when Rajah Man Sing marched in from Rotas, passed through Palaoon (Palamow), and established his authority in the country; on the disturbances which followed the death of Akbar Shah, the Zemindars regained their independence A.H 1042 (A. D. 1632). Shah Jehan gave the country Palamow as a Jagheer to Buzurgatmed Cawen, Subadar of Patna, and settled the revenue at Rupees 1,36,000; in A. H. 1096 he was turned out and Ibrahim Cawen succeeded; Beharry Dass, the Fouzdar of Ibrahim Cawen, raised the revenue to 1,60,919, and of this settlement an account is given in which Coira Orissa, or Nagpore, with Currunpoor or Badam, is rated at Rupees 40,505; the rest of the revenue is made up from the other parts of the country.

In the reign of Mohomed Shah, 1131 F.E. (A. D. 1724) Scabullened Cawen was Subadar. He marched against Rajah Nagbundy Sing, who was then Zemindar of Nagpore, and to whom the Ghatwalls of Palaoon, Ramghur, and Badam were subject. The Subadar had reached the hills, when he was met by Bedman Dass Tacoor, the Raja's agent, and his further progress arrested by payment of a Nuzzeranah of a lakh of Rupees, 4,500 in cash, the rest in diamonds. Tribute was afterwards withheld, and in 1137 F.E. (A.D. 1731) Fughyrul Dowlah, the then Subadar, marched to the foot of the hills by way of Koonda. He met with considerable resistance, and was glad to compromise his claims by receiving rupees 12,000 from the Ghatwall of Ramghur on account of the Nagpore Rajah, and 5,000 from the Ghatwall of Palaoon. In 1141 (A. D. 1735) Aliverdi Khan with some difficulty enforced this payment, and it was continued afterwards till the British occupied the country.

As for the internal history of the country during the period, we have no written records to guide us. But inferences from established facts enable us to reconstruct this history with a certain degree of certitude.

As the Rajas through marriage with proud and high-born Rajput families like that of Pachete, gradually came in contact with the great Aryan world outside their hillgirt plateau, they began to imbibe ideas of worldly grandeur and royal pomp to which hitherto they had been perfect strangers. A change came over the spirit of their regal dreams. And, in course of time, they too, it would seem, chose to have about them a pompous court attended by Brahmans, courtiers, omlahs and servants and all the other paraphernalia of Hindu royalty.

The dazzling splendour which the royal court gradually assumed deeply impressed the simple Mundas occasionally summoned to Doisa or to Khukra to render military service, and their impressions found vent in songs like the following :

JADUR

Sona leka disumea, lipi
Okorem lelada, lipi ?
Rupaleka gamaia, lipi,
Chimaire Chainadam ?
Sona leka disumea, babu
Doinsareing nelada, babu-
Rupaleka gamaia, babu,
Kukuraing Chainada.
Sona leka disumea, lipi,
Mapatanakoa lipi,
Rupaleka gamaia lipiko
Tupuingtana.

TRANSLATION

O Where's the land that shines like gold ?
　　Say where such land didst see.
O where the land like silver gleams ?
　　Say where such land may be.
Ah ! bright as burnished gold the land
　　In Doisa realm I found.
There gleams the land as silver white,
　　In Khukra all around.
But in that golden land, my dove,
　　Oh ! men each other slay !

And in that land of silver, love,
Oh ! deadly arrows fly !

These Brahmans, Rautias[8] and other courtiers and servants
who now flocked to the Raja's place mostly from Bihar and the
Central Provinces,[9] had to be provided for. Circumstanced as
the Raja then was, what better expedient could he devise, or his

[8] The Rautias, some say, were invited by the Raja to keep down the Mundas.

[9] The Biru family claim to be an offshoot of the Orissa Raj family. Their
ancestor Hitambar Deo is said to have been one of the sixteen sons of a Maharaja
of Puri. Hitambar, it is said, owing to some dispute about succession to the
throne, removed to Sambalpur and obtained a grant of twelve villages from Maharaja Balaram Deo the then Maharaja of Sambalpur. Hitambar's Son Hari Deo
in pursuance of a mysterious divine direction left Sambalpur about the year
A.D., 1557 and went to Bijadih in Pargana Kesalpur which was then included
within the dominions of the Raja of Chota Nagpur. While here he presented a
diamond (one of many diamonds which he recovered from river Mahanuddy
under the directions of Shiva) to Raja Bhimcoran, the 29th Maharaja
of Chota Nagpur who was then living at Khukra-garh. The Maharaja made a
Jagir grant of the whole of Pargana Kesalpur to Hari Deo on whom the title of
Raja was now conferred, Raja Hari Deo was succeeded by his eldest son Kolha
Deo as Jagirdar of Biru. After Raja Kolha Deo came successively Raja Pitambar
Deo, and Raja Bhir Sing Deo. Raja Demo Deo and Raja Bhim Sing Deo.
Bhim Sing and his relatives assisted Raja Durjan Sal when the Mahomedans
invaded Khukra, Subal Sing, a nephew of Raja Bhim Sing, was killed in the
battle, Bhim Sing and his brother were taken captives to Delhi along with Raja
Durjan Sal. And it is said that it was with the help of Bhim Sing that Durjan
Sal was able to tell a real from a false diamond and thereby regained his liberty
and secured the title of Maharaja. In return for his services Bhim Sing
obtained from Maharaja Durjan Sal the title of Raja and a Jagir grant of the
entire pargana of Biru in addition to Pargana Kesalpur. Raja Bhim Sing was
succeeded by his eldest Son Raja Keso Deo, and Keso Deo by his own eldest
son Raja Narain Sing Deo. Raja Narain Sing by his failure to embank the Sankh
permanently, incurred the displeasure of the then Maharaja of Chota Nagpur,
and the latter refused to invest Narain Sing's successor Ram Sing with the title of
Raja. Accordingly Ram Sing was called Bahera, and a rental of Sicca Rs. 375 was
henceforth to be paid annually to the Maharaja for the jagir of Parganas
Kesalpur and Biru. After Bahera Ram Sing came successively Bahera Balaram
Sing, Bahera Gondal Sing, Bahera Dham Sing, Bahera Ghan Sing, Bahera Hari
Ram Sing, and Bahera Indarjit Sing. Bahera Indurjit's son Gajraj Sing was
given back the old title of Raja by the present Maharaja of Chota Nagpur.
The present zemindar, the eldest son of Gajraj, is locally known as Raja Hikim
Sing, to whom I am indebted for this family history. The local traditions
regarding the origin of the Biree family, are perhaps not quite so probable
as those regarding the origin of the Sahanis of Gidra and the Baraiks of
Pargana Panari.

advisers suggest than that of making service grants of his rights in a number of villages to these new-comers ? This system of service-grants was an exotic idea probably imported by these alien adventurers themselves. And thus arose the class of jagirdar under various denominations such as Bhaiyas, Baraiks, Brittias Pandeys, Jamadars, Ohdars and so forth.

In the beginning, it would appear, the change was imperceptible. The evil fruits that might spring from such imported seeds were not perhaps foreseen by the Raja. As Mr. Rakhal Das Haldar in his account of the village system of Chota Nagpur appended to a Resolution of the Bengal Government of the year 1880, writes :

> It is probable that when he (the Maharaja) gave away villages in this manner, he meant no more than to relinquish his claim to the supplies in favour of the Jagirdar.

The oldest pattah or lease which Mr. Rakhal Das Haldar could discover was dated A.D. 1676. And Mr. Haldar, as the then manager of the Maharajah of Chota Nagpur, had free access to the archives of the Raja's Sheristah or Record-office. It has been occasionally argued on the strength of the terms of some of these pattahs that the Maharaja must, at the time of granting these jagirs, have possessed absolute proprietary right over the Chota Nagpur villages. But a moment's reflection will show that this cannot be a sound view of the matter. The draftsmen and scribes of these documents, as indeed all literate people of the Maharaja's Court, were, and even now mostly are, men from Bihar. And these men naturally employed the set forms for such documents they had known in use in their own country.

To return to our account of the disintegration of the ancient land-system of Chota Nagpur. The Jagirdar who thus got an inch was determined to take an ell. As Mr. Rakhal Das Haldar, who can by no means be accused of any partiality to the ryot, ays :

> The grantee could not possibly remain contented with the Maharaja's share of the produce. His natural desire was to grow rich and powerful, within his own sphere at least; and he was not long master of the village before he commenced attacks on the most vulnerable points of the system. The lands held by

the *raiyats*[10]—naturally came first within his grasp. The people could be easily persuaded to believe that as the Maharaja was entitled to supplies from the villages, and the ryots provided the bulk of the supplies, and as the Maharaja had made over these to the grantees, the latter had an absolute right to them. Thus a certain proportion of the produce of the lands held by the ryots was collected by the Jagirdars, the same being gradually commuted into money, and the foreign idea of 'rent' introduced. The Jagirdar's right to such lands came to be recognised also, and hence originated the Rajhas tenure. Out of the Rajhas the grantee took some lands for holding himself; such land came to be known as Manjhihas.

In villages that still retained the *Khuntkatti* system, the annual dues levied by the superior landlord on the village community was made up of the rent payable by the *Parjahoroko* or *eta-haturenko*, the outsiders, who held lands under the Khuntkatti brotherhood. As the demands of the foreign landlords went on increasing, the balance required to meet those growing demands was made up by subscriptions or *chandas* from among the khuntkattidars themselves.[11]

It was probably at this period that the Mahto was introduced as a new functionary and gradually a Mahto Khunt was evolved in many villages probably out of the Munda Khunt. The new Jagirdars shrinking perhaps from introducing any officers of their own, sought to conciliate the villagers by allowing a member of their original village family to manage the affairs of the village in its relation to the new landlord. Even to this day, in the intact Khuntkatti villages of Parganas Sonepur, Tamar and Siri, the Mahto and his Khunt are unknown.

It was in the villages inhabited by the comparatively docile Uraons that the division of the cultivated lands of the village into Bhuinhari, Rajhas and Manjihas appears to have been first intro-

---

[10] i.e. the *Parja-horoko* or *Etahaturenko* described in our last chapter.

[11] Thus, from the very nature of the thing, the *chanda* was in earlier years a variable and fluctuating amount, the proportion paid by the different khunt-kattidars being determined according to their circumstances. When, in course of time the demands of the inferior landlords came to be fixed, the proportion of the *chandas* to be borne by the different khuntkattidars attained some sort of fixity.

duced. The Mundas, always zealously tenacious of their own
institutions and averse to any change, naturally resisted tooth and
nail all attempts at a disintegration of their village communes.
Their blood boiled with indignation at the sight of these foreigners
whom the Maharaja let loose over the country and who sought to
reduce them from their position of village-proprietors to an inferior
status. And their fierce hatred of these aliens, the Mundas
expressed in indignant songs like the following in which the unwelcome strangers are compared to the greedy vulture, the rave-
nous crow, the upstart peacock, and the ominous owl :

JADUR

Notem tirubachi sirmam sangin,
Kokordojanaji marangenjana.
Notemtirubachi sirmam sangin,
Kokordojanaji rajanjana.
Mara dojanaji marangenjana.
Kokordojanaji rajanjana.
Natu Natu Kauko diguarjana.
Mara dojanaji maranjenjana,
Disum disum Kauko kotoarjan.
Natu Mundako nekelatana
Natu natu kauko diguarjana.
Natu Mundako taiurtana.
Disum Buiarko taiurtana,
Natu Mundako nekelatana,
Borote gegako nekelatana.
Chiritegegako taiurtana.

TRANSLATION

Look where thou wilt, dear, wherever eye gazes,
Up to the sky or below to the earth,
(Men of mean blood wilt thou meet in high places,)
Owls pose as lords, dear, the owls of low birth.
Struts the vain peacock in glory of plumage,
Owls pass for lords, dear, the owls of low birth.
Look how the crow rules as *diguar*[12] each village,
Peacocks are grown great beings on earth.

[12] The *diguar* is a village-watchman or chowkidar.

> Rules the vile crow now as Kotwar[13] all over,
> Now hath each village for *diguar* a crow,
> Mundas of hamlets now tremble and shiver,
> They that were owners of hamlets erenow.
> Bhuinhars all over now quake and quiver,
> Mundas of hamlets now tremble with fear.
> Terror supreme now doth reign the land over,
> Mundas of hamlets have lost their old cheer.

Long and strenuous must have been the efforts these indignant Mundas made to prevent any breach in the fortress of their village communes. And in the end only the Munda settlements nearer the Uraon country and in closer contact with Uraon settlements, succumbed to the onslaught. The Khuntkatti nature of a number of villages hitherto held by the descendants of the original settlers in common ownership was at length seriously impaired. As the result of this mutilation, the proprietary right of the village community over a large part of the *done* and *tanr* lands of the village was materially affected, the Jagirdar usurping the right to levy a rent on these lands in lieu of the supplies hitherto given as the Raja's dues. These lands now came to be called the *Rajhas* (or *Rajangs* literally the share of the Raja, and the Mundas assert that up till the Bhuinhari settlement under Bengal Act II of 1869, these consisted in not a single village of more than half the cultivable lands, the other half at least being still left as the Bhuinhari lands of the descendants of the original settlers, and for this latter no such rent had to be paid. This arrangement gave rise to the expression still in use among the Mundas of what are known as the Bhuinhari *pattis*[14], *adha dam adha kam*, meaning "rent is payable only for half the (cultivable) village-lands and for the other half only (feudal) service." Such is the origin of the *Rajhas* lands[15]

---

[13] The *Kotwar* is a royal officer who keeps guard over a town or village to prevent breaches of the peace, thefts and other like offences.

[14] Among Bhuinhari *pattis* in Pargana Sonepur are the Bamni *patti*, the Sundari *patti* and the Zirath *patti*.

[15] This process of creating *rajhas* and subsequently subdividing the *rajhas* into *majhias* and *rajhas proper* may still be seen going on in portions of Tamar Pargana. In many Khuntkatti villages there the Raja or his lessors have got hold of a plot or plots of lands and begun by cultivating them *khas* or through tenants and styled such lands *rajhas* and the name *manjhihas* is yet unknown in such villages. But these *rajhas* lands in Tamar are what would be called *majhas* in the Bhuinhari pattis.

which at first included no more than the lands of the *parjahoroko* or *etahaturenko* (outsiders) described above and was in course of time swelled by the inclusion of portions of lands owned by the Khunt-kattidars as well, till at length in many villages the total amounted at one time to half the cultivable lands of the village. Out of these *rajhas* lands[16] the Jagirdar and later on the Thikadar who is a subsequent creation gradually laid hold of some of the finest plots, and began to cultivate them through his own servants, and these came to be known as the manjhihas (literally, the share of the manjhi). The waste lands or jungles remained, as before, the common property of the village community. To console the Munda and the Pahan for their loss of status, to them were alloted specific plots of rent free lands called respectively Mundai and Pahanai including Dalikatari and Panbhara lands. Whereas the Bhuinhari lands of the Munda and Pahan were heritable tenures, the Mundai, the Pahanai and the Dalikatari lands were to be held during the continuance of the incumbents' services to the village community. As a rule, however, the offices of the Munda and Pahan are hereditary. Thus, the Bhuinhari, as Mr. Rakhal Das Haldar says, is but "the remnant of the old *Khuntkatti* tenure". The present Bhuinhari villages are, what has been aptly styled 'broken *khuntkatti*,' villages.

It must have been after a long and painful struggle that the Mundas yielded even so much of the ground as they appear to have done. And thus, by slow degrees, a number of what were originally intact Khuntkatti villages were at length reduced to what are now known as the Bhuinhari villages. But even in the area popularly known as the Bhuinhari area to which operations under Bengal Act II of 1869 were extended, not a few villages succeeded in resisting their conversion from Khuntkatti villages into villages of a lower status. In such villages, the villagers would not allow the landlord to convert any of the village-lands into his rajhas or manjhihas. The Bhuinhari Commissioners had conse-quently to desist from measuring and preparing any record with

---

[16] "Out of the *rajhas*," Mr. Rakhal Das Haldar writes, "the grantee took some land or lands for holding himself; such land came to be known as *manjhihas* from '*manjhi*' the headman of a village. As the grantee was mostly resident proprietor, he required agricultural services from the ryots, and created the *betkheta* 'out of the *rajhas*'. Colonel Dalton, however, adds in a marginal note to the report of Mr. Rakhal Das Haldar, 'or out of his *majhas*'.

respect to such villages. And the descendants of the original settlers have retained their Khuntkatti rights in the lands of these villages.[17]

But the majority of the villages in the Bhuinhari area were not so fortunate. And, consequently some of the more unyielding among the Mundas of these villages appear to have retreated to the jungles further south rather than submit to such ruthless expropriation. Thus, we hear of Gaasi Munda of the Purthi Kili then living in village Hasa, not far off from Khunti, emigrating to the mountainous and jungly tract further to the south-east, and his descendants founded villages all around them, where the Khuntkatti system is still in full vigour. In this way from the furthest north-west of the Ranchi District, the Mundas at length made their way to the furthest south-east.

It was perhaps at this period in the history of the Ranchi District that Hindu Ahirs, Kumhars, Nowas, and a few other low class Hindu castes immigrated into the plateau in the train of the Hindu Jagirdars or at their invitation, just as some low class Mahomedans such as the Jolhas appear to have found their way into the country in the train of the Mahomedan troops who invaded Khokra in the 16th century.[18] The Ghasis, a tribe who earn a precarious livelihood by fishing and begging appear to have come to the country earlier. For, the Mundas tell a story that when Fani Mukut was installed as Raja, the Ghasis asked him, "What shall become of us ?", and the new Raja replied, "Go ye and beg from door to door". And since then, it is said, the Ghasis have lived by begging. This incident is said to have given rise to the common saying among the Mundas :

[17] Among these may be mentioned village Bargari, about eighteen miles to the south of Ranchi, and villages Posea and Burju not far off from Khunti, and the majority of villages in Pargana Siri.

[18] It is not altogether unlikely, however, that a portion of the lower class of the Chota Nagpur Mahomedans were originally converts. It appears that a few Mahomedan adventurers who came in the train of the Mogul army or the descendants of such adventurers succeeded in securing Jagir grants from the Maharaja, and it may be to their proselytising zeal that the origin of a small fraction of the low class Mahomedans of the Ranchi District has to be traced. Traces of these ancient Mahomedan grantees exist in the names of certain villages such as *Samsera*, *Rahamsera*, etc. A large number of the present Mahomedan residents of the Ranchi District appear to be the descendants of the Mahomedan traders who came here in the beginning of the Nineteenth Century.

Nagbansi Raja,
Kompat Munda,
Duarsing Ghasi.

The attacks on the land-system of the Mundas and on their rights to the villages that they had themselves eastablished, appear to have commenced in the eighteenth century, and have been in active progress till the present day.

Great as has been the success the Hindus have since achieved in impairing the original land-system of the Mundas, their attempts in making the Mundas converts to their own religious faith appears to have been attended with much less success. Buddhist monks, if they ever worked among them, have left no traces whatsoever of their activities in the Munda country.[19] It is only some Vaisnav preachers who appear to have once chosen the land of the Mundas as the field of their work, and seem to have met with a temporary success.

From the seventeenth Canto of *Sri Chaitanya Charitamrita* we learn that the great Vaisnav reformer and devotee of Nuddea on his way from Nilachal to Mathura passed through Jharkhand and made conversions among its aboriginal population. Thus we read :

মথুরা যাবার ছলে আসি ঝারিখণ্ড,
(ভিল্ল প্রায় লোক তাহে পরম পাষণ্ড ।)
নাম প্রেম দিয়া কৈল সবার নিস্তার ;
চৈতন্যের গূঢ়লীলা বুঝে সাধ্য কার ?
বন দেখি ভ্রম হয় এই বৃন্দাবন,
শৈল দেখি মনে হয় এই গোবর্দ্ধন ।

Again :

ঝারি-খণ্ডে স্থাবর জঙ্গম আছে যত,
কৃষ্ণনাম দিয়া কৈল প্রেগেতে উন্মত্ত ।
যেই গ্রাম দিয়া যান, যাঁহা করেন স্থিতি,
সে সব গ্রামের লোকের হয় প্রেম ভক্তি ।

[19] It appears probable enough that during the reign of the great Buddhist monarchs Asoka, Maurya and Kanishka, the Mundas of Jharkhand had to acknowledge the suzerainty of the paramount power. And the great Hindu monarch Samudra Gupta in the second quarter of the fourth century, appears

Subsequent Vaisnav preachers appear to have made earnest attempts to convert the Mundas. One of them was Binand Das by name whose memory is still preserved in songs he composed in the Mundari language with a view to facilitate the conversion of the Mundas. The elevated ideas expressed in the songs about *pap* and *punya* and about the vanity of earthly enjoyments, the style and composition[20] and the characteristic mannerisms of Vaisnav poets[21] in these songs, leave no doubt as to their Hindu origin. Such is the well-known song beginning *Bhatiora pitipiri honortanaking jurijuri*.[22] The small number of Bhagats among the Chota Nagpur Uraons and the Vaisnavs among the Mundas of Bundu and Tamar Parganas bear testimony to the partial success that attended the efforts of the Vaisnav preachers. And even among the unconverted, Vaisnavism has left its mark on songs and religious festivals. The *Karma* festival with its *Lahusa* songs can be clearly traced to Vaisnav influence. Unlike other festivals, the *Karma* puja is not presided over by the Pahan, no fowl or other animal is sacrificed but only *ghee* and incense are used as in Hindu festivals.

Some *Karam* songs sung by the Sonepur Mundas who have forgotten even the name of Vaisnavism, appear to have been composed at a time when the influence of Vaisnav teachings had died out but the memory remained. Thus in the following widely known *Karam* song we hear of the wide-spreading Kadamba (*naucleas*) tree on the banks of the Jumna associated with the *lillas* of Srikrishna.

> *Jamuna gara japa, Buru gitil Kadam Suba,*
> *Tiri riri rutu-saritana*
> *Mand sakam chora rera*[23]

---

to have actually carried his victorious arms through the land of the Mundas in his Southern Expedition. The autonomy of the Mundas do not however appear to have been ever interfered with.

[20] Such as the rhymes at the end and caesura in the middle.

[21] Such as the characteristic line towards the conclusion of each song—"Binandas Kajitanae," 'Thus saith Binand Das'.

[22] Among other songs of Binand Das may be mentioned those beginning "Hohore Kuri banoama muri," and "Nawa Samay rakabtana", etc.

[23] *Mand sakam* is the Mundari name of a fish which looks like a bamboo leaf (the *banspata* fish of Bengal)—*Chora* is the *chang* fish and *rera* is the *magur* fish so common in Bengal.

Among the Mundas of the Panch Pargana one still hears distinctively Vaisnav

Soben haiko nirtana,
Karakom do duar-re dubakana
Landatanae.

TRANSLATION

By Jumna's bank on sandy hill,
There stands a Kadamb tree.
How sweet the flute the air doth fill
With notes of *tiri riri.*
Lo ! fish of every size and shape
There move so gay and free,
And there the crab with mouth agape
Doth sit and smile in glee.

In genuine Munda villages, one is sometimes surprised to hear
the Munda youngmen and women ending their songs with lusty
shouts of *Radhe-Radhe.* The Mundas as we have found by personal
interrogation, have not the remotest idea as to what this exclamation means, all that they know being that it is the customary signal
that the song is ended. But every Hindu knows what it means.

In the Panch Parganas, a number of well-to-do Mundas, ambitious of rising in the social scale, have adopted the faith of their
more civilised Hindu neighbours, by preference—the Vaisnav form
of the religion. And it seems that if ever Hinduism once more
earnestly seeks to bring the Mundas into its fold, the Vaisnav
sect will have a greater chance of success than any other sect of
Hinduism. Some of the comparatively wilder Mundas of the south
may perhaps take kindly to the worship of *Sakti.*

---

songs about *Krishna-Lila* in which Bengali words are freely used. As an instance
we may cite the following *Karam* song composed by Budhu Babu, the well-known
Munda poet of Tamar Paragana.

Ogo ogo Duti, okotea Brajapati ?
Mage mage bachhar murijan,
Oro gating kae hijua.
Amgodo thorkia.
Nokore letagirijan ?
Nalita Brinda-duti, okotia Brajapati ?
Nidasingi Kurambhitar aege urutan
Dumburleka ji aenagin otang biurtan.
etc.   etc.   etc.

Although the bulk of the Mundas have, hitherto rejected Hinduism, clear traces of Hindu influence are observable in many of their social ceremonies and religious festivals. Thus, the *Sindurdan* or besmearing of vermilion on the foreheads of the bride and bridegroom by each other, the use of *Sasang* or turmeric in marriages, the fasts and ceremonial ablutions practised in Munda religious festivals, besides some other practices[24], are evidently borrowed from the Hindus.

Such in brief, is a rough and imperfect outline of the earlier history of the Mundas of Chota Nagpur. We have here presented nothing more than the dry skeleton of a subject abounding in living interest. We have included in our hurried survey, a period extending over many centuries. We started, in the first chapter, from a period when the Chota Nagpur Plateau was covered over with primeval forests. We have seen in the second chapter the Mundas, hounded down by successive bands of alien enemies, fly from country to country till at length they penetrate the jungles of Jharkhand. In the third chapter, we have seen them in clear jungles, establish villages of the patriarchal type, and for the first time break the virgin glebe. And we have seen how the Uraons, a few centuries later and under circumstances not unlike those that brought the Mundas to Chota Nagpur followed the lead of their Munda precursors, entered the country from the north-west, settled among these Munda pioneers, adopted their village organisation and *parha* government, and at length gradually crowded the Mundas out further to the east. And we have seen how at length both Munda and Uraon, in utter ignorance of future consequences, placed a king over their own heads. The more docile Uraons, as we have seen, quietly submitted, though not perhaps without an inward pang, to the evils that followed in the wake of kingship.

But the most striking phenomenon in the History of Chota Nagpur is the unbending conservatism of the more strong-willed Mundas. We have seen in the present chapter how this remarkably tenacious tribe in their anxiety to protect their sacred birth-right, their ancient village-organisation and land-system—made a gradual tour of the entire country from one end of it to the other. And at

---

[24] Among the Mundas of pargana Tamar, even the use of the *baran-dala* as in Hindu marriages has been adopted. After a marriage ceremony is over the Mundas of the Tamar and Siri parganas, curiously enough, will utter lusty shouts of 'Haribol'.

every stage of their migrations, we have seen, how the Mundas
left behind them indelible signposts of their former presence in the
names of places and in sepulchral and memorial stones which exist
to this day.   Well may the Mundas adapt the words of the poet
to thier own case and exclaim with legitimate pride :

> Tread where we may on Nagpur ground,
> From farthest west to wild Tamar;
> Or north or south, but still is found,
> Some ancient ruin, rath or mound,
> To tell of things that were.

CHAPTER V

THE MODERN HISTORY OF MUNDAS AND THEIR COUNTRY
[1765—1910]

Sit down, old men, together,
Old wives, in quiet spin,
Henceforth the Anglo-Saxon
Is the brother of the Finn.

Whittier's 'The Conquest of Finland'

WE now come down the stream of our narrative to what may be called the Modern Period of the History of the Mundas. The commencement of this epoch may be taken to correspond roughly with the occupation of the country by the British. This period saw the introduction of the alien *ticcadars* or temporary lessees in several Mundari villages.[1]

The *Ain-Akbari*,[2] that excellent account of the institutes of the great Emperor Akbar, written by his able Prime Minister Alamy Sheikh Abul Fazl, tells us that in the time of Akbar Shah, Kokrah, as Chota Nagpur was then called, formed part of the Subah of Bihar. When in the year 1765, the grant of the Dewany of Bengal, Bihar and Orissa, was made to the East India Company by the Emperor Shah Alam, Chota Nagpur, as part of the Subah of Bihar, necessarily passed to the British.

In the beginning, however, this obscure part of the Dewany does not appear to have attracted any particular notice. It was in the year 1770 that the first entry of the British into Chota Nagpur seems to have taken place. In that year, a British Officer of the name of Captain Camac, at the head of a troop of soldiers, appeared at Palamau to reinstate Gopal Rai, the local Raja, who had been driven out from his dominions by the Thakoor. The Satburu fort is still pointed out as the place where the Raja, Gopal

---

[1] The name *ticcadar* however subsequently came to be employed indiscriminately to the permanent or rather the *putraputradik* jagirdars as well.

[2] The *Ain-Akbari* forms the Third Part of Abul Fazl's great work the *Akbarnamah*.

Rai, had an interview with this representative of the East India Company. The Raja acknowledged himself a vassal of the British Lion, paid a *Nazarana*, received *Khillat*, promised to pay an annual tribute of three thousand rupees, and undertook to assist the Company against the Marhattas.

An exchange of head-dress, it is said, sealed the compact. The year 1771 also witnessed the conversion of the then Maharaja of Chota Nagpur into a vassal of the Honourable East India Company.

As we learn from the Minute prepared in April, 1832 by Mr. Thomason, who was then Deputy Secretary to Government :

During the operations of Captain Camac in Palamau,[3] Muchchun Singh, the Raja of Ramgarh, intrigued to prevent the success of the British to whom Durpnath Shahi of Chota Nagpur rendered essential service.

The Rajah of Ramgarh then used to pay an annual tribute of Rs. 27,000 to the British Government, and this amount included Rs. 4,000 levied by him from the Raja of Chota Nagpur.

The Minute of April, 1832, says :

Captain Camac, represented to the Provincial Council at Patna the importance of securing in our interests the Raja of Chota Nagpur, whose country would form an effectual barrier to the incursions of the Marhattas, thus covering Behar and Beerbhoom, and at the same time, giving us the command of the passes into the Deccan, through which, he stated, that Mr. Law had retreated after his defeat in Behar.

With this view, Captain Camac recommended that Raja Durpnath Sahi should be allowed to pay his *malgoozaree* direct to Government, instead of through Muchchun Sing, the Raja of Ramgarh, whose conduct he represented to have been most arbitrary and oppressive.

---

[3] Captain Camac was employed in reducing the Zamindars at Khurakdiha and the Junglebury District in 1769-70, and in 1771 to reinstate Raja Gopal Roy in Palamau and bring Palamau entirely under subjection to the British.

If this request were granted, the Rajah was ready to pay Rs. 12,000 in lieu of Rs. 6,000, which had been before extracted from him. On this occasion Durpnath Sahi himself addressed a letter to the Provincial Council at Patna, which commences thus : "I have been from old a *Malgoozar* (or renter) of the Government, and the Rajah Muchchun Sing, has long been a servant of me and my father." He proceeds to state that Muchchun Sing had acquired power by being employed for the Nizamut, and had usurped authority over him : and he prays that he may be allowed to hold the country as formerly, and that he will be responsible for the rents.

The Patna Provincial Council acceded to the propsal of Captain Camac, and accepted Raja Durpnath Sing's offer, making a settlement with him for three years at Rs. 12,000 per annum. On this occasion he received a Khilat from the Patna Council and a Perwannah from the Chief and Raja Shital Roy. In 1772 the Raja of Nagpur afforded our troops much assistance in the reduction of Ramgarh, but suffered himself much from the incursions of the Marhattas and the disturbances occasioned by Nanna Sam, a pretender to his Raj. The revenue appears to have been irregularly paid and balances to have accrued. The authority of the Rajah over the Jagirdars in his country was very imperfect, the Subordinate Rajahs of Toree and of the five Pergunnahs, Tamar, etc. seldom paid him any thing.

Thus Maharaja Durpnath Sahi, the then incumbent of the Chota Nagpur *guddi* obtained his first *patta* or *sanad* under which he was to pay to the Company six thousand rupees a year as *Nazarana* or tribute and another six thousand rupees as rent. This was subsequently raised to Rs. 14,100,15as, 3 pies at the Decennial Settlement, and later on to Rs. 15,041. The internal administration of his dominions was left entirely in the hands of the Maharaja, who thus became a tributary chief.[4]

[4] The Maharaja seems to have been repeatedly in arrears in paying his tribute. And on June 7, 1785, a *parwana* was issued to him by the Committee of Revenue "reprimanding him for his obstinacy, and desiring that he will personally attend at the Katchari of the Collector of Ramgarh and settle his balances". Again, we find a *parwana* issued on December 22, 1785 threatening to dispossess him if he does not pay up his revenues regularly. In 1787, it is said, the Raja having been in arrears, troops were sent against him, and the Raja was reported to have fled to the Maratha country, Vide *Cal. Rev.*, July, 1869, p. 115. On November 12, 1792

Eight years later, in 1780, however, a District under the name of the 'Ramgarh Hill Tract' was established with its headquarters alternately at Sherghatti (now in the Gaya District) and Chatra (now in the Hazaribagh District). The first officer placed in charge of this new District was one Mr. Chapman, and he combined in himself the functions of a Judge, a Magistrate and a Collector of Revenue. A force of native infantry called the Ramgarh Battalion under a European Commander was also stationed at Hazaribagh. The newly formed district comprised the present districts of Hazaribagh, Palamau, and parts of the present districts of Gaya, Manbhum and Monghyr, while Chota Nagpur proper under its own tributary chief owned a vague allegiance to the East India Company and formed but a nominal part of this huge district. In the year 1781, we find Mr. Grant, the then chief Sheristader describing the dominions of the Rajah of Chota Nagpur as "an elevated region which forms part of Suvah Behar, containing nearly 18,000 square miles, though proportionally (to Behar and Tirhut) of very inconsiderable value. This highland district, including the modern subdivisions of Palamau, Ramghur, and Chutia Nagpur, bounded on the west by the Subah of Allahabad, on the south Orissa, and on the East Bengal, hath since the age of Ptolemy been geographically termed the Three Bellads and Cantons, in Arabic."

In the beginning, the Bengal Regulations were in force in this

---

we find the Board of Revenue recommending to the Governor-General that the Collector of Ramgarh be authorised to suspend for the present the Government demands upon the Zamindar of Nagpur. Again on Aug. 13, 1793, the Collector of Ramgarh recommended to the Board of Revenue certain measures to be adopted for the recovery of balance due from the Raja of Nagpur. In 1795, again, we find the Maharaja applying for suspension of revenue owing to disturbances in Tamar Pargana. And on May 30, 1797 the Collector of Ramgarh again reports about balances due by the Maharaja. In 1798 we find the Maharaja unsuccessfully seeking remission of Revenue on the ground of depredations said to have been committed by the Marathas in his dominions. In 1799, too, we find him in arrears, and the Board directed the Collector of Ramgarh not to levy any interest on arrears due by the Maharaja. In 1800, the Raja sought remissions on the ground of incursions of the Raja of Sirguja on his Estate, and in 1801, a remission of Rs. 1500 was granted on that ground. On July 21, 1801, we find the Secretary to the Government, directing the Board that no coercive measures should be used to recover balances from the Raja of Nagpur, without a reference to Government. The letters of the Collector of Bihar to the Board of Revenue, dated the 27th May, 1803 and the 8th January, 1805, speak of further accumulated arrears. [Vide *Bengal MS. Records*, 4 vols., edited by Sir William W. Hunter.]

unwieldy district, without any consideration for the widely different conditions of these parts from that of Bengal. Appeals from the decisions of the District Officer who combined in himself the offices of Judge, Magistrate and Collector, lay direct to the Governor-General. In the year 1800, the Collectorship of Ramgarh was abolished, and the Board of Revenue, by their letter of the 15th April, 1800, to the Collector of Bihar, informed him that the Ramgarh Collectorship was annexed to his District. A Magistrate and Judge remained at Ramgarh. Not long afterwards, we find the Collector of Bihar visiting Ramgarh and stating in his letter of the 22nd July, 1800, to the Board of Revenue that he sees no grounds for exempting Nagpur (Chota Nagpur) from the operations of the ordinary Regulations, proposes measures for the realisation of excise-tax there and the issuing of licenses. Stamp papers were introduced in that year into Nagpur (Chota Nagpur). With foreigners from Bengal and Bihar unacquainted with the customs, the land tenures, and the languages of the people in all the subordinate Government posts, and with alien landlords lording it over in the villages, the Mundas had indeed a very trying time of it. Signs of unrest among the aboriginal population all over Chota Nagpur *proper*, were abundantly in evidence. Now and again, serious riots broke out which drew the attention of the authorities. In 1789, there was an insurrection in Tamar which was not quelled until Lieutenant Cooper made an expedition against the insurgents and reduced them in the beginning of July. Again, on the 28th November, 1794, we find the Collector of Ramgarh reporting to the Board of Revenue regarding "the refractory conduct of the people of Tamar", and the Board, in reply, directing him to "apply for a guard for the protection of the peace of that part of his District". The disturbances in Tamar continued unabated till late in 1795.

In the year 1806, Raja Deo Nath Sahi died, and his son Raja Gobind Nath Sahi was recognised as Raja and Zamindar of Nagpur by the Government. In the year 1809, the Raja of Chota Nagpur was ordered to keep up police stations in his dominions and appoint Thanadars and Chowkidars.[5] But this measure, as it was soon discovered, tended to aggravate the discontent rather than allay it. There was a rising of the Mundas and Uraons in the year 1811. And, about the year 1817, the country of the Mundas and Uraons had to

[5] See *Regulation XX of* 1793 *and Reg. XVIII of* 1805.

be brought under the direct administration of the East India Company as part of the Ramgarh District, and the Maharaja of Chota Nagpur had to be deprived of his position as a Tributary Chief.

The grievances of the Mundas and Uraons were not, however, directly concerned with the Maharaja. The financial embarrassments in which Raja Jugernath Sahi Deo, a youth of about nineteen years who succeeded his father Raja Govind Nath in July, 1822, on the Chota Nagpur *guddi*, before long involved himself led to the creation of a new class of *Dikus* or alien landlords styled *Thikadars*. These were mostly Mahomedan traders of valuable clothes and other articles who stuffed the young Maharaja full with their merchandise, but could not ultimately be paid in cash. And so villages had to be granted to them on *thika* or temporary lease. It was against the new class of Thiccadars or Jagirdars who, armed with a grant of the Raja's or his *khorposhdars'* rights in the villages, wanted to encroach upon the immemorial rights of the villagers which the Maharaja had never dreamt of questioning, that the aborigines were mightily incensed. Some of the *khorposhdars* and *Jagirdars* of the Maharaja, too, appear to have followed the example of the new *Thikadars*. As Mr. Bradley-Birt writes:

Everywhere the Zamindars had been giving grants of lands to the new-comers, Hindus, Sikhs and Mussulmans, who were fast ousting the original holders of the soil. The new land holders, ignorant and unmindful of local traditions, had inflicted great oppression on the rayats.

A Report to the Governor-General's Agent by his Principal Assistant at Kishanpur—Dr. Davidson, dated the 29th August, 1839, gives the following account of the rise of the various classes of middlemen under the Maharaja of Chota Nagpur :

The great mass of the population of Nagpur, known by Europeans under the name of Coles, consists of Mundas, Khareas and Uraons. The uniform tradition states, that the Mundas originally cleared the country and brought it into cultivation. There was no Rajah of the whole country which was divided into *purhas* (or patches) from 15 to 20 villages each under a Rajah. It is impossible now to say what these Rajahs received from their subjects, most probably only assistance in war and *salami* at festivals. Finding, I suppose, that this system of managing the country by means of so many Rajahs did not answer, the Mundas elected the ancestor of the present Palkote family to be Rajah of the whole country, since which 62 Rajahs of that family are stated to have sat on the *Guddi* with a few adoptions in the same family. The Rajah's family and friends pretend they were Rajputs at the time of the election, but there can be no doubt that their ancestor was a Munda, and the family prospering, they managed by force to get married into the Rajput families of Pachete and Singbhum, and eventually into others, and now pass for as good Rajputs as any in India.

The remains of the former system of Cole Rajahs are still visible in Pergannah Khookra and other parts of Nagpur. They have still their *purhas* and nominal Rajahs, who are always men of influence and in their festivals the members of the *purha* assemble to hunt, amuse themselves and decide disputes, etc. on which occasions the Rajahs' authority is still recognised.

Each *purha*, in general, has its distinguishing flag or ensign, any attempt to make use of which by the Coles of another *purha*, at their festivals, immediately leads to serious quarrels.

The custom in those remote days was, that whoever cleared the land became the owner of the same, free of rent, only in return rendering to the head of the villages such services as the common good required.

* * *

To enable the Palkote Rajahs[6] to keep the peace and carry on the wars in which they were constantly involved, a certain rent from each village[7] came gradually to be paid, but the right of property of the head Mundas of the villages[8] appears to have been long recognized.

[6] The seat of the Maharaja of Chota Nagpur was then at Palkote.

[7] This is obviously an inaccurate statement. The Maharaja did not originally receive a rent from the headman or Munda of each village, but from each Manki or head of a *patti* or group of villages considered as a unit. Even to this day, in such Manki-*pattis* as still survive, it is only the *Manki* or *patti*-head who is liable to pay a quit-rent for the entire *patti* to the Maharaja.

[8] This again is an inaccuracy. Neither the Munda nor the Manki had any 'right of property' in the villages. Such proprietary right belonged to the village community collectively and not to any one individually and exclusively.

On the Palkote family becoming Hindoos and regularly marrying into the neighbouring Hindoo families, it became a great object with them to induce other Hindoos to settle in Nagpur. The only mode of doing so, in their power was, to grant villages, by which means, all the *Suds* or foreign proprietors in Nagpur have been established. Burraicks, Rajputs Brahmins, Rowteeas, etc. are all foreigners brought in by the Palkote family as a sort of military force to enable them to support themselves against the neighbouring Rajahs, and also to control the Coles. The *Suds* being more civilized than the Kols were not long in obtaining the mastery and have kept it. And now in all the more open parts of Nagpur, there is hardly such a thing to be met with as a Cole proprietor of a village. In the southern parts of it they have been more fortunate; and the Mankees and Mundas of Sonpur exhibit to this day much the same state of society as formerly prevailed all over Nagpur, only the Mankees and Mundas pay more rent, than was ever paid by the Cole proprietors in Pergannah Khookra in former times.

I say nothing of the Mankees and Mundas of Tamar and the five Pergannahs as those countries did not form any part of the Nagpur family's possessions till modern times.

In all the various changes of rulers in India no Government seems to have interfered in the internal management of Nagpur until our own times. The paramount power appears to have been always contented with getting a moderate rent for the country, and when that was not paid, a force was sent to collect as much as it could, but no attempt ever appears to have been made to interfere with the police or administration of justice, which was left entirely to the Rajah. The consequence was that only those of the original heads of villages, who were strong enough to inspire fear such as those in Sonpur, etc. were able to keep their villages, the others were entirely dispossessed and replaced by *Suds*, or their villages resumed by the Rajah himself long before our time.

*   *   *   *

The persons to whom lands have been granted in Nagpur by the Rajahs may be divided into three classes :

I. The younger brothers of the different Rajahs and their descendants. On a Rajah succeeding to the estate, his younger brothers always received a grant of lands subject to a small rent.

II. Burraicks, Rajputs, Rowteeas, etc. who hold Jagirs granted originally on payment of a fixed rent for the performance of military services. The latter are now little required, and they pay in general a somewhat higher rent than they did at the time of the introduction of the authority of our Government.

III. Brahmins and individuals of other castes who have come from below the *ghats* and got grants of lands, generally by purchase at fixed rents from the different Rajahs, sometimes also rent-free,—and also grants of rent-free lands for religious purposes, in the mode usually given by Hindoos.

Almost the whole of the lands above-described with the exception of those for religious uses are held on what is called in Nagpur, *putraputradik* tenures, i.e. the grantee and his direct male descendants are entitled to hold the lands on payment of the rent stipulated as long as there are any direct male descendants, on failure of which the Rajah is entitled to resume the estate.

To this classification, however, a fourth class has to be added— viz. tenures held by some 'Dependent Rajahs' whose tenures were not originally created by the Chotanagpur Raja. Of these Mr. Cuthbert in his Report of 1826, writes :

Six subordinate Purganas were incorporated with Chotanagpur, viz. Tamar, Bundu, Rahe, Baranda, Silli, and Barwe. How or when these Purganas became dependent on the Rajah of Chotanagpur, I cannot ascertain, but it would appear that for a long time the dependence was little more than nominal. It was not until the country came into the British possession that these Rajas were permanently and actually incorporated with Chotanagpur. The revenue which these Rajas pay at present to the Raja of Nagpur was fixed by Major Crawford in 1840 Sambat and is as follows :—The Raja of Tamar possesses about 185 villages and pays as *malguzari* 26,660 rupees, Raja of Rahe 83 villages, pays 1,500 rupees, Raja of Bundu 88 villages, pays

705 rupees, Raja of Silli 87 villages, pays revenue 647 rupees, Raja of Baranda 255 villages, pays 1,462 rupees, Thakur of Barwe 29 villages, pays 846 rupees.

The Raja of Chotanagpur has no right in these Purganas saving the revenue payable to him, and thus these Rajas may be considered in the light of Talukdars. The Rajas, however, still acknowledge the Raja of Chotanagpur as their feudal chief, and on the death of a Raja, his successor waits on the Raja of Nagpur, pays homage and presents a considerable *Nazzerana*, generally 1,000 rupees, and receives the title from him.

The same feudal rights and customs prevalent in Chotanagpur proper are exercised by these Rajas.

The position of these 'Dependent Rajahs' and 'their relation to their chief' appears to have since undergone a considerable change, as the following extract from Mr. Webster's well-known Report of the 8th April, 1875, shows. After quoting a few passages from a letter of Mr. Nathaniel Smith to the Secretary to the Government, Mr. Webster says :

It may be gathered from this extract that the tenures of these dependent Rajahs were not creations of the Maharajah of Chotanagpur, but that they had been gained by conquest.

Tamar, indeed, was at one time subject to Orissa, and it seems probable that it was brought under subjection when the Chotanagpur chief accompanied the Mahomedans in their invasion of Orissa. Bundu and Rahe were not finally reduced and made tenants of Chotanagpur under regular covenants till 1793, when Major Farmer compelled their rulers to give *Kabuli-yats*. Silli, as far as I can learn, was fully under the power of the Chotanagpur estate some time before the country was ceded to us, as I find in some old papers that rent was assessed on each village in that Purganah.

Barwe was originally subject to Sirguja and was not finally brought under the power of Chotanagpur till A. D. 1799. The traditional origin of the Barwe family is as follows : A Benares Brahmin came to see the Raja of Sirguja in his Kutcherry. Just before he entered, it so happened that the Rajah had gone out, but his *chamar*-bearer was sitting close to the Rajah's seat. Now the *chamar*-bearer was dressed in the Raja's cast off clothes, and the Brahmin seeing him, mistook him for the Raja, and addressed him as Maharajah-Sahib. When he discovered his error, he begged the real Raja not to let him fall under the imputation of having told a lie, and to make his words come true. So the Sirguja potentate in order to save the honour of the holy man, made his servant a Raja, and settled him in Barwe. His descendants quarrelled with their old patron and went over to Chota Nagpur. The present holders are not the legitimate descendants of the original Jagirdars.

All these estates are held under what are called Bhandowa-pottahs, and on the failure of heirs-male of the original holder, they fall into the Chota Nagpur Estate. Tori and Rahe have already so fallen in. It is generally held that all under-tenancies created by the holders determinate with that of the grantee....

The present possessors of Bundu and Tamar are not legitimate descendants of the men who were in possession at the time of the Permanent Settlement, so that now these tenures may be considered as creations of Chota Nagpur.

The correctness of the opinion expressed in this last sentence is however open to question.

As to the general character of the Jagirdars of those days, Mr. S.T. Cuthbert then Collector of Zilla Ramgarh, submitted in the year 1826 a report[9] to Government in which he observed:

The Jagirdars (with few exceptions) have always been considered a turbulent description of people....The half-deserted villages, which one frequently meets with evince the oppressive conduct of these people as land-holders.

The number of these *jagirdars*[10] amounted in 1856 to about six hundred, "who hold each from a portion of a village to 150 villages" as we learn from a Memorandum by the Principal Assistant Captain Davies. It is no wonder, therefore, that in the year 1820 the ferment of unrest that had been so long seething all over the country, again burst forth in open revolt. The leaders of this revolt were two

[9] Mr. Cuthbert's Report was published in the *Journal of the Royal Asiatic Society of London*, Vol. VIII, pp. 407-16.

[10] In earlier reports and other papers the words *Jagirdar* and *Thikadar* are often used indiscriminately for the Subordinate tenure-holders under the Maharaja.

Mundas named Rugdeo or Roodan (Rudu, according to Colonel Dalton) and Konta (Kantoo according to Colonel Dalton). The Mundas still preserve the memory of the admirable skill in archery that Rugdeo possessed. His arrows, it is said, were each two cubits and a half in length, and he could ply these arrows while leaping backwards at a vehement stride.

The immediate cause of the insurrection was however rather curious. In the year 1819, there was a great drought in the pargana of Tamar, and the Mundas with their universal belief in witch-craft assembled to discover who the witch was that caused the calamity. The 'arrow-shooting test' pointed to one Treeb-hooban Manki as the miscreant. The Manjhi, however, managed to escape, but one of his sons was murdered, and his house and village burnt. Once the vial of the Munda's pentup wrath gainst the *Sads* was tapped, it burst out with destructive fury. A crusade against the alien *thiccadars* and *jagirdars* was proclaimed. The insurrection spread from town to village, and from village to hamlet. And at length, military operations on an extensive scale had to be undertaken to put down the revolt. It took Major Roughsedge with the Ramgarh Battalion several months to quell the insurrection and restore tranquillity. Roodan and Konta were at length arrested and they ended their lives in prison. In the year 1823, the Maharaja was prohibited to collect *sayer* duties. And in the year 1826, the charge of the Armai and Govindpur thanas were taken out of the hands of the Maharaja.

But the seeming tranquillity that now ensued was nothing more than a temporary lull. The horrors of the insurrection of 1820 were still green in the memory of the authorities, when towards the close of the year 1831, another outbreak vastly more formidable in its magnitude, convulsed the entire length and breadth of the country. This was, in the words of Colonel Dalton, but the "bursting of a fire that had long been smouldering". Not long before this a fresh cause of discontent had arisen. As the Bengal Government Resolution of the 25th November, 1880 tells us:

The oppressions of these men (i.e. the Jagirdars), however, were borne with, but a far worse class of men had obtained a footing in the country about the year 1822, when the late Maharajah Jagarnath Sahi Deo, obtained his ancestral *gaddi* on the death of his father in July of that year. These men were

8

Mussalmans, Sikhs and some others, who came to the country as horse-dealers and shawl and brocade merchants, fetched enormous offers for their goods from the Nagvansi Chiefs, and obtained farms of villages instead of cash, of which latter the Chiefs were always in want. The foreign farmers having but a temporary interest in the villages, squeezed as much as possible from the ryots in the shape of rents, *abwabs* and *salamis*. But this was not all. They proved their yoke to be galling indeed, and rendered the very name of *thikadar* in Chota Nagpur infamous. "The Pathans have taken our *hoormat*, and the Sikhs our sisters. Our lives are of no value, and being of one caste, let us stand fast to each other, and commence to plunder, murder, and loot." This resolve culminated in the insurrection of 1832.

The principal leaders of this revolt hailed from Porahat in the adjoining District of Singbhum, and were named Topa Suyu, Binrai, and Kate Sardar[11] Sing Rai Manki, Doonda Munda and other of Sonepur Pargana with hordes of followers joined the insurgents. Between three to four thousand Mundas and Hos assembled at the Sadom Gootoo Pahar. Among other leaders may be mentioned Samad Manki, Rara Munda, Mathura Munda and Ganga Manki. The immediate cause of the revolt in Sonepur was the grants made by the Maharaja's brother of a number of villages in Pargana Sonepur over the heads of the Mankis and the Mundas, to certain Mahomedans, Sikhs, and Hindus. Twelve such villages belonging to Sing Rai Manki and Mohan Manki, proprietors of Silgaon and eleven other villages, had been granted to some Sikhs, and, as Colonel Dalton says, "not only was the Manki dispossessed but two of his sisters were seduced or ravished by those hated foreigners".[12] Village Chalom and eleven other villages belonging to Byjonath Manki were given to one Hossein Khan and the Manki was not only reduced to destitution but on a false pretext taken to the Daroga of Gobindpur and sent in irons to Sherghatty.

At a large gathering of the Mundas convened at village Lankah in pargana Tamar, it was unanimously decided that the injuries

[11] Some Mundas also name Khanda Pator as one of the Singbhum leaders who joined the Munda Insurrection of 1832.

[12] In the recorded deposition of Byjonath Manki before the then Magistrate of Sherghatty, in the presence of Mr. Commissioner Lambert, we read that the daughters of Sing Rai Manki were kept in concubinage by the Sikhs.

inflicted and the indignities heaped up on the Mundas were past all bearing and that they had no alternative but to 'burn, plunder, murder and loot' their oppressors.

On the 20th December, 1831, a group of villages of the Sanrigaon *Patti* that had been farmed out to two Sikhs named Hari Sing and Dayal Sing, were robbed, burnt and devastated.   On the 25th December, 1831, a number of villages leased out to Kale Khan and Saifullah Khan were plundered and burnt, and a servant of the Thikadar was burnt alive. A plundering incursion was made on the 2nd January, 1832, into village Kamrang which had been farmed out to one Muhamed Ali Naik.   The next day another village, Gingira in pargana Sonepur, which had been granted to one Jafar Ali Khan was reduced to ashes and ten inmates of his house, including a Munda woman he had seduced, were burnt to death. The Porahat Mundas had a special grievance of their own against this infamous Jafar Ali Khan. This Jafar Ali Turuk (as he is called by the Mundas), it is said, used to buy iron in large quantities from the Murhu Bazar for exportation.   And the Munda women Poraha side who came to sell most of this iron complained on their return home, to their leaders or *sardars*, that the Turuk used forcibly to take away all their iron and indignantly throw into their baskets only two pice for each seer of iron taken, although the women would protest that the iron was worth considerably more.   The spirit of insurrection spread like wild-fire from one end of the country to the other. The Uraons joined the Mundas and the Hos, in their attempts at destroying the *Sads* or Hindus and the 'Dikus' or foreign landlords.

Colonel Dalton says :

In every Paragana the villages in which *Sads* (Hindus) resided were destroyed and all *Dikus* (foreigners) who fell into the hands of the insurgents were murdered. The Zemindars of Rahe, Bundu, Tamar, and Barwa, though neither Sads nor Dikus, narrowly escaped with their lives, when those places were all sacked and destroyed.

When the Nazir of the Sherghatty Court came up and proclaimed that if the Kols would desist from their campaign of rapine and bloodshed they would get back all their lands, the insurgents indignantly replied that they would obey none but the Maharaja alone and would not leave a single foreigner alive in Nagpur. And for a time the insurgents had all their own way. The Nazir's indiscretion in arresting Byjonath Manki, one of the most influential men amongst the Mundas, and sending him in chains to Head Quarters, appears to have aggravated the situation. In an Official Report from the then Acting Magistrate, Mr. R. Kean, made in January, 1832, we read :

The insurgents are stated variously to amount to from 1,000 to 1,200 men, but they will in all probability have increased by the time your force will have reached them; they are possessed of no arms, but bows, and arrows and axes, in the use of which they are exceedingly expert, and they further possess the advantage of fastnesses of the hills to which they retire, and to dislodge them is a task of great difficulty.

The apprehensions of Mr. Kean were soon realized and the number of insurgents went on swelling with a fearful rapidity. On the 14th of February, 1832, Captain Impey, who arrived with five companies of Sepoys, attacked the insurgents at village Sillagaon and killed Bhagat Sing, one of the Munda leaders. Seven sons of Bhagat Sing and 150 followers of his are said to have been killed in the action. A number of Munda villages were burnt down by the troops. But the Larkas and the Mundas remained as undaunted as before.

The Mundas triumphantly narrate how a captain who had come from Calcutta with British soldiers and encamped at village Selda in pargana Sonepur proved a sorry match for the resourceful Larka Hos. The Larkas, it is said, would remain in hiding in jungly recesses during the day and would come out at nightfall and shoot at the British soldiers from behind when the latter would return to their encampments after a day's futile search. And in this way, so the Mundas will boastingly and with evident exaggeration tell you, all the British soldiers were killed one after another, till at length the Captain had to go back with the severed heads of his soldiers. The Mundas still commemorate in their songs the delusive victories of the Larkas in their struggles with the British troops.

The following is an instance of such songs :

JADUR

Telengako jamanjana
Pithouria parganare,
Larakako hundingjan
Goa Balangare.
Mare Hoko tupuingjan
Jikilata pirire.
Mare Hoko mapajan
Ichahurang Dombaghatre.

Telengako haratingjan.
Jikilata pirire,
Larakako darijan,
Ichahurang Dombaghatre.

TRANSLATION

Within Pithouria bounds,
The soldiers mustered strong.
Balanga Goa saw
The fighting Larkas throng.
At Jikilata then
The Larkas' arrows flew.
At Dombaghat Ich'rung,
Their foes the Hos shot through.
Ah ! then, on Jik'lata field
The soldiers vanquish'd lay.
At Dombghat Ich'rung
The Larkas won the day.

It was not till March 1832, nor without some loss of lives on the part of the British, that Captain (afterwards Sir Thomas) Wilkinson[13] with the collective help of all available forces, succeeded in bringing back order.   Many are the stories that the Mundas still relate about Alkisun Saheb, the name by which they remember

[13] Captain Wilkinson took charge at Hazaribagh from Mr. H. G Mackenzie as officiating Political Agent of the South Western Frontier Agency.   On the 1st March, 1839, he made over charge to Mr. J. Davidson, and himself went to Nagpur as officiating Resident.

Captain Wilkinson.   The Captain encamped at Tamar and there,
it is said, cultivated the acquaintance and friendship of the Mundas,
and learnt their language.   The chiefs of Tamar and Bundu—
who, the Mundas maintain, were originally of Munda extraction,—
the Mankis of Tarai, of Sargaonpatti, Gorapatti, Chalompatti
and Kulipiripatti, were all summoned by the Captain and they as
well as the Nagbansi Maharaja who went to the Captain's camp
to attend at the inquiry regarding the succession to the Tamar
Estate on the death of Tikait Mani Nath Sahi, were all enjoined
to keep out the Larka Hos from the Maharaja's dominions.   The
Rautias of Sundari, Khunti, Thorpa, Bamni and other places who
attended Alkisun Saheb's *durbar* were, it is said, honoured with the
title of Baraiks and directed to help the Nagbansi Raja and the
Kompat Mundas to keep out the Larkas from the realm.   From
Tamar, the Captain, it is said, went to Selda and thence to Porahat
where he managed to make friends with some of the Larka Sardars.   Suyu and Khanda Pator became great friends of the
British Government, and it was through the latter that Dasai
Manki, one of the rebels of Kochangpir in Kolhan, was captured
in 1836.   Of some of the more unyielding sardars, such as Katey
and Binji Rai or Binrai, it is said, that while they were enjoying
themselves at a dinner party a number of British soldiers suddenly
came up and arrested them and took them in chains to Calcutta.
And thus the Larkas were finally subdued.   The memory of the
capture of the Sardars is preserved in the following short song one
occasionally hears in the southern parts of the Ranchi District :

> *Hohore Binji Rai saredar,*
> *Hore berime kandai.*
> *Hore hakimke hajure*
> *Hore berime kandai.*

TRANSLATION

> Alas ! for thee, O Binji Rai,
> Alas thou weepest in chains !
> Alas ! in presence of Hakim high,
> Alas ! thou weepest in chains.

Thus ended this insurrection or rather *Jacquerie*, as a writer in the

Calcutta Review for July 1869[14] calls it. As the same writer remarks, "it scarcely deserves the name of an insurrection when a body of men, goaded by the apparent want of redress, rose not against Government but against the Zemindars, seeking the wild justice of revenge". That this was so is abundantly borne out by more than one authoritative contemporary account. Thus, we read in a Report, of the year 1832, by Major Sutherland, Private Secretary to the Vice President in Council, that the land-tax which had been increased three-fold in a few years was one ground of dissatisfaction, the insurgents insisting on an assessment of not more than eight annas on each plough. We are also told that seven taxes were extremely obnoxious, in consequence of which the insurgents, it is said, used to inflict seven cuts on such of their oppressors as they could lay their hands on, one cut for each tax, namely,—*batta* or exchange-compensation for changing copper into silver,—an excise-tax on spirits, a proposed tax on opium which Government proposed to cultivate,—village *Salamis*—forced labour on the roads, fines for supposed or real crimes,—and postal taxes on villages (*dak masohara*).

Major Sutherland continues :

The hatred of the *Kols* seems to have been excited by the conduct of the Hindu and Mahomedan inhabitants of their country, whom they call *Sud* or foreigners, in a degree hardly inferior to that which they felt towards our Police and Tax-gatherers. The Mahomedans were mostly the farmers or Thikadars of the villages which had been resumed by the Raja or his chiefs, or which were mortgaged to others; the original possessors rented land which was formerly their own from these farmers, &c., and the 'Routeas and Kols' bore that sort of hatred to him which the Irishman bears to the interloper who gets possession of his hut and crop. The Hindus were mostly traders and money-lenders. Long stories are told of the enormous profits made by the former and of the usurious interest levied by the latter (money-lender), with the impossibility of the simple Kol ever getting out of the clutches of either, backed as they were by our Police and Adalat. The vengeance which he sought and inflicted on all is but too apparent at such towns as Choreah,

[14] P. 143.

Chutia, Burkagur and others of that description, where the foreigners principally resided. The sight most humiliating to our Government that I have ever witnessed, was such of the inhabitants
of these places as had returned, standing with their childern
in the midst of this scene of desolation, with occasionally an
old man or woman whose infirmities had prevented their accompanying the rest in their flight, and who, by the savages who
had risen to desolate their houses and ravage their fields, had
been tortured or burnt to the verge of death,—all calling in one
loud voice for redress of the grievances they had suffered, and in
reproaches on our Government for having left them unprotected.
They were told not inscorn, that their Raja should have protected
them, and they replied significantly enough, we had a "Raja",—
(meaning, the ancient Munda Rajah).

Again, Mr. Blunt, who was at the time (1832) a Member of the
Governor-General's Council, and had been previously (1805)
located in the District, in his very able Minutes on the causes of
the insurrection of 1832, said :

I am decidedly of opinion, that the insurrection originated
in the dispossession of the Mankis and Mundas of Sonepur,
Tamar, Sillee, Bundu, and the adjacent Perganas from their
hereditary lands, countenanced, if not instigated, by some influential person or persons in the District. To restore and permanently secure tranquillity, the same measures must, I think, be
adopted for reinstating the hereditary proprietors who have been
dispossessed from their lands in Chota Nagpur....
I am clearly of opinion that the system of Civil Administration, which may be well calculated to protect the rights, and to
promote the happiness of the people in our Regulation Provinces,
cannot with like advantage or safety, be extended to the Jungle
Estates; and that, for many years to come, the extension of our
laws and of the jurisdiction of the ordinary Courts of Justice
into such tracts will be both premature and injurious, both to the
peace of the country and to the welfare of the people; and I
think a serious error was committed in introducing our Regulations into Chota Nagpur, or in attempting to create a revenue
from taxes to be levied from subjects so uncivilised and so poor.
It is worthy of remark that the insurrection which occured in

Palamau in 1817-18 was produced by the illegal or fraudulent dispossession of the hereditary proprietors of some of the jagir lands in that Pergunnah, combined with other local causes. It now appears that in Pergunnahs Sonepur, Tamar, Silee, Baranda and Boondoo, in which quarter the insurrection in Chota Nagpur commenced, most of the hereditary proprietors, the Moondas and Mankis, have been dispossessed of their lands, which have been transferred in farm to foreigners (theekadars and mahajuns) whose expulsion and destruction appears to have been a primary object of the insurgents.   It further appears that the most grievous oppression and exactions have long been practised by the native officers of Government, especially the Police Darogas, which alone, amidst a people so poor, might well account for any general feeling of discontent.

Mr. Blunt thus concluded his very interesting and instructive minutes:

To secure the future peace of the disturbed Pergunnahs, the first measure necessary appears to me to be the restoration of the Mankis and Mundas to their hereditary possession; and then subjecting the police establishments to the most vigilant control.

An inquiry into the origin of the insurection reveals the following facts :

Many Mankees of Sonepur for some years had been deprived of their hereditary estates by Harnath Sahai, the Kumar of Go- bindpur who had farmed them to Thiccadars.   Those Thicca- dars had rendered themselves obnoxius not only to the Mankees but to the tenantry.   They would not permit the former to have even the fruits of the trees which themselves and their fore- fathers had planted, and having only a temporary interest in the land they naturally raised from it the highest possible rents. Two of the Singbhum Sardars, Bindrai of Kutma and Soyu Munda of Gondulpur had been ill-treated by two of the Sonepur Thiccadars and a relative of one of them in the service of the Singbhum Rajah.   These two sardars, it would appear, having consulted with their brethern the Mankees of Sonepur called in the assistance of the Bandgaon Koles over whom Bindrai appears to have had great influence, and of those of Kochang, and were

Tāmār. They resolved to rid themselves of the obnoxious class of Thiccadars, and with this view commenced plundering and burning their property and murdering them and their dependants wherever they could meet them. In the villages which were first attacked, the Koles were heard to say they would not leave a Thiccadar alive in Sonepur as they were enriching themselves on the Koles' lands while they themselves were starving. They did not molest, or carry off from the villages which they attacked, the property of the Koles by whom they were generally joined. The news of this forbearance and of the cruelties practised towards the *suds* spread rapidly and induced the latter to desert their houses and their property with the exception of what they could carry away about their persons. The Raotia Zemindars of Sonepur had recently had their rents raised and the Kooar had deprived some of them of their estates and of others had farmed, mortgaged or granted villages in Mokuraree tenures. When they were called on to collect their followers to resist the Koles, not a man came forward and they were left unmolested by the Koles, which leaves but little doubt but that they were from the first aware of the course to be pursued, and latterly they actually joined the insurgents. The insurrection spread to the Palamau; Tori and Ramgar parganas.

The Koles throughout Nagpore had within the last few years had their rents increased by their Ilaquadars, Zemindars, and Thiccadars 35 *per cent*. They had to make roads through the Pargana without payment, as *Begaris*. The Mahajans who advanced money and grain managed within twelve months to get from them 70 *per cent* and sometimes more. The Mundas disliked the tax upon liquor which was fixed at 4 annas per house, but more than that amount was actually levied besides a Rupee salami on almost every village and a *Khasi* or goat. There were several Mankees, Mundas, and other Zemindars in the jungly tracts of Chota Nagpur who were little civilized, but whose estates had been in their families for generations. Several of these had been deprived of their Zemindaris by the Kooar of Sonepur, and others of them had given villages on their estates to monied men to induce the latter to advance them cash. The insurgents, numbering 8,000, were finally dispersed on the 25th February 1833, after their defeats at Bali Nagar, Chatna pass and Sunhatee.

The quelling of this insurrection ushered in a new epoch in the administration of the country. The ordinary Regulations that had hitherto been in force in the district were withdrawn from it. And by a new legislative enactment, Regulation XIII of 1833,the parts of the country known as Chota Nagpur Proper, as well as Palamau[15] Kuruckdeha, Ramgarh, and Korunda, were separated from the old district of Ramgarh, and these together with the Jungle Mehals[16] and the dependent tributary Mehals, were formed into a 'Non-Regulation' Province and called the South-western Frontier Agency. By S. 3 of the New Regulation, the new Agency was withdrawn from the operation of the general Regulations. Up to this time the nearest Court was at Sherghatti (now in the Gaya District). Now, the District of Lohardaga was constituted "to dispense justice over 12,500 square miles from one centre". The system of Zamindary Police was introduced. Police *thanas* were established and began to be maintained at the *sadar* stations at Government expense. Zamindary *thanas* were established at Palkote where the Maharaja had then his seat, and also in the Estate of the Thakur of Govindpur and of the Zamindars of Bundu Tamar, Sili, Borway, and Banta Hajam.

The Maharaja, though originally bearing all police expenses, came to receive an addition of 4 per cent, on their quit rents from the subordinate Zamindars and, still later, both the Maharaja and his ilaquadars came to receive a police cess of from Rs. 2 to Rs. 3 from each village from the immediate holders of the villages. And thus arose the 'abwab' known as *Police Pacha* still realised from the ryots in some villages, although the necessity and justification for it no longer exists.

Captain Wilkinson was appointed the first Agent to the Governor-General. By way of conciliating the Mundas and Mankis of the Panch Parganas and the Manki *Pattis*, he granted them confirmatory *pattas*, confirming their titles and fixing the rent for ever.

[15] In 1853, Palamau was made a subdivision of the Lohardaga District, the subdivisional head-quarters being fixed first at Kornda, and removed in 1859 to Lesliegunj, and in 1863 to Daltongunj. On the 1st January, 1892, Palamau was constituted a separate District with Mr. W. R. Bright as its first Deputy Commissioner.

[16] This included the present District of Manbhum and the pargana of Dhalbhum. By S. 3. *Reg. XVIII of* 1805, parganas Pachet, Bagmundi, Baigankudar and the twenty-three parganas were transferred from Zilla Birbhum and Dhalbhum from Midnapore to Zilla Jungle Mehal.

Hazaribagh, Manbhum, and later on, Singhbhum, formed subordinate districts of the Agency, and were each administered
by a Principal Asistant to the Agent to the Governor-General.
Civil justice was administered by Munsiffs and by a Principal
Sudder Amin stationed at Golah.   Later on, in the year 1842,
the administrative head-quarters of the District were transferred
from Lohardaga to Kishanpur so called, as tradition states, after
Captain Wilkinson himself who was popularly named Al Kishun
Saheb.

It was here that Captain Wilkinson, the first Agent had, in 1834,
fixed the head-quarters of the South Western Frontier Agency.
Kishanpur then covered that part of the present town of Ranchi,
on which the old Jail buildings stood, and which is now occupied
by the Executive Engineer's office-building.   In a letter, dated
the 25th December, 1845, the Governor-General's Agent thus
describes the duties of his own office and that of the Deputy
Commissioner :

The Agent and Commissioner has the superintendence of every
department, is Superintendent of Police and performs all poli-
tical and revenue duties, and some Civil in the three Regulation
Districts, (Police cases, such as dismissal and fine, excepted).
All the Civil cases, excepting those involving succession in large
Zemindaries, and those between the Estates are with the Agent.
Formerly   appeals   from   the   decisions   of   Principal   Sudder
Ameens in Civil suits were heard by the Principal Assistants,
now they are heard by the Deputy Commissioner.[17]

[17] The Principal Assistant Agents came to be called Principal Assistant Commissioners from 1855.   These Principal Assistants were the District Officers, the
same as the Deputy Commissioners of our days.   The post of the Deputy Commissioner, created in 1843, was in those days equivalent to that of the Judicial
Commissioner of our days.   The Agent was the Divisional Commissioner.   Captain J. C. Hannyngton appears to have been the first Deputy Commissioner of
Chota Nagpur and acted as such from 1850 to 1856.   He was succeeded as Deputy
Commissioner by Captain W. H. Oakes (who became a Major in 1858) who
acted as Deputy Commissioner of Chota Nagpur up to the 30th April, 1861.
By Government Notification, dated the 30th April, 1861, the Deputy Commi-
ssioner of Chota Nagpur came to be styled the Judicial Commissioner, and the
Principal Assistants became Deputy Commissioners of their respective Districts.
Thus Major W. H. Oakes was the first Judicial Commissioner of Chota Nagpur.
The list of successive Judicial Commissioners is as follows :

Old sicca rupees ceased to be legal tender from the 1st of January, 1838. And, later on, the unstamped copper coin known as pucca pice was substituted by pice of Government mint coinage. These changes in the administration, though an improvement on the system that preceded it[18] do not, however appear to have done much to ameliorate the condition of the aborigines of the country. As one account says :

Major W. H. Oakes,		1860—1861.
Major (afterwards Lt. Colonel) J. S. Davies,		1861—1877.
[Mr. T. E. Ravenshaw (offg.),		1862—1864.
Lt. Col. W. Agnew (offg.),		1867.
Mr. H. L. Oliphant (offg.),		1874—77.]
Mr. H. L. Oliphant,		1677—85.
[Mr. R. M. Towers (offg.),		1878—80.
Mr. J. Whitmore (offg.),		1881.
Mr. G. E. Porter (offg.),		1884—85.]
Mr. G. E. Porter,	1-1-1886 to	13-9-1887.
[Mr. F. W. R. Cowley (offg.),	1-3-1886 to	12-12-1886.
Mr. G. W. Place (offg.),	5-8-1887 to	24-8-1887.
Mr. F. W. R. Cowley (offg.),	25-8-1887 to	13-9-1887.]
Mr. F. W. R. Cowley,	14-9-1887 to	13-10-1897.
[Lt. Col. E. G. Lillingston (offg.),	8-7-1888 to	7-9-1888.
Lt. Col. E. G. Lillingston (offg.),	1-12-1889 to	30-11-1889.
Mr. C. M. W. Brett, (offg.),	10-4-1891 to	1-9-1891.
Lt. Col. Lillingston (offg.),	2-9-1891 to	13-9-1891.
Lt. Col. A. Evans Gordon (offg.),	2-4-1893 to	24-5-1893.
Mr. R. H. Anderson, (offg.),	12-3-1895 to	14-5-1895.]
Mr. F. B. Taylor,	14-10-1897 to	12-5-1902.
[Mr. W. S. Lee (offg.),	17-9-1898 to	1-10-1898.
Mr. F. S. Hamilton (offg.),	18-3-1899 to	26-10-1899.
Mr. S. N. Huda (offg.).,	29-1-1901 to	28-2-1901.
Mr. H. C. Streatfeild (offg.),	25-3-1901 to	16-5-1901.
Mr. R. R. Pope (offg.),	17-5-1901 to	12-5-1902.]
Mr. R. R. Pope,	13-5-1902 to	10-11-1904.
[Mr. W. Maude (offg.),	22-7-1902 to	2-10-1902.
Mr. H. C. Carnduff (offg.),	11-4-1904 to	21-2-1905.
Mr. W. H. H. Vincent (offg.),	22-2-1905 to	22-3-1906.
Mr. E. E. Forrester (offg.),	25-3-1906 to	30-11-1906.]
Mr. W. H. H. Vincent,	1-12-1906 to	13-3-1909.

[18] Hitherto the officer in command of the Ramgarh Battalion acted also as the Governor-General's Agent for the South Western Frontier Province. Thus Major E. Roughsedge, who was appointed in 1817, was succeeded in 1822 by Lieutenant Colonel W. R. Gilbert and he in his turn was succeeded by Major W. G. Mackenzie in 1828. Major Mackenzie was succeeded in 1830 by Captain Wilkinson.

"From this time the fight between the two races, the Hindus and the aborigines in Chutia Nagpur took another form, that of calling in the aid of the Police and the Court of laws, an arena on which the Hindus soon became the masters of the field; for the Police were chiefly men of Bihar, the same Province the Zemindars had originally come from and in the Courts their own language Hindi was spoken, besides their having more intellectual power and pecuniary means than the Kols. The latter almost accustomed already to the position of a downtrodden and half-enslaved race received a severe shock from the mighty grip of the English Militia and lay prostrate at the feet of their Zemindars and Thikadars."

[Mr. A. W. Watson (offg.),   13-9-1907 to 5-10-1907.]
[Mr. J. Reid (offg.),   29-7-1908 to 29-9-1908.]
Mr. D. H. Kings ford,   25-3-1909 till the present time.
[Mr. J. D. Sifton (offg.),   1-9-1909 to 12-10-1909.

By the same Government Notification of April 30, 1861, the then Principal Assistant Commissioner of District Lohardaga (as of the other Districts of the Division), came to be called the Deputy Commisiner. The first Deputy Commissioner of District Lohardaga was Captain J. S. Davies who had succeeded Captaine G. N. Oakes as Principal Assistant Commissioner in 1858. The list of successive Deputy Commissioners of the Lohardaga District (which came to be called the Ranchi District from the 9th January, 1899) as follows :

Captain J. S. Davies,   1861.
[Lt. R. C. Money (offg.),   186.].
Captain A. P. S. Moncrieff,   1861—12.
[Lt. R. C. Money (offg.),   1862 ; Cap. H. M. Boddam (offg.), 1866.]
Captain R. C. Birch,   1862—18623
[offg. in 1863 ;—Lt. R. C. Money, Lt. G. N. Oakes, and Mr. J. F. K. Hewitt.
offg. in 1864 ;—Mr. J. F. K. Hewitt, and Mr. H. L. Oliphant, (also 1865)].
Mr. H. L. Oliphant,   1865—1877.
[offg.—in 1868, Lt. E. G. Lillingston, and Cap. R. C. Money ;
    —in 1869, Cap. R. C. Money, and Cap. E. G. Walcott ;
    —in 1870, Cap. E. G. Walcott, and Lt. E. G. Lillingston ;
    —in 1873—75, Cap. N. Lowis ;
    —in 1876, Cap. E. G. Walcott, Mr. R. H. Renny, Cap. C. H. Garbett, and
            Mr. J. J. Livesay ;
    —in 1877, Cap. E. G. Walcott, and Cap. C. H. Garbett].
Mr. A. W. B. Power,   1878—1785.
[offg. in 1881, Mr. R. M. Waller,
    in 1882-1883, A. M. Mackie,
    in 1884, Lt. Col. W. L. Samuells,
    in 1885, Lt. Col. Samuells, Mr. E. G. Lillingston].
Lt. Col. E. G. Lillingston,   1-1-1886 to 15-3-1892 .
[offg. Mr. G. W. Place,   9-2-1887 to 22-2-1887 .

As Colonel Dalton says :

It often happened that the unfortunate Kol, who with difficulty made his way to the far off station, found the tables turned on him when he got there. A posse of witnesses in the pay of the opposite party were already on the spot, prepared to prove "that he had not only no rights to the land, but was a turbulent rebel besides.

A writer in the *Calcutta Review* of July 1869, thus graphically describes the situation :

When the oppressor wants a horse, the Kol must pay ; when he desires a palki, the Kols have to pay, and afterwards to bear him therein. They must pay for his musicians, for his milchcows.

Mr. D. J. Macpherson,	12-7-1889 to 2-9-1889.
Mr. R. H. Renny,	27-10-1889 to 1-12-1889.
Mr. T. W. Richardson,	12-8-1891 to 15-11-1891.
Mr. T. W. Richardson,	23-12-1891 to 28-12-1891,]
Lt. Col. A. Evans Gordon,	16-3-1892 to 25-3-1896;
[offg.—Mr. C. H. Bompas,	8-4-1893 to 26-5-1893;
Lt. Col. A. Evans Gordon,	27-5-1893 to 11-4-1894.
Mr. C. Cuthbertson,	12-4-1894 to 18-6-1894.
Mr. C. F. Manson,	4-9-1894 to 1-11-1894]
Mr. H. C. Streatfield,	26-3-1896 to 16-10-1901.
[offg. Mr. H. T. Forrest,	11-8-1898 to 7-11-1898
Mr. W. S. Coutts,	25-11-1900 to 1-1-1901.
Mr. W. S. Coutts,	25-3-1901.]
Mr. W. Maude,	17-10-1901 to 15-3-1905.
[offg.—Mr. W. S. Coutts·	7-1-1902 to 14-2-1902,
	3-5-1902 to 10-6-1902, 22-7-1902 to 2-10-1902.
Mr. E. Lister,	7-6-1903 to 7-10-1903.
Mr. A. W. Watson,	25-4-1904 to 9-5-1904,
Mr. E. Geake,	10-5-1904 to 16-9-1904,
Mr. T. S. Macpherson,	16-3-1905 to 29-4-1905,
Mr. R. G. Kilby,	30-4-1905 to 21-12-1905,]
Mr. H. L. Stephenson,	22-12-1905 to 11-10-1908.
[offg.—Mr. S. C. Chatterji,	12-10-1907 to 22-10-1907,
Mr. P. S. Settle,	23-10-1908 to 19-1-1908,
Mr. A. W. Watson,	14-3-1907 to 24-3-1907,
Mr. E. H. Berthoud,	25-3-1907 to 5-5-1907.
Mr. A. W. Watson,	6-5-1907 to 11-9-1907.
Mr. E. H. Berthoud,	12-9-1907 to 5-11-1907.]
Mr. W. B. Thomson,	20-1-1909 till the present time

for his *pan*. Does some one die in his house ? he taxes them; is a
child born ? again a tax ; is there a marriage or puja?
a tax.[19] Is the Thikadar found guilty at Cutchary and sentenced
to be punished ?   The Kol must pay the fine.   Or does a
death occur in the house of the Kol ? The poor man must pay
a fine. Is a child born ?   Is a son or daughter married ? The
poor Kol is still taxed.   And this plundering, punishing, robbing
system goes on till the Kols run away. These unjust people not
only take away everything in the house, but even force the Kols
to borrow, that they may obtain what they want, reminding one
of Sidney Smith's account of the poor man taxed from birth to
his coffin.   Again, whenever the Thikadar has to go to Cutchary
or to the King, to a marriage, on a pilgrimage, however distant
the place, the Kols must accompany him and render service
without payment.

It must have been for want of adequate information that this
state of things was suffered to continue. And in 1854-1855, we
find Mr. (afterwards Sir Henry) Ricketts, as a Member of the
Board of Revenue, making an inspecting tour through Chota
Nagpur. In the Report submitted by him to Government,
Mr. Ricketts observes :

Though there was no complaint preferred to me, there seems
reason to apprehend that the people of the District, the Coles,
suffer much injustice at the hands of the foreign middlemen
introduced by the Rajah, their Zamindar. Dr. Davidson
who was a person of much intelligence, and studied the condition
of the Province with much attention writing in 1839, says :
"In point of fact, there was no regular Police or Administration
of Justice till the present Agency was established in 1834, that
they (the Kols) are frequently imposed on by their land-holders
is not for want of comprehension, but that they have been so
long completely left to their mercies, and so entirely deprived
of any protection from them, that it is difficult for them to make
up their minds to resist."   Major Hanyngton now tells me that:
"In Chota Nagpur the Bhooi has lands which exist in every

---

[19] In the course of time many of these taxes came to be permanent and hence
the many curious items of inequitable cesses misnamed Rakumats that we now
meet with in the Jamabandies of many villages.

village, have been exposed to the rapacity of the middlemen, aliens who are hated by the people, and who, to obtain these lands, spare no species of force or fraud. Against these our Courts do not afford any facile remedy, and the day may not be distant when the people, goaded beyond endurance, may take the law into their own hands. To protect these undertenures is, therefore, not only as a duty important, but it is also essential to the permanent tranquillity of the country. For this end, it would be necessary to ascertain what the tenures chiefly are, and how far they should be recognised: this being done, and the result made known by authority, the Courts would do the rest : the inquiries would demand some time and care and caution but it is practicable, and in the end would requite any labour that might be bestowed on it."—This evidence from a very intelligent officer, who has been many years in the Province, appears to me to be deserving of much attention. I have shown in another place, that alien Omlahs monopolise the public offices ; that though Dr. Davidson declares that "the Kols are an intelligent people, as much if not more so, than the labouring class of any part of India which I have visited," they have been with very few exceptions, regarded by the authorities as unfit to run with a message or carry a spear. With alien farmers, alien Omlah, and alien Subordinates in all Departments over them, doubtless the Kols must have much to endure.[20]

In proposing a Pargana-wari Investigation and Record of Rights for the protection of the Kols, Mr. Ricketts observes :

Immediate settlement under Regulation VII of 1822, the Zamindars remaining in possession, might be some avail, but it cannot be concealed that it must be a hopeless contest between a middle-man of any degree and a Zamindar in charge of the Police. However carefully his rights may have been ascertained and recorded, if the Zamindar Darogah is resolved he shall go, he must go ; his ruin may be effected in a hundred ways, and if he resist, will be effected, though the officer in charge of the District be his friend.

As a Result of the Report of Mr. Ricketts a further change in

[20] Vide *Selections from the Records of the Bengal Government*, no. XX.

9

the form of Administration was introduced in the year 1854. By Act XX of that year, the Agency was abolished and Chota Nagpur passed under the Lieutenant-Governorship of Bengal as a 'Non-Regulation Province'. And ever since then the country has been administered as a Division of Bengal under a Commissioner.[21]

The first Commissioner was Mr. W. J. Allen appointed as such on the 25th April 1854, and his successors have been[22] :

Colonel	E. T. Dalton,	1857—1875
Mr.	W. L. Robinson,	1875—1877
Mr.	V. T. Taylor,	1877—1878

[21] The term 'Non-Regulation' should not however be understood to mean that the ordinary laws are not in force in the country which was now for the first time designated the 'Chutianagpur Division'. Except in the Kolhan pargana in the District of Singbhum, most of the General Legislative enactments in force in other Divisions are now in force in the Chota Nagpur Division, but there have in addition to these been enacted some special laws for the protection of particular classes or for particular purposes. Thus, there is a special enactment for the relations between land-lord and tenant, and one for the protection of encumbered Zamindars. There is also a special law for the rural police. Another important difference between the 'Regulation' and the 'Non-Regulation' districts is the difference in the designation of the District Officer. Whereas the District Officer in an ordinary (or 'Regulation') district is called the 'Magistrate and Collector' the District officer of a Non-Regulation district is styled the Deputy Commissioner. And the Deputy Commissioner is vested with some powers which the district officers in the Regulation districts do not possess. The Commissioner of this Division has besides his ordinary duties (as in other Divisions), the superintendence and Judicial and Executive control over the Tributary States (the 'Political States') in the Division.

[22] *The Agents to the Governor General were* :

Major E. Roughsedge,	1818—1821
W. R. Gilbert,	1822—1827
W. G. Mackenzie,	1828—1829
Captain (afterwards Major) T. Wilkinson,	1830—1839
[Mr. John Davidson was in charge from the 2nd March to the 4th April, 1839]	
Major J. R. Ouseley,	1839—1849
Captain J. Hannyngton, 23rd April to 16th August	1849
Mr. J. H. Crawford,	1849—1853
Mr. W. J Allen,	1853—1854
when he was appointed the first Commissioner.	
Mr. A. C. Mangles,	1878
Mr. J. F. K. Hewitt,	1878—1882
Mr. ((afterwards Sir) John Edgar (offg.)	
(25th April to 5th November).	1882
Mr. J. F. K. Hewitt,	1882—1885

All the time that the various forms of administration described above were being successively tried in the land of the Mundas and Uraons, the Jagirdars and Thikadars were actively engaged in reducing these original "holders of villages to holders of the plough". Mr. Ricketts, in his Report (para. 47) tells us that he was informed by the local officers "that the class of indigenous village Zamindars is gradually, or rather quickly, disappearing in that character though still existing as discontented ryots brooding over their wrongs". But if for a while, the Mundas and the Uraons lay stunned and stupefied by the constant blows inflicted on their ancient rights, they were not long in gathering new strength to offer fresh resistance to the aggressions of their alien landlords. This fresh accession of strength was imparted by a strong ally which now came to them as a God-send. This new ally was the religion of the Cross. With the Christian Missionary came the Christian School master. And with the dawn of education came a vivid realisation of their present position as well as of their lawful rights and privileges. As Captain Davies, the then Senior Assistant Commissioner, wrote in 1859 :

With Christianity has naturally come an appreciation of their rights as original clearers of the soil which rights in many instan-

Mr. (afterwards Sir) C. Stevens	1885—1889
Mr. J. A. Hopkins Offg. 5th July to 6th Oct.	1888
Mr. W. H. Grimley	1889—1896
Col. E. G. Lilingstone, Offg. 12th August to 10th November,	1891
Mr. H. A. Wace Offg., 30th May to 25th October	1892
Lt. Col. A. E. Gordon, Offg. 4th September to 1st November,	1894
Mr. C. R. Marindin (Offg.) 2nd August to 8th December,	1896
Mr. G. Toynbee (Offg.) 2nd April to 1st August,	1896
Mr. A. Forbes	1896—1902
Mr. J. G. Ritchie Offg. 27th July to 25th October,	1899
Mr. W. C. Macpherson (Offg.) 16th April to 25th June,	1901
Mr. W. Maude, Offg. in 1002 in 1903, and again in	1904
Mr. P. C. Lyon, Offg. March to April,	1904
Mr. C. A. Radice, (Offg.) October and November,	1905
Mr. F. A. Slacke	1902—1905
Mr. E. A. Gait C. I. E.,	1905—1907
Mr. F. W. Duke, March to April,	1907
Mr. L. P. Shirres	1907
Mr. H. J. Mc. Intosh	1907—1911
Mr. W. B. Thomson Offg. 15th April to 13th May,	1909
Mr. E. Geake (Offg.) April to October.	1910

ces they have asserted and established ;—this, independent of other causes which induce the higher castes of natives to view with displeasure the spread of Christianity, caused great alarm amongst the land-holders and farmers, who were not slow to use against these converts every means of persecution they could safely venture on, but with no other effect than the spread of conversion.

Though conversions of the Mundas and Uraons into Christianity, when once commenced, went on multiplying with wonderful rapidity,—it took some time before any converts could be made. The four pioneer Missionaries, Pastors E. Schatz, F. Batsch, A. Brandt and H. Janke, who arrived at Ranchi in November, 1845, preached and prayed, amongst the Uraons and Mundas for about five years before they could bring any one into the fold of Christ. These first German Missionaries were attracted to Ranchi by the docility and light-heartedness of a few Kol *coolies* they came across in the streets of Calcutta. The historic spot on which they pitched their first tents in Ranchi now forms part of the Lutheran Mission grounds and is marked by a memorial cross inscribed with the names of the four pioneer Missionaries.

Although Mission Stations were established at Ranchi (1845), at Domba—9 miles south-west of Ranchi (1846), at Lohardaga—48 miles west of Ranchi (1848) and at Govindpur—30 miles south-west of Ranchi (Domba having been abandoned in 1850), it was not till the 9th of June, 1850, that the only four Uraons named Kasu, Bandhu, Gurha and Nawin Porin, received baptism. These were the first converts made in Chota Nagpur, by the German Evangelical Mission sent out to India by Pastor John Evangelist Gossner of Berlin. It was several months later, on the 26th of October, 1851, that Sadho Munda, a bhuinhar of village Bandhea and Mangta Munda of village Balalong were baptized by the Rev. Mr. Schatz. These were the first Munda converts to Christianity. It was on the 18th of November, 1851, that the foundation-stone of the picturesque Gothic Building popularly known as the German Church, on the Ranchi Chaibassa Road, was laid. This Church, consecrated at Christmas, 1855, and called the Christ Church, is the first Christian Church built in Chota Nagpur. By this time, the congregation swelled to about eight hundred inquirers and over four hundred baptised members. The Report of April, 1857, shows an enormous increase of converts which then amounted to 900 baptised members and 2,000 inquirers.   And this, in spite of the strenuous opposition of the Jagirdars and Thikadars.   As we learn from a Report of the German   Evangelical Mission of Chota Nagpur :

The Kols were a thorn in their (i.e. the Jagirdars' and Thikadars') eyes.   In 1855, a Hindu Thikadar with a large crowd of armed men had made a sudden attack upon the Missionary Hertzog and beaten him so dreadfully that he fell down unconscious and was dying.   Though the Thakur was fined and threatened to be executed if he would repeat such an act of cruelty, on the whole, things did not change.   The Hindu Zamindars and Thikadars had the crops of the Christians cut, their cattle taken away, set fire to their houses and properties, and instigated false law suits against them.   Once it occurred that in more than thirty villages, the Christians were assaulted at one and the same time, oppressed and abused in various ways : conferences were held by the Zamindars to consult how to stop the growth of Christianity, and it was resolved, "out with the Christians and the Missionaries, out with them."

When therefore the Sepoy Mutiny broke out in 1857, the Christians had to fear the worst.   At first it seemed as if Chota Nagpur would be spared, for when the news of the fall of the old Mahomedan capital Delhi came, all had been quiet in Chota Nagpur.   But the Sepoy regiment at Hazaribagh began to join the mutineers, and after four days it was reported to Ranchi that the town had been plundered and burnt down. All Europeans fled to Calcutta and the Missionaries had to leave their stations and their congregations to save their own lives and those of their wives and children.   It was on July 31, that the missionaries assembled all Christians then present at Ranchi and having prayed with them and explained how things stood, bade them farewell and let them and the school children retire to the villages.   It was in the worst time of the rainy season, and anybody acquainted with the trouble of travellers in the rains can imagine what hardships the Missionaries with their families had to undergo before they reached Calcutta (August 17).   In the meanwhile Ranchi was plundered by the Sepoys. Above all, they sought to destroy the Ranchi Church. Cannons

were put up before the building, but of the four cannon balls
that were fired on it, only one, without doing any damage, hit
on the tower wall, where it is still visible.   The interior of the
church was all plundered ; benches, chairs, candlesticks taken
away ; the beautiful organ valued at Rs. 3,000, and all windows
dashed to pieces ; much damage done to the Christening font and
the pulpit ; but the building itself was not destroyed. The cannon shots on the church were, for the mob, the signal to seize
upon the other mission buildings.   All furniture, stores, utensils,
windows, doors, even the nails out of the walls and the fences
round the garden were taken away and the emptied rooms
served first as quarters to the soldiers, then as stables for cows and
oxen.   In a similar way fared the other mission stations.   The
Christians were persecuted and illtreated. The Christians'
houses and villages to which the mutineers could proceed were
plundered, the inhabitants had to flee and to spend six weeks
in the jungles, mountains and caves without any other food than
roots and leaves; many of the fugitives died or got ill.

It will not be out of place here to describe briefly how the wave of
Sepoy insurrection travelled to distant Chota Nagpur, what course
it took and how it was eventually pacified.   Ranchi was then the
headquarters and artillery of the Ramgarh battalion, of which one
detachment was stationed at Chaibassa and another at Purulia.
In July 1857, a detachment of the 8th Native Infantry came to be
quartered at Hazaribagh.

The news of the mutiny of the native garrison at Danapur and
of the rising of Kunwar Singh, reached Hazaribagh on the 30th
July.   The detachment of the 8th Native Infantry at once
mutinied, driving their officers and the civil authorities from the
station.

Those were still the days of confidence.   Almost every officer
of the native army, whilst admitting and deploring the disaffection of other regiments, believed implicitly in the loyalty of his
own men.   When, then, intelligence reached Doranda, the
civil station adjoining Ranchi, that the troops at Hazaribagh,
only sixty miles distant, were shaky, the officer commanding
at that station despatched Lieutenant Graham with thirty
horsemen of the Ramgarh Irregular Cavalry, two companies

of the Ramgarh battalion, and two guns, to Hazaribagh to disarm them. Graham marched, but he had not reached the second stage before Captain Oakes met him with the information that the detachment of the 8th Native Infantry had mutinied the previous day. That same night his own infantry mutinied, seized, in spite of his protestations, the guns and ammunition, as well as four elephants, the property of Captain Dalton (then acting Commissioner of Chota Nagpur), and marched back to Ranchi, breathing hostile imprecations against the Europeans there stationed. The cavalry remained staunch.

Captain Dalton and a few European officers were at Ranchi. They received timely information of the revolt. The defence of the place was impossible. They remained there, however, till the latest safe moment, and then proceeded to Hazaribagh, now abandoned by the rebels, and whither Lieutenant Graham with a few horsemen who had remained faithful had preceded them.

The stations of Ranchi and Doranda fell into the hands of the rebels, who plundered the treasury, fired cannon at the church, released the prisoners, and destroyed private property.[23]

The court-house of the Principal Assistant was destroyed. Before the mutineers left Dorunda they had set fire to all the bunglows there except Dr. Brougham's. Rapine and plunder was the order of the day. "In famous characters released from the jail by the mutineers, some of them of considerable influence", complains Colonel Dalton, "are raising bands of dacoits and are plundering in all directions". Thakur Bisnath Sahi of Barkagarh, one of the rebel leaders of Ranchi, went out with 150 followers and cut several trenches in the road leading over the Ramgarh ghat or pass with the obvious intention of making it difficult for the troops advancing against Doranda. An influential ghatwal of Ramgarh was reported to have joined Bisnath Sahi. Some other Zamindars had attempted to close the ghats to prevent the ingress of the troops under Major English, and to assist the mutineers in obtaining supplies. At first, Colonel Dalton, with the aid of the officers of the Ramgarh battalion and the cavalry as well as a few faithful native horsemen and foot-soldiers, and supported by his own subordinate Civil Officers, Captains J.S. Davies and W. H. Oakes,

[23] *History of the Indian Mutiny*, by Col. G. B. Malleson, *C. S. I.* Vol. II, pp. 134 *et seq*

succeeded in partially restoring order to Hazaribagh, and captured many of the rebels.   But within a few days, matters came to such a pass that he had to fall back on Bagodar.   This was on the 13th of August.   And there he remained till 150 men of Rattray's Sikh regiment under Lieutenant Earle arrived, and with their help he once more occupied Hazaribagh.   But the mutineers were still at large, and Colonel Fischer, commanding a detachment of Madras troops was ordered by the Government to march by way of Doranda to Hazaribagh.   Before the orders reached Colonel Fischer at Barhi on the night of the 13th September, it was believed that the mutineers had proceeded in the direction of Rhotasgarh. Colonel Fischer despatched Major English with 150 soldiers of the 53rd and 150 Sikhs towards Doranda, where he reached on the 22nd September.   Whilst English was making for Doranda, Rattray, with 200 Sikhs, was intrenched at Dehri, and Fischer, with the main body, was moving towards Japla.   The enemy had been known to have passed through Tiko Ghat, Pundri and Balumath to Nowadch —which they reached on the 27th September. Fischer correctly guessed that Chatra would prove to be their place of refuge.   But Fischer was now relieved from the charge of the operations against the insurgents, and ordered to protect the Trunk road, the campaign in Chota Nagpur being entrusted to Major English, under the direct orders of the Commander-in-Chief.

Major English met the insurgents, now numbering three thousand at Chatra, and completely defeated them, the loss on his side having amounted to 42 killed and wounded.   This was on the 2nd October, 1857.   Chota Nagpur was now left to the protection of Rattray and his Sikhs, who "proved themselves fully competent to make head against the insurgents in Chutia Nagpur and in the districts immediately to the north and east of it."

Although the courts had been re-opened after Dalton's return to Ranchi on the 23rd of September, and business proceeded as usual, desultory warfare continued for sometime longer, for the local rebels were still at large.   The leading local rebels who took the most active part in the mutiny of the Sepoys of the Ramgarh battalion were Thakur Bisnath Sahi of Burkagarh, and Pandey Ganpat Rai of Bhaunro.   The outbreak at Doranda is believed to have been preconcerted by Thakur Bisnath Sahi, who, it is said, was elected by the mutineers as their Chief, and Pandey Ganpat

Rai was, it is said, formally installed by them as their Commander-in-Chief.   The Thakur would sit everyday in one of the cantonment bunglows to administer justice.   Jamadar Madho Sing was, however, the prime mover of the Ranchi Mutiny.   As the Bengal Government Administration Report for 1857-58, states:

The risings in Chota Nagpur were by no means general, and occurred often as much from personal animosity amongst the chiefs and people themselves as from any dislike to British rule.

The same Report observes: It is a matter of wonder, that the ignorant and savage population, seeing the troops in open mutiny, the prisoners forcibly released from the jails, the treasuries plundered, the stations abandoned by the authorities, should not have risen *en masse*, as, had there been any widespread feeling of dissatisfaction with the British rule, they would undoubtedly have done.

Among the petty skirmishes and affrays that took place in the district since the return of the officials may be mentioned the affray of the 5th November, 1857, in which, one Amir Ali Khan was killed and some other men wounded.   Three followers of Pandey Ganpat Rai, namely, Ruthu Sing, Golam Ali, and Kanee Ahir, were recognised as having taken part in the affray.   In March, 1858, depredations were committed by the local insurgents on some villages in Pargana Nawagarh, and the Borway Police Station was looted.

To operate against the local insurgents, Colonel Dalton assembled an escort of the Ramgarh Irregular Cavalry under the command of Captain Nation and 200 of the new Kol Levy.   These Kol recruits had been fully drilled and instructed in musquetry under Lieutenant Reeves.   The embers of disaffection were not finally extinguished in the district of Lohardaga (Ranchi) till Thakur Bisnath Sahi and Pandey Ganpat Rai were at length captured with the assistance of Bisnath Dubey and Mohesh Narain Sahi.   Thakur Bisnath and Pandey Ganpat were placed on their trial before the Deputy Commissioner (since styled Judicial Commissioner) for various acts of rebellion and other crimes, and were both hanged, the former on the 16th April, and the latter on the 21st April, 1858. Ninety-seven villages, including *tolas* or hamlets, which constituted Thakur Bisnath's estate had already been confiscated by the

Government on the 10th December, 1857. The Government generously made compassionate allowances to various members of the rebel's family. The property of Pandey Ganpat Rai consisting of eleven villages and shares in two other villages were also forfeited to Government. Bhola Sing, a Zamindar of Chorea, was, it is said, put to death by the residents of Chatra. Thus ended the Ranchi episode of the terrible Mutiny of 1857. As Colonel Maleson observes:

No officers deserved better of their country than those who served in Chutia Nagpur, none exhibited greater zeal, greater energy, greater self-reliance, greater devotion.

By the close of 1857, the mutiny so far as Ranchi was concerned, was practically, at an end, and the German missionaries returned to Ranchi. As Sir Willam Hunter tells us:

During the Mutiny the native Christian community was broken up but their dispersion over the district seems to have given a considerable impulse to Christianity, as the number of converts largely increased after the restoration of order.[24]

Here is the account given in the Mission Report :

The next ten years after Gossner's death[25] or after the Mutiny, were a period of rapid progress in Chota Nagpur. People came in crowds to get enlisted as inquirers and many who had been instructed were desirous of being baptized. The fifty Christian villages that were counted before the Mutiny had grown in November 1858 to 1905, and at Christmas about 1500 Christians had come to Ranchi and more than 150 families manifested by breaking the caste their willingness to give up heathenism. These were followed by sixty families who came on New Year's Day 1859. And it was said that the whole tribe of the Mundas would turn at once and altogether to Christianity. The movement against the heathen was so mighty that the aborigines feared lest their landlords, the Hindoo Zemindars, also should become Christians and that then things would be worse than ever, since they never would give up the habit of depriving poor people of their land.

[24] *Statistical Account of Bengal*, Vol. XVI., p. 424.
[25] Gossner died on March 30, 1858.

Making the utmost allowance for the optimistic zeal of the Missionary writer, the Report, we may take it, gives us a substantially correct account. For, we find some official corroboration of these statements. Thus, in a letter dated the 15th March, 1859 already referred to, from the then Senior Assistant Commissioner of Lohardaga to the Commissioner of Chota Nagpur, we read :

During the disturbances which followed the Mutiny of the Ramghur Battalion in August, 1857, the Zemindars, etc. taking advantage of the absence of the authorities, oppressed and plundered the whole of the native converts, many of whom preserved their lives only by seeking with their families, the protection of the jungles. On the restoration of order, the Zemindars, apparently afraid of what they had done, ceased to molest them for a time; and as they received assistance from the Relief Fund to enable them to cultivate their lands, they assumed an independence which irritated the landholders; and when the time came for cutting the rice-crops for the past year, they again came into collison.

In the meantime the number of new converts in this and the adjoining Pergunnahs of Busea, Belcuddee, and Doessa, all unbaptized, had greatly increased.

The German Mission Report from which we have already quoted gives the following Statistics of the converts :

At the end of 1860 there were 1700 baptized converts, to whom were added in the following seven years on an average 1225 every year, viz. 522, 809, 1296, 2100, 1994, 829, 1024.

The same Report candidly informs us :

It must be admitted that most of the new inquireres looked to the secular benefit the Christians enjoyed rather than to the spiritual side of the new religion : 'Let us give up demon-worship, become Christians and be instructed, that assisted by the Padris, we may be saved from the unjust oppression of the Hindus and regain the land that we have been deprived of'. Such-like thoughts were almost common and were specially expressed by the leaders of the people. But the more the Christians increased in numbers the more violent grew the hatred of the landlords, for they were afraid that the aborigines, getting out of their stupidness, would no longer patiently bear whatever the Hindus pleased to do to them. So they began to oppress and persecute the Christians in various ways. These, it must be admitted, did not suffer the wrong in a Christian spirit but showed themselves disobedient and obstinate against their masters and openly opposed them.

Contemporary official reports show that in these conflicts the aborigines were as much to blame as their landlords. In some instances, the former attempted to take forcible possession of lands which they claimed as their ancestral property since wrested from them by the Thikadars. And the latter in their turn retaliated by instituting false cases of dacoity and plunder against the aboriginal tenants and subjecting them to illegal confinements and duress. Towards the end of 1858, the conflict assumed a serious aspect, and a detachment of native infantry had to be sent from Ranchi to Govindapur for the preservation of order in pargana Bussea and Sonepur, both largely inhabited by Mundas.

The origin of the disturbances is thus related by the Senior Assistant Commissioner in his letter of the 15th March, from which we have given more than one quotation :

In the month of October last, Baboo Seebnarain Sae, a Zemindar of this Pergannah, proceeded to the village of Jhapra, in which and several adjoining villages a great number of the recent converts reside, ostensibly to collect his rent. The Christians assert that he seized and oppressed several of them, demanding dues he was not entitled to; on which the Christians of all the surrounding villages assembled to resist these proceedings, and there was an affray, in which the zemindar and his people were driven out of the village, the Christians capturing his horses, &c., and two men brought them to me at Ranchi, lodging a complaint against the Zemindar. This was the commencement of all the recent disturbances. I treated the case as one of ordinary affray, intending to proceed against both parties. Immediately after this I made over my office to Mr. George, Sub-Assistant Commissioner, and proceeded to Palamow.

That Sub-Assistant Commissioner, who was new to the office and unacquainted with the people, owing to the absence of the parties in the case struck it off his file.   Of this I was not aware till my return the other day from Palamow.   Emboldened apparently by this, other Zemindars appear to have attempted to coerce the Christians, which was successfully resisted by the latter and their relatives amongst the Kols, and thus disorder prevailed more or less thoroughout the Pergannah, and in many instances the nominal Christians of this and Pergannahs Bussea, Belcuddee, and Dooesa, taking advantage of this confusion for-cibly re-possessed themselves of lands claimed as their Bhoo-nearee, of which they undoubtedly had been out of possession for periods varying from ten years up to one or two generations and extorted refunds of the value of property of which they alleged the Thicadars and Zemindars plundered them during the dis-turbances or of which they asserted that merchants and others had defrauded them.   Many of these claims I believe to have had some foundation, though others were doubtless ficti-tious.

Besides the affray above noticed, the only serious one which has occurred in this Pergannah was in November last.   In this case, Anund Sing, Jagirdar of Bala, assisted by others, amongst them some servants of Thakoor Judunath Sahi, Illaquadar of Police, attempted to coerce his ryots of that village many of whom are nominally Christians.   They, assisted by those of adjacent villages, opposed force to force; an affray ensued, and two men were killed on the side of the Jagirdar; three men, one a servant of the Thakoor, and a horse belonging to another one besides some arms, were captured and taken by the Christians to the Sub-Assistant Commissioner at Ranchi, together with the body of one of the men slain in the affray, and there lodged their com-plaints.

Of another Zamindar who was also a Magistrate, the Senior Assistant Commissioner writes :

Acting on a Perwannah received from the Sub-Assistant Commi-ssioner, he assembled his Jagirdars with their followers, numbering not less than 200 people, ostensibly to assist the Police.   These with his subordinate Police officers, proceeded to several villages apprehended the whole of the Christians and their relatives, and carried them off to the Thakoor's house, where some, against whom false accusations of dacoity and plunder had been preferred, were thrown into stocks, and the houses of many of the Christians were plundered in the village of Jhabra. The Christians seeing the approach of this force, all fled, so the party contented themselves with setting fire to the house of one of the Christians, containing a quantity of grain, &c. I myself visited the spot, and found the blackened ruins and burnt grain.

In more than one instance the Illaquadar of Police has been guilty of detaining prisoners in his own custody for a most unwarrantable time. On my arrival I found at his house, which is in fact the Thannah, a man who had been in confinement for one month, and this man, a Christian, is the owner of the house at Jhabra which had been burnt, as noticed in the preceding paragraph; probably he would not have been then sent to me, had I not issued a peremptory order for all prisoners under trial being forwarded without delay. To make matters worse, a false entry was made in the calendar, to the effect that the man had been apprehended only three days before he was sent to me. It is not difficult to guess why this poor man was detained so long ; and when I came to enquire into the charge against him, I found there was no evidence whatever tending to implicate him. Immediately on my arrival at Govindpur, a complaint was made against the Illaquadar of Police, that he had allowed a prisoner to be so maltreated while in confinement that he died under it. The fact of the case I find to be that the unfortunate man did die whilst in confinement in the stocks and with handcuffs on. I caused the body to be exhumed and found the latter still on it. The Illaquadar reported the death to have occurred from natural causes, and of course had plenty of witnesses to prove it. On the other hand, the companions of the deceased all declare that he died from ill-usage and want of food. One thing, however, is clear ; the deceased and his companions were illegally detained in the stocks for six days, and if the Illaquadar's report be true, the poor creature was laid up for five days with fever and a bad cough, and yet he was left to die hand-cuffed and with his feet in the stocks; and it would appear that the charge on which he was confined was a false one. This man was also a Christian.

It was not against the Zamindari Police alone that the Mundas and Uraons had serious grievances. The Hindu judiciary of that time, in some instances, would seem to have betrayed an undue partiality towards the Hindu landlords. Here is an instance that was published in November 1856 in a Berlin periodical of the name of Biene :

> The other day a poor tenant lodged a complaint against a Brahmin Zemindar in his court, on account of cruel treatment and oppression. The Medical Officer being called in as a witness, gave us a description of the transaction. As soon as the guilty Brahmin robber came into the court of this judge to be heard, the honest judge rose from his seat, and in the most humble position, crouching on all fours before the accused Brahmin Zemindar, touched and kissed his feet, saying "Thy blessing my father", and after having received his blessing, he put a chair for the accused close to his own, whilst the accuser, the Christian tenant, with his witnesses, had to stand far off at a distance, being treated as if they were the criminals. The crime in this instance was too glaring, the medical man gave evidence as to the dangerous nature of the wounds inflicted, others as to the robbery committed, and the Brahmin Zemindar was fined five rupees.[26]

Another source of irritation to the Mundas and Uraons was the system of Begari or forced labour which they were made to render to their landlords. Of this, the Senior Assistant Commissioner in his letter of the 15th March, 1859, writes :

> If the owners of villages would content themselves with merely what they are entitled to, there would be no discontent, but the instances are rare in which they do so, and the refusal of the Christians to render more than they are bound to do, is another cause of their being persecuted by the landholders. In some villages I have found that the *bhetkeyta*, given nominally as payment for their labour, has been resumed by the owner, who

---

[26] The translation of the letter is from the *Calcutta Review*, Vol. XIIX, p. 131 In a footnote in the article in the *Calcutta Review* (July 1869), several instances of oppression are quoted from a journal kept by a Missionary in 1856. The possibility of such a state of things as is revealed in the quotation above is, of course, not to be dreamt of in our days.

still, however, continues to exact the labour from his ryots. This difficulty there will be no trouble in adjusting, though it is quite impossible effectually to control the proceedings of the landowners, where, as in the case here, their ryots are generally so much in their power, that they dare not complain against them, but as Christianity spreads, and spread it inevitably will, these ryots will be able to assert their own rights.

That such aggressions at this period led to several serious riots, we have already seen. A serious case took place in 1859 at a village called Ghagari. In consequence of a land-dispute between a Munda Christian named Bari and one Karam Singh, a jagirdar, a free fight ensued, in the course of which the jagirdar and two of his followers were killed, and Bari was wounded, and soon afterwards died in jail. The Sudder Court to which the case went up in appeal held that the Jagirdar's party were the aggressors, and the sentences of transportation for life on Bari and another were reduced by Mr. Justice Loch to ten years' rigorous imprisonment.

It is refreshing to turn from these dismal accounts of riots and affrays to the philanthropic efforts of the first two Christian Missions to educate and civilise the aborigines of Chota Nagpur. We speak of two missions instead of one ; for, in the year 1868, there occurred a split in the German Mission in consequence of a disagreement between the senior German Missionaries at Ranchi and the Home Committee at Berlin, regarding the constitution and organisation of the Mission. The Home Committee sent out a band of younger missionaries from Germany ; and the then senior missionaries Messrs. F. Batsch, H. Batsch, H. Bohn, and Wilhelm Luther Daud Sing[27] along with a large number of Christian converts petitioned Bishop Milman of Calcutta to receive them into the Church of England. The Bishop, after due enquiry, granted their request and on Sunday, April 19, ordained Messrs.

---

[27] This was an Indian Rajput Missionary. Originally of Bundelkhand district, his father Ganeshi Sing settled at village Kotari, 16 miles west of Ranchi. When about 11 years old, William Luther Daud Sing (then known as Maninath Sing) joined the Ranchi English school and was baptised three years later in 1854 by Rev. E. Schatcz who treated him as a son and brought him up. He was married seven years later to an Uraon girl named Mariam. His ministerial life was passed mainly in Chaibassa where he was loved and respected by all. He died on the day of Pentecost in the year 1909.

F. Batsch, H. Batsch, H. Bohn, and Wilhelm Luther as Deacons in the presence of a congregation of 1,100 persons of whom about 600 received the Holy Communion. At the same time 41 Indians were baptised and 633 were confirmed. The four newly ordained Deacons were made priests a few years later.

On the 21st of June, 1869, the Rev. (afterwards The Right Rev.) J.C. Whitley, B. A., arrived at Ranchi from Delhi, where he had been working for seven years. He came here by the orders of the Bishop, "to comfort and sustain the German Clergy", as the S. P. G. Mission Report for 1869 tells us. In 1890, Chota Nagpur was formed into a separate Diocese under the Right Rev. J. C. Whitley as its first Bishop. From his arrival in 1869 till his sudden death in October, 1904, the late Bishop Whitley remained the life and soul of the S. P. G. Mission in Chota Nagpur. He learnt the language of the Mundas, compiled the first Mundari Grammar written in English, and translated portions of the New Testament and the Prayer Book into the Mundari tongue. These works as also the translations of portions of the Gospels and the Apostles by the Rev. A. Nottrott of the German Mission were amongst the earliest books published in the Mundari tongue. But the first documents ever written in the Mundari tongue appear to have been a Mundari Primer and a Mundari Hymn-book written by the Rev. Mr. (afterwards Dr.) Nottrott as a first step towards the education of the Mundas. These books were printed at Benares in the year 1871. In 1881, the Rev. A. Nottrott published the first Mundari Grammar in the German tongue to assist young German Missionaries coming to the Ranchi District. This book has since been translated into English by the Rev. P. Wagner.

It is mainly due to the indefatigable exertions and wise guidance of the Rev. Dr. Nottrott who arrived at Ranchi from Germany in the year 1867, that the German Evangelical Lutheran Mission—to give it its full name—is the great success amongst the aborigines of Chota Nagpur that it is at present. And similarly the Anglican (S. P. G.) Mission owes its success amongst the same people in a great measure to the untiring zeal and fatherly guidance of the late Bishop Whitley. By a curious coincidence both these reverend gentlemen were born in the year 1837, the year which saw the accession to the throne of England of our late beloved and revered Queen Victoria.

We shall now proceed to give a short account of the splendid

10

work done by the two Missions amongst the Mundas, Uraons, and Kharias of Chota Nagpur. From the very beginning of their existence, schools were established by the Missions to educate boys and girls. The German Mission School at Ranchi, which originally taught up to the Primary Standard, was raised to the Middle Vernacular Standard in 1884, and to the Matriculation Standard in January, 1896. From their commencement this School as well as the German Mission Girls' School have been entirely boarding schools. The substantial and spacious building in which the Boys' School is held was built forty-three years ago—"a solid testimony", as Mr. J. A. Cunningham, Inspector of schools of the Chota Nagpur Division writes,—"to the wise fore-thought of those pioneers in education". Of this School Mr. Cunningham writes :

Since coming to Chota Nagpur I have been in search of a helpful standard by which I might test the quality of work being done in its schools, and I think I have found such a standard-guage this morning at the German Evangelical Lutheran High School. (In name only would it seem capable of profitable pruning). In almost every really essential respect I am satisfied that it may serve as an excellent 'model' school towards which others may with advantage aspire.... All the boys[28] seemed to be the very picture of health and happiness. Their choir entertained me in a way that I have not been entertained for a very long time and which I shall not easily forget. Altogether I am impressed with the school as a master-piece of educational organisation, and only those who have attempted such organisation in India can appreciate in some small degree, what that means—in India. In such a work as this, the German Mission School at Ranchi, the civilisation of the West really justifies itself in the East.

Besides the High English School with its 179 pupils, the German Mission has within Chota Nagpur 26 boarding schools with 1,974 pupils including 626 girls. Of these boarding schools, four, namely those at Lohardaga, Govindpur, Koronjo, and Takarma, teach up to the Middle English Standard. Besides these, the Mission has twelve Kindergarten Schools with 423 children. Of village schools in the Chota Nagpur German Mission, there are

[28] Refers to the Uraon and Munda boys in the Boarding House of the School.

at present 175, with 3,229 pupils including 462 girls. The teaching-staff of these village schools are all Christian converts of the Mission, —chiefly Mundas and Uraons. For preparing teachers for this large number of village schools, the Mission maintains at its head-quarters in Ranchi, a Normal Training School. To qualify abori-ginal students for Missionary work, the Mission opened as early as 1867 a Theological Seminary at Ranchi. In the year 1907, a Girls' Training School was opened in which aboriginal girls qualify themselves for employment as teachers in the girls' schools at the various Mission stations and elsewhere. In the year 1905, two aboriginal girls were sent by the Rev. D. Dr. Nottrott with the help of a Government grant of Rs. 200 to Kalimpong for learning lace-work, and on their return in 1906, the German Mission Lace School was opened at Ranchi. In this school about thirty abori-ginal Christian girls are now receiving practical instruction in lace-making. Besides the large number of village churches, the Mission has 36 associations for Young Christian Men and two for Young Christian Women, known respectively as Y. C. M.'s and Y. C. W.'s. Ever since 1873, the German Mission has got a stone Lithographic Press of its own at Ranchi. In the year 1882, however, a Printing Press was established, and this is at present the best of its kind in Ranchi. There is also a Book-binding establishment attached to the Press. As early as the year 1877, a fortnightly journal in Hindi, styled the *Ghar-Bandhu*, was started which still continues to supply Mission news and general information and instruction to the Christian converts of the Mission. Numerous religious and educational books in Mundari, Uraon, and Hindi have been published by the Mission since its establishment. In the year 1908, 45,135 copies of books on the Christian religion in the Hindi, Mundari, and Uraon languages were printed by the Ranchi German Mission Press, and as many as 11,564 copies of books bound in the Mission Book-bindery. Under the auspices of the Calcutta Bible and Tract Society, Dr. Nottrott brought out several years ago a translation of the New Testament, and his voluminous translation of the Old Testament has recently been published by the same Society.

Amidst all its multifarious activities, the German Mission has not neglected the sacred work of relieving the sick. The German Mission Hospital and Dispensary at Ranchi was built about the year 1890. Here medicines are distributed *gratis* to Christians as

well as non-Christians.   At this hospital alone 4,220 cases were
treated during the year 1908, and at the German Mission Hospital
at Lohardaga 1,918 cases during the same year.   The total number
of men, women, and children who received medicines during the
year 1908 from the different hospitals appertaining to the Chota
Nagpur German Mission amounted to 19,004.   An Asylum for
Lepers was started at Purulia in the year 1887 by the Rev.   Mr.
Uffmann.   Already, in 1882, a Leper Asylum had been opened at
Lohardaga in the Ranchi District by the Rev. F. Hahn.   But
the Purulia Asylum is the biggest institution of its kind in India,
and maintains about 600 lepers as indoor patients.   On the death
of the Rev. Mr. Uffmann, the management of the Purulia Asylum
was taken up by the Rev. Mr.   Hahn, who was awarded a gold
medal by the Bengal Government in recognition of his splendid
services to suffering humanity.   Both of these Leper Asylums are
mainly supported by the Edinburgh Society for Lepers in the East.
In September 1907,   the Rev.   E. Muller started Co-operative
Credit Banks in the Ranchi District for the amelioration of the
material condition of the Christian converts of the Mission, and
under the able supervision of the Rev. P. Wagner, a Co-operative
Bank has been since organised at every mission station in the
Division.

Besides the three old Mission stations at Ranchi, Lohardaga,
and Govindpur, there are now Mission stations at Burju (established
in 1869), Takarma (1873), Chainpur (1892), Khuntitoli (1895),
Gumla (1895), Kinkel (1899), Tamar (1901), Koronjo (1903),—all
within the Ranchi District.   Outside the District, the German
Mission has stations at Hazaribagh (1853), Purulia (1863),
Chaibassa (1865), Porahat (1867), Chakradharpur (1893),
Rajgangpur (1900), Karimatti (1902), and Jharsuguda (1904).
Of the European working staff of the Mission, there are in the
Ranchi District alone, 22 ordained missionaries and 3 unordained
missionaries, 4 single-women missionaries, besides 18 married
ladies (wives of missionaries) who are all engaged in mission-work
of some kind or other. Besides these, as many as 797 native converts,
mostly Mundas and Uraons, were employed in Mission work
during the year 1909.   An idea of the results of the educational
efforts of the German Mission may be gathered from the following
statistics for the year 1909.   During that year Christian converts
of the Chota Nagpur German Mission educated in the mission

schools were employed as follows : Native Pastors 34, Catechists 447, Colporteurs and Bible women 36, Pandits and Boarding School Masters 87, Female Teachers and Kindergarten Teachers 24, Doctors and Compounders 7, Trained Nurses 2, Government Servants 209 (including one Uraon Sub-Deputy Collector and one Munda Sub-Registrar), Clerks and Sub-overseers in Municipal offices 9, Railway employees 37, and skilled artisans 110. Besides these, there were, in the year 1909, fifteen aboriginal candidates for the Ministry. The total number of baptised converts of the Mission was 74,626 at the end of the year 1909. Of this number, as many as 55,650 belonged to the Ranchi District, besides a large number of Uraon and Munda Christians working in the Duars and in Assam as coolies. It is quite a remarkable fact that in a single year (1909), the contriibutions made by the Indian converts, mostly aboriginals, towards mission expenses amounted to Rs. 24,440.

We now come to the good work done and doing by the English Mission of Chota Nagpur under the auspices of the Society for the Propagation of the Gospels. The construction of the fine cathedral known as the St. Paul's Cathedral (popularly called the English Church) was taken in hand in the year 1869, but it was not completed and consecrated till the year 1873. The same year witnessed the ordination of three Mundas—the first of their race —as Deacons. They were named Markas Hembo, Prabhu Sahay Bodra, and Athanasius Tuti. At the same time M. Kachchap, the first Uraon Deacon, was also ordained. One after another School-houses and other Mission buildings were erected in the town of Ranchi and in the interior of the District, till at the present moment the Mission has altogether 15 *pucca* masonry churches and 101 *kachcha* shapels within the Diocese. The number of clergy now amount to 35, of whom 14 are Europeans and 21 Indians—mostly Mundas and Uraons. Of the 21 Indian clergy, 14 are priests and 7 deacons. It is worthy of note that the Indian Ministry are remunerated partly from the Native Pastorate Endowment Fund and partly from the offerings of the congregations, no contribution whatsoever being received for the purpose from Mission Funds. During one year, 1909, a sum of Rs. 3,642 was raised by the Indian (mostly aboriginal) congregation alone for Church purposes, including Rs. 1,577 towards the support of their clergy. The Pastors are assisted in their work by Preachers (*pracharaks*). At the end of the year 1909, there were 132 Christian and 26 non-Christian teachers, 56 Christian mistresses of schools, 108 Readers, and 9 Bible women, working in this Mission amongst aboriginal Christians scattered over no less than seven hundred villages in the Division.

The Anglican (S. P. G.) Mission Schools of all sorts number 118 with 4,248 pupils, about 2,000 of whom are non-Christians, and 979 are girls. Of these girls 300 are non-Christians.[29] At the head of the Anglican Mission Schools stands the St. Paul's High School at Ranchi with its 400 pupils including 184 boarders. This institution was raised from a Middle English School to the Matriculation Standard only two years ago. In the very first year of its affiliation to the Calcutta University, this school sent up for the University Examination six candidates all of whom successfully matriculated. As early as 1878, a Theological class was added to the school, with the Rev. Oscar Flex and the Rev. Roger Dutt as tutors. The Boys' Middle English School at Murhu with its 74 boarders and 58 day-scholars is doing excellent work amongst the Mundas. Nor has female education been without its due share of attention. The English Mission Girls' School at Ranchi, with its 282 pupils including 125 boarders, is an excellent institution and is under the able management of a European Lady Missionary. It prepares girls, Christian as well as non-Christian, for the Upper and Lower Primary Scholarship Examinations. Towards the end of the year 1908, a Lace School was opened for young women and girls who number over twenty at present. A Female Normal Training Class was opened in the year 1909 to prepare female Teachers for girls' schools. A nice masonry building has been recently constructed at Ranchi to house the Lace School and the Female Normal Training Class. Besides secular and religious training, physical training is imparted to the girls and young women by regular drills and by various games, notably the 'Basket Ball'. It is worthy of note that there is a girls' Debating Society in connection with the Female Normal Class. Besides the Ranchi schools, the English Mission maintains fourteen day schools for girls within the Diocese, the majority of them being however within the Hazaribagh District. Besides these there

---

[29] The number of pupils in the English Mission Schools was 865 in the year 1880, 1209 in 1890, and 2153 in 1900.

are 64 mixed schools in which boys as well as girls receive education. Of these over 50 are in the Ranchi District alone.

In the matter of female education, it may be noted, the Munda is extremely conservative. "What is the use of a girl learning to read and write," asks he, "when she will only have to mind her husband's hearth ?" And, thus, out of some 2,500 Christian Munda girls of the Mission, hardly more than 160 are attending the English Mission Schools. Within a mile of the Ranchi Railway Station, Miss F. E. Whipham, a Zenana Missionary of the Anglican Mission, who is well-known to the Ranchi Bengali community for her former excellent educational labours in the zenanas, opened a few years ago a day school which has now developed into two, one for boys and another for girls. These schools are doing excellent work among the non-Christian boys and girls of the essentially Hindu village of Chutia.

As in the Ranchi and Chaibassa Boarding Schools, the pupils of the village Boarding Schools too have regular daily services in Church and live amid healthy Christian surroundings. Side by side with intellectual culture and religious training, physical development is encouraged by regular games of football and hockey. More than once, the Ranchi Anglican Mission Aboriginal Boys' Hockey Team won Hockey Challenge Cups at Ranchi as well as in Calcutta. In 1895, a Blind School was started at Ranchi in connection with the English Mission by Mrs. O'Connor. In this school blind men are trained in industrial work in cane and bamboo, and blind women are taught mat-making. Reading and writing are also taught on the Braille system. A quarterly journal called the Chota Nagpur Diocesan Paper is regularly published in English. The English Mission, like the German Mission, has a Hospital and Dispensary whose ministrations are extended not only to Christians but to non-Christians as well. The English Mission Hospital and Dispensary at Murhu under the Rev. Dr. Kennedy, in the very heart of the Munda country, is numerously resorted to not only by the Mission converts but by non-Christian Mundas as well as by Hindus and Mahomedans all around. In 1909, as many as 2,960 patients were treated and 99 surgical operations made at this Hospital.

And in this connection we must not omit to mention Miss Ingle's Home for Orphans at Ranchi. Although a Mission institution, it is now supported mainly, if not solely, by Miss Ingle from her own private funds.   Last, but not least, is the good work that is being done by the Village Co-operative Banks opened by the Mission, chiefly amongst the Uraons.   Of the many philanthrophic activities of the Christian Missions of Chota Nagpur, there is none which is more highly appreciated by the people than these Banks, which, besides their great educative value, are calculated to save an unthrifty people from the unrelenting clutches of the notoriously usurious Chota Nagpur *Sahu*.   In the matter of Co-operative Credit Banks, the extensive organisation of the Chota Nagpur Roman Catholic Mission is unique in India.   We shall describe that noble institution in detail in our account of that Mission.

The English (S.P.G.) Mission Stations in Chota Nagpur at present number 23, and are located at Ranchi, Maranghada, Murhu, Ramtoliya, Kander, Biru, Bargari, Phatayatoli, Dorma, Soparom, Jargo, Chaibassa, Katbari, Purulia, Hazaribagh and Chitarpur.   The number of Christians of the Mission rose from 5,733 baptised converts and 1,900 communicants in 1870, to 11,000 baptised converts and 4,700 communicants in 1880.   The number further rose to 12,500 baptised converts and 6,000 communicants in 1890, and to 14,000 baptised converts and 6,564 communicants in 1900.   At the end of the year 1909, the number of baptised converts of the Anglican Mission was 18,117 and of communicants 8,349.

The month of January 1892 witnessed the arrival in Chota Nagpur of another mission known as the Dublin Univerisity Mission. Its centre has been, from the very beginning, in the picturesque town of Hazaribagh.   And to the Hazaribagh District they confined their activities up till the year 1900.   In 1901, at the invitation of the late Bishop Whitley, the work of the Dublin University Mission was extended to Ranchi, the English (S.P.G.) Mission having placed the Dublin missionaries chiefly in charge of the medical and educational work of the Ranchi centre.   About two years ago, however, the Dublin Mission found it necessary to withdraw their missionaries back to Hazaribagh.   The Bishop of Chota Nagpur is the ecclesiastical head of the Dublin University Mission of Hazaribagh as of the S. P. G. Mission, which has its chief centre at Ranchi.   The present Bishop of Chota Nagpur is the Right Rev. Foss Westcott, M.A.

Such is but a brief account of the work of the Protestant Missions of the Ranchi District.   In Mundari and Uraon villages of the

Ranchi District, the most careless observer can tell the house of a Christian convert of some year's standing from that of his non-Christian fellow tribesmen by the greater cleanliness of the Christian's house and the general neatness and orderliness of everything about it.   The contrast illustrated by the various pictures given in this book of Munda and Uraon Christian men and women, boys, and girls on the one hand, and, on the other, of non-Christian Mundas and Uraons at their feasts and elsewhere, will, we hope, help the reader towards an appreciation of the brilliant achievements of the Christian Missions in their noble work of civilising and educating the aborigines of Chota Nagpur.

If the Missionaries have spared no efforts to ameliorate the material condition of the aborigines of the district, the British Government has been no less sincere and unremitting in its endeavours to improve their condition and restore permanent peace and prosperity to the country. After the conflicts and affrays that had occurred in the parganas of Sonepur and Basia in the year 1858, were suppressed, the Government seriously discussed the question of registering the special tenures of Chota Nagpur. The authorities at length saw that the only effectual mode of preventing a repetition of such affrays and riots would be to remedy the grievances that had given rise to them. And accordingly, under Government orders, dated the 15th April 1858, Lal Lokenath Sahi, a local Zamindar and a Sub-Assistant Commissioner was deputed to prepare a register of all Bhuinhari lands. This officer began his operations in August 1860, and continued his work till his death on the 13th August 1862. During this period his enquiries extended to 572 villages, out of which he could complete the registers of 429 villages only, while those of 143 villages were left incomplete. The parganas in which carried on his investigations were,—Lodhma, Khukra, Udaipur, Sonepur, Doesa, Korambe, and Basia.   The Lal appears to have exempted all 'danr' (high) lands from his registers as he seems to have been of opinion that no land except low or 'don' lands could be Bhuinhari. He was, moreover, not vested with powers to adjudicate finally on questions of disputed title. His decisions might be either upheld or rejected by the oridinary Civil Courts. The idea however, that some operations were going on to protect their rights, pacified the Mundas and Uraons for the moment. But with the death of Lal Lokenath Sahi and the withdrawal by the India Councils Act (1867) of the power of passing summary

orders in Non-Regulation provinces, disputes between landlords
and tenants broke out afresh. And, at length, with a view to
an authoritative settlement of the title to Bhuinhari lands, the
Chota Nagpur Tenures Act (Act II of 1869) was passed by the
Bengal Council on the 26th July 1869.

The scope of the Act was thus described in a Bengal Government Resolution of the 25th November, 1880 :

The disputes which had assumed so chronic a character in connection with these (special) tenures were attributable to encroachments, generally on the part of the landlord, but, sometimes, on
the part of the tenants, to claims advanced by tenants to lands
alleged to be *bhuinhari*, and resisted by the landlords; and to the
exaction from the tenants of services in excess of, or other than,
those which they were bound to render according to the custom
attaching to their tenures. It was therefore provided by Act
II (B.C.) of 1869, with the view of stopping these causes of dispute,
that the tenures should be defined and recorded, and a register
made of all rights, privileges, immunities and liabilities affecting
the holders. The tenures mentioned in the Act were, however,
only the Bhuinhari and Manjhihas, the latter including Betkheta,
and thus the large class of Rajhas tenures were not specifically
dealt with in the operations which ensued. The Lieutenant-
Governor was empowered to appoint one or more persons as
Special Commissioners to carry out the provisions of the Act.
Each Special Commissioner was to investigate claims to the
tenures and demarcate the lands, and then make for each village
an accurate register of all the tenures specifying the conditions to
be fulfilled, the rent and services to be rendered, and the rights
and privileges to be enjoyed. He was authorised to restore to
possession all persons (or their heirs) who had been wrongfully
dispossessed within 20 years of the passing of the Act, and to
enter their names as occupants of the lands in the village register.
Tenures which had come into existence within twenty years
were not to be registered unless they were created in revival
of previous occupation. Tenants who were bound to fulfil
certain conditions, or to give certain services in respect of their
tenures, and the persons having the right to exact such conditions
and services, were authorised to apply to the Special Commissioners for the commutation of the conditions and services

for a payment in rent. Provision was made for the hearing and decision of such applications by the Special Commissioners, with the help of two Assessors appointed by each party respectively. The procedure for the filing and hearing of appeals against the decisions of the Special Commissioners, and for the disposal of applications for review of judgment, was also laid down in the Act. The decisions of the Special Commissioners were made appealable to the Commissioner of the Division, whose judgment was declared final. Petitions presented in relation to any matter cognisable under the Act were exempted from Stamp duty.... A copy of each entry was to be furnished to the tenant, and a copy of each register to the farmer or proprietor of the village. The register, when finally revised and corrected, was to be submitted to the Commissioner of the Division for confirmation and it was directed that one copy should in future be kept in the Deputy Commissioner's office and another in the office of the Board of Revenue.

The operations under the Act were extended to as many as 2,482 villages situated in 35 parganas[30] of the Lohardaga (now the Ranchi) District. As many as 13,473 claims were disposed of, besides 1,161 applications for commutation of services and 3,544 miscellaneous cases. Of the 13,473 claims, 7,423 were contested. The Special Commissioners granted review of their own judgments in 294 cases, and 844 appeals from their decisions were preferred to the Divisional Commissioner. Out of the appeals, 636 resulted in the confirmation, 28 in the modification, and 14 in the reversal of the orders passed by the Special Commissioners. As many as 68 were summarily rejected, and in 98, the cases were remanded for further hearing. The operations under the Chota Nagpur Tenures Act of 1869 commenced on the 1st of April 1869 and continued up till the 31st of March 1880. The total expenditure of these operations amounted to Rs. 2,69,887 besides minor charges for tents and surveying and mathematical instruments. The registers of lands recorded as privileged tenures under the Act fill 13,720 pages of sixty-nine volumes.

The high hopes entertained at its introduction into the Council were, however, far from being fulfilled. The sanguine expect-

[30] Parganas Tamar, Rahe, Bundu, Baranda, Sili, Borway and Biru in the present Ranchi district were exempted from the operations under the Act.

ations of the framers of the Act as to its success in removing all grievances and allaying all disturbances, were soon found out to have been but illusive. And the reasons are not far to seek. In the first place, the Act came too late. As early as in 1839, we find Dr. Davidson, then Principal Assistant to the Governor-General's Agent, urging the necessity of an authoritative investigation into the claims of Bhuinharis. Said he :

> The value of the Bhoonears attach to their land is very great : nothing will ever reconcile them to be deprived of it. They are always buried in the villages where their Bhoonearee lands are situated, and even if they die at a distance, their heirs consider it a necessary act of piety to transport their bones to their own village, that they may be buried in the Harsali, or burying-ground of the village. The disturbances in Nagpore of 1832, were caused by no one cause so much as the dispossession of the Mundas and Mankies, who are the Bhoonears of Sonepur, of their lands; and until the Bhoonears are protected in the possession of their lands, we never can be certain of the peace of the country. For this reason, I would strongly recommend that you should authorize the Assistants of the Division to investigate all cases for dispossession of Bhoonearee lands as miscellaneous cases, and when satisfied of the justice of the Bhoonears' claim, and that he has not been more than twenty years out of possession, to decree in his favour, and give him possession, allowing the opposite party to appeal to you. A reference to a regular suit is not at all applicable to a Kol; and if so ordered, in nine out of ten cases, the powerful Zemindars will thereby be able to defeat the poor Bhoonears.

These apprehensions were, alas ! fully justified by subsequent events. The results of the 'Bhuinhari' settlement under Bengal Act II of 1869, revealed how great had been the havoc committed on the 'Bhuinhari' lands in the half a century that preceded the passing of the Act. In the beginning, as we have seen, the villages of the Mundas were of the Khuntkatti type, and even to this day as many as 156 Munda villages have succeeded in retaining their ancient Khuntkatti nature intact. It was in such Mundari villages as entirely succumbed to the aggressions of the Jagirdars and Thika-dars, that the descendants of the original Khuntkattidars were deprived of their rights to the village itself, but were allowed to hold their original clearances which now received the name of Bhuinhari lands.   At first these Bhuinhari lands would appear to have covered a very large area,—in fact, the greater portion of the cultivated lands of the village.   But, by continual encroachments of the Zamindars on these lands, the Bhuinhari area shrunk into less and still lesser area and the Majhas and Rajhas lands increased in direct proportion to the diminution of the Bhuinhari area. And the varying proportion of Bhuinhari to other classes of lands found in different villages during the Bhuinhari Settlement, would go to show this.   Thus, Mr. Rakhal Das Haldar, the First Special Commissioner appointed under Act II of 1869, says in his able Report :

It may be broadly stated that the proportion of 'Bhuinhari' to 'Rajhas' varies from even less than the hundredth part of the cultivated lands to more than three-fourths. In some villages, it may be correct to say that one-fourth of the lands is 'Bhuinhari', in others one-third, one-half, two-thirds, or even so much as three-fourths.

Thus, in a single village, namely, Dorma in pargana Sonepur, the Special Commissioners demarcated more than 1,500 bighas (495 acres) of Bhuinhari lands.   In one village in pargana Lodhma and in four villages in pargana Sonepur, the Bhuinhari lands demarcated under the Act exceeded 1,000 bighas (330 acres) in each, but were less than 1,500 bighas.   The Bhuinhari lands in village Bargari measured over 3,200 bighas (1,056 acres) out of a total area of 4,300 bighas (1,419 acres) of lands in the village. Village Lalgunj with a total area of about 2,600 bighas (858 acres) was found to contain as many as 2,000 bighas (660 acres) of 'Bhuinhari' lands.   Out of a total area of 4000 bighas (1,320 acres) of land in village Nagri, as many as 3,000 bighas (990 acres) were demarcated as Bhuinhari.   On the other hand, two villages in pargana Lodhma and twenty-three villages in pargana Sonepur were found to have each less than 100 bighas of Bhuinhari lands.   In six villages in pargana Lodhma and twenty-two in Sonepur, only Pahanai lands, varying from a bigha and a half to not more than thirty-four bighas, could be found for demarcation under the Act.

The second cause which seems to have contributed to the failure of the Tenures Act of 1869, in allaying the unrest, is to be sought in the ignorance and stupidity of the aborigines. As one account says :

It must be borne in mind that only a few of the 'Bhooinhars' fully relied on the good intentions of the Government and understood the purpose of the Act. A great many of them looked with suspicion on the proceedings of the surveyors and the Special Commissioners thinking that nothing but the imposition of a new tax, or something like it, was contemplated, and this superstitious fear of the 'Bhooinhars' was turned into account by the land-lords and 'Thikadars,' who tried their utmost to dissuade them from putting forward their claims. In pursuing their objects they had recourse to promises or threats or gifts or money for the sake of spending it in the liquor shops; and last but not least contrived means to disunite the' Bhooinhars', according to the maxim *divide et impera*. Government officials and the Missionaries too tried their utmost to enlighten the people on the purpose of Government in passing the Act. The Missionaries even translated it into their language and admonished them to be of one accord and after all to speak the truth; but only the Christians listened to what was told them and the non-Christian 'Kols' for the most part either omitted to claim their 'Bhuinhari' lands in full or in part and in many places combined with the Zemindars against the Christians and thus against their own cause. It must be admitted that in some instances the Christians put forward exorbitant claims and therefore made their statements unreliable, thereby losing instead of gaining something.

The Vorstand of the G.E.L. Mission from whose Representation[31] to Her Majesty Queen Victoria, made in 1889, we quote the above, mention several such cases. One of these cases was communicated to them by the chief Special Commissioner, the late Mr. Rakhal Das Halder himself. Mr. Halder is reported to have said :

All the cultivators in a certain village stated before me in court,

[31] This representation was signed by the Rev. Dr. A. Nottrott, Rev. J. F. Hahn and Rev. Mr. Betzler.

that there was no "Bhuinharee" land in their village and that
they were simply Rayats and not Bhuinhars, I knew better how
matters stood in their village, and that by a good quantity of pork
and liquor they had been prevailed upon by the Zemindar to deny
their claims.   I therefore adjourned their case for 8 days,
telling them, that if they after the expiration of this time, had not
come to their senses and would even then abide by their present
statement, their Bhuinharee would be gone for ever.   They returned after 8 days and told the same story; so I could do nothing
for them.   A long time after this, these villagers again came to
me complaining that the Zemindar had dispossessed them of all
Bhuinharee lands. Of course it was too late to help them and
they owe it to their own folly, if in this village no Bhuinharee
lands have been recorded.

The third cause why the Chota Nagpur Tenures Act failed to give
satisfaction to the Mundas and Uraons is that the Act left untouched several other classes of tenures and a number of other rights
to land or their produce, about which these aborigines have always
been very keen.   Thus, no provision was made in the Act for the
protection of the immemorial rights of these people to cut and appropriate wood from the village jungles for building and repairing
their houses, making and mending their agricultural implements,
as well as for fuel and other domestic uses. No provision, again,
was made for securing to the Buinharis the mango groves and topes
of other trees said to have been planted by them or their ancestors
on uplands, and over which they claimed to have been always
in possession. 'Sarnas' and 'Korkar lands', too, were similarly left
out of the record. Although the tenants have in many cases
succeeded in preserving their rights to these, instances are not
rare in which landlords have wholly or partially dispossessed the
tenants from such lands. Another most objectionable omission
of the Chota Nagpur Tenures Act of 1869 would appear to have
been the exclusion of Khuntkatti tenures from the scope of
the Act.

It was not till late in the year 1903 (August), that by Bengal Act
V of that year, special provisions were made to protect the Mundari
Khuntkatti tenancies from the unscrupulous aggressions of landlords and money-lenders, and the suicidal acts of the Mundas
themselves. But in the meanwhile what a considerable number of

Khuntkatti tenancies had been destroyed by avaricious landlords as well as through the folly of the Mundas, it is difficult now to estimate. Writing in 1871, (August 21), Mr. Rakhal Das Haldar, the distinguished Bhuinhari Commissioner, says :

I have reason to believe that one Mankipatti in Sonepur has been extinguished probably more than sixty years ago—the Jiwripatti, owned by the Thakoor of Tilmi. The Mundas and Pahans exist only in name, have not yet forgotten the time when their ancestors were the sole undisputed owners of the villages. Another Mankipatti—that of Chalom, exists in name as belonging to a Manki,—although the head of the patti has been reduced to the position of an ordinary makararidar.

In his speech in the Bengal Legislative Council on the 18th July 1903, the Hon'ble Mr. F. A. Slacke, said :

Owing to the non-recognition of their rights, the Mundaris for more than three-quarters of a century have been in a state of agitation, which from time to time has culminated in outbursts. This (discontent among the Mundas) found a vent in the great rebellion of 1832-33, the immediate cause of which was an attempt by the Thakur of Sonepurgarh to destroy Khuntkatti rights in Bandagaon and Kochang in the district of Ranchi. The attempts to destroy the Khuntkattidars' rights did not then cease, and they were the cause of the disturbances between landlords and tenants in that district in the year of the Mutiny. Both sides took advantage of the disorder that then prevailed,— the landlords to oust the Khuntkattidars who were holding at low permanant rentals, the Khuntkattidars to recover the Khuntkatti lands which the landlords had previously succeeded in making rajhas or manjhihas, i.e. rayati or sir.
Eventually the Chota Nagpur Tenures Act of 1869 was passed, and effected some improvement. But it omitted to deal with all the privileged lands, as it took no notice of intact Khuntkatti villages. This omission left such villages at the mercy of the spoliator. The destruction of the Khuntkatti tenancies went on, and the discontent thereby created brought about the outburst of 1888, when what is locally known as the Sardar Larai began and has not yet ceased.

To this effect also were the observations of the then Settlement Officer of Ranchi made in May, 1903. Said he :

Of the disturbances of 1857, the Bhuinhari Act of 1869 was the direct fruit. This Act dealt with certain privileged agricultural lands known as Bhuinhari, Pahanai, etc., on the one side and Manjhihas and Bethkheta on the other. It provided for their survey and record; and it totally failed to effect any real amelioration of the condition of the Mundaris. It is not difficult now to see why it was foredoomed to failure. In the first place it dealt with a portion only of the privileged lands. Bhuinhari is merely another term for Khuntkatti; and, from the scope of that Survey were excluded precisely those areas of the Munda country where Khuntakatti rights still most vigorously flourished. Only the miserable *disjecta membra* of what had once been intact Khuntkatti villages were dealt with and the Five Parganas and the Mankipatti, the heart of the Munda country, were left to become the sport of the Ranchi law courts. Further, the optional character of Clause IX of the Act left open the running sores of abwabs and begari. And finally... the Bhuinhari tenures, which were not customarily alienable by sale, were not made legally inalienable.

On the other hand, the passing of the Registration Act (XVI of 1864) which came into force on the 1st January, 1865, and the Registration Act, XX of 1866, which came into force on the 1st May 1866, would seem to have given an impetus to such alienations.[32]

We have now indicated the main causes that led to the failure of the Chota Nagpur Tenures Act. Though it was productive of some amount of good, the Act did not deal with all the irritating causes of dispute between the Mundas and the *dikus*. More than one numerously signed memorial was sent up to the Local and Imperial Governments and even to the Secretary of State by or on behalf of several thousands of Mundas and Uraons.

[32] The first Ex-officio Registrar of Dt. Lohardaga was Mr. H. L. Oliphant, and the first Ex-officio Deputy Registrar of Ranchi was Lieutenant Lilingstion. No document seems to have been registered in the District before 1865. Before that the Deputy Commissioner used to endorse documents from time to time, but no copies of such documents were kept.

11

The simple aborigines were the unsuspecting dupes of a band of unscrupulous agitators, since known as Sardars, and, deceived by the false hopes held out by them, spent a good deal of hard earned money in getting up these petitions. As the Hon'ble Mr. Slacke said in his Council speech of 1903 :

Utilising the bitter feelings of the Mundaris, some of their fellow clansmen persuaded the people that the Hindus had not right to the lands, that the lands belonged to the Mundaris, that no rent should be paid, and that the Sovereign had given a decree to this effect.

The extravagant claims put forward in these petitions defeated their own object.[33]

[33] Here is a specimen of the recklessly rabid petitions submitted by these Mundas.

To

The Commissioner of Chota Nagpur.
Dated Ranchi, the 25th March, 1879.

We, the Mundas of 8 Parganas of Chota Nagpur beg most respectfully to lay before your Honour the following prayers, and hope you will be good enough to consider them duly. That the measurement of Bhooihurree lands in Chota Nagpur made by the special Commissioner Babu Rakhal Dass and others is not rightly done. He measures the land which the Ticcadars say ; they do not measure what is not measured (mentioned ?) to them by the Ticcadars ; they strike off the claim of the Mundas from their ancestral land. Therefore we the Mundas do not at all agree with the measurement made by the Native Special Commissioners. They have put aside the claim of many from their ancestral land and the Ticcadars consequently began to oppress us excessively. And therefore the inhabitants fly to Assam to escape oppression, their lands being dispossessed by the Elakadar. How the rights of the Elakadars are come to be settled and that of the Mundas not ? If Chotanagpur does not belong to the Mundas, it belongs to none,—neither to Ticcadars or Elakadars nor to the Nagbunsis. Chotanagpore was established by the Mundas and possessd by them. Nagbunsis, now the ruling power of Chotanagpore, were servants of the Mundas. Afterwards by dishonesty they usurped the Raj and they falsely declared that it was given to them by the Mundas. What worthy deeds they performed to the Mundas that they gave it to them ? What, had the Mundas no appetite or hunger that they gave it ? Nobody can give to any even $\frac{1}{4}$ of a seer of rice, then how the Mundas gave such a vast Raj to the Nagbunsis ? If the Raj is given to the Nagbunsis they ought to bring their babus (bahis ?) or Saboot before Government. The Nagbunsis were only Bhuinharies and Tahsildars of the Mundas : Such was our primeval state ; but by time it has undergone a calamitous change. At present even the little possession under the name of Bhuinhari land is going to be in the danger of being dispossessed.

Their principal prayer, that of being allowed to form themselves into village communities directly under Government, was, under the changed circumstances of the country, found to be unreasonable and extravagant, and the petitions were all necessarily rejected.

The heads of the Missions sought in vain to convince these memorialists, of the futility of prosecuting their hopelessly time-barred claims. The infuriated Sardars (who called themselves Christians) resented the remonstrances of the missionaries and severed their connection with the Missions. The Missionaries of the German Evangelical Lutheran Church in Chotanagpur forwarded a Memorial to the Bengal Government regarding certain grievances of the aboriginal tenants of the District and the Lieutenant Governor by his Minute, dated the 5th July 1876, informed the Memorialists that "he did not share their apprehensions that the Kols may be tempted to resist authority or disturb order." But, unfortunately, Sir Richard Temple's optimism was not borne out by the event. The agitation soon assumed a threatening aspect and riots and other disturbances of the public peace were not long in coming.

Some of the leaders, it is said, attempted to coerce their tribesmen into seceding from the Churches and withdrawing their children from the Mission schools. One of the agitators himself made an unauthorised celebration of a marriage according to Christian rites.

The year 1881 witnessed a ludicrously comic show at village Doisa, which had once been the seat of the ancestors of the Maharaja of Chotanagpur. A small band of malcontents styling themselves the 'Children of Mael', and their leader 'John the Baptist,' established themselves on the ruins of the *garh* of Doisa[34] and proclaimed a Raj of their own.

Yours most obediently,
JUGDEEP, JOSEPH,
MANMASEE
CHUMNA etc.
14,000 Christians.

The memorials they forwarded to the Local and Supreme Governments are too lengthy to be quoted, but all are in the same strain as the above.

[34]These Munda sardars went to the length of claiming the *Doisa garh* as having been founded by their ancestors. Thus in a memorial to the Lieutenant Governor of Bengal submitted in 1884 by about 12,000 Mundas, we read :

Threatening letters were sent to the Munsiff of Lohardaga. Some of the ringleaders were promptly prosecuted and punished by the Deputy Commissioner, Mr. Power. But the agitation went on unabated for the next few years. The excitable Kols of the villages were easily drawn into the movement, and thus commenced what is now known as the 'Sardar Larai'. As the Settlement Officer of Ranchi observed in May 1903:

The Sardars—an unscrupulous and dishonest gang of cheats obtained so great a measure of support because of the growing discontent of the Mundaris with the enhancement of begar and abwabs, with the extension of the 'Manjhihas' of the landlords, and, above all, with the constant sapping of Khuntkatti rights in village after village.

To one who has not been among them it is difficult to realise the passionate attachment of these savages to the grove and graveyard of their clan and to the fields which their ancestors cleared among the forests, and equally difficult to realise how sensitive they are to the degradation from the honourable rank of Khuntkattidar to that of mere raiyat. To lose all this or to see neighbour after neighbour sinking into this pit,…was calculated to set on fire a far less excitable people than the Mundas.

The unrest and the agitation grew every day more and more acute. One band of agitators stopped the Bara Lal of Palkot, a near kinsman of the Maharaja, on a journey, when the Bara Lal with great presence of mind, succeeded in making good his escape by temporising with them and acknowledging their pretended claims. Meetings were held by the Mundas at different places in the south and south-west of the district and in Porahat, and it is said that the 'thirty-five Sardars[35]' gave out that as they

---

Many monuments still exist of big stone-slabs and foundation-stone-pillars, high above the ground, in Sutiamba Ghar, and also in several other Ghars, in several Pergunnahs of Chota Nagpore, to bear testimony to the ancient deeds of the Mundas, wherever they at different times and places first established them-selves in a body, and long before the family of the now-called Rajahs settled there,—specially the two stupendous old monuments respectively in Pergunnahs Doisa and Khukra, known as Nava-Ratnas.

[35] The signatories to the Memorial of 1834 appear to have been thirty-six in number, viz :

had filed strong petitions against the 'thirteen hakims' of the district, the people should resist the authority of the local officers and seize 'Manjihas lands'. These dangerous counsels do not appear to have been extensively acted upon. It was probably owing to the precautions taken by the authorities, the strengthening of the Police force, and the exemplary punishments awarded in the few cases that came up to the Courts, that there were not many instances of riots or serious disturbances in the harvesting season. Only one case of paddy cutting at Tilma, and cases of trespass on the Manjihas lands of the Rani of Tamar, besides a few other cases in the Parganas south and west of Ranchi, were reported to have occurred. The causes of the disputes that survived the operations under the Chota Nagpur Tenures Act of 1869, were thus pointedly explained by the then Deputy Commissioner of the District:[36]

No doubt can possibly exist as to the beneficial effect resulting from these coveted tenures (the Bhuinhari) being ascertained and demarcated. It is a pity, however, that the opportunity was not taken of measuring and settling each whole village instead of Bhuinhari and Manjihas lands only. The Bhuinhars generally claimed their entire holdings, and often other lands, of which they were out of possession, as being all *bhuinhari*. When a decree was given for a portion only, no finding was come to with respect to the remainder beyond recording that it was not *bhuinhari*, but *rajhas* (rent-paying) or *manjihas*. When held to be of the latter description, it was demarcated under the Act, but when declared to be *rajhas*, a door was opened for

1 Samuel Munda, 2 Munmasi Munda, 3 Paulus Munda, 4 Patras Munda and 5 Boas Munda of Pargana Basia ; 6 Biswas Munda, 7 Jakria Munda of Pargana Belsia ; 8 Nikodim Munda, 9 Barnabas Munda, 10 Paulus Munda, 11 Manmasi Munda, 12 Nikodim Munda, 13 Doah Munda, 14 Rijha Munda, 15 Mansid Munda, 16 Obed Munda, 17 Lita Munda, 18 Mansid Munda, 19 Gidhone Munda, 20 Samuel Munda, 21 Gopal Mnnda, 22 Reda Munda, and 23 Mani Munda of Pargana Sonepur ; 24 Johan Munda , and 25 Jhirga Munda of Pargana Belkadi ; 26 Daud Munda and 27 Mansue Munda of Pargana Lachra ; 28 Tinga Munda of Singbhum ; 29 Gidhone Munda of Porahat ; 30 Thinga Munda, and 31 Singa Munda of Tamar Parg; 32 Samuel Munda, 33 Asab Munda, 34 Markus Munda and 35 Amus Munda of Pargana Doisa ; and 36 Joseph Munda of Pargana Khukra.

[26] Quoted in *Bengal Government Resolution* (Revenue Department), dated the 25th November, 1880.

numerous complications. The Special Commissioner had no power to determine *whose rajhas* it was, nor what rate of rent was payable for it. Usually it was either in possession of the claimant rightfully, or had wrongfully been taken ' possession of by him when operations under the Act commenced and held by him since without payment of rent. As soon as the Act came into force, it was not uncommon for Bhuinhars to combine and take forcible possession of lands which, according to their rights, they were entitled to claim as Bhuinhari, withholding payment of all rents. Active and solvent Illaquadars protected themselves well enough by resort to the Criminal Courts ; but when, owing to the incompetence or poverty of Illaquadars resistance was feeble, these combinations were frequently successful. As the *bhuinhari* cases came to an end, the struggle for the *rajhas* commenced. Whether lands really belonged to the Bhuinhar or not, the Illaquadar might be supposed to say to a Bhuinhar,—"You claimed all your land as Bhuinhari and have only got a decree for a fraction ; you have put me to expense in contesting the Bhuinhari case, you are not a tenant to my mind. I can get a higher rent for the *rajhas* from Ramjiwan Kurmi or Baksu Jolah, so turn out and let me settle the land with a man after my own heart". The reply would be: "Decree or no decree, the land was brought under cultivation by my ancestors, the village is ours, and the country is ours, not yours. If compelled to do so, I will pay rent, but turn out I will not." Then ensues the usual litigation, first in Criminal, then in Revenue and Civil Courts, to carry on which the demarcated Bhuinhari is probably mortgaged or sold to a *mahajan*. The Illaquadar registers a pottah in favour of Ramjiwan Kahar or Baksu Jolah, who, with two or three witnesses, formally scatters some seed on the land either before or after the Bhuinhar has done so. When the crop is ripe, a report is made by one party or the other to the thana that there is a likelihood of a breach of the peace, and whichever party reaps the crop is charged with theft. At specified seasons, the Courts are almost swamped with criminal trespass and paddy-cutting cases. It may generally be said that, when Illaquadars are intelligent, and powerful, they are in the wrong ; and that, when they are otherwise, the Bhuinhars are at fault. The result, however, is seldom satisfactory ; for, in protracted litigation, intelligence, length of purse, and influential position will, in the long run, carry the day. When an Illaquadar accepts a Bhuinhar as tenant for lands claimed as Bhuinhari but declared to be *rajhas*, even then disputes arise about the rate of rent. When the ordinary rates are demanded, the Bhuinhar is clearly wrong in declining to pay rent accordingly, but he almost always invariably does so, contending, even in the face of a final decree, that the lands are Bhuinhari still. It often happens that there are two rates of rent in a village—the old customary rate paid by the native cultivators, and the contract rate paid by new ryots settled on vacated lands by Illaquadars. Illaquadars always try, naturally enough, to level up to the contract rate without the tedious process of measuring the whole village.

Thus disputes between the Mundas and their landlords continued, and, now and again, assumed a serious aspect. Although at this period, several special Acts relating to Chota Nagpur were passed by the Legislatures, none of them grappled with the most crying grievances of the people. In the beginning of the year 1879, *Act I of 1879*, known as the *Chota Nagpur Landlord and Tenant Procedure Act*, was passed by the Bengal Council. The *Act of 1879* closely followed the provisions of the *Bengal Rent Act of 1859*, and failed to effect any appreciable improvement in the relations between the Mundas and their landlords. *The Chota Nagpur Encumbered Estates Act* passed by the Supreme Coucil in 1876 (*Act VI of 1876*) and amended in 1884 by Act V of that year, affected the Mundas but remotely. The abolition of the Zemindari Police and the introduction in 1863 of the new constabulary under *Act V of 1861*, proved a real boon. The *Hazaribagh and Lohardugga Rural Police Act* was passed by the Bengal Council in 1878 (*Act VIII of 1878*) and was superseded in the year 1887 by the *Chota Nagpur Rural Police Act (Act V of 1887)*.

In the meanwhile a fresh body of European Missionaries and philanthrophists had appeared in the District. These were the Missionaries of the Society of Jesus. No book on the Mundas and their country can be complete without some account of the noble work of the Christian Missions in educating and civilizing the Mundas and other aboriginal tribes of the District.

Of the several Christian Missions at present working in the Ranchi District, the Roman Catholic Mission, though latest in point of time, now counts by far the largest number of adherents. We shall here attempt to give a rough account of the establishment and work of this Mission amongst the Mundas, Uraons and other aboriginal tribes of Chota Nagpur.

As early as the year 1859, the Catholic Mission of Western Bengal was constituted by His Holiness Pope Pius IX, and entrusted to the Belgian Section of the Society of Jesus. It was not, however, till ten years later that the Mission started work in Chota Nagpur. In fact, Chota Nagpur was the last province to which the Society turned their attention. Almost the first work of the Mission after its arrival in India was the establishment of the well-known St. Xavier's College in Calcutta which celebrated its golden jubilee last year with befitting grandeur. The Mission next extended its sphere of work from the metropolis to the Sunderbans on the one hand and to Orissa on the other. It was in the year 1869,—the same year in which the Church of England (S. P. G.) Mission of Chota Nagpur was established at Ranchi, —that the Rev. Father A. Stockman, S. J., arrived at Chaibassa and there opened the first Catholic Mission station in the Chota Nagpur Division. The work of the Catholic Mission, in the beginning, lay almost entirely amongst the Hos and the Mundas. The progress was necessarily very slow at the commencement. And, indeed, organised missionary work in Chota Nagpur was not undertaken by the Society until another fifteen years had elapsed.

In the meanwhile, the colony of Catholic Munda converts established at Chaibassa was, in the year 1874, removed to Burudi, a village in the Khunti thana of the Ranchi (then called Lohardugga) District, and here the first Catholic chapel in the Ranchi District was built. In the same year, a Catholic clergyman of the name of the Rev. Father De Cock, who had come a few years earlier as Military Chaplain to the Madrasi soldiers stationed at Dorunda, finally settled at that cantonment station, and began missionary work. In the year 1882, a new mission station was opened at village Sarwadag, about twelve miles south of Khunti. The same year, the Rev. Father Stockman removed to Jamgain, about twelve miles south of Ranchi and there opened a Mission station. It was in the year 1883, that a central Mission station was established at Dorunda, and regular mission work commenced.

By the year 1885, the number of baptised Mundas of the Chota Nagpur Catholic Mission amounted to 2,092. On the 14th of

March of that year, a young and energetic Missionary of the name of Father Lievens[37] arrived at Dorunda, and, in the following November, opened a mission station at village Torpa. Two years later, in the year 1887,the Rev. Father Motet, removed the central Mission station from Dorunda to the town of Ranchi. By August, 1888, the Roman Catholic Mission had established 77 schools and employed 189 Catechists in the Ranchi District, and counted as its converts, 11,291 baptised persons and 39,060 catechumens. This remarkably rapid success of the Catholic Mission was mainly due to the exertions of the Rev. Father Lievens, who was now appointed the Director of the Mission and whose zeal for mission work was unbounded. He was assisted in his work by a band of devoted Missionaries[38] some of whom are still working in Chota Nagpur. Before long, Father Lievens began to preach the religion of the Cross to the ruder Mundas, Uraons and Kharias in the remote southern and south-western parts of the Ranchi District. Father Lievens mixed with the people as friends, instructed them in the elements of religion, and helped them in their temporal difficulties. The aborigines of the Ranchi District had suffered cruelly and long. They had hitherto been looked down upon by their neighbours as untouchable Pariahs ; now they came to know that they too were men and fit to be treated as such. When the missionary appeared on the scene, they were groaning under many wrongs and indignities. With their conversion to Christianity came a better appreciation of their rights as men and as tenants. They saw a happier era dawning before them. Besides having all the attraction of novelty, Christianity

[37] The Rev. Father Const. Lievens, was born in Belgium in 1856. He reached India in 1880. After three years spent as a *Seminare* at Asansol, and one year as a Master at the St. Xavier's College in Calcutta, Father Lievens was transferred to the Chota Nagpur Mission. Here he worked so hard that his health broke down, and, in 1892, he had to sail for Europe for the benefit of his health. But the strain on his constitution had been too heavy, and, shortly after his arrival in Europe, he died at the early age of 37.

[38] Amongst these may be mentioned the Rev. Father J. Hoffmann, whose Mundari Grammar is the standard work on the subject, the Rev. Father P. Dehon (who died in 1905) whose excellent paper on the "Religion and Customs of the Uraons" published in the *Memoirs of the Asiatic Society of Bengal*, is the only elaborate contribution on the subject in English, and the Rev. Father Grosjean who was then Superior General of the Bengal Mission and subsequently came to Ranchi as Superior of the Chota Nagpur Mission and, a third time as Rector of the Manressa House.

seemed to these aborigines the only means to drag them out of the
miserable pit into which they had fallen. They felt that while
their landlords oppressed them, they would no longer have to sit
still with folded hands and curse their lot in silence. Hope was
in the air. There was a frantic rush to the fold of Christianity.
One sees in imagination the Munda and Uraon converts of those
days joyfully exclaiming,—

> 'Tis coming on the steps of time,
> And this wide world is growing brighter !
> Though we may not see its dawn sublime,
> High hopes make the heart throb lighter!

The numerous conversions to Christianity naturally made the
Zamindars anxious and angry. Father Lievens, in a printed
letter to the Catholic Archbishop of Calcutta, dated the 19th
February, 1890, cited the instance of a rich landlord of the
district offering him on several occasions a sum of one thousand
rupees on condition of his refusing to admit as Christians the
tenants of five of his villages. In the year 1889, a number
of landlords sent up a petition to the authorities alleging that the
Roman Catholic 'Padri Sahebs' were unsettling the minds of their
ryots and converting them to Christianity by the hundreds in the
Parganas of Panari, Kasir, Nawaghar, Borway, Ardhe, and Korambe, in the west and south-west of the District. Hitherto many
landlords of these Parganas had had their own way with the tenants
whose backs had been bowed under long years of submission to
their demands, just or unjust. No wonder, therefore, that such
landlords should have viewed with alarm and indignation the
conversion of their tenants and a consequent growth of manly
independence in them. We can picture to ourselves the wailing
and gnashing of teeth in these landlords' camp. It cannot, however,
be denied that drunk with hope, these excitable aborigines occasionally exceeded the bounds of moderation. Tingling with the
pulsations of a new life, some of the new converts appear to have
attempted to coerce their unconverted brethren into accepting
their new faith and sharing in the larger life that seemed to open
out to them. Like the young hillstreams of the District, after heavy
showers of rain, heaving and swelling till they overflow their banks,
the upheaval amongst these enthusiastic neophytes of an excitable

race, appears occasionally to have led them into reprehensible excesses. But the reports that reached the authorities through the police and the Zamindars, of the disturbances that took place in these parts appear to have been exaggerated. And in the beginning these exaggerated alarmist accounts appear to have been too credulously accepted. The *Indian Daily News* of Calcutta appears to have first drawn the attention of Government to certain insinuations against the CatholicMission. And soon afterwards we find the Lieutenant-Governor Sir Steuart Bayley visiting the district to see things with his own eyes. The result of the Lieutenant-Governor's inquiry exposed the baselessness of the suggestions against the missionaries.[39]

Already the *Englishman* newspaper of Calcutta in its issue of the 23rd Dec., 1889, wrote :

It now seems that the story of a rising of the Kols, is pure moonshine.

And it was afterwards authoritatively declared, that the actual disturbances which occurred were not really serious. There was only one case of resistance to the authorities, and the rest were mostly cases of disputed rights to lands or crops.[40] The Assistant Commissioner, who was deputed to try the cases locally inflicted excessively heavy punishments on the accused Christians. *The Indian Daily News* of the day wrote :

[39] Vide *Government of Bengal Resolution*, Judicial Department, Dated Ranchi the 15th March, 1890.

[40] We have examined the copies of the records of most of these cases, and they do not appear to have been generally more serious than the generality of cases between landlords and tenants in the District both before and after that period. Here are samples of some of those cases. The case of Jaisri Sing vs. Ghumrua, Jhirga Uraon and others under s. 447, I.P.C. for ploughing up complainant's Bahera Sokra land ; the case of Mahendra Sing vs. Jhirgu and others under s. 447 I.P.C.; the case of Mahendra Sing vs. Pandea and others under s. 379 I.P.C. for cutting wood in the village-jungle; the cases of Babu Rambin Rai vs. Lenda Master, and Babu Ramdin vs. Timra, both withdrawn under s. 248, C. P. C., the case of Gokhul Sing vs. Punai under s. 145, Cr. Pr. Code; the case of the Rev. Fr. Dehon vs. Mahadeo Sing and others under s. 506, I. P. C.; the case of Babu Nobo Kristo Ray vs. Abraham Arlandu ; the case of Sohor Sahi vs. Bisram Christian under s. 324, I. P. C.; the case of Empress vs. Bhuka and others (the Urmi pony case); the case of Nakul Sing vs. Dukhia Uraon under s. 147 and 379, I. P. C.; the case of the Rev. E. Huyghi vs. Mathura and others;

From the action taken by the Lieutenant-Governor it is clear that there had been great want of consideration in the hearing of the charges and some perfunctory confirmation of the senten--ces even by the Deputy Commissioner.

The accused in some cases appear to have been dragged about from camp to camp and obtained no legal assistance at the trial. A number of the convictions were found to be unsustainable, and were set aside in appeal by the Judicial Commissioner, and of some of the rest, the Lieutenant-Governor during his visit to Ranchi, by his Resolution, dated the 15th March 1890, remitted the larger part of the sentences. In that Resolution, in connection with the case of Gandura, Uraon and others, Sir Steuart Bayley observed :

Although the prisoners had no legal advice, the Magistrate made no endeavour to ascertain by examination of the witnesses whether the claims put forward by the prisoners to the ownership of the *dhan* had any foundation, and if so what it was.

In the same case, Sir Steuart Bayley observed with much dis-satisfaction that all the accused in this case were in the first instance sent to Ranchi for trial, a distance of 95 miles and then sent back to the camp of the Deputy Commissioner at Bhusur, where the case was disposed of. This procedure seems to have been unnecessary and harassing. Again, in the portion of the Resolution dealing with the witch-craft case, we read :

An attempt was made at the trial to throw the blame of the ill-treatment of these women (suspected witches) exclusively on the Christian Kols of the villages and to connect two of the servants of the Rev. Mr. Lievens with the occurrence. The Lieutenant-Governor considers this to have been perfectly

the case of Lodro vs. Ramdhan Gour and others; the case of Emp. vs. Chutia Uraon and others under ss. 147 and 225, I. P. C.; the case of Abhiram Sing vs. Gandura and others under s. 337, I. P. C.; the case of Gajadhar Ram vs. Jhirga and others under s. 379 for cutting paddy of a field claimed by him. The case of Emp. vs. Mahadeo Ram Tewary and others, and the cross-case against Fr. Cus, in June 1890, do not come within the category of cases between landlords and tenants.

gratuitous, and he is constrained to express his dissatisfaction with the manner in which the case was tried by the Assistant Commissioner.

In another part of this Resolution which dealt with the petition of Dasso Bhuini and others, the Lieutenant-Governor observed :

That officer (the Judicial Commissioner) has remarked that certain comments made by the Magistrate on the conduct of some Roman Catholic Missionaries ought not to have appeared in his judgment, as they were in no degree justified by the evidence on the record. The Lieutenant-Governor fully concurs in this condemnation, and the expression of his disapproval will be conveyed .[41]

Although the actual disturbances were not serious, Sir Steuart Bayley felt the pulse of the times with exactitude when he observed that :

The spirit of antagonism between landlord and ryot was so strong and generally diffused throughout the district, that it might at any time cause a breach of the peace on a large scale.

The opinion one sometimes hears, that it does not concern the clergymen how his congregation fare in the world, appears to us to betray a poor idea of the priest's duty to his flock. In fact, the Missionaries would have been unworthy stewards of the spiritual well-being of their Christians, if they merely stood by and wrung their hands in silent despair while their converts were sinking deeper and deeper in the miry depths of abject helplessness and impoverishment—a condition which could not but re-act on their moral and spiritual lives. The hearts of the Missionaries naturally went forth to their down-trodden converts in their earthly sufferings. The head and front of their offending seems to have been that they occasionally loosened their purse-strings in response to piteous appeals for help in their law-suits with the landlords. And it was indeed the natural discontent of the ryots which sometimes took

[41] The cases dealt with in this Resolution were the Tangartoli case, the Pony case, the Rescue case and the Witch case. The Resolution was published in the Calcutta *Statesman* and quoted in the *Indo-European Correspondence* of the 26th March, 1890.

the form of law-suits.   But more often it was the ryots who were
harassed by frivolous litigation used as a weapon of persecution.[42]
True, a vague idea seems to have prevailed amongst the aborigines
that by conversion to Christianity,   'they will better themselves
somehow or other'.   The origin of this idea was correctly explained
by Colonel Dalton when he observed :

[42] By way of illustration we here give extracts from a few judgments of Courts.
Thus, in his judgment in *Rent Suits Nos.* 132 *to* 135 *of* 1887, Mr.G.W. Place, Asst.
Commissioner of Lohardugga, said: "The suits seem in these cases of a vindictive
nature, as the plaintiff sues also for ejectment.   The defendants have not done
anything to deserve such vindictive proceedings, as they have all paid something
as the plaintiff himself admits."   The same officer in his judgment in rent suits
Nos.   142 to 147 of 1887, wrote, "The evidence has considerably reduced the
plaintiff's preposterous claims.   Indeed, I am only beginning to learn the...of the
Chota Nagpore Zemindars, who invariably claim in rent suits a higher rent than
was ever paid and virtually turn a suit for rent into one for enhancement, However,
the plaintiff has been exposed in this case."   This general remark in the above
quotation was perhaps too sweeping, for there must have been some exceptions
amongst the Zemindars.   But of the prevalence of the practice noticed by here,
most officers of the time speak in more or less marked language.   Thus, Mr.
F. W. R. Cowley, Judicial Commissioner of Chota Nagpore in Rent Appeal No.
94 of 1888 wrote :   "When a ryot becomes liable to pay an enhanced rent.
the law provides a procedure to be followed, and a Zemindar should take steps, if
he wants more rent, under section 21, & c., Act I (B.C.) of 1879.   Doubtless it is
simpler to come into court and to demand a certain rate as one for excess lands,
but if a Zemindar does so, the onus is strongly upon him of proving that the
ryot has consented to pay him the rent claimed. In the present instance it is
admitted that it is only within the last four years that any attempt has been made
to assess the excess tanr lands of the village."   Similarly, Mr. A.W.B. Power,
Deputy Commissioner of Lohardugga, in his judgment in rent suit No. 4 of
1879-80 referred to a case of the same nature, as follows,—"I fully believe that
defendants were put to all the expenses of previous litigation on a false issue, i.e.,
plaintiffs sued them for arrears at an enhanced rate, to which enhancement defendants had never consented, and represented that enhanced rent as the normal
and established one."
    Among other classes of harassing litigation were suits for possession of lands
formerly waste and brought under cultivation by ryots and Bhuinhars (under local
custom) but claimed as nij-jote by the landlords, and claims to raiyati lands of
refractory tenants as Zemindar's *nij-jote* or as raiyati of some creatures of the
landlords.   But it must at the same time be admitted that cases are not rare in
which the tenants by way of retaliation for aggressive acts and harassing suits,
have actually claimed what was not their own or what had ceased to be their
own for a long time past, and denied liabilities sanctioned by law.—Their apologi-
sts attribute this "to despair or dogged obstinacy, the natural outcome of prolonged
ill-treatment endured by them."   That such ill-treatment was a matter of

When matters came to an issue between the simple Kol and the Zemindar or the foreign farmer, the Kol had no chance, and indeed he appeared to think so himself, for he seldom sought redress. But the Kols who embraced Christianity imbibed more independent notions and in several instances successfully asserted their rights. From this the belief unfortunately spread through the District that when Kols go to court as Christians, they are more uniformly successful than those who have not changed their religion. The next step was to profess Christianity, and going up to Ranchi to the Mission they returned with their hair puritanically cropped, and were ready to assert their rights and defy their landlords.

This was said of the converts of the German Mission long before the Jesuit Fathers came to the district. And it was for the very same reasons that a similar idea prevailed amongst the Kols when the Roman Catholic Mission appeared in the country. Such an impression will naturally prevail "whenever a class of men that take a real interest in the welfare of the people come amongst them and show sympathy for their misery and sufferings".

No wonder, therefore, that there was a large accession to the Catholic Mission when the missionaries began to work amongst these people with a degree of self-sacrificing zeal which attracted the admiration of Mr. (afterwards Sir) Charles Cecil Stevens, who was Commissioner of the Chota Nagpur Division from 1885 to 1889. But there does not appear to be any ground for supposing that the missionaries held out any hopes of the nature we have

---

frequent occurrence is testified to by the resolutions passed at a meeting held at Ranchi on the 14th January, 1890, when an Association was formed with the senior local barrister (Mr. Ray) as Secretary and a Senior Pleader (Mr. Aikath) as a prominent member. In the printed proceedings of this Association, styled "The Chotanagpore Reform Association"(now defunct), we read, "Extortion, ill-treatment, torture, and forced labour to which ignorant people are subjected, to which we can bear testimony, are shocking to our eyes." In the Calcutta *Statesman* of the 24th May, 1891, we find a long letter from Rev. F. Hahn, Secretary, German Mission, about "Affairs in Chotanagpore," in which after an account of the grievances of the tenants the correspondent said, "The wonder is only how the Kols are bearing up with their present position. They do it in this way; they like a good drink ; and whenever the Zemindar requires them to be in good humour, or to forget an injustice done to them, he has recourse to giving them pice for drink."

alluded to. Their self-sacrificing devotion to the cause of humanity would preclude such an unjust supposition. In a paper on *Some Reminiscences of Chutia Nagpore*, read by Sir Charles Stevens, K. C. S. I. in February, 1901, in the Jehanghir Hall of the Imperial Institute (London), that ex-Commissioner of Chota Nagpur and Ex-Lieutenant-Governor of Bengal, spoke in high terms of the self-sacrificing zeal of the Catholic Fathers of Chota Nagpur, and by way of illustration, he gave long extracts from the diary of his wife during their tours in the interior of the Ranchi District. In that paper, Sir Charles thus describes the origin of the agrarian disturbances :

I have found them (the Kols) most tenacious of what they believe to be their rights. Their comparative ingorance and stupidity have attracted oppression at times. Rajas and land-lords have called in the help of cleverer and stronger people from outside, and this process is still going on. But oppression is not tolerated beyond a certain point, and in the past has led to rebellion and much bloodshed. At the present day, too, most troubles and difficulties in the administration arise from the encroachments of the outsiders and the dogged resis-tance of the people.

Mr. Grimley who succeeded Mr. (afterwards Sir Charles) Stevens as Commissioner of Chota Nagpur traced the origin of the agrarian disturbances of the period to the same causes. In 1896, Mr. Grimley said :

The result of the enquiries begun by Mr. Renny and continued by Colonel Lillingston is to establish the fact that the unsettled relations of landlords and tenants have been brought about in a great measure by the greed and rapacity of the former. The investigating officers travelled over a large tract of country and wherever they went had to listen to the same story of oppression, in the form of illegal exactions, excessive enhancement of rent, unlimited demands of beth-begari, and the withholding of re-ceipts for rent.

Again in his Administration Report for the year 1895-96, Mr. Grimley writes :

Primitive people are by nature singularly tenacious of purpose and cling to old traditions, and this feeling among the Kols led up to the Agrarian agitation of 1889, when they made an effort to free themselves from the yoke of middlemen, the thraldom of beth-begari, and other unpleasant incidents connected with the cultivation of land.

With a view to remedying the evils, Mr. W. Maude, I.C.S. was, in the year 1890, specially deputed to the district to report on the working of the law then in force regulating the relations between landlords and tenants in Chota Nagpur. The Lieutenant-Governor during his visit in Ranchi in March, 1890, himself held more than one conference with representatives of the tenants and landlords. On the 14th of April, 1890, the following Proclamation was issued in the District by the Commissioner, Mr. W. H. Grimley:

For some years past there have been agrarian disputes between the ryots of the Lohardugga district and their landlords on the subject of *beth-begari*, which has seriously interfered with the good government of the country. The Commissioner has lately been making enquiries into the causes of these disputes, and is most anxious to secure their final settlement. Until this can be effected, it is necessary for the sake of peace to draw attention to the limits within which, according to the custom of the country, Zemindars may demand labour from certain ryots. The following scale, founded on the ancient custom of Lohardugga, as ascertained by Government, is therefore published for general information. The Commissioner warns all Zemindars that, if they forcibly exact labour in excess of the amount prescribed by custom, they may be liable on complaint to a prosecution for wrongful restraint under section 341 of the Penal Code. He also calls upon those ryots who have hitherto rendered *beth-begari* to grant the labour willingly and ungrudgingly according to the prescribed scale, or the decision of the *Bhuinhari* Special Commissioners, as the case may be.

Prescribed scale for each holding : Three days' ploughing; Three days' digging; Three days' sowing or planting rice; Three days' cutting rice; One day's threshing corn; One day's assisting in the making of a granary; Carrying loads for the

landlord on journeys within Chota Nagpore,—the labourer
to be supplied with food.

It is a relief to turn from this sickening narrative of the unsatisfactory relations between the aborigines of the Ranchi District
and their landlords, to an account of the expansion of the Catholic
Mission in that district. Wonderfully rapid, indeed, has this
expansion been ! The Chota Nagpur Catholic Mission has
not only attracted to its fold the unconverted by the thousands,
but have drawn in many aboriginal converts from the Protestant
Missions working in their country. An idea of the rapid expansion
of the Mission may be gathered from the following statistics:
The number of Catholic converts rose from 15,000 in the year
1887 to 39,567 in 1897. Of this number, 22,728 were baptized
converts and 16,839 were neophytes. The figures for the next
three years are 53,908 (including 17,602 neophytes) in 1898,
58,311 (including 20,838 neophytes) in 1899, and 71,270 (including 29,658 neophytes) in 1900. In another five years the
number swelled to 101,630 including 43,350 neophytes. At
the end of the year 1909, the Chota Nagpur Catholic Mission
counted as many as 147,366 converts, of whom 72,943 were neophytes. Out of this total number as many as 91,345 belong to the
Ranchi District alone, 1,763 persons to the Singbhum District,
6,230 to the Palamau District, 35,791 and 18,222 respectively to
the two tributary estates of Jashpur and Gangpur. The number
of Catholic converts of the Munda tribe alone now exceeds 30,000,
as against 2,092 in the year 1885. The Catholic Mission centres
in the Ranchi District are now 16 in number and are located at
Ranchi (established in 1887), at Sarwada (1882), at Torpa (1885),
at Mandar (1893, when it took the place of the older centre at
Dighia, established in 1886), at Noatoli (1890, when it took the
place of the older centre at Basia, established in 1888), at Karra
(1888), at Khunti (1891), at Katkahi (1892), at Rengarih (1901),
at Soso (1901), at Kurdeg (1903), at Samtoli (1903), at Nawadih
(1907), and at Majhatoli (1907). The Mahuadanr mission station
in the Palamau District was opened in 1896.

There are, at present, as many as 53 European priests, over 500
aboriginal catechists, and more than 200 school-masters employed
in the Chota Nagpur Catholic Mission. Fifteen solid brick-built
churches and over 400 chapels have been already erected in Chota

Nagpur and some others are in course of construction. Of these Catholic Churches, not a few are very fine specimens of ecclesiastical architecture, such as the splendid Church at Ranchi known as the Church of the Immaculate Conception and the fine Church at Sarwada in the heart of the Munda country.

We shall now proceed to describe some of the educational and other institutions organised by this Mission. Besides the central school at Ranchi known as St. John's School of which we shall presently give a short account, the Catholic Mission has established no less than 140 boys' schools all over Chota Nagpur in which as many as 7,683 pupils are now receiving education. The majority of these schools are located within the Ranchi District. Sixteen of these schools teach up to the Lower Primary Standard, and 4 up to the Upper Primary Standard. The Mission maintains in Chota Nagpur 21 Girls' Schools with a total of 4,760 girls on their rolls. Of these four are big Convent Schools, each with a strong staff of European 'Nuns' and aboriginal 'Sisters'.

Of the educational institutions of the Chota Nagpur Catholic Mission, the most important is the St. John's School. This School was started in the year 1887 by Father Motet as a Lower Primary School; and was originally meant to impart elementary education to the children of the Catholic converts in Ranchi and its suburbs. It was soon deemed necessary to admit into this school, boys from the Catholic Mission centres in the interior of the district with a view to training them for the posts of Catechists and Schoolmasters. In the year 1903, the St. John's School was raised to a Middle English School, and in 1905 to a High English School. This institution has from its commencement, been a boarding-school for Catholic boys. Since 1904, however, non-Christian boys are also being admitted as day-scholars. At present the number of boarders,—mainly Munda and Uraon Christian boys, is 170, and of day-scholars, mainly Hindu and Mahomedan students, is about 70. The boarders each pay only a nominal fee which represents but a small fraction of the expenses incurred by the Mission for their board, lodging and tuition. A Government grant-in-aid as well as private donations and the school-fees paid by the non-Christian pupils help the Mission in meeting the current expenses of this school. The St. John's School was affiliated to the Calcutta University in 1908, and in that very year one Munda boy successfully passed the Matriculation examination.

In connection with the St. John's School, we must not omit to mention the theatrical performances of its aboriginal boys. It was in 1890, that these performances first began. In those days, there were very few aboriginal converts who could read or write. And it was with a view to instructing the converts and their children in the elements of religion that these dramatic performances in imitation of the mystery-plays of the Middle Ages in Europe, were introduced. It is mainly Biblical incidents and parables that are dramatised in Hindi by competent missionary gentlemen for this theatre. Among the more important plays may be mentioned those of 'the Birth of Christ', 'the Death of Christ', 'Cain and Abel', 'Joseph', 'Daniel', and 'The Prodigal Son', Incidents of the lives of the Saints, such as St. Clement and St. Nicolas, have also been dramatised and played. Occasionally, the Catholic boys play, on their school stage, some farce specially translated for them into English or into Hindi from the works of eminent French dramatists like Racine and Moliere. In these plays, the Catholic Fathers have introduced some imitations of the choral songs of ancient Greece. The airs of the songs are either Chota Nagpurian or European. An excellent musical band has also been organised by the boys of the Ranchi Roman Catholic Schools. St. John's School has also a well-equipped infirmary attached to it. Besides these school infirmaries, every Missionary centre has a dispensary of its own where the clergyman in charge distributes medicines to Christians as well as non-Christians.

The same year in which St. John's School was raised to the Middle English Standard, a more ambitious institution was started by the Rev. Father Grosjean, then Rector of the Mission. This was the Apostolic School of Ranchi. Originally housed in a small building by the side of the St. John's School, it was removed two years later to a fine building constructed to accommodate the pupils and the Principal. Besides a large hall, several class-rooms, dormitories, and Principal's quarters, it has a nice chapel and an infirmary attached to it. This school aims at preparing for the priesthood such of the comparatively intelligent boys amongst the Christians as feel spontaneously called to it. It began with nine boys and now counts twenty pupils on its rolls. And it is worthy of note that the institution is now so popular amongst the Mundas and Uraons that several applications for admission had to be recently rejected for want of accommodation. The majority of its *alumni* are Munda and Uraon boys of the Ranchi District, and only a few are Eurasian boys from the Calcutta and Darjeeling Mission Schools. After a five years' course in Latin, English, Mathematics, History, Geography, Declamation, Music, Solfeggio, Gymnastics, etc. in the Ranchi Apostolic School, the successful students are sent to the Papal Seminary at Kandy in Ceylon for a further seven years' course—namely, a three-year course in Philosophy and a four-year course in Theology. It is reported that the Munda and Uraon students of the school generally show great aptitude for these studies and are very hard-working. The success of this school will be watched with great interest by all well-wishers of the aborigines.

The central Girls' Schools of the Chota Nagpur Catholic Mission are those at Ranchi, Khunti, Rengari in Pargana Biru, and Tongo in Paragana Borway. These are all excellent institutions under the efficient management of European nuns who are assisted in their work by a band of Munda, Uraon, and Kharia 'Sisters'. Of these schools we shall only describe the one at Ranchi which may be taken as typical of the rest. The Ranchi Catholic Girls' School was started in the year 1890 by an Irish congregation of nuns called the Lorettine Nuns well known in Calcutta for the great boarding house and Loretto School in Chowringhee and the excellent Orphanage at Entally. In January, 1903, a second congregation of nuns known as the Ursuline Nuns came out from Europe and took charge of the Catholic Girls' School and boarding house at Ranchi. This school is divided into three departments. The first department is conducted in accordance with Government regulations and is attended by about two hundred girls who receive education up to the Upper Primary standard. The second department counts over four hundred girls on its rolls during the cold season (from November to February) when the girls are no longer required to assist their parents in agricultural work. These girls receive only an elementary education. All the girls in these two departments are aboriginals and free-boarders. The third and lowest department is attended by native Christian children of ages varying from two to seven years. The parents of these children are generally day-labourers in the town of Ranchi. Instruction is given to these children on the Kindergarten method. The number on the rolls of this Kindergarten department is now sixty.

The next institution we shall describe is the first as also the best of its kind in Chota Nagpur. This is the Ranchi Catholic Mission Lace School, which was started in the year 1905. This school is meant for Indian Catholic women living in the town of Ranchi and its suburbs. At present more than one hundred aboriginal women daily attend this Lace School. Most of these pupils are married women with children to look after. To suit their convenience, the hours of work are so arranged that they can go home and attend to their domestic duties twice in the day and finally return home in the evening. Nor is daily attendance compulsory. It is reported that these aboriginal women learn the art of lace-making in an incredibly short time. And the excellent laces they turn out are said to be in great demand in Calcutta and even in far-away Europe. Every pupil of the Lace School is paid by the school authorities at a fixed rate for every yard of lace she turns out in the week. And thus, these poor women who could formerly earn but a few pice a day by cutting and selling grass or by working as day-labourers in the town of Ranchi and its suburbs, now earn a decent livelihood by attending the Lace School. And a visit to the Ranchi Catholic Lace School will convince you that it will be hard to find anywhere else a happier and more contented group of hundred women than those who find work there.

From the very commencement of their work in Chota Nagpur, the Catholic Fathers perceived that unless effective means were devised to improve the material condition of their converts, religion will have very little hold on their minds. Agriculture has formed the main, and practically the sole, occupation of the aborigines of the Ranchi District. But the lands of the district are not particularly fertile, and about a quarter of the entire area of the district is unculturable. The Munda or Uraon has generally a large family to maintain, and the agricultural holding of the aboriginal ryot hardly yields produce sufficient for the consumption of himself and his family even for six months in the year. And, as a consequence, many an aboriginal ryot of the district live in a state of chronic indebtedness. With a view to the amelioration of the economic condition of the Christian converts of the Mission and to train them for some other occupation besides agriculture, the Catholic Mission Industrial School was opened at Ranchi in the year 1894. It was intended to turn out good carpenters and masons. This institution which did good work in its time was discontinued after a few years, when a more ambitious industrial school was started by this Mission at Khunti in the centre of the Munda country. At Ranchi, however, a large tile factory was opened by the Rev. Father Hoffmann in the year 1908, which now trains a number of Munda and Uraon boys and young men in the manufacture of roofing and flooring tiles with cement and sand. The secrets of the art of polishing, colouring and enamelling tiles and making floral decorations on them are also being taught in the factory.

The Khunti Roman Catholic Industrial School to which we referred in the last paragraph, was started by the late Rev. Father Vandaele who was himself proficient in Mechanics. This institution consists of four principal departments, viz. the weaving and dyeing department, the carpentry department, the iron-works department, and the silk-worm-rearing department. Of these four departments the first deserves special mention. The proud and conservative Mundas have a strong prejudice against weaving, which is done in a Munda village by a caste called *Penrais* or *Panrs*. A Munda who weaves cloth with his own hands loses his caste. Father Vandaele cast about for some means to break this prejudice and a happy idea struck him. He thought of the Japanese improved handlooms which are worked by the feet alone, and inquired of a number of Mundas if they would have any objection to weaving with a machine in which the hands would not have to be used. On the Mundas agreeing to handle such machines, he procured a number of them, and all the looms were soon occupied. Under Father Vandaele's directions, a few more looms of the same pattern as the imported Japanese looms, were also made in his own Industrial School. On the sudden death of the Rev. Father Vandaele, the school was placed under the Rev. Father De Staercke who had once been connected with a big factory of weaving and spinning looms in Europe. Again and again the Mundas have made difficulties about working at these looms, so that at present the weaving department of the school is mostly attended by Uraon young men. What will be the ultimate success of this department, it is difficult to predict. But, at all events, splendid efforts are being made, and no trouble is being spared by the Catholic Fathers. Father De Staercke effected great improvements in the weaving department and also in the carpentry and iron-works departments. He procured another dozen Japanese looms, and had six plain looms of European pattern made in the Khunti school workshop. He also began giving practical instructions in the art of dyeing both cotton and silk. For the iron-works department, an up-to-date lathe was brought out from Europe about two years ago. The silk-worm-rearing department was added only last year, and thousands of mulberry trees have since been grown to rear silk-worm cocoons. The outturn this year has amounted to about fifty thousand cocoons. This industry is a very profitable one and is now in great favour in England, France, Italy, Russia, Turkey and Japan. It has been an old industry in Lower Bengal and in various other parts of India. Although this industry has been known in the adjoining districts of Singbhum and Manbhum, it does not seem to have ever before been introduced in the Ranchi District. And this department of the Khunti Catholic Industrial School promises a bright future for the Catholic Munda youth.

If the Khunti Industrial School is calculated to effect a great improvement in the material condition of the Catholic Mundas, by far the grandest philanthropic organisation of the Catholic Mission is the Chota Nagpur Catholic Co-operative Credit Society, started by the Rev. Father J. Hoffmann. Of this institution, the Government Report on the working of the Co-operative Societies in Bengal for 1909-1910, writes :

The scheme cannot fail of ultimate success, and it is bound sooner or later to effect an economic revolution in Chota Nagpur. It is doubtful, however, whether such an ambitious scheme will succeed anywhere else or under any other circumstances. To carry through a scheme like this requires Father Hoffmann's singleness of purpose and devotion, and an organisation such as that possessed by the Roman Catholic Mission in Chota Nagpur.

In fact, Father Hoffmann's scheme is a unique experiment, for it reverses the ordinary method of organising co-operative societies as isolated autonomous societies, and begins with the formation of a Central Banking Union and then seeks gradually to evolve autonomous rural units out of it. With regard to the constitution of this society, the same Government Report writes :

To make any impression on the aboriginal tribes by means of work of ordinary lines would be a slow and tedious process. And the problem before us is how to give the aboriginal tribes the full advantages of co-operation in order to prevent their further exploitation by their more advanced and pushful neighbours and to enable them to hold their own in the economic struggle. Father Hoffmann's Society in Ranchi...offers a practical solution of the problem. It is a large centralized society embracing the whole Roman Catholic population of Ranchi and formed with the object of enabling the members of the Mission to constitute themselves into a system of federated and autonomous societies within the central institution. The Society is managed by a central committee of management which sits in Ranchi town and conducts all its affairs. The area of operation is divided into some sixteen circles corresponding to Missionary circles, each in charge of a Missionary. The circles again are divided into villages or groups of villages, each of which forms a rural unit. The unit is in form practically a small Reiffeisen Society. It has its own punchayat and supervisors, and keeps its own accounts and administers its own loans. For the present, each rural unit conducts all business on behalf of the Central Society.

The Chota Nagpur Catholic Co-operative Credit Society was registered under Act X of 1904, on the 2nd December, 1909. By the end of June 1910, as many as 229 rural units were constituted and the Society had realised a capital of Rs. 22,845 3as, and every succeeding month is bringing in additions to this capital.[43] For the Society's headquarters at Ranchi, a fine two-storied building with a strong-room, rooms for the stores department, the banking department, the Director's office, the accountant's office, and so forth, was erected last year. Tracts in Hindi and Mundari written by Father Hoffmann to explain the system and its advantages have been printed and circulated amongst the Catholic population of Chota Nagpur. Again and again, Father Hoffmann has been making long tours throughout the Ranchi district to preach to his Christians the advantages of co-operative banks. In these preaching tours he himself practises what he

[43]By March 1911, the capital rose to Rs. 37,709.

advised other members of the Co-operative Credit Societies' Conference that sat at Calcutta last year to do.   He then said :

> You must yourself be imbued, as it were, with the inner spirit and the high aims and the enthusiasm of a Reiffeisen, and then, in a language and a style adapted to the present mental condition of the Indian cultivator, write, so to say, on his mind in clear lines and vivid colours the deeply human beauty of the Reiffeisen system and its palpable and immense advantages.

We have written at comparative length about this Society, because to us it appears to hold out the brightest promise for the future social and economic regeneration of the Mundas, Uraons and Kharias who form a considerable portion of the population of the Ranchi District.

When one thinks of the ever-increasing and splendidly organised educational and benevolent institutions of the Catholic Mission, the self-sacrificing zeal with which each Missionary devotes himself, heart and soul, to the work entrusted to him, the obviously simple and even ascetic habits of life of the Catholic Fathers and Brothers, approximating to Oriental ideals of a religous life, and the picturesque forms and ceremonials connected with Catholic worship, which are calculated to appeal to the Oriental mind,—one is inclined to believe that by degrees the Catholic Mission may not improbably draw into its fold the majority of the aboriginal population of the Ranchi District.   An eminent Church-of-England Divine, the Venerable H. B. Hyde, Archdeacon of Madras, in a recent article in the *Guardian*, traces the expansion of the Catholic Mission in India to almost the same causes that we have indicated above.   Writes he :

> The majority of Christians in India thus belong to the Roman Communion.   The Roman Catholic community in India is now elaborately organized, is in command of immense resources in money, and is administered with admirable ability and always with a view to its expansion by means of missionary enterprise and the absorption of Christians of other confessions through the influence of ever-multiplying and ever-improving educational institutions....
>
> The treasury of the Propaganda and those of the great

Missionary Associations of Paris, and Milan, of the Society of Jesus, and of several missionary Orders pour funds into the country; while convents of foreign nuns, admirably equipped as seminaries of female education, are becoming numerous everywhere. Roman Brotherhoods and Sisterhoods carry on also other benevolent works by means of hospitals, charity homes, dispensaries, orphanages and refuges of all kinds. But the main streams of influence are connected with education, both primary and secondary, and also academies of the highest standard....The influence quickly established over their pupils, particularly by the nuns, is profound and life-long. The influence of the Irish Christian Brothers and that of the Jesuit teachers is scarcely less penetrating. The authority exercised over the heart and imagination of an impressionable boy by a teacher (even though he be a foreigner and an indifferent athlete), who has obviously no other aim in life than to be a school-master for the sake of the cause of Christ, is naturally far greater than that even of an English graduate who is teaching for the sake of a salary.

With regard to the evangelization of the heathen and the harvest of converts from Protestantism, Roman missionaries rely much more than we do upon the natural instincts of Oriental races. Our missions undoubtedly hold up a high and strict standard of morals and devotion, but we, for the most part, provide for religious expression by even more austere forms of the already austere forms of public worship approved by puritanized English taste. On the other hand, the Roman missionary system provides the Oriental with something to see and to do as well as something to say and to hear; and full advantage is taken of all that can be made picturesque in the Church Festivals, particularly by public processions.

To return to the political and social history of the Mundas and their country. Although, after the pacification of the agrarian disturbances of the years 1889 and 1890, the unrest in the Ranchi District had, to all appearance, subsided, a good deal of fermentation was seething below the surface. And outward signs of ferment were not long in coming. The months of July and August, 1895, witnessed a strange movement in the heart of the Munda country. The discontent of the Mundas once more found exaggerated and distorted expression in the preachings of one Birsa Munda, a youth of about twenty-one years of age, an inhabitant of village Chalkad in Thana Tamar.   This young man possessed remarkably attractive features for a Munda, —a face intelligent and smiling, and withal pensive and thoughtful.   He had received a little education and a smattering of English in the German Mission School at Chaibassa. From German Protestantism, the boy soon reverted to the old Munda faith of his ancestors.   These were but unconscious preparations for a new religion he himself was ere long to preach. Hindu ideas, too, of external and internal purity appear to have exerted a strong fascination over his mind.

The first idea of propagating a new religion was apparently accidental and rather curious.   In the early monsoon of the year 1895, this future prophet was out in the jungle with another Munda youth of about his own age, but much inferior to him in intelligence.   A thunder-storm overtook them in the jungle, when a brilliant flash of lightning passed over Birsa's features.   Just at that moment, Birsa's companion happened to turn his eyes towards him, and was struck with astonishment at seeing Birsa's face changed for the moment from its ordinary brown-black colour to a glowing red and white ! On his companion describing to Birsa the marvel he had just witnessed, the quick-witted Birsa was put in mind of his old Biblical studies, and promptly declared he was just having a revelation from the Deity, and that more miracles were forthcoming!

On his return home, Birsa's companion lost no time in spreading the news of Birsa's marvellous interview with the Deity, with such additional details as a dazed imagination could suggest. A Munda mother first arrived with her baby, whom the fond mother fancied to have been ailing.   Birsa solemnly touched the baby, calmly breathed over it, sonorously chanted some *mantras* in an unintelligible jargon, and confidently declared the baby cured; —and, lo and behold! the baby was found all right from that moment! The supernatural powers of the young miracle-worker were now established beyond doubt.   His fame spread to the remotest corner of the Munda country.   Expectations ran high. The credulous Mundas and even non-Mundas flocked in from all directions to see the young prophet newly arisen in the realm. It was in the depth of the rainy season.   Birsa's village was in the heart of a jungle tract.   There were no spare huts in the small

village in which the large crowds who came up every day could
seek shelter from the rain.   Heedless of the inclement weather,
the inconvenient journey through the woods, and the not less
inconvenient camping under trees or under bamboo umbrellas
planted on the ground to serve as protection against the rain,
the pilgrims stayed on at Chalkad as long as the scanty store
of rice they had carried with them lasted.   The lame, the halt,
the blind, the sick, came in shoals to Birsa to be healed.   Birsa
calmly repeated his strange-sounding incantations, and solemnly
gave his assurance that they would soon get well again if only they
had faith enough in him.   When complaints reached the young
miracle-worker that certain persons who had received his ministrations were not yet cured, he silenced such sceptical suggestions
with the solemn assurance that those people had not approached
him in the proper attitude of reverence !

The intelligent Birsa before long perceived that his hold on the
people's mind required some more stable basis than a shaky reputa-
tion for miracles.   For a few days, he sat solemn and silent, revolving the matter in his mind.   And, at length, the prophet
opened his lips.   Out came the message he had received from
Sing Bonga Himself for the salvation of his tribe.   Hundreds of
Mundas listened with eager and reverent attention to every word
that fell from his hallowed lips.   The Mundas were henceforth
to worship one God only.   They were to give up their customary
sacrifices to a multitude of *Bongas* or deities, abstain from eating
any animal food, lead good lives, observe cleanliness in their
personal habits, and wear the *janeu* or sacred thread in the manner
of the twice-born Hindu castes.   Such were the doctrines of his
new religion,—apparently a mixture of Christianity and Hinduism.
It would have been all right if the young propagandist had stopped
here.   But mad fanaticism soon took hold of him.   It was perhaps
his overzealous followers who at length spoiled him.   For, Birsa
counted within a short time a large following of devoted disciples,
which, in the beginning, included almost the whole of Mundadom,
even Christian converts not excepted.   These, with the love of apotheosis so natural to some men, soon came to regard him as *Bhagwan*
or God Himself.   *Dharti Aba*, or the Father of the World, was a
favourite name applied to Birsa by his disciples.   In keeping with
his new position, Birsa now announced that on a near date which he
named, fire and brimstone would descend from heaven and destroy

all men on earth save and except those who had the good sense
to repair to Chalkad and stay near him on that day. They were
to put on new clothes for the occasion. And, it is said, that, for a
time, the demand for clothes became so great in the Murhu and
other neighbouring markets that it considerably exceeded the
supply.

The appointed day at length arrived. At sunrise on that day,
village Chalkad presented a unique spectacle. Thousands
of Mundas,—men, women, and children,—from far and near,
might be seen waiting in breathless suspense for the arrival of the
fateful hour. As morning wore on, the excitement grew more and
more intense. Just when the crowd were on the tiptoe of expectation, the *Bhagwan* stood up to speak. The vast assembly were all
ears. But,—good heavens !—what disappointing news was this !
The *Bhagwan* intimated that there was some probability that the
catastrophe might, after all, be postponed for a time ! It all
depended upon whether a piece of string which he now tied up
between two trees, snapped or not. To the utter disappointment of
the assembled Mundas, neither did the string give way nor did
the non-Birsaite world come to an end on that day.

The authorities now saw that Birsa's pretensions had exceeded
the bounds of permissible nonsense. A number of Police constables
who had been deputed to watch his proceedings were roughly
handled by Birsa's followers. Their bedsteads and other belongings were thrown into a river by the foolish fanatics.
Matters gradually began to assume a serious aspect. The
rumour got abroad that the massacre of all unbelievers was
decided upon and a date fixed for the purpose. Attempts at
arrest were, for a time, strenuously resisted, till at length, one night,
mounted on an elephant, the District Superintendent of Police
with twenty armed policemen at his back made his appearance in
the village, and, with great courage and adroitness, pounced upon
the sleeping Birsa in his den, gagged his mouth with his pocket
handkerchief, took him up on his elephant before the sleeping
multitude of Birsaites at Chalkad could get up and offer resistance.
When, in the morning, Birsa's followers woke up to find their
Master mysteriously spirited away in the night, they remembered
Birsa's recent prophecy that even though the Government might
capture him and send him to prison, he would transport himself
bodily back to his home at Chalkad on the fourth day from his

arrest, leaving a log of wood at the jail for his substitute.   The prophecy was now circulated by those who had heard it made. This announcement naturally brought the whole country-side once more to Chalkad.   Streams of men and women again began to pour in from all directions to the *Bhagwan's* village. And, on the fourth day from the arrest, as many as seven thousand people, it is said, once more assembled there.   When, however, the prophecy was falsified by the event, a number of Birsaites wavered in their faith.

Reports of a fresh incident, however, now opportunely arrived from Ranchi, and helped sustain the faith of a large number of Birsaites in their *Bhagwan*.   In the Ranchi Jail, there had been a small barn with mud-walls.   In it a large quantity of grain stored in gunny-bags had been stowed away, supported against the wall. The weight of these sacks proved too much for the thin mud-wall which gave in, the very day Birsa was taken to the jail.   A distorted version of this incident found its way into the Munda country, and the rumour spread that the jail-walls came down the very moment Birsa *Bhagwan* entered the jail-gates.

Some of Birsa's principal followers were, however, presently afforded the opportunity of personally testing the value of this story about the jail-walls.   For, they were soon afterwards arrested and incarcerated in the same jail with their Master.   Birsa and his arrested followers were now taken from Ranchi to Khunti.   A trial at Khunti, in the heart of the Munda country, would, it was expected, give an object-lesson to the people who had been deluded by Birsa's pretensions.   After the trial had commenced, on the 24th of October, on Birsa's followers appearing to threaten violence, the proceedings had to be stopped.   A number of these followers were promptly arrested, and Birsa and the arrested Birsaites were led back to Ranchi to take their trial there.   It was in November, 1895, that Birsa was sentenced to undergo rigorous imprisonment for two years and a half.   His followers who had been co-accused with him were also sentenced to various terms of imprisonment, while those who had been arrested during the trial at Khunti were acquitted, as it was found that they really meant no harm but that their language had been misunderstood.   The Rev. Father Hoffmann, than whom no one knows the Mundas better, rendered great assistance to the authorities by explaining the real state of things.

The last embers of the fire of enthusiasm which Birsa *Bhagwan* had kindled had hardly died away, when, on the occasion of the celebration of the Diamond Jubilee of the reign of Empress Victoria, Birsa Munda was released from jail, sometime before the expiry of the term of his sentence. And Birsa lost no time in gathering around him once more a large number of followers. His first move after his release was to occupy the old Hindu temple at Chutia. The object of this visit was probably to assert his supposed claim to the Chota Nagpur Raj of which Chutia was an ancient seat. Some of the Hindu images in the temple, Birsa and his followers wantonly desecrated. They next proceeded to perform some ceremonies of their own in the temple. While the fanatics were thus engaged at dead of night, the Hindu residents of Chutia surprised them and managed to arrest four of Birsa's followers. In the confusion and darkness, Birsa himself managed to escape. This happened in the last week of January, 1897. The arrested Birsaites were duly tried and punished for this outrage on the religious feelings of the Hindus of Chutia.

For nearly two years after this, although the agitation in connection with the apotheosis of Birsa was going on among the Mundas in the south and south-east of the Ranchi district, the *Bhagwan* himself did not stand out prominently before the public. His followers gave out that the *Bhagwan* had left the world for a while.

For a time, indeed, things appeared to have quieted down, and the police officers who had been stationed in the villages which Birsa used to frequent, were withdrawn. The Government, ever anxious to promote the welfare of its subjects, now applied itself to devising measures to ensure permanent peace and unbroken prosperity to the district. With a view to achieving this end, a Bill for the commutation of prædial services in Chota Nagpur was introduced into the Bengal Council and passed into law as Act IV of 1897. And the people were assured that this measure was a preliminary, and a preliminary only. The Lieutenant Governor, Sir John Woodburn, visited the District in November, 1898, and his Chief Secretary who accompanied him fully explained the views of the Government to the leaders of the Sardar Agitation and their Counsel from Calcutta.

It was not in Birsa's nature, however, to remain idle for any length of time. In the year 1899, he once more emerged from his temporary eclipse. He felt the pulse of his people with tolerable accuracy and now made a dramatic bid for renewed popularity by adding dangerous political tenets to his innocent religious teachings. Taking advantage of the seeming sense of security of the authorities, Birsa began to flit about here and there in the south and south-west of the District, stirring up the minds of a large number of Mundas to a frantic pitch of infatuation. He also appointed 'Prachars' or preachers of his own to disseminate his religious and political cult amongst his fellow tribesmen. The then state of sullen discontent amongst the Munda tenantry probably suggested, as it certainly helped, the dissemination of his revolutionary teachings. It is said he also compiled a book of prayers for the use of his disciples, amongst whom the book was circulated in manuscript.

Of the strained relations between the Mundas and their landlords in those days, the Report of the Land Revenue Administration of the Lower Provinces for the year 1897-98 said :

In Lohardugga, the Zemindars are said to take all they can in the way of rent and labour out of the raiyats, especially the aboriginal raiyats, whom they coerce by threatening to oust them from their lands. The raiyats, on the other hand, try to evade payment of their just dues.

And in the Report of the following year, we are told :

There is no change to report in the relations of landlords and tenants (of the Lohardugga District), which continue most unsatisfactory, the landlords trying to get all they can out of the raiyats, legally or otherwise; the raiyats where they resist at all, refusing to pay their lawful dues....Disputes as to rights in jungle are also becoming very common, and unless something in the way of a settlement of such rights can be made, either the old rights of the cultivators or else the jungles themselves will shortly disappear over a great part of the district.

Besides grievances as to rights in land, the tenants had other sufferings and tribulations during these three years. They suffered from a severe famine in 1897,—the severest in the District

13

within living memory ; the year 1898 was marked by a widespread epidemic of cholera ; and before the tenantry could recover from the effects of the terrible famine of 1897, the winter crop, in 1899, too, proved a total failure.   Birsa and his 'Prachars' made capital out of this state of general discontent and suffering.   In the last three months of the year 1899, numerous meetings were held in different parts of the Munda country.   Either Birsa himself or one or other of his principal followers presided over each of those meetings.   The principal meetings were held on Dumari Hill in October, 1900, at Marihatu about the same time, at Satal and at Poje about the middle of December, at Bartoli, a fortnight before Christmas, at Kotagara two days before Christmas, and at Bicha- kuti on Christmas-Eve, 1899.   All these meetings were held at night, at all these meetings the grievances of the Mundas were recounted, and vehement language was used to inflame the passions of the people and stir them to blood and mutiny.   The coming Christmas-Eve was fixed upon as the date for commencing their revenge against Rajas, Hakims, Zemindars, Christians and Samsars (non-Christians).   The Christian Mundas were to receive especial attention, as they had deserted the *Bhagwan* since his first arrest and imprisonment.   Here is a description of the meeting on Dumari Hill given by one of Birsa's own followers in Court :

We arrived at the meeting place before midnight.   The meeting place was on the top of the hill.   When we arrived we found about sixty or eighty persons assembled.   Birsa sat on a stone.   There was cloth spread on the stone on which Birsa sat.   Birsa sat facing the east and the rest of the people sat around him.   About midnight everyone had assembled and shortly afterwards the moon rose.   When everyone was assemb- led, Birsa asked what troubles we suffered from.   Jagai of Kudda and three or four others whose names 1 do not know said that we suffered from the oppression of Zemindars and Jagirdars and the Thikadars.   Birsa then told us to make bows and arrows and *baluas*, as we were greatly oppressed.   We all said we would make them and Birsa said that he had given a similar order at the other meetings in different parts of the coun- try, and that everyone who belonged to his religion was making weapons. Birsa said that the weapons were to be used for killing Thikadars and Jagirdars and Rajas and Hakims and Christians.

Some of the persons assembled asked if the Rajas and Hakims and Christians would not shoot with their guns and kill us. Birsa replied that we would not be struck, that the guns and bullets would turn to water, and said that on the day of the great Christian festival two weeks later, he would come, and that we were to have the weapons ready. The meeting broke up at cock-crow.[44]

In November, 1899, Birsa left his village on a new errand. With a few chosen followers, he visited the *Nawratan* buildings at Doesa, and from there brought what he called *Bir-da* (literally, hero-water). This water he sprinkled on the persons of his followers with certain ceremonies, and assured them that thenceforth they would be matchless in fight, and that the Rajas, Hakims, Zemindars, Jagirdars, Padris and Prachars would all be defeated and slain. "When these would all be destroyed," said he, "the country would be ours." A number of more sensible Birsaities were not convinced by this insane logic, and naturally shrank back from such mad teachings, and finally gave up Birsa's religion.

In meetings held on Christmas-Eve, 1899, different persons were told off to different directions to commit murders and arsons. And a large number of preconcerted murderous attacks and cases of arson occurred simultaneously in different parts of Thanas Khunti, Tamar, Basia and Ranchi. Over one hundred instances of such attacks were deposed to at the subsequent trials. Among other places, an out-house in the Sarwadag Mission compound, was burnt down that Christmas-Eve.

At Ranchi a few barbed arrows were shot in the dark near the German Church, and a carpenter was so severely wounded that he died shortly afterwards in hospital.

A German merchant of the name of Mr. Caesar was shot dead in a village in the depth of a jungle in pargana Sonepur. Two arrows flew into the Murhu Anglican school-house where the Rev. Mr. Lusty, who had been, to some extent, instrumental in the first arrest of Birsa, was listening to the hymns of the boys that Christmas-Eve; but fortunately the arrows missed their aim and did no harm. The Rev. Father Carbery, then of

[44]This is from the recorded deposition of Ratan Munda of Kuda, prosecution witness No. 1 in the case of Emp. *v.* Dukhu Pahan and 31 others (the third batch of Birsaites), before the Committing Joint Magistrate.

Sarwadag, received an arrow on his chest, and narrowly escaped death. The Rev. Father Hoffmann was likewise providentially saved, two arrows shot at him that evening having missed their aim. At village Burju, a police constable and four chowkidars were put to death by the Birsaites.

For a few days there was something like a panic in Ranchi, and it was apprehended that the Birsaites might any day assail the town on a sudden. On the 7th of January, 1900, news reached the authorities at Ranchi that a body of three hundred Mundas, armed with bows and arrows, battle-axes and spears, had attacked the Khunti police station, killed one of the constables, and set fire to some houses. The Commissioner of the Division, Mr. Forbes, and the Deputy Commissioner of the District, Mr. Streatfield, at once hastened up to Khunti with 150 men of the Native Infantry then stationed at Doranda. On the 9th of January, they came up with the Munda 'army', now stationed on Dumari Hill, three miles south of Saiko, and close to villages Janumpiri, Gutuhatu, and Kurapurthi. To defend their position, the Mundas had erected a large number of stockades at intervals. Mr. Streatfield at first tried his best, by explaining the position to the insurgents in their own language, to induce them to lay down their arms. The infatuated fanatics derided his proposals and defied his strength. And thus there was no help for him but to order the troops to fire. The defenders of the position now ran down a deep gully into the jungle beyond. And it was then discovered that behind their fortification of stockades they had with them women and children and large stores of clothing, food and cooking utensils. "Four Mundas were found to have been killed, and three wounded, and the dead bodies of three women and a boy were discovered in the jungle."[45]

One hundred and fifty military police were now despatched to the disturbed parts and a large number of Birsaites were soon captured and sent up to Ranchi for trial. Birsa was traced to the bordering district of Singbhum and brought to Ranchi under arrest. During the pendency of the case, the *Bhagwan* departed this life in the Ranchi Jail. Of the eighty-seven Birsaites who had

[45] Vide Administration Report of the Lower Provinces for the year 1899-1900, p. 4. See also articles on The Advent of Birsa by the Rev. G. H. Lusty in the *Wide World Magazine* for October, 1910, and in the *Chota Nagpur Mission Paper* for October, 1895.

been committed to the Sessions, capital sentence was inflicted on two for murders committed during the revolt, while others were sentenced to various terms of imprisonment or transportation. On appeal to the High Court, a few were let off, and the sentences on a few others were reduced.

Thus ended the last of Munda risings in Chota Nagpur, known as the 'Birsaite Rebellion' of 1899-1900.

The authorities were now more anxious than ever to devise some radical cure for the discontent amongst the Mundas which had now become chronic. Sir John Woodburn came to the conclusion that "the essence of the whole business was to get a correct record of existing facts in tenants' holdings. And it was decided, in 1901, to effect a survey and settlement of the Munda country. By Bengal Government order of the 18th February, 1902, Survey and Settlement operations commenced in the 1,846 square miles constituting the Munda country. This comprised the whole of thanas Tamar, Khunti, and Bano, one-third of each of the thanas of Basia and Karra, and one-fourth of thana Kolebira, besides 645 acres in the south of the Ranchi thana. And in the light of the results of the investigations made by Mr. E. Lister, the eminently able officer to whom the settlement of the Munda country was entrusted, the Chota Nagpur Landlord and Tenant Procedure Act of 1879, and the Commutation Act of 1897 were amended by Bengal Act V of 1903. The Rev. Father Hoffmann did yeoman's service to the cause of the Mundas by explaining most lucidly to the authorities the true nature and extent of their rights in Khuntkatti villages and lands. The amending Act dealt chiefly with the rights of the Mundari Khuntkattidars or original clearers of the soil, as the treatment hitherto accorded to them was, in the words of the Select Committee, "one of the chief causes of the agitation which has long disturbed the people locally known as the Mundaris'.

When these amending Acts were being discussed and passed, it was understood, that a consolidated Act would be passed at an early date. It was reserved for Sir Andrew Fraser's Government to give the long-promised Act to the district. Sir Andrew evinced almost a personal interest in the welfare of the Ranchi district, and, by his wise measures, succeeded in quieting the unrest of a century. Here is the account given in the Government Report[46]

[46]The Administration of Bengal under Sir Andrew Fraser,K.C.S.I. pp. 60.-64.

of Sir Andrew's legislative and other measures for the Ranchi
district :

Briefly, the position when Sir Andrew Fraser assumed charge[47]
of the Province was as follows : For generations the aborigines
of Chota Nagpur had been in a state of unrest owing to their
inability to protect what they believe to be their rights in the
land.   They enjoy special rights and privileges in respect of the
lands cultivated by them, and these are recognised by the indigenous landlords.   But, for many years past, these landlords
have gradually been losing their estates to aliens, chiefly of the
money-lender class ; and the latter when they came into possession, always endeavoured to break down the rights of the cultivators and to enhance their rents.   The result was that there
had been constant disputes between landlords and tenants, and,
occasionally, armed risings of the latter.   To remedy this state
of affairs, the Tenures Act of 1869, and the Landlord and Tenant
Procedure Act of 1879, were passed; but subsequent events,
culminating in another uprising of this clan, showed that further
measures were required to put an end to the legitimate grievances
of the Mundas.   The Government accordingly determined to
have a record-of-rights prepared for the Ranchi District, and the
enquiries thereby originated showed that the aborigines had no
confidence or trust in the Courts, owing chiefly to their mental
inferiority as compared with the Aryans opposed to them.
They were, therefore, made to understand that Government
would, as far as possible, deal with their claims by special enquiry
on the spot, so that there should be no doubt in regard to those
that were recognised.   Accordingly, Act V of 1903 was passed,
and a part of that Act dealt with the subject of Mundari Khuntkatti tenancies.   The Settlement Officer began operations in
the most disturbed portion of the Ranchi District, and succeeded
in restoring, to some extent, confidence in the minds of the aborigines, who had unfortunately been made most suspicious by
past events.

At his first visit to Ranchi in September, 1905, Sir Andrew
Fraser made especial enquiries regarding the progress of the
Settlement and the working of the laws above mentioned.   He

[47] On the 2nd November, 1903

found that through the ignorance of the Courts, aided by the apathy of local officers until more recent years, immense injustice had been done to the Mundas by the agency of the law. The feeling created in the minds of many of them was one of great bitterness against the Government, whose failure to interfere on their behalf they had not been able to understand. This feeling had been fomented by unscrupulous men, who, for their own purposes and pecuniary gain, assisted in overreaching the Mundas, while pretending to be their friends.

Special laws had been made, and an expensive Settlement undertaken in order to check this mischief. But there was a danger of the former being rendered fruitless by the entire ignoring of it by officers trying suits between landlords and tenants and by their want of knowledge of the peculiar customs and tenures existing in Chotanagpur. His Honour, therefore, requested Mr. H. W. C. Carnduff, C. I. E., whom he had appointed to be Judicial Commissioner of Chota Nagpur, to bring out an annotated edition of the local Tenancy Act, and publish, as an appendix, a paper by Mr. E. Lister, I.C.S., the Settlement Officer, and the Rev. Father Hoffmann, S.J., a local missionary with great knowledge of the people, in which a full account was given of the land-system of the Mundari country in Ranchi.... These measures have been attended with excellent results.

The enquiries made by Sir Andrew Fraser also showed that, although much good was being done by the Settlement, other measures were still necessary, and it was arranged that Mr. F. A. Slacke, C.S.I., Commissioner, should draw up with Mr. Lister a joint note showing what further remedial action was required. This note was received by His Honour in August, 1905, and the measures therein indicated as necessary are now in course of being taken. One new sub-division has already been opened at Khunti, and it is in contemplation to open two others in the north and south-west of the Ranchi District.

Finally, Sir Andrew Fraser was satisfied that the agrarian law of Chotanagpur needed thorough revision. The experience gained in the Settlement made it clear that the local Tenancy Act failed in various important respects to take due account of the rights enjoyed by the aboriginal cultivators...A rough draft of a revised Bill was prepared in consultation with the officers possessing most knowledge of the agrarian condition of Chotanagpur; and its provisions were discussed in detail during a visit of His Honour at Ranchi in August, 1907, at a series of conferences attended by the local officers and selected representatives of the landlords and tenants of Chotanagpur. The last conference was presided over by His Honour....Practical unanimity was obtained regarding most of the matters dealt with in the revised Bill. This Bill was further revised in accordance with the conclusions then arrived at. It was decided to re-arrange and consolidate the whole of the principal enactments relating to landlord and tenant in Chotanagpur in an entirely new amending Bill. The Bill was introduced in Council and passed into law in 1908.

This Act is intended for the protection of the aboriginal peasantry of Chotanagpur against alien adventurers. Another measure has been brought forward for preserving the status of the large hereditary landlords....The ruin of the old hereditary families also reacts on the peasantry. In Chotanagpur, the landlord is not the absolute owner of the land. The aboriginal ryots enjoy speicial rights in respect of the enjoyment of forest produce, the clearing of waste, and the like. Their rents, also, are very low. The hereditary landlords acquiesce in their enjoyment of these customary rights. But when estates fall into the hands of aliens, the latter invariably claim full proprietary rights, and do all they can to enhance rents. The cultivators are unable to hold their own in the law courts or to cope with the chicanery brought to bear against them. They give way for a time, but, at last, turn on their oppressors and on other foreigners. There have been repeated instances of this in the history of Chotanagpur, the last being the Munda rising of 1899-1900. In circumstances like these, the case for special legislation appeared to the Lieutenant-Governor to be overwhelmingly strong. A Bill to amend the Encumbered Estates Act has accordingly been introduced with provisions enabling the Government to assume the management of estates in such cases.

This amending Bill was passed into law (Act III of 1909) in the opening year of the administration of our present Lieutenant-Governor, Sir Edward Baker.

In the present chapter we have attempted to give a rough outline of the history of the Mundas and their country during the

British period. It is, as we have seen, mainly the history of a constant struggle between the descendants of the original clearers of the soil and the new class of Dikus or alien landlords. This new class of landlords, though in the beginning only entitled to collect the nominal tribute which used to be paid by the different village communities to the Maharaja of Chota Nagpur, in course of time, gradually arrogated to themselves extensive rights to lands, rents, and services. Their continual efforts at breaking the foundations of the old Khuntkatti system, though strenuously resisted from the very outset, have, in most parts of the district, eventually met with more or less complete success. In their barbarous ignorance, the Mundas failed to adapt themselves to their new environment, neglected in the beginning to have recourse to the newly established British Courts of Justice, and, by explaining their position and their grievances clearly to the English officers, to seek redress at their hands. Unmindful of the changed circumstances of the country, heedless of consequences, taking no measure of their own powers, the Mundas foolishly and recklessly sought to end their woes by taking up arms against the sea of troubles that encompassed them. And heavy indeed has been the penalty they have paid for their folly.

The authorities at length had a clear insight into the root of their troubles and grievances. Ever ready to administer impartial justice, and to promote the welfare of all classes of its subjects, the Government finally ordered the preparation of a Record of existing rights which has just been completed. And it is to be expected that the troubles of the Munda country will henceforth be a matter of past history.

To make amends for their loss of many ancient rights, now past all remedy, Providence has vouchsafed a new boon to the Mundas. This is the inestimable boon of education, for which the Mundas must remain forever grateful to the British Government and the Christian Missionaries. The rapid progress in education which the Mundas made in a single generation, attracted the admiration of Lieutenant-Governor Sir John Woodburn, who visited Ranchi in 1898. On his return to Calcutta, he thus described his impressions in a speech on the occasion of St. Andrew's Dinner, in December of that year:

"And while I was speaking of Chotanagpur, I was thinking of

the surprise that awaited me there, even so old an Indian as myself. We are accustomed to hear of, and to speak of, the savage tribes in those hills as almost irreclaimable from the naked barbarism of their nomad life. What did I find ? In the Schools of the Missionaries there are scores of Kol boys, rapidly attaining University standards in education. It was to me a revelation that the savage intellect, which we are all apt to regard as dwarfed and dull and inept, is as acute and quick to acquire knowledge as that of the sons of generations of culture. It seems incredible, but it is a fact, that these Kol lads are walking straight into the lists of competition, on equal terms with the highbred youth of Bengal. This is a circumstance so strange even to me, so striking, so full of significance for the future, that I could not refrain from telling you of this last surprise of this wonderful land we live in."

Since Sir John Woodburn visited Ranchi, education has been spreading much faster amongst the Munda and Uraon youths of Chota Nagpur. It is no longer confined to the sons of the Christian aboriginals alone. The improvement in the material condition and social position of the educated Kol Christians has opened the eyes of his non-Christian brethren to the advantages of education. And, in some of the Government schools and Mission schools of the district, you may now find a sprinkling of non-Christian Munda and Uraon boys eagerly emulating their Hindu, Mahomedan or Christian class-fellows. The boarding-house for non-Christian Kol boys recently started at Ranchi by some patriotic Mundas and Uraons, if properly managed and financed, may ultimately prove an eminently useful institution. It is not to matters educational and spiritual alone that the Chota Nagpur Christian Missions have confined their attention. Thanks to their many-sided activities, and to the ever-ready assistance and encouragement of our benevolent Government, a number of Munda and Uraon young men, trained in the Government and the Mission Industrial Schools, are now making good carpenters, draughtsmen and surveyors. Lace-making and embroidery are now the favourite occupation of an increasing number of Munda and Uraon females. Trade in lac is being pursued by a number of Mundas in Sonepur and the Panch Parganas. Much has been done and is still being done to save the Mundas from the clutches of the usurer, the liquor-seller and the coolie-recruiter.   Co-operative Societies started under the auspices of the Government and of the Christian Missions are eminently calculated to ameliorate the material condition of the tenantry and contribute to their social evolution.

If the advent of the Christian Missions in Chota Nagpur has been a Providential boon to the Mundas and Uraons in having expedited their social and intellectual evolution, the introduction of the Hindu landlords and other Hindu settlers amongst them has not been an unmixed evil.   No dispensation of the Divine Ordainer of things is without some beneficent purpose.   For one thing, it has been their long contact with the Hindus that has raised the Mundas of the eastern parganas of the Ranchi District in the scale of civilisation.   In fact, at the census of 1901, as many as 164, 162 Mundas described themselves as Hindus.   Many of the Hinduised Mundas of the Panch Parganas are, in their manners and intellectual capacity, now hardly distinguishable from other Hindus of equal social status and intellectual culture.   And their comparative freedom from the proverbial Mundari vice of drunkenness is quite remarkable.   Even the earlier phase of the Birsaite movement, before it degenerated by assuming an agrarian and anarchic complexion, affords striking evidence of the influence which Hindu ideas of ceremonial purity and moral life exerted on the religious consciousness of these people.   Nor can the ruder Mundas of the southern and western parganas disclaim all indebtedness to the Hindus.   The influence of Hindu ideas on their religious beliefs and practices, their social customs, their folk-tales and their songs, though not ordinarily apparent on the surface, has been as beneficial as it is deep-seated.   This silent influence is, however, apt to be overlooked in the presence of the crying evils of Zemindary aggression and oppression which afflicted the Mundas during the last two centuries.   But, in this world, rights grow and die, property is acquired and lost, persecution suffered and forgotten, and even bad influences work their evil and wear away in time.   The elevating influences of religion and morals, culture and manners, however, get absorbed in the life-blood of the nation, and endure to the end of time, unless destroyed by strong counteracting influences.

It is to the British Government and the Christian Missions, however, that the Munda owes the heaviest debt of gratitude.

One sometimes fancies that when during years of oppression and persecution in the past, the pitiful groans of the Mundas rent the air, Heaven in His infinite mercy decreed that out of the ashes of those ancient Munda peasant-proprietors there should in time emerge a better class of their descendants, educated and enlightened and capable of competing on equal terms in the race of life with their more civilised fellow-men : And the British Government and the Christian Missionary were the selected agents for the execution of this Divine decree. The Mighty Voice went forth 'They must not go, the ancient race !' And still :

> The cry swells loud from shore to shore,
> From emerald vale to mountain hoar,
> From altar high to market-place.

THEY SHALL NOT GO, THE ANCIENT RACE !

CHAPTER VI

THE ETHNOGRAPHY OF THE MUNDAS

"The proper study of mankind is Man."

—Pope

(1) COUNTRY, APPEARANCE AND MATERIAL CONDITION

Introductory

IN the south-western corner of the Province of Bengal, high above the din and bustle of the plains, reposes the picturesque land of the Mūndās, *in* Bengal yet not *of* it. In its physical features, in its geological formation, in its botanical products and its mineral wealth, in its ethnological peculiarities, in its social and political history, Chōtā Nāgpūr presents a striking contrast to the rest of the Province of which administratively it forms a part. Remarkably refreshing is the contrast its blue hills and rugged ravines, green sal jungles and terraced fields of yellow paddy, limpid hill-streams rushing down their narrow beds of rock and sand, and picturesque water-falls leaping over abrupt precipices, present to the monotonous stretch upon stretch of Bengal plains, broken here and there by some muddy meandering creek or 'khāl' or by some mighty river tardily rolling down with its load of loam and silt into the sea.

If the difference in external features between the Chōta Nāgpūr plateaux and the rest of the Province is thus great, the difference in the races and tribes that people the two tracts, their languages, their manners, their religions, their social customs and political history, and last, but not least, their systems of land tenure, is, if possible, still greater.

Number and Habitat

The Mūndās are the most numerous of the so-called Kolarian tribes inhabiting the Chōtā Nāgpūr Division. In the census of 1901, the total number of Mūndās in India, excluding Christian converts, was found to have been 466,668. In Bengal, the total number of Mundas was 438,143, of whom 296,218 were returned

as Animists, 85,410 as Hindus, and 56,575 as Christians. Of
these the whole of Chōtā Nāgpūr contained 344,373, and the
Ranchi District alone 287,105. Although less numerous than the
Dravidian Urāons of the Ranchi District, the Mūndās, as the same
Census Report observes, "have a universally admitted precedence
over the other aboriginals by virtue of their older occupation of the
country, their traditions of rule in it, and their establishment of the
Nāgbansi Maharajas". The Ranchi District, the principal home
of the Mūndās, has an area of 7,103 square miles, and is situated
between 22°20′ and 23°43′ North Latitude, and 84°0′ and 85°54′
East Longitude. It is bounded on the north by the Districts of,
Hāzāribāgh and Pālāmāu, on the east by the District of Mānbhūm
on the south by the District of Singbhum and the Tributary State
of Gāngpur, and on the west by the Pālāmāu District and the
Jāshpūr and Surgujā States.

The great bulk of the Mūndās occupy the south ern, south-western,
and eastern parts of the Rānchi District. The percentage of
Mūndāri population in the different thānās of the District was
ascertained at the Census of 1901, to have been as follows : Khunti,
72 per cent; Tāmār, 72 p. c. ; Bāno, 52 p. c. ; Basia, 39 p.c. ; Kōlebirā,
36 p. c.; Kārrā, 28 p. c.; Silli, 22 p. c.; Rānchi, 18 p. c.; Kōchedegā,
11 p. c.; Māndār, 9 p. c.; Chainpur, 5 p. c.; Toto and Sisai, each
3 p. c.; Palkot and Kūrdeg each 2 p.c.; Lohārdāga, and Bishenpur,
each 1 p. c.

Natural Aspects

The Ranchi District naturally divides itself into two distinct
plateaux, resting respectively at average elevations of 2,000 and
1,000 feet. The higher plateau comprising nearly two-thirds of
the area of the District covers its northern and western parts,
and is connected with the lower plateau lying on the extreme
southern and eastern borders of the District, by rugged precipitous
passes locally called 'ghats'. The plateaux are generally undulat-
ing, and a large number of hills and hillocks, generally of gneiss
formation strike up on every hand. A peculiar hill-feature of the
District is the large number of pāts or isolated tablelands perched
up on lofty hills averaging 3,600 feet above sea-level, which rise
abruptly out of the higher plateau in its north-western corner.
About one-third (32.10 per cent) of the area of the District is still
covered by jungle. The jungles, especially about the ghats or

passes, often present a highly picturesque scenery. The rivers of the District are generally narrow streams of water, usually almost dry except during the rainy season. But some of the 'ghāgs' or waterfalls of the District are magnificent, and any one of them, as the *Imperial Gazetteer of India*[1] observes, would "in a Western country be regarded as worthy of a visit even from a distance". The geological formation of the District is the Archaean or Pre-Cambrian, except a narrow strip on the south which is of Gondwana formation. As for minerals,—limestone, mica, and quartz occur in veins in beds of gneiss, and iron of an inferior kind is to be found throughout the District. In some places in the south-eastern parts of the Tamar Pargana, a soft kind of stealite allied to soapstone is dug out of small mines. The climate of the District is dry, and except in certain portions below the 'ghāts', generally very healthy. The average mean temperature rises from 62.2 in December to 87.8 in May. The mean minimum in the cold season is 51° and the mean maximum in May is 100°. The average annual rainfall varies from 50 to 65 inches.

Names

The name *Mūndā* appears to have been given to this people by their ancient Hindu neighbours. The Mūndās call themselves 'Haro-ko' (men) and their race the Horo (man).[2] The name '*Kōl*' generally applied to the Mūndās and other allied tribes, may not improbably be a transformation of the name *Horo* the initial *h* sound having been emphasised into *k* and the *r* sound softened into *l* by well-known rules of phonetic transition. But whatever be the origin of the name, the Mūndās now strongly resent the appellation *Kol* which appears to have acquired an opprobrious suggestion. They have no objection to the name 'Munda', which in their own language has come to signify a man of substance and, in its special sense, refers to the temporal village-headman. The

---

[1] New Edition (*1908*), Vol. xxi, p. *198*.

[2] Cf. *Arleng* (man), the national name of the Mikirs of Assam, the *Mande* (man), the national name of the Garos of Assam, the *Chingpho*(man), the name of an aboriginal tribe of the Upper Dehung valley of Assam, the *Boro* (man), the national name of the Kachari aborigines. Several other races in various parts of the world call themslves by equivalent words (meaning 'men'), and thus ignore the other families of the human race. Cf. the name Deutsch for the Germanic race.

name Mundari is used as an adjective by British administrators for convenient reference.[3]

As for the name of the country they now inhabit, the Mūndās of our days have no recollection of any name by which it was known prior to the establishment of the Nāgbansi Rājās, after whom it came to be called Nāgpur. It appears probable, however, that the names 'Pulinda-Des' or Paulinda, and 'Dasārna' which occur in early and medieval Sanskrit literature, included the present home of the Mūndās. And it seems pretty certain that the 'Jhārkhand' country of later Sanskrit literature included modern Chōtā Nāgpūr. To the Mahomedan rulers of India the country was known as 'Kokerah'; and the names 'Nagpur' and 'Coira Orissa' also appear to have been occasionally used. The French traveller Tavernier who during his third visit to India in 1643 appears to have passed through the present Rānchi District in his journey from Rudas (Rohtasgarh) to Sumelpour (Sambalpur) seems to refer to this country where he says :

All these thirty leagues you travel through woods is a very dangerous passage, as being very much pestered with robbers.[4]

The earliest British administrators knew the country as Nagpur.[5] But, shortly after British occupation, the country came to be also called 'Chota Nagpur', to distinguish it from the more important Nagpur in the Central Provinces. Thus, in James Rennel's *Map of Hindostan*, prepared in 1792, we find a special map of "The Conquered Provinces on the south of Behar containing Ramgur, Palamow, and CHUTA NAGPOUR with their Dependencies". Walter Hamilton in his *Geographical, Statistical, and Historical*

---

[3] Thoroughly Hinduised Mundas in the Panch Parganas sometimes call themselves 'Bhuinhar Chhatris". In certain parts of the Panch Parganas, however, the Hinduised Mundas as also the Bhumij Mundas arrogate the name 'Munda' exclusively to themselves and call the Mundas of a lower status as 'Mundaris'. and sometimes as 'Urang Mundas' probably to indicate their objectionable Uraon-like habits of eating beef, and other food regarded unclean.

[4] Vide *Tavernier's Travels*, Book 11, Ch. XIII., (Ball's Edition, Vol. 1.)

[5] Vide Captain Camac's letter to the Governor of Bengal, containing "A Narrative of Pallamow and Nagpore Countries", dated Ramgur, the 12th August, 1774.

Description of Hindostan and Adjacent Countries[6], published in London
in the year 1820, as also in his East India Gazetteer,[7] spells the
name of the country as 'Chuta Nagpoor', and explains the name
as meaning 'Little Nagpoor'.   In Sir John Shore's famous Minute
of the 18th September, 1789, the country is called simply 'Nagpore'.
In the *Fifth Report of the Select Committee on the Affairs of the East
India Company*, published in London in 1812, the orthography of
the name is changed into 'Chutea Nagpoor'.   And the Report
goes on to say, "It is also sometimes generally described under the
appellation of Kokerah, more commonly called Nagpoor, from the
diamond mines of that place".   From 'Chutea Nagpoor', the
spelling was soon changed into 'Chutiya Nagpore', and then into
'Chutia Nagpore'.   And it came to be supposed that the name
was derived from village 'Chūtiā', a suburb of the present town of
Ranchi.   Against this derivation it may be pointed out that
Rennel, although spelling the name of the country as 'Chutia
Nagpur', adopts a different spelling, namely, 'Chuttiah', for the
village.   It is also a significant fact that in vernacular documents of
that period, the country was generally described as 'Nagpur
Khurd' or the 'Little Nagpur'.   The spelling 'Chutia Nagpur'
was subsequently abandoned in favour of 'Chota Nagpur' which is
now the accepted form of the name.

Physical Appearance

The physical characteristics of the Mūndās are asserted by
modern Anglo-Indian Ethnologists to be of the Dravidian type.
The colour of the Mūndā's skin is black-brown, not unoften of a
shade approaching black.   The head inclines to be long (doliko-
cephalic), the nose is thick and broad and sometimes depressed
at the root, the lips thick, the facial angle comparatively low, the
face wide and fleshy, the features irregular, the figure squat, the
limbs sturdy and well-formed, and the stature rather short.   The
Mūndā has strong muscles, a good chest, powerful jaws and stomach,
and strong white teeth.   Both men and women, when young,
are comely in appearance.   Of the one hundred Mūndā specimens
whose measurements are given by Sir Herbert Risley,[8] the average

[6] p. 288.
[7] p. 415 (2nd Edition).
[8] Vide Risley's *Tribes and Castes of Bengal*, Vol. 1, pp. 385-393, and *Poeple of
India*. App. IV. p. cxiii.

14

head-measurements are as follows : Length, 185.2, breadth 138.6, and cephalic index 74.5. The highest cephalic index measured was 80.5, whereas the lowest was 68.9.[9] The average nasal index was found to be 89.9, whereas the maximum was 112 and the minimum 74. The average stature was 158.9 centimetres, the maximum height among the hundred specimens having been 171.8, and the minimum 144.6. Of Sir Herbert Risley's one hundred subjects, we may take No. 35 (Ram Sing Munda, aged 39) as a fine specimen. His measurements were—nasal index, 85.1; naso-malar index, 113.2; cephalic index, 75.5; fronto-zygomatic index, 82.6; vertico cephalic index, 74.3; vertico-bimalar, 60.4; vertico-frontal index, 56.1; vertico-bizygomatic index, 67.9; facial angle 69; nasal height, 47; nasal width, 40; bimalar breadth, 113; naso-malar breadth, 128; cephalic length, 184; cephalic breadth 139; and minimum frontal breadth 105. Modern Anglo-Indian Ethnologists would seem to classify the Mūndās and allied tribes raciallly as Dravidians—the same race to which their neighbours the Urāons belong.   More reasonable and correct, however, appears to be the following account given by Dr. A. C. Haddon :

The Munda-speaking peoples are a very ancient element in the population and appear to have been the original inhabitants of the Ganges in Western Bengal. After many wanderings, they settled mainly in Chota Nagpore. Everywhere they have been more or less modified by the Dravidians, and while scattered relics of the languages are preserved, the original physical type appears to have been assimilated to that of the Dravidians, but perhaps it was originally a closely allied type. They may belong to the primitive Indonesian races.[10]

For a better understanding of the principal anthropometric indices, we may mention that Anthropometrists class heads giving cephalic indices (which represent proportion of breadth of skull to length taken as *100*) under *70* as Hyper-dolico-cephalic (very long-headed), from *70* and under *75* as Dolico-cephalic (long-headed), from *75* and under *80* as Meso-cephalic (medium-headed) and from *80* and over as Brachy-cephalic (broad-headed). Similarly noses giving nasal indices (proportion of breadh of nose to its length taken as *100*) of from *50* to *70* are called Leptorhine (fine-nosed), from *70* to *85* as Mesorhine (medium-nosed), and from *85* upwards as Platyrhine (broad-nosed).

[9] In measurements taken by ourselves the lowest cephalic index of a Munda subject measured 67.

[10] *The Races of Man and Their Distribution* (XXth Century Science Series), pp.*64-65*.

Dress

The dress of the Mūndās is very simple and scanty. Their men ordinarily wear loin cloth called *botoi*. This is from six to nine cubits long and has coloured borders at the two ends. On festive occasions, young men and boys wear a longer *botoi*, two ends of which called *bondols* are allowed to hang gaily before and behind almost down to the feet. Young men also wear around the waist a sort of belt called 'kārdhāni.' These are sometimes made of cocoon-silk and called 'lumāng kārdhani'. When made of plaited thread, they are called 'gālāngkrādhāni.' Very old men who sit at home and are unfit for work wear only a piece of cloth about a yard long. This is called 'bāgoā' or 'bhāgoā' in Mundari (*Kowpin* or *langoti* in Hindi), and is passed between the legs and over a string encircling the waist. A small portion of the 'bāgoā' is allowed to hang in front. Besides his loin cloth, the Mūndā uses a piece of cloth as a wrapper for the upper part of his body. This is of two varieties. The larger variety, called *barkhi*, measures about six yards in length, and is doubled up in wearing. The shorter variety is called *pichowri* and is from five to six cubits in length. In the cold weather, the Mūndā generally uses a blanket as a wrapper over his body. But those who cannot afford to buy blankets, use only the *barkhi*. The use of coats and cloaks, is generally unknown except to Christian converts, Hinduised Mūndās and other Mūndās who generally frequent the civil stations.

As for the dress of Mūndā females, they generally wear a long piece of cloth called 'pāriā' round the waist, allowing a portion of it (called 'pailā', in Mundari) to pass diagonally over the upper part of the body so as to cover the breasts. Little girls wear a shorter cloth, without the ornamental borders of the 'paria' This is called 'Khānri'ā.' In the interior of the Mūndā country, however, one not infrequently meets with Munda women going about with no other wearing apparel than a piece of cloth called 'lāhāngā' round the waist. The legs of men as well as of women are generally uncovered, and shoes are seldom worn. Sometimes, however, people whose feet are wearing away, put on a sort of leather sandals called 'Kharpa' or 'ūhūr-kharpā' consisting only of a sole with a strap passing over the feet. Wooden shoes called 'Kātsū' are often used during the rains. The head, like the feet, is usually uncovered. Occasionally however, well-to-do Mūndās while going to the markets (*peet*) or to the towns wear 'pāgris' called in Mundari *bened*. A long piece of cotton cloth wound

round the head in coils serves the purpose of a *bened*.   Young men,
too, on occasions of dancing festivals, generally wear coloured
beneds.   In his journeys from one village to another, the Munda
carries a stick (sōtā), a purse (sutam-thailā), a lime-box (*chunauti*),
and a small box for carrying powdered tobacco and generally
called by the Hindi name of 'nās-dāni.'   In the rains, bamboo-
umbrellas (chātōm) as also circular rain-hats called 'Chūkūri'
made of leaves of the gūngū creeper are used.   At present, these
are being gradually replaced by cloth-umbrellas imported from
Calcutta.   Women, in particular, use elongated rain-hats called
gūngūs which cover the back down to the feet.

The Mūndā's clothing is generally made of cotton (Kāsōm).
The Mūndā woman spins cotton at home and gets this home-spun
cotton made into clothes by some men of the semi-aboriginal
Penrai of weaver caste.   Some Christian Mūndās, and more
particularly those living in or near the towns of Ranchi, Khūnti
and Būndū, are taking to the use of imported Manchester clothes.
The Hinduised Mūndās of the Pānch Parganas generally imitate
their Bengali neighbours in the matter of clothing.

Jewellery

Young Mūndā women are fond of decorating their person
with a large variety of ornaments.   These ornaments are generally
made of brass, for very few Mundas can afford to go in for jewellery
of a more costly material.   Ear-rings made of silver, and even of
gold, are, however, occasionally used.   The ornaments ordinarily
worn are,—for the arms,—brass bracelets called 'sākōm' and
'kākāna'[11], lac-bracelets called 'lāhti', brass armlets called 'tār'
and glass armlets called 'chūrlā', for the neck,—brass-necklets
called 'hāsuli', and for the legs,—brass anklets called 'āndu'.
Besides these, *tarkis* or ear-rings made of brass and occasionally of
silver, or even gold, 'mudāms' or finger-rings, and 'polās' or rings
for the large toe and 'jhūtiās' or rings for the other toes, all made of
brass, are generally used.   All these brass ornaments are manufa-
ctured by the country braziers of the Kāsgariā or Kaserā caste.
Occasionally, well-to-do Mūndā females, such as Mānkiāins,
will use gold nose rings called *noths*, and, over the forehead, thin

---

[11] A number of *sakoms* are worn on each arm with one *kakana* (which is larger
than the *sakoms*) at the end. Sometimes iron bracelets called *beras* are also used.

circular bits of gold called 'pātwāsis'.   On one side of the nose, a small brass-pin called 'chhūchi' (resembling the Bengali 'nāk-chābi') is occasionally worn.   The poorer Mūndā women use a peculiar ear-ornament called 'tār-sākōm'. This consists of a roll of palm leaf or some similar leaf, about an inch and a half long and about three-fourths of an inch in diameter, dyed red and set off with tinsel and lac.   Young Mūndā females use a kind of hair pin made of iron or brass and called 'khōngsō', to hold together their wealth of black hair which is tied up in a knot or chignon (sūpid) with twists of false hair (nāchā) at the back of the head.   Wooden combs called 'nākis' are also used for the same purpose.   Necklaces or *hisirs* made variously of coral (tijū hisir), of 'kāsi' grass (Kāre hisir), of *birni* reed (sirūm hisir) and of glass-beads (mūngā hisir) are also worn by young women.

This love of personal decoration is, to some extent, shared by young men as well.   It is not unusual to meet a Mūndā youth wearing long hair which is well oiled and combed and tied up at the side in a knot (sūpid) with a wooden hair comb (nāki) stuck into it, strings of coral beads (mūngā-mālā) or China beads (mohan mala) or beads of kāsi grass (Kāre-mālā) adorning his neck, and brass or iron armlets (*beras*) on his wrists.   Mūndā young men and women are particularly fond of flowers, with which they decorate their hair profusely whenever they can.   Garlands of flowers in the form of necklaces (bāhā hisir) are also worn.   The Mūndās appear to have formerly worn their hair long, as some of their young men do to this day. But the example of the numerous Christian converts amongst them is influencing most Mūndās in cropping their hair short.   Non-Christian Mūndās, however, must keep a pig-tail (chūndi).   In some instances, this chundi is allowed to grow very long, when it is tied up in a small knot called 'rōtōd'.

Tattooing

The Mūndās *tattoo* their girls by way of ornamentation.   A girl at the age of eight or nine years has her forehead pricked over with a needle and three parallel lines of prickings made, and into these a kind of black vegetable-dye is injected.   Similarly, two parallel lines of prickings on each of the two temples and two or three pricks over the chin are made, and the same dye injected. The back, the arms, the hands and feet are likewise tattooed. This process of tattooing is called 'sāngā' by the Mūndās.   In

former times, Mūndā boys at about ten years of age, used to have
the flesh of a portion of their arms scalded with a red-hot iron-rod
(sikhā) into a circular mark, which was regarded as a decoration.
This process, known in Mundari as the 'singā', is now falling into
disuse.

Weapons

In a list of the weapons used by the Mūndās, the first place
must be given to the bow and the arrow. The former they call—
'ā-ā' and the latter 'sār', and the two together 'ā-sār'. The handle
of the arrow is called the 'tūti' and the end the 'māil'. These,
as well as the battle-axe (kāpi) and the spear (balam) are, in these
peaceful days, principally used in hunting. The shield (phiri) and
two kinds of swords, namely, the 'khāndā' which is a straight sword,
and the 'tarwāri' which is crooked at one end, are now used only
at Paiki dances in marriage festivals. The iron-bound stick
(mered-sōtā), generally of bamboo, is carried by the Mūndā in his
journeys from one village to another. Small pincers (chimtā)
are carried at the waist and used, as occasion arises, for extracting
thorns which often prick the feet in his jungle roads and pathways.

Agricultural And Other Implements

The Mūndā is essentially an agriculturist, and, naturally, uses
a large variety of agricultural implements. To prepare the land
for cultivation, the Mūndā uses the plough which consists of the
wooden frame (nāyāl), an iron ploughshare (pahal), and a yoke
(ārānā), the harrow (ārāgom or atragom), a long earth-remover
(kārhā) made of wood and driven by cattle, the hoe (kulām),
and occasionally, the crowbar (soboro) with which rocky soil is
opened up. The yoke-rope and the iron yoke-hooks are called
respectively the joti and the 'kānābāsi,' and the mallet which is
made either of rope or of buffalo-skin is called the mundri. The
sickle (dātrom) is used in reaping crops, and a sort of sling called
dhelkhusi or hurang is used in field-watching. On the threshing-
floor (kolom), a pitch-fork called 'ānkri' is used. Three different
kinds of husking-instruments are used by the Mūndas. The first
is known as the 'dārusehel' or wooden mortar. This is constructed
by hollowing out a piece of wood, and inserting it upright in the
ground with the scoop turned upwards in the form of an inverted
bell. The grain is put in this scoop or hollow, and husked with a

wooden pole called 'tūkū'. The second variety is the 'dirisehel' or stone-mortar. This consists of a small basin-like hollow made in a block of stone or on a flat hillock. The grain is placed in this hollow and husked with a wooden *tuku* or pestle. The third variety is the ordinary wooden *dhenki* acted on by the feet. The principal appliances used by the Mūndā in wood-cutting is the axe or 'hākay', which is of two sizes, a bigger one—the 'hākay' proper— used in felling timber and splitting wood, and a smaller one called 'hūding hākay', used in chopping off small branches and twigs. The Mūndā usually manages his own carpentry. For this, his principal tools are the adge (*kisla* or *bassila*) for chipping wood, and the 'rūknā' or chisel to make holes in wood. Munda women, as we have seen, spin the cotton (kāsōm) grown on their fields. The appliances used for this purpose are the wooden spinning-wheel, 'charkhā', the cotton-cleaner called *tisri*, the thread-making shuttle called 'dherā', and a small thread-twister made of stone and called a 'karāt'. The different parts of the spinning-wheel are the spindle called *karad*, the thread-gatherer called 'māl', and the iron spinner called *karan*. The instrument with which Mūndā women separate (*rid*) the seeds from the cotton is called the *dainri*. The Mūndā housewife not only spins her own cotton, but often presses her own oil. In every village, you will meet with an oil-press (kūhū) in the courtyard (rāchā) of some well-to-do Mūndā's house. This is used not only by the owner but by his neighbours as well. Although the Mūndā now-a-days catches fish only occasionally, the varieties of fishing traps and nets he uses, appear to point to a time when fishing and hunting were his principal occupations. The generic Mūndāri name for a net is 'jālōm', which is curiously almost sound for sound the same as in Sanskrit. The Mūndā uses a push-net called *pilni*, a drag-net called *charguria*, a small circular proddling fish-net called 'girā' fixed on three sticks joined together in the form of a triangle, and bamboo fishing-traps called *janjid* and *kumni*.

Household Utensils and Furniture

The household utensils and furniture used by the Mūndās, are neither numerous nor costly. To cook his meals, the Mūndā uses earthen-ware pots (chātū) made by the Kūmhārs or potters, and mud-hearths (chūlhās) made by his own women-folk. The Mūndā's service of plate consists of a few bell-metal cups (dūbris) and bell-metal dishes of three sizes called 'thāris', 'duvās', and 'chipnis' respectively in the descending order of size. Stone plates (pāthrā) and cups (pāthri) are sometimes used. Wooden-bowls called 'katlas', are sometimes made and used to hold curries, etc. Wooden spoons (dāru lūndi) and iron ladles (karchūl) are used to turn rice and curries in the cooking-pot. Earthen jars (dā-chātū) are used to hold drinking water. A large earthen jar to hold water is called *sorol*. Those who cannot afford to buy brass lōtās', use earthen 'chūkās' for holding water to wash their hands and faces with. Mūndā women in carrying water from the well, tank, or spring (dāri) generally place the earthen jars (gharās) on a small straw-pad (bindā) over the head. 'Pūrūs' or cups made of sāl-leaves are occasionally used to drink liquids from. On his travels, the Mūndā often carries a 'tūmba' or pumpkin-gourd to hold drinking-water. Various sorts of bamboo-baskets are used as cupboards for storing household goods. Paddy is stored in 'pōtōms' or bundles made of straw-strings. A smaller pōtōm (as in the illustration) is called a *tipsi*. Large bamboo-baskets called 'chatkās' are also used for the same purpose. Smaller chatkās are called *dimnis*. Grain is carried and kept in big baskets called 'khānchis' ; smaller baskets, called 'tūnkis' are used in carrying paddy-seeds to the fields, and to hold cereals, vegetables, and the like. Very small baskets, called 'tūpās', are used by children in gathering sāgs or edible leaves. All these baskets are now generally made by men of other castes such as the Bāns-Mālhis and the *Doms*. The Mūndā measures his grain in wooden 'tenrās' or 'pailās' made by the *Barhis* or carpenters. A set of scales called 'tūlā-dāndi' is kept in every well-to do Mūndā's house. To store his belongings the Munda uses *pitis* or boxes made of bamboo split very thin. Boxes made of bamboo split less thin than in a *piti*, are called 'harkās'. *Pitis* and 'harkās' are provided with lids of the same material. A 'harkā' without a lid, is called a 'dāli'. The Mūndā's lamp is made of a thin round wick placed in a small mud-cup filled with oil. Brooms or *jonos* made of the *birni* grass are used by Mūndā women to sweep the floors of their houses and courtyards with. Knives (kātū) and meat-cutters (*bainthi*) are among the household implements of a Mūndā. Among his house-hold furniture, are the 'mānchi',—a stool with wooden frame and string bottom,—and the 'gāndū' (Bengali,—*pinri*) of two varieties,—'dārū-gāndū' or wooden seat, and 'būsū-gāndū' or straw-seat. String bed-steads called 'pārkōm' (Hindi—Khātiā) are used by well-to-do Mūndās. Those who cannot afford to go in for 'pārkōms', spread their palm-leaf mats on the floor, for beds. Occasionally, some cast-off or tattered cloth (*ledra lija*) is spread over the mat for a more comfortable bed. The richer Mūndā sometimes indulges in the luxury of a 'kūtūnri' or pillow stuffed with cotton. For the ordinary Mūndā, a 'gāndū' (wooden or straw *pinri*) placed underneath the mat, serves the purpose of a pillow for the head. In many cases, however, no such head-rest is used at all. The tolerably well-to-do Mūndā uses a 'kamrā' or blanket as a wrapper in winter. The poorer Mūndā uses only the 'pichowri' or the *barkhi* as a protection against cold.

Musical Instruments

The Mūndā is fond of music and uses a variety of musical instruments. Among these are the 'dhōlki'—a small drum made of wood and goat-skin, the 'nāgerā'—a large drum made of iron and the hide of an ox or a buffalo, the 'dūmāng'—another variety of the drum having an earthen framework with the top and the bottom made of monkey-skin, the 'dhānplā' or tambourine made of wood and goat-skin, the 'karetāl' or cymbal made of brass, the 'sārāngā' or fiddle made of wood and goat-skin with strings of horse's tail, the 'tūhilā' or banjo made of pumpkin gourd and wooden handle with a string of silk, the 'bānōm'— another variety of the banjo consisting of two gourds and two strings and brass-guaze, the *rutu* or bamboo-flute, and the 'mūrli'—a smaller flute also made of bamboo. On occasions of *Paiki* dances, young men wear ankle-bells called 'ghūgurā'. In marriage festivals, musicians of the Ghāsi tribe are employed by the Mūndās. The principal instruments played upon by these Ghāsi musicians are the 'dhānk'— a large drum made of wood and leather, the 'narsinghā' or horn made of copper or brass, and the *perened* or pipe made either of brass or of bell-metal.

Food

The staple food of the Mūndā is boiled rice. For a side-dish, the more well-to-do Mūndā uses boiled pulse or 'dāl'; but, except on special occasions, the poorer Mūndā has only some boiled green herb or 'sāg'. As a partial substitute for rice, the poorer Mūndās use 'gōndli' (*panicum miliare*) and 'māruā' (*eleusine crocana*),

for a few months after those millets are harvested. The maize or
'makāi' is also similarly used. The daily meals of the Mūndā are
three in number,—the 'loāri' or morning meal, the 'tikin mandi' or
mid-day meal, and the 'āyūb māndi' or evening meal. The 'loāri'
consists of stale rice preserved in water overnight, and a pinch
of salt. This is generally taken at about 8 A. M. by adults, and a
little earlier by children. The poorer people cannot often afford to
have 'loāri' but take for their 'tikin māndi' some stale rice with 'sāg'
and 'mār' or the thick starchy liquid drained off the cooked rice.
In more well-to-do Mūndā families, the 'tikin māndi', which is taken
at about noon, consists of hot rice and some boiled 'sāg' and 'dāl'
or pulse. The 'āyūb māndi' is generally taken between 6 P. M.
and 8 P.M., and consists of hot rice with 'sāg' or 'dāl' or both. Fowls
and goats are reared for food, but are killed and eaten chiefly
at festivals and sacrifices. Except among the Mūndās of the
Pānch Parganās, and only the more respectable portion (such as
the Mānkis, etc.) of the Mūndās of other parts of the district,
the use of beef, pork, and buffalo-meat as food is not altogether
in disfavour. The varieties of pulse ordinarily eaten by the
Mūndā are—'urid' (*Phaseolus Mungo; Var. Roxburghii*), 'kūrthi' (*Dolichos Biflorous*), 'bōdi' (*Vigna Catiang*), 'barāi' (*Phaseolus Mungo*), and
'rahār' (*Cujanus Sativa*). Besides green herbs or 'sāgs', the more
well-to-do Mūndā occasionally uses vegetables grown on his
lands. Among these vegetables are onions, brinjals, radishes,
tomatoes, pumpkins and gourds, *dherases* or lady's fingers (*Hebiscus
Esculentus*), beans, varieties of arum such as the 'sāru' and *pechki*,
and vegetable roots such as the sweet potato (*Ipomea Batktus*).
The corolla of the flowers of the *madkam* or *mohua* (*Bassia Latifolia*)
is also used for food. The oil used in cooking is extracted either
from mustard or from niger oil-seed (*sūrgūjā*). For condiments,
turmeric or *haldi* (Mundāri, *sasāng*), and chillis are used. As
in Hindu families, the female members of the Mūndā's family
will not sit down to eat before the men have finished their meals.
At each meal, the Mūndā, like the orthodox Hindu, will drop a
few grains of rice on the ground in the names of his deceased ancestors. The right hand is used in eating and the use of knives and
forks at his meals is unknown to the Mūndā.

Drink etc.

The favourite drink of the Mūndā is rice-beer or *ili*. Each family brews its own *ili*. This is made of boiled rice which is fermented and mixed with certain kinds of vegetable roots (*ili-ranu*). This liqour is stored in earthen jars and becomes ready for use in about five days. In the cold season, the *ili*, if left untouched, will keep good for a month or even more; but, in the hot weather, it will not do so for more than three or four days. The distilled-liquor shops too are now-a-days frequented by a large number of Mūndās, but less so by them than by the Urāons. It is a most remarkable fact that the majority of Hinduised Mūndās have given up their age-long habit of drinking. In the whole of Pargana Bārāndā there is practically not a single grog-shop. The Mūndā does not ordinarily smoke tobacco, except in the eastern parts of the district where powdered tobacco rolled up in sāl leaves in the form of cigarettes, is smoked. The Mūndās of other parts of the district take powdered tobacco with lime. The use of betel or betel-nut is practically unknown except to the Hinduised Mūndās of the Pānch Parganās.

(2) The Munda Village

The village basti

Looking down from the top of one of the numerous hills with which the Ranchi District is studded, you see the surface of the country thrown up into long undulations. The highest level space here and there generally forms a village-site. Here the Mūndā homesteads are huddled together without any orderly arrangement. And an apology for a road (*hōrā*) threads its labyrinthine way in and out of the village-basti or aggregate of homesteads.

Houses

Except the poorest amongst them, the Mūndās have gene-rally commodious houses. The residence of a well-to-do Mūndā family consists usually of three or four houses with a quadrangle called 'rāchā' in the middle and a 'bākri' or compound at the back. The majority of Mūndā houses consist each of at least two huts. Of these one is called the 'giti-ōrā' or the sleeping-house, and the other the 'māndi-ōrā' or the eating house. The 'giti-ōrā' in which the family-members sleep, usually comprises also the 'merom-ōrā' or goat-pen where goats are kept during night.

Mūndās who cannot afford to have a separate cattle-shed or 'ūnri-gōrā' use a portion of the 'giti-ōrā' for the purpose. The 'māndi-ōrā' in which the Mūndā's meals are cooked, includes also the 'āding' or sacred tabernacle where the spirits of departed ancestors are worshipped. No one save and except a member of the family is allowed to enter the 'āding', which is partitioned off from the 'sārē' or the rest of the 'māndi-ōrā' by a low mud-wall about three feet high. A portion of the 'sārē' is marked off as the 'jū-ūla' or kitchen, which no man of a different caste may enter. Any Mūndā may enter the 'sare', but only relatives and members of the family may sleep in it. The sacred 'āding' further serves the purpose of a store-room. A small space at one corner of the 'sārē' is usually staved off as a fowl-pen or 'sim-kūsli' in which the Mūndā's poultry are kept at night. Well-to-do Mūndās have verāndās or 'oāris' on one or more sides of the main house. These 'oāris' are often enclosed wholly or in part with low mud-walls and uti-lised as lumber-rooms and sometimes as additional sleeping-rooms. The houses are supported by wooden posts and have often tiled roofs, but the poorer Mūndās thatch their houses with a sort of grass called 'sāuri'. The posts and rafters are generally made of sāl wood obtained from the village jungles. The walls of the houses are generally of mud, but sometimes, especially in the western parganas, walls of split bamboos are met with. The houses generally have heavy wooden doors usually consisting of two roughly hewn planks, each revolving on a socket at one end of the door-step. Windows are conspicuous by their absence in Mūndā houses. The floor of a Mūndā's house is usually raised one or two feet above the ground. For ropes used in house-building, the Mūndās gather 'chōp' or the fibre of a leguminous creeper (*Bāuhiniā purpureā*) which grows wild in their jungles. Occasionally some Mūndā cultivator grows a little hemp called *jinri* in Mūndāri (*Crōtōlāriā juncea*), and 'kūdrūm' called *ipil* in Mūndāri (*Hibiscus cannabinnes*), for making ropes with. Attached to every decent Mūndā house, there is, as we have said, a plot of *bari* land (M., bākri-piri) in which maize (M., jonheār), chillies (M., mārchi), brinjals (M., toko), pumpkin (M., kākārū), and other kitchen vegetables are grown. Every cultivator has a manure-pit (M., sāra-gārā) close to the *basti* and often close to each indi-vidual homestead. In this pit, cowdung, decayed vegetation, and all sorts of refuse are deposited from day to day, and finally

burnt and carried to the fields as manure. These manure-pits add
to the filth and stench of the village which, even without them, is,
in places very trying indeed to the nostrils of a foreigner.

Dormitories for unmarried boys and girls

The unmarried young men and girls of a Mūndā family do not
generally sleep at night in the family-residence. And to strangers
and foreigners it is at first a mystery where they pass the night.
But once you succeed in gaining their confidence, the Mūndā of a
village will tell you where the 'giti-ōrā' of their young bachelors
and that of their maidens respectively are. Although Mūndā bachelors, except in some localities such as in parts of Parganā Lodhmā,
have no institution exactly like the Urāon *Jonk-erpa* or 'Dhūm-kūria',
all young bachelors of a Mūndā village or hamlet (*tola*) have a
fixed common dormitory in the house of a Mūndā neighbour who
may have a hut to spare for the purpose. And, similarly, all the
unmarried girls of a village or a hamlet sleep together in the night
in a house belonging to some childless old Mūndā couple or to
some lone elderly Mūndā widow. The matron of the house exer-
cises a general superintendence over the morals of the girls. These
'giti-ōrās' for boys as well as for girls are, in their own humble way,
seminaries for moral and intellectual training. When young
bachelors and young maidens are assembled in their respective
'giti-ōrās' after their evening-meals, riddles (nūtūm-kāhāni) are
propounded and solved, folk-tales (kāji-kāhāni), traditions and
fables are narrated and memorised, and songs sung and learnt,
until bed-time. Besides these dormitories, the other noticeable
places in a Mūndā village are the Sarnās, the Akhrā, and the
Sasān.

The Sarna

Although the greater portion of the primeval forest, in clearings
of which the Mūndā villages were originally established, has since
disappeared under the axe or under the jārā-fire,[12] many a Mūndā
village still retains a portion or portions of the original forest
to serve as *Sarnās* or sacred groves. In some Mūndāri villages,
only a small clump of ancient trees now represents the original

---

[12] By the 'jara' system, land is prepared for cultivation by burning down
portions of jungles.

forest and serves as the village-*Sarnā*. These Sarnās are the only temples the Mūndās know.[13] Here the village-gods reside, and are periodically worshipped and propitiated with sacrifices. Besides the Sarnās,—there may be more than one in the same village,—the other important places in a Mūndā village are the Akhrā or dancing-meet and the *Sasān* or burial-ground.

The Akhrā

The Akhrā is usually located almost in the middle of the village-*basti*, and consists of an open space under some old wide-spreading tree. Here, public-meetings are held, the *Panchāyat* hold their sittings, offenders against social rules as well as suspected witches and sorcerers are brought to justice, and the young folk of the village assemble in moon-lit nights and on festive occasions to dance and sing. A number of large stone-slabs placed underneath the tree serve as seats for actors and spectators.

The Sasān

The village Sasān, too, adjoins the village-*basti*, and consists of a number of big stone-slabs lying flat on the ground, or propped up on small chips of stone at the corners. Under one or more of these stone-slabs, lie buried the bones of the deceased members of each family of Khūntkāttidārs or Bhūinhārs of the village. The bones of a Mūndā, dying away from his khūntkātti or Bhūin-hāri village, will, if possible, be conveyed by his relatives, as a pious duty, to his ancestral village and there ceremonially buried under the family *Sasān-diri* or sepulchral stone-slabs in the Sasān of the *Kili* or sept. No outsiders, not even resident Mūndāris of the village who do not belong to the original village-family, will be allowed to use the village-*Sasān*. And the Mundas very properly regard these sepulchral stones or *Sasan-diris* as the title-deeds of the Khūntkāttidārs and Bhūinhārs of each village.

[13] In rare instances, such as in village Goa or Gora near Murhu (*Thana--*Khunti), more than one *kili* or sept established the village, the different *kilis* (the Mundhu *kili* and the Chutia Purthi *kili*) of Mundas arriving in successive bands and each *kili* clearing a separate block of lands which they occupy still. As no member of one *kili* may be buried in the *Sasan* of another *kili*, there are necessarily more than one *Sasan* in such villages. Similarly in village Khatanga in *Thana* Khunti, the different tolas were founded separately by men of the *Tuti kili* and by men of the *Sarukad Purthi kili* respectively.

Village Fields

Leaving the village *basti* behind you, you come first to the *dihāri-dānr* (M., *hātū-jāpāpiri*) lands. These are cultivable uplands nearest the *basti*, and are regarded as part of the village-site itself. These *dihāri-dānr* lands are mostly used as *chirā-bāris* in which various *rabi* crops besides onions, garlics, and sometimes potatoes and similar other crops are grown. Portions of *dihāri-dānr* lands are also used as *birā-bāris* (M., *bianr bakri-ko*), on which paddy-seedlings are reared for transplantation. Beyond these *hātū-jāpāpiri* lands, and further from the *basti*, you see stretches of uplands with their sides sloping down in step-like terraces into the bottom of intervening hollows. The uplands are locally called *dānr* or *tānr* (M., *piri*), and the terraced low-lands are called *dōn* (M., *lōyōng*). The former are suitable for dry cultivation and the latter for wet cultivation. Lands standing midway between the *dōn* and the *dānr* lands are called *tariā* fields. These latter are, properly speaking, low-lying por-tions of *dānr* lands. The drainage of the high lands further up passes over these *tariā* lands, rendering them capable of growing the earlier and lighter varieties of lowland rice such as the *karhāni* paddy. The *dōns* or lowlands are sub-divided, according to their respective elevation, into (1) the *gārha lōyōng* or the lowest dōn lands at the bottom of the depressions between the ridges, (2) the *sokrā* lands or terraces of middle elevation, and (3) the *bādi* or *chowrā* *dōn* lands situate further up the sides of the slopes and immediately below the *tāria dānr* lands. In the Bengali-speaking portions of the Pānch Parganās, the *gārhā dōn* lands are known as *bahāl* or *dōbar*, the *sōkrā dōn* lands as *kānāli*, and the *bādi* or *chowrā* *dōn* lands as *bāid*. A sub-division of *gārhā dōn* lands is the *kūdar-dōn* which, owing to the water of some spring flowing over it or some streamlet irrigating it, receives moisture throughout the year. It is on such lands that, besides the usual winter rice-crop, a summer crop called *tewa* rice is grown.[14] The terraced dōn lands testify

---

[14] These '*dofasli* don' lands are classed as 'first-class don,' and the middle terraces are sub-divided into 'second-class don' lands which yield harvest in Aghan, and 'third-class don' lands yielding harvest in katik. In the worst or 'fourth-class don' (chowra don) lands the paddy ripens in Bhado or Aswin. Similarly the *tanr* lands nearest the *basti* and growing vegetables, etc. are classed as 'first-class danr' and the uplands further from the *basti* are sub-divided into 'second-class danr' lands which are comparatively level and free from stones, and 'third-class or ruguri danr' lands which are stony and more sloping.

to the dogged perseverance and indefatigable industry of the Mūndās. Years of patient labour of whole families of Mūndās are spent in embanking hill-streams, levelling river-beds and valleys, cutting into stubborn ground higher up and forming them into little terraces of dōn lands. Generation after generation of Mūndās have toiled in the heat and in the rains to prepare these terraced rice-fields. And still they go on patiently reclaiming waste lands and preparing dōn lands, as their forefathers had done before them. Dōn lands in the cultivation of the tenant who prepared them or his heirs and transferees, are known, in non-khūntkatti villages, as 'kōrkar' lands and have special privileges attached to them.

(3) AGRICULTURE

Soil

The principal varieties of soil in the Mūndā country are—(1) the *pānkuā* (M. *pank loyong*) or alluvial soil, found mostly in the Pānch Parganās, and best suited for rice; (2) the *nāgrā* (called *nāgdhā* by the Sonepur *Mūndās* and *chite* in the Pānch Parganās),—a kind of black sticky clay soil; (3) the *khirsi* consisting of equal proportions of clay and sand; (4) the *rūgūri loyong* or gravelly soil; (5) the *bālā* (M., *gitil ote*) or sandy loam; and (6) the *lāl*, *mātiā* (M., *ārā hāsā*) consisting of a red ferruginous sandy loam found only in *dānr* lands.

Crops

Of food-crops, the staple is rice, which is grown both on *dōn* as well as on *dānr* lands. The general name for upland rice is *gōrā* (M., *gōdā bābā*) which is reaped in August and September, and includes several varieties of coarse rice only—such as, the *alsāngā*, the *kārāngā*, etc. Besides *gōrā* rice, other important *Bhādōi* crops, such as *gōndli* (M.,*gūdlū*), *kūrthi* (M., *hōre*), *marūā* (M., *kōdē*), and other millets and pulses are grown on *dānr* lands. The third harvest of the year is the *rabi* harvest gathered in February and March. Among the more important *rabi* crops grown on *dānr* lands are the *rahar* or *cajanus sativa* (M., *rāhāri*) and the mustard or *sinapis nigra* (M., *māni*). The upland crops are generally sown by rotation. Thus, after the *māruā* crop is gathered from a field in October-November, *gōra* paddy will be sown on it in the following May and harvested in September. In the next year, the same field will be sown with the *ūrid* (M., *rāmbārā*) pulse which will be harvested in September or October. This will be followed next June by a gōndli crop which, in its turn, will be reaped in August. A month or two later, either *sūrgūja* or *kūrthi* will be sown on the same field. Frequently *rahar* pulse, which is reaped in March, is sown along with *gōra* or *gōndli* on the same *dānr*, and *bōdi* is sown along with *mārua*. This usual cycle of upland cultivation is sometimes varied according to the usage of a particular village or the convenience or inclination of individual cultivators. In most *Mūndāri* villages, the uplands are poor in quality, and are therefore generally left fallow, by turns, for one, two, or three years at a time.

The low-land rice (M., *lōyōng bābā*) may be broadly divided into two main classes; namely the *garuhān* (M., *hambāl bābā*) or *barkā* rice grown on the lowest *dōn* lands and reaped in November and the *lauhan* (M., *ramāl bābā*) or light rice grown on the upper terraces known as *chowrā-dōn* lands. The former class is the great winter crop of the year which is reaped in November and December, and comprises a large variety of fine rice such as the *Kalamdāni*, the *Tilāsār*, and the *Rāi-chuni*. The latter class is reaped in autumn and comprises several varieties of coarse rice such as the *Jhālar-gendā* and the *Mūgdhi*. In speaking about *Kūdar dōn* lands, we have referred to *tewa* rice which is grown on lands which retain moisture throughout the year and are therefore capable of yielding two crops in the year. *Tewā* fields are found only in *Thānās Khūnti*, *Būndū*, and *Ormānjhi* and measure altogether 1.18 square miles in the whole of the Rānchi District. Including *dofasli danr* lands, the entire area of lands, *dōn* as well as *dānr* within the Rānchi District, cropped more than once in the year is only 39 square miles. Out of a total area of 7,103 square miles in the Rānchi District, 3,614 square miles or 50.88 per cent are nominally under cultivation. But, making allowance for *dōfāsli dōn* lands and the cycle of cultivation in *dānr* lands, the total net cropped area of the district does not exceed 2,483 square miles. Of this, 1,530 square miles (or 61.6 per cent of the cropped area) produce rice, *urid* is grown on 127 square miles, *gōndli* on 300 square miles, *mārūā* on 110 square miles, *sūrgūja* on 157 square miles, and other crops on 255 square miles. Only 43 square miles in the whole of the district are covered with fruit trees.[15] The average

[15] We are indebted for the above statistics to J. Reid, Esq, I.C.S., late Settlement Officer of Ranchi.

15

gross produce of one acre of '*dōn*' land, would, in a good year, amount to about 17 maunds of paddy.

Agricultural operations

The Mūndā's methods of cultivation are very simple. There are two processes for the cultivation of low-land paddy, viz. the *būnā* (*Mūndāri*, *hèr*) or sowing broad-cast, and the *rōpā* (*Mūndāri*, roā) or transplantation. The former is generally made in June and the latter in July and August.

(*i*) *Buna* : The *būnā* process, again, is of two kinds, namely, *dhūri-bunā*. (M., *her-jeteā*) or sowing in dust, and *lewā* (M., *āchāra*) or sowing in mud. Before sowing or transplantation, the fields are generally ploughed up three or four times. The first ploughing, known as chirna (M., *si-chātā*) is made, if possible, soon after the winter-rice is harvested, or, at any rate, immediately after the first shower of rain in the month of *Māgh* ; the second and third ploughings known respectively as *dōbārnā* (M., *si-rūrā*) and *uthāōnā*, follow, in *būnā* fields, shortly afterwards—either in *Māgh* or in *Fāgūn*. These *būnā* fields are generally manured in the month of *Chait*, by distributing over them cowdung[16] in small heaps, and then spreading out this manure either with the spade or with the plough. The third ploughing is followed by harrowing and levelling with an implement called the *kārhā* or *mher*. The last ploughing is called the *purāonā* or finishing. The *purāonā* and *uthāōnā* are often the same. The land having been thus prepared for the reception of paddy-seeds, *dhūri-būnā* is made in May or June by casting dry seeds on pulverised ground.

(*ii*) *Lewa* : In June, after the regular rains set in, *lewā* or moist-sowing is made. The field which was once ploughed in Māgh (January-February) is thoroughly ploughed up again after a heavy shower of rain in *Asārh* (June - July) so as to work up the soil into a state of liquid mud. The mud is then allowed to settle down for a day or two, after which the water which comes up above the mud is drained off. The seeds which have already been made to germinate by being soaked in water for about twenty-four hours, and put

---

[16] Other manures used by the Mundas are ashes, mud from old tanks, karanj flowers, and oil-cakes.

into a covered basket, is now scattered on the surface of the mud. They are carefully watched until they take root and a few leaves spring up.

(*iii*) *Ropa* : The last process in point of time is the *rōpā* (M., *rōā*) or transplantation. On the day of transplantation, the field is once more ploughed up by the men with the help of the *chowk*, and soil and water are mixed up into a uniform puddle. The paddy seedlings brought in bundles from the nursery where they were reared, are washed clean of all earth and one by one separately inserted in the mud by the women. It is indeed a very pleasing sight to see the Mūndās, men and women, some with their picturesque rain-hats on and others bare-headed, cheerfully working in their fields in the rains all the day long.

(*iv*) *Weeding* : The paddy fields are weeded three times. The first weeding takes place before the field is sown. Grass and other noxious plants that have come up since the field was last ploughed up are carefully picked up by the hand. This process is called *tūsāng* in Mūndāri. The second weeding takes place in the month of *Sāwan* (July-August) when the paddy-fields generally get infested with grass. This weeding is done with the help of the plough and the harrow. This process is known as *bidhāonā* in Hindi, and *kārāe* in Mūndāri. The last weeding is made in the month of Bhādo (August-September), when such of the grass as escaped the previous weeding, are carefully picked up with the hand, and taken home to be used as fodder for cattle. This weeding is called *hered* in Mūndāri.

(*v*) *Watching* : When the crops are ripening, they require to be watched. In the day-time, this is done generally by the women and the children, but at night the watching is always done by men who stop in small temporary sheds erected for the purpose on or near the fields. These huts are made of straw spread over branches of trees, and are locally known as *kūmbās* (M., *gūiū*).

(*vi*) *Harvesting* : The harvesting is done both by men and women. A threshing-floor or *kharihān* (M., *kōlōm*) is prepared beforehand by scraping grass off a suitable plot of land, and making it clean and tidy with a coating of cowdung (M., *gūri*) mixed with water. Rocky places or *chātāns*, if available, are preferred. Otherwise, a plot of *bāri* land or some mango-tope or other uncultivated land is utilised as a *kharihān*. The paddy stalks, as they are

reaped, are left on the ground in small bundles, and are carried to
the threshing-floor.   Here the paddy stalks are arranged in circular
heaps called *chakars* (M., *chāki*) with the ears on the inside.

(*vii*) *Threshing* :   The threshing is done at the *kharihān* described above. The paddy-stalks are first spread out on the ground,
and a few bullocks tied in a line are driven round and round over
them.   As the threshing goes on in this way, the straw is sifted
with a pitchfork called *ākāin*.

(4) TRIBAL ORGANISATION AND ITS DEVELOPMENT INTO SOCIAL AND POLITICAL ORGANISATION

Tribes and Sub-tribes

The Mūndā tribe is divided into a large number of *exogamous
groups* called *kilis*.   According to Mūndā tradition, all the members
of the same *kili* are descended from one common ancestor.   But
such a tradition may not be quite correct with regard to the original
kilis.   Though exogamous as regards the *kilis*, the Mūndās are
endogamous so far as other tribes are concerned.   Thus, there
can now be no valid marriage, according to Mūndā custom,
between a Mūndā and the member of any other 'Kolarian' tribe,
such as the Sāntāls, the Khāriās, the Asūrs, or the Bir-hōrs.

(*i*) *The Bhumijes* :   It is only with the Bhūmijes of Pargana
Pātkūm which adjoins the Tāmār Pargānā of the Rānchi District,
that the Mūndās of Tāmār side still inter-marry.   In fact, the
Bhūmij-Mūndās of Tamar and the adjoining parganas of the
Mānbhūm District would appear to belong to the same tribe as the
Mūndās.

(*ii*) *The Khangars* :   But a Mūndā will not marry even in a
Khāngār family, although the Khāngārs are believed to have
originally formed one tribe with the Mūndās.   The reason asserted
is, that the Khāngārs were excommunicated in the days of tradition
for having eaten unclean meat.[17]   In Parganās Būndu and Tāmār,

---

[17] The story goes that two Munda brothers were travelling with their wives
from one place to another.   One of the brothers and his wife preceded the other
brother in the journey.   On the way, the former brother's wife was brought to
bed of a child.   While leaving the place, the Munda couple buried the placenta,
etc. in the hearth they had improvised at their temporary lodging.   Soon afterwards, the other brother came up there with his wife.   On opening up the hearth,

these Khāngār Mūndās are known as Pātor Mūndās, in parts of Khūnti Thānā as Māhli Mūndās,[18] in Singbhūm as Tāmāriās, in Gāngpur as Būndūars, and in Pargānā Belkāddi by the significant name of Marāng Mūndās.

(iii) *The Konk-pat Mundas* :   The Mūndās of the Central Plateau and its neighbourhood are distinguished from other Mūndās by the appellation of Kōnk-pāt (corrupted into Kōm-pāt) Mūndās. The origin of the term is lost in obscurity.   The derivation suggested by Mr. R. D. Haldar in the Appendix to a Government Resolution of the 25th November, 1880 (published in the *Calcutta Gazette* of the 1st December, 1880), from the Hindu words *kanak* (gold) and *pata*, does not appear at all probable.   The name may not improbably have some connection with the term *Pat Munda*—an appella· tion still used to signify a head-Mūndā belonging to particular Munda families reputed to be descended of the original Mūndā Rājās and accorded precedence over other Mūndās in social matters. We have heard old Mūndās explaining the origin of the name by asserting that it was given to them when the first Nāgbansi Rājā of the country adopted a snake-shaped *pagri* as his royal insignia, leaving the chief *Mūndās* to wear *pagris* of *pat* (M., *lumang*) or cocoon silk as their distinctive head-dress.   Such a *pagri* is still worn by the village Mūndā in many villages when he succeeds to Mūndā-ship and receives the Mūndāi *pagri* at the hands of the Manki, and in some villages at the hands of the Zamindar.   The Bhūinhār Mūndās of the west would seem to be an off-shoot of the Kōnk-pāt Mūndās.

Kilis and Their Origin

According to modern authorities on Sociology, from tribes and sub-tribes was evolved the Family, when communal marriage was superseded by individual marriage and the Matriarchal Age was superseded by the Patriarchal.   After the hunting and fishing stages of savagery were passed, and the nomadic savage settled

---

he discovered the placenta, etc., buried there, and thought that his brother had bagged some game, and left a portion of the meat for him to cook and eat.   And so the couple unsuspectingly ate the unclean meat.   When the brothers met, and the truth was known, the brother who had eaten the unclean meat was excommunicated.   And his descendants became the Khangars.

[18] The *Mahli Mundas* should not, however, be confounded with the *Bans Mahlis*, also known as *Turis* or *Oreas*.

down and first took to agriculture, the institution of individual
marriage appears to have developed or perhaps to have been re-
established once more and it soon took root.   Descent came to
be traced through the father and no longer, as before, through
the mother.   The wife was no longer the common property of
the tribe, the sub-tribe, or the matriarchal group.   The child no
longer belonged to the community or to the mother alone, but to
the father as much as to the mother.   And kinship came to be
traced not, as before, through a common female ancestor, but
through a common male ancestor.   Even in the Matriarchal Age,
descendants by the same mother came to be regarded as brothers
and sisters betwixt whom sexual union was at first looked upon
with disfavour, and afterwards altogether forbidden.   Women
were generally captured or taken from other tribes or sub-tribes,
and septs first arose in the Matriarchal Age when sexual union
between descendants of the same mother came to be interdicted.
A relic of that period may perhaps still be traced in the important
position assigned to the maternal uncles of the bride and the
bridegroom in Mūndāri marriages.   Even if the division of the tribe
into *kilis* or totemestic septs had existed in the Matriarchal Age,
those divisions are no longer recognisable unless indeed they be
represented by the different allied tribes and sub-tribes such as the
Hōs, the Khārias and the Bhūmijes who once formed the same
people with the Mundas.   Be that as it may, it must have been
after the institution of individual marriage that the present division
of the Mūndās and other allied tribes into *kilis* or totemestic septs
on the traditional basis of paternal consanguinity arose.   The
fraternal ties of mutual affection engendered by residence under
the same roof sharing the common hearth, and growing under the
fostering care of the same parents, made brothers hold together, and
their children and children's children and subsequent generations
came to regard themselves as knit together by ties of common
descent, and bound to stand by one another in weal or woe, share
the same property in common, join in common worship, and bury
their dead in a common *Sasān*.   Injuries to any member of the
family caused from outside came to be looked upon as common
injuries and would be resented and avenged by all the members.
Many are the stories still told by the Mūndās about the members
of a *kili* combining in ancient times to punish wrongs committed
by outsiders to individual members of that *kili*.   The repugnance to

consanguinous marriages already developed in the Matriarchal
Age, was accentuated by improvement in manners and civilisation
which necessarily followed agricultural life.   Marriage between
descendants of the same common paternal ancestor was interdicted.
And all the supposed descendants of one ancestor came to be
described as belonging to one *kili*. Distinctive *kili* names came
to be coined, either from some memorable incident connected
with the clan, or from some other circumstance connected either
with religion or superstition.   As time went on, and generations
multiplied, each *kili* became enormously enlarged, and the unwieldy brotherhoods came to be further sub-divided into separate
kilis. This sub-division was probably effected to avoid the necessity
of the members of one *kili* having to travel a long way off into the
domain of another *kili* to seek wives for their sons or husbands for
their daughters.   When the Mūndās entered the Chōtā Nāgpūr.
plateaux, the number of their *kilis* appears to have been very small.
As a proof of this may perhaps be mentioned the very small number
of *kili* names (such as the Hemrom, the Hāsdā, the Soien) which
the Mūndās have in common with the Sāntāls and the Bhūmijes
who formed one people with the Mūndās before the latter entered
Chōtā Nāgpūr.   And the legends connected with the origins
of most Mūndāri *kilis* of our days would leave no doubt that the
number of *kilis* swelled enormously by sub-division, since the
Mūndās migrated into Chōtā Nāgpūr.   We shall content ourselves
with giving here the stories connected with the origin of a few
of these *kilis* only.   Though mostly fabulous in origin, some indications of historical facts may perhaps be gleaned from them.

(*i*) *The Tuti Kili* : The origin of the *Tūti kili* is stated to be[19] as
follows : The ancestors of the sept lived in village Chūtiā near
Rānchi, whither they had migrated from Sutiāmbe-Kōrambē.
While migrating again further to the east, from Chūtiā they had
to cross a swollen river in the depth of winter. One batch of
the emigrants first crossed the river, but began to shiver terribly
with cold when they reached the other bank. They, therefore,
shouted out to their relatives on the other bank to send them some
burning charcoal which the latter had with them.   The men on
the other bank, finding no other means of helping their kinsmen,
put some burning charcoal into a fork made of a twig of the

---

[19] There are two or three slightly different versions of this story.

tuti plant which abounded in the vicinity, and sent the twig with the charcoal to the other bank with the help of a bow and arrow. The Mundas on the other bank thus relieved from the biting cold, vowed not to eat the *tuti* plant any more, and thenceforth formed a separate *kili* called the *Tuti kili*.[20]

(*ii*) *The Mundu Kili* : The origin of the *Mundu kili* is narrated as follows: While coming to Sōnepur side from the Eastern Parganās (whither they had first migrated from the Central plateau), the head of the migrating family was carrying a lighted twist of straw (*bōr*) at night. While he was nearing the end of his journey, the straw-light burnt down to its lower end (*lo mūndū jānā*). From this circumstance this Mūndā and his near kinsmen constituted the Mūndū *kili*.

(*iii*) *The Soe Kili and Its Sub-divisions* : The story of the origin of the different sub-divisions of the *Soe kili*, is somewhat interesting. The story goes that a Mūndā had grown *kāpās* cotton (*kāsōm*) on his field close by a river named, *Chilua lkir*. A large *Sōe* or *Sōel* fish made a subterranean passage from the river up to this cotton-field, and every night the fish would stealthily come to the field through this passage and damage the cotton. Unable at first to trace the thief, the owner of the field ultimately remained watching the field one night, and at length discovered the *Soe* fish eating his cotton. Forthwith, with an arrow, he killed the fish. But the fish was so large and heavy that he had to call in the aid of all his *hāgās* or *bhāyāds* to carry the huge fish to the village. The fish was then chopped into pieces, and the meat distributed amongst all the *hāgās*. The Mūndā who had killed the fish with his arrow came to be called *Tuing-Sōe*[21] and his descendants formed the *Tuing-Sōe kili*.[1] The man who chopped the bones came to be called *Jāng-Sōe*[1] and his descendants constituted the *Jāng-Sōe kili*. The Mūndā who divided the meat into different shares came to be called *Til-Sōe*[1] and his

---

[20] So great is the Munda's respect for his totem, that he will not, if he can, allow his totem to be eaten even by men of other castes, in his presence. Thus, not long ago, in village Tilma, inhabited mostly by Mundas of the Tuti *kili*, a Mahomedan neighbour had grown *tuti* plants on his *bari* land. The Mundas when they saw the *tuti* plants coming up, offered threats of violence to the Mahomedan who at length pacified the enraged Mundas by uprooting the *tuti* plants.

[21] Tuing is the Mundari word for 'shooting an arrow', *Jang* means 'bone', *Til* is 'to divide', *Or* means 'to distribute', and *Patra* is 'a leaf-plate'.

descendants formed the *Til-Sōe kili*. The Mūndā who distributed the shares came to be called *Or-Sōe*, and his descendants
became the *Or-Sōe kili*....The Mūndā who brought the leaves
on which the different shares of meat were placed came to be styled
Pātrā Sōe and his family the *Pātrā Sōe kili*. One of the *Bhāyāds*
had taken his own share of the meat in a piece of cloth dyed with
gamcha earth (a kind of ochre-coloured earth called *gerua mati*)
and came to be called *Gāmchā Soe* and his descendants came to
constitute the *Gāmchā Sōe kili*. The men of the *Gāmchā Sōe kili*
will not use cloth dyed with *Gāmchā* earth, and no Mūndā of the
different branches of the *Sōe kili* will eat the Sōe fish. The other
sub-divisions of the *Soe kili* are the *Mandi-Sōe*, the *Chiki-Sōe*, the
Tulā Sōe, the *Adoa Soe*, the *Rura Mandi Soe* and the *Bāndā Sōe*
kilis, each of which *kilis* is somehow or other connected with the
legend given above.

(*iv*) *The Horo or Kachua Kili* : In the legends connected with
the origin of a few of the *kili*-names, some supernatural elements
have been introduced. Thus the origin of the *Hōrō* or *Kachuā*
kili is given as follows. The ancestor of the *kili*, while on a
journey, had to cross a swollen river. His *hāgās* or kinsmen
crossed the river safely. But he himself did not venture to do
so unaided, and exclaimed, "Whoever will take me safely
across the river, will be my kith and kin for ever." In those
days all animal and vegetable creation could understand
human speech and could themselves be understood by man. A
tortoise who heard the Mūndā's appeal for help, came up and
offered to carry him across the river. The tortoise succeeded in
carrying on his back not the Mūndā alone but all his family and
luggage safe to the other side of the river. True to his promise,
the Mūndā thenceforth assumed the name of *Horo* or 'Kachuā', and
his descendants came to form the *Horo* or *Kachua kili*. No Mūndā
of the *kili* will kill a tortoise or eat its flesh.

(*v*) *The Nag Kili* : The story of the origin of the well-known *Nāg*
kili (the same as the *Pāndu Bing kili*) is as follows : A Mūndā
snake-charmer had tamed a white Nāg snake (*Pāndu Bing*) which
he used to take with him in his itineraries. At length while returning home from a distant village, the sanke-charmer died on the
way. The Nāg-serpent now coiled itself round the corpse and carried
it home to the bereaved sons. Out of gratitude to the faithful *Pāndu*
Bing. the deceased snake-charmer's sons kept the snake in their

house, and gave it plenty to eat and drink every day. And the snake, too, would do them no manner of harm. Thenceforth the descendants of the deceased snake-charmer came to be called the men of the *Nāg kili*.[22] No member of the *kili* would injure a Nāg serpent. The Hinduised Mūndās of this *kili* in some localities, such as the Mānkis of village Mānkidi (*thānā*— Sonāhātu) seek to derive the name from a supposed Nāg Rishi, but also recount the story of a huge Nāg serpent protecting their ancestor with its expanded hood.

Transformation of Kili Names

In many cases, the Hinduised Mūndās of the Pānch Parganas have succeeded in transforming their *kili*-names almost beyond recognition. Thus *Sāndi kili*[23] has been changed into *Sāndil gōtra*— a gōtra or clan-name common to many genuine Hindu families and said to be derived from Sāndilya Rishi. This sept-name is in so much favour with the semi-Hinduised Mundas of the eastern parganas that instances have been known in which a Munda of the *Sāndil gōtra* has married in the same *gōtra*. This probably shows that this new *kili* name has been adopted by several originally distinct *kilis*. The majority of Mūndās in the *Sonāhātū Thānā*, now belong to the *Sāndil gōtra*. The only other Mūndāri *kilis* within that *Thānā* appear to be the *Nāg gōtra*, the *Tau* (sparrow) *gōtra*, and the *Sāngā*[24] *kili*. A curious instance of the transformation of *kili* name is that of the *Jom Tuti kili* into the Bhōj-Rōj-gōtra of Parganā Tāmār (as for example, in village Kota).

Change of Kili

In a very few instances families of one *kili* have been known to have been incorporated into another *kili*. Thus, the Mūndās now residing in villages Chiūr and Chāldāndu in Pargana Sōnepur (Thānā, Karra) originally resided in village Chenre (a tōlā of Ulātu in Thānā Rānchi), and belonged to the Bando (wild cat) *kili*. It is said that a large venomous snake used to trouble the men of the Pātrā Mochiā Parhā, who long unsuccessfully sought to establish villages where the present village of Bingāon stands, and round

---

[22] The Bhumijes have also got this *Kili* amongst them. The *Tau* (*sparrow*) *Kili* of the Mundas is the same as the *Tessa gotra* of the Bhumijes.

[23] *Sandi* in Mundari means the male of an animal, a bullock.

[24] *Sanga* is the Mundari name for the pith of a particular plant.

about it.   An ancestor of the present Mūndāri residents of village Chiūr succeeded in killing the snake, and was allowed to settle down in that locality, and the village he established was named Bing-hātu (the snake-village), since known as Bingāon. His descendants afterwards removed to villages Chiūr and Chāldandu. But to this day they have their *sasān* or graveyard at Bingāon. The man who killed the snake was admitted to the *Herenj-kili* to which the Mūndās of the Pātrā Mochiā Pārhā belong. And his descendants, now the Mūndāris of Chiūr and Chāldāndu, are not permitted to enter into marital relations either with men of their original *kili*—the *Bāndō kili*, or with men of their adopted *kili*—the *Herenj*. Among other *kilis* of the Mūndās may be mentioned the following : the Pūrthi *kili* with its sub-divisions—the Chūtu Pūrthi, the Hūni Pūrthi, the Sārūkad Pūrthi, the Hāsā Pūrthi, the Engā Pūrthi, the Sāndi Purthi *kilis*, the *Oreā kili*, the *Rundā kili*, the *Kāndir kili*, the *Bōdrā kili*, the *Surin kili*, the *Hai kili*, the Bārlā *kili*, the *Bhēngrā kili*, *Langchere kili*, the *Hurumsuku kili*, the *Hāsārā kili*, the *Hēmrōm kili*, the *Bodoso kili'*, the *Mundri kili*, the *Gomi Buru kili*, the *Sankura kili*, the *Chāmpi kili*, the *Hāns kili.*, the *Bābā kili*, the *kūlā kili*, the *Dere Sāngā kili*, the *Bārlānga kili*, the *Sāl gotra* and the *Kamal gotra*.

Parhas and Pattis

In course of time, as the members of each *kili* increased, and one village proved insufficient for the residence and cultivation of all the members, other villages were founded in the neighbourhood by different members of the same *kili*.   In the beginning they appear to have buried their dead in the common *sasān* in the parent-village, joined in certain public *Pūjās* (worship) in the *Sarnā* of the parent village, and otherwise maintained their former association in almost all respects except residence and culti-vation.   But, in course of time, they, too, came to have their own public worship at the *Sarnas* of their new villages, and established their separate graveyards in their respective villages.   But in social and administrative matters, they continued to act as one body.   And to this day, this association for common social and administrative purposes has been maintained, though not by all the villages belonging to one *kili*,—for that would be impracticable, but by each group of villages of the same *kili* that left the parent village together and settled side by side.   This brotherhood of allied and associated villages constituted a *pārhā*.[25] The *pārhā* now became the unit of social as well as political organisation. And by degrees this organisation attained almost ideal perfection. But here their further progress naturally stopped. With his limited ideas, the semi-barbarous Mūndā could not extend his vision beyond the limits of his *Pārhā* and conceive of wider organisations. Naturally, therefore, they succumbed to the first Nāgbansi leader who arose amongst them with a more extended vision—the more comprehensive and grander scheme of a 'state',—of an organisation which should confederate these isolated *pārhās* under the leadership of a chief of chiefs. The Nāgbansis succeeded in their noble ambition only because they sought to build a mighty state upon foundations already existing, and did not seek to destroy the 'pārhā' organisations and other established institutions of the Mūndās. The early Nāgbansi chiefs appear to have seen that such a course of destruction and vandalism would not be tolerated by the proud and untameable Mūndās, and, would ultimately involve the ruin of the state or kingdom which they might succeed in establishing for a time. And thus it is that we find the *pārhās* still existing in more or less pristine vigour, so far at least as their social authority is concerned, although their administrative and political authority has been, in course of time, naturally undermined to a great extent.

Bhuinhari Pattis

The new Nāgbansi Rājās found in these Pārhās ready-made, political divisions which they utilised as so many revenue circles and the *Pārhās* promised, or were obliged to give, him tributes which, in course of time, came to be fixed. The only innovation which the Nāgbansi Rājās sought to introduce was to apply the name of *Pattis* to the *Pārhās* and of Bhuinhars to the *Mānkis* or the former political chiefs of the *Pārhās*. Though the term 'Bhuinhārs' is now-a-days applied to all descendants of the first aboriginal founders of villages in Chōtā Nāgpūr proper, it appears to have been originally equivalent to the appeallation 'Mānki'. This view explains the tradition amongst the Mūndās that formerly there were, in the whole of Sonepur, only "eight Mānkis and nine Bhūinhārs".[1] With the gradual undermining of the political

---

[25] The *pir* of Kahhan (Singbhum) appears to be a variant of the name 'Parha'.

authority of the *Pārhās* the name 'Mānki', as the political head of
the ancient Pārhā, gradually dropped off in the entire Mūndā
country west of the present Rānchi-Chāibāssā Road.   The memory
of the name still lingers here and there within that tract.   When,
still later, the Bhūinhār-heads (the representatives of the ancient
Mānkis) of the Mūndāri *pattis* of these parts lost all political power
over their respective *pattis*, and the Nagbansi Raja or his Jagirdars
came to collect their annual tributes direct from each individual
villager instead of through the Bhūinhār-head, all the descendants
of the original settlers of these villages came to be indiscriminately
called Bhūinhārs.   The Mūndās of these parts, by reason of their
comparative nearness to the Raja's court, gradually came to add
office-bearers to their *Pārhās* in imitation of those they found in their
Raja's Court which strongly impressed their imagination.   And
the designations of the many dignitaries of their Raja's court
such as those of 'Lals' 'Thakurs', 'Kotwars', pleased their fancy
and were adopted by them for the added office-bearers of their
Pārhās.

Manki Pattis and Other Khuntkatti Pattis

The more untameable and uncompromising Mundas, who
migrated to the south and south-east of the District, clung to the
original form of their ancient institutions, and it is amongst them
that the name of *Manki* is still in use.   The circumstances of
their colonisation, however, necessitated a striking difference in
constitution between the present *Manki pattis* and the *Bhuinhari
pattis.*   Whereas each *patti* in the Bhuinhari area was co-extensive
with a Pārhā, and comprised exclusively of members of one *kili*, the
later-colonised *Manki pattis* could not have been so.   And the
reason is not far to seek.   When an adventurous Mūndā family left
their former home in what is now the Bhuinhāri area and entered
the then primeval forest in the south and south-east and established
one or more villages, they began to feel keenly the separation from
their relatives.   The natural gregariousness of man prompted these
pioneer settlers to invite other families to come and live in their
neighbourhood, where unreclaimed jungles then abounded.
Relatives by marriage, who must necessarily have belonged to
kilis different from their own, were naturally amongst those invited to come and settle by their side.   The first pioneer settler
naturally became the political head or Mānki of the villages founded

all around by members of his family or by families of relatives who
came and settled at his invitation. When the Nāgbansi Rājā
came to assess a tribute on these newly established blocks of villages
which he called *pattis*, he naturally looked to this Mānki as responsible for the tribute. The distance of these new colonies, and their
inaccessibility naturally deterred the Rājā from seeking to collect
his tribute from each village-Mūndā separately. Thus, we see
how it happened that whereas in the older or Bhūinhāri area, the
kilis are more or less geographically grouped, they are not so in the
later-colonised Khūntkātti area.

Parha Government

In the Bhūinhāri area, each *Pārhā* now consists of about
a dozen villages, the Bhūinhārs of which all belong to
one and the same *kili*. In the Manki pattis, the Pārhās,
as we have seen, are not co-extensive with the *pattis*,—the
Mūndās of a single pārhā often hailing from two or three
separate *pattis*. Nor do the *parhas* in the *Mānki pattis* always
consist exclusively of Mundas of one and the same
kili.[26] By way of justification for this, the Mūndās of such
mixed *pārhās* suggest that social matters cannot be properly
decided by *kili-hūgās* (clan brethren) alone, but that the opinion of
'kūtūmbs'—men of other *kilis* with whom alone matrimonial relations can be entered into,—must needs be consulted. But the
real reason, as we have seen, was different.

The executive authority of the pārhā and its judicial authority
are vested in a select body known as the *Panchāyat*. The 'Pancha-
yāt' in a Bhūinhāri pārhā is a fixed body with a permanent
president styled the Rājā and a permanent staff of officers— such
as the Kuār, the Lāl, the Thākur, the Kartā, the Dewān, the
Ohdār, the Pānre, the Kōtwār, and the Sipāhis,—titles evidently
adopted later in imitation of the Hindu Rajas and Jagirdars. The
Panchayat of a pārhā in the Khūntkatti area is neither a fixed
body nor has any permanent officers except the president called
by them the 'Pāt Mūndā', the social head of the *pārhā*, whose office
is hereditary. The judicial authority of the 'panchāyat' is now

---

[26] Thus, in the *Hahab Parha*, consisting of villages Hahab, Singasari, Kakara,
Ulatu, Kolad, Bandua Bundubera, Hating Chauli, and Maipatdi, there are
Mundas of no less than three *kilis*,—namely, the *Runda kili*, the *Jom-tuti kili*,
and *Patra-kukuri kili*. The Munda of Hahab is the Pat Munda.

exercised only in cases of breaches of marriage-laws and other social rules, disputes regarding the right claimed by a family to bury their dead in the village sasān, disputes about inheritance and partition, and boundary disputes between two Mūndā villages. Occasionally the 'panchāyat' assumed jurisdiction over persons declared to be witches and sorcerers by the Sokhās or professional witch-finders.

The Panchāyat in the Bhūinhāri Area

(i) *Constitution* : Each Pārhā in the Bhūinhāri area has, as we have seen, a standing *Panchāyat*. All the male members of the *Pārhā* may attend its deliberations, but the principal officers who conduct its business are the *Pārhā* Rājā and his two Sipāhis, the Dewān and his two Sipāhis, the Thākur, the Lāl, the Pāndé, and the Kartā. The *Pārhā* Rājā is the President of the Panch, the Pāndé convokes it, and the Pāhān or Kartā offers the necessary sacrifices and at a *pārhā* feast, eats the first morsel before the other Mūndās present can commence eating. Each of these offices is generally hereditary, or rather is borne by the Mūndā, or the Pāhān, or the Māhāto for the time being, of some particular villages comprised in the *Pārhā*. The offices of the *Sākām-heāni*—who gathers the 'Sāl' leaves on which rice is served to the assembled Mūndās at the Panchāyat-feasts, the *Chārichātāni*—who makes the leaf-cups used in drinking from, and the *'pān-khāwās'* who distributes chūna or lime, tamaku or tobacco, and in some instances pan or beetle-leaves, are similarly held each by some headman of a particular village. And the villages themselves are also called the Rājā, the Dewān, the Lāl, etc. as the case may be, of the *Pārhā*. Each *Pārhā* is known by the name of the village where its *Pārhā* Rājā resides.

(ii) *Proceedings of the Panchayat* : A Mūndā wishing to make any serious complaint to the standing *Panchayat* against another Mūndā of a village of the Pārhā, or to refer any dispute to the decision of the *Panch*, will notify his intention to the Pārhā Rājā, through the Mūndā or Pāhān of the complainant's own village. The Rājā will thereupon direct the Pāndé of the *Pārhā* to assemble the members of the *Pārhā* on a certain date in the village of the man complained against. When the *Panchāyat* meet, the complaint or cause of the dispute is explained by the President, and the *Panchāyat* hear the evidence and explanations (statements) of both sides somewhat in the same manner as in a Court of Law. And the verdict of the *Panchāyat* is pronounced by the President. Fines imposed by the *Panchāyat* are realized by the Dewan and his Chāprasis by force, if necessary. Pitiful indeed is the condition of the convicted offender who refuses to bow to the decision of the *Panchāyat* or pay the fine imposed. The recusant is often severely thrashed, and always outcasted. He cannot find wives for his sons or husbands for his daughters, and is turned out of his lands, in certain cases, if possible.

The Parha Panch in the Khuntkatti Area

A *Pārhā Panchāyat* in the Khuntkatti area differs only in its constitution from the *Panchāyat* of a *Pārhā* in the Bhūinhāri area. As we have already noticed, a *Pārhā* Panchāyat in the Khūntkātti area is not a standing committee as in the Bhūinhāri area. A Pārhā Panch in the Khūntkātti area is composed of one or two headmen (the Mūndā or the Pāhān or both) from each of the different villages constituting the Parha. The 'Pāt Mūndā' of the *Pārhā* presides over the deliberations of the Panch thus constituted.

With regard to the proceedings of the *Panchāyat* and the mode of execution of its orders, there is very little difference between those of a *Pārhā Panchāyat* in the Khūntkātti area and those of a Pārhā Panch in the Bhūinhāri area.

Private Panchayat

The *Pārhā Panchāyat* described above is convened only to decide serious disputes or punish serious offences. In ordinary private disputes, a private Panchāyat is convened by the disputants to decide the dispute. We shall now describe the constitution of such a private *Panchāyat* and its mode of procedure. Each party calls a number of Mūndās generally of the same *kili*, but sometimes a few men of other *kilis* too are called. The men called by each party are called the *Panches* (*Pach-ko*) of that party. Out of the two sets of *Panches* thus called, the Munda and the Pahan of the village to which the disputants belong, or the assembled *Panches* themselves, nominate three or more men on each side as the *select Panch* of that side. The *Panches* of the two sides, thus selected, will now join heads together and elect one amongst themselves as the *Sir Panch* or President. The nominated *Sir Panch* with the select *Panch* on both sides will now take their seats in a central position. The other men of the assembly (also called *panches* of the parties) will now remove to some distance, the two disputants each with his respective partisans (called his *panches'*) withdrawing one to the right and the other to the left of the *Sir Panch* and his associates, but beyond hearing distance from them. Two or three persons are selected by the *Sir Panch* and his associates to act as 'Kaji-idiāgūs' or messengers. The *Sir Panch* will then proceed to question two or three men called from amongst the partisans (*Panches*) on each side. The *Kāji-idiāgūs*[27] will explain the depositions of these witnesses on each side to the opposite side and also recapitulate the evidence, for the benefit of the *Sir Panch* and his associate-*panch*. Now-a-days, when one or more of the *Kāji-idiāgūs* are literate, the depositions are sometimes recorded in writing and read over to the parties and to the *Panch*. The *Sir-Panch* and his associate *Panches* will, last of all, retire to some distance to consider the evidence, each by himself. Then the *Sir Panch* will call each of his associate *Panches* one by one and ask his opinion about the matter in dispute and the reasons for his opinion. He will next send for, or himself go to, the *Panches* or assembly of partisans on each side, and question them as to their opinion with reasons. Finally, after considering all these depositions and opinions, the *Sir Panch* will pronounce his decision and give his reasons. The *'hūkūm'* or decree will be passed accordingly. And, when some members of the Panchāyat are literate, the decision will generally be put down in writing. In former times, the decision of the *Panchāyat* was regarded as an inspired decree, and no Mūndā would have dreamt of disregarding it. But now-a-days, this is not always the case. A party dissatisfied with the *Panch-faisal* (decision of the *Panch*) now sometimes seeks his remedy in Courts of Law. The *Panches* do not get any remuneration, but are entertained with food and drink by the party who calls them. When any fine is realised from an offender, part of it, at least, goes to provide for a general feast to the *Panches*, and to the other Mūndās of the village.

Oaths and Ordeals

The favourite methods sometimes employed by a *Parha Panch* as well as by a private Panch to find out the truth about a

[27] *Kaji-idiagu*, literally means 'word-carrier'.

dispute or to detect a culprit are the *oath* and the *ordeal*. These are preceded by certain religious ceremonies conducted by a member of the *Panch* in which *Sing-Bōngā* (the Sun-God or Supreme Deity) is invoked to bring the false claimant to grief. Oaths are commonly taken by touching or rather taking on the head a tiger-skin (*kūlā-ūhūr*), or bamboo leaves (*mād-sākām*) or *jitiapipar* leaves (*tepel-hesā sākām*), or fire (*sengel*), or cowdung (*guri*), or 'ātap' or *ārūā* rice (*ādoā chāuli*), or a clod of earth from the deponent's hearth (*jū-ūlā*). In land-disputes or disputes about a *sasān* or graveyard, the oath is often taken on a clod of earth (*hāsā*) from the land or the '*sasān*' in dispute. Oaths, taken on the cow's tail, and on copper and *tulsi*-leaves, are also in vogue, and appear to have been borrowed from the Hindus. When any oath is taken, an appropriate formula is pronounced by the deponent. Thus, while swearing on the tiger's skin, he will say, "May tigers devour me if I be guilty" (*neāing gūnhā-kāredo kūlā jōmte jōming kā*). While swearing on the cowdung he will say, "May all my cattle die if I be guilty, or if my claim be not true". While swearing on copper and *tulsi*-leaves, the deponent will say, "May I not get money (copper) any more".

The Lolo-Da (hot water) and the Kata-Topana (foot-burying) Ordeals

A common ordeal by which suspected culprits are tested is to put a coin of copper or silver into a vessel filled with boiling water, and to ask each suspected person successively to dip his hand into the water and take out the coin. The Mūndā believes that the real culprit's hand will get scalded in the process, but that the innocent man will come out unscathed from the ordeal. Another curious ordeal sometimes employed in deciding a boundary-dispute is that known as *kātā-topānā* in Mundari and as *gōr-gāri* in Hindi. The procedure is as follows: Two holes are dug, one on each alleged boundary line. Two men are selected, one by each of the two disputing parties from amongst themselves to undergo the ordeal on their behalf. The representative of each party will then put one leg into the hole dug on the boundary line claimed by his party. Powdered ārūā rice (*ādoā-chāuli-hōlōng*) will then be thrown in upon the leg inside the hole. The two holes being thus filled to the brim with rice-dust, the two representatives, each with one leg buried in a hole, are to remain in this situation until one of them, either through sheer exhaustion or being unable to stand the biting of ants or other insects, begs to be released. The Mūndā believes that the false claimant is sure to have his leg in the hole wholly eaten up by white-ants, if he remains in that situation for some length of time. The man who shows the greater fortitude and holds out longer and comes out unhurt by insects, wins the case for his own party.

Special Oaths

Sometimes boundary disputes are decided by a combination of arbitration and ordeal. The disputing parties undertake to abide by the verdict of a person expected to know the correct boundary, provided he will point out the boundary after taking certain religious vows and in certain specified methods such as, by walking along the boundary line with an untanned cowhide on his head, or by driving a heifer along the line, or by carrying along the line a basket filled with earth and wheat or other grain on his head. One party may also undertake to give up his claim in case his opponent will go round the boundary line he claims, in one of the methods aforesaid, or by leading his son by the arm along the line.

Customary Law[28]

Having thus examined the indigenous Mūndari method of administration of justice, we shall now proceed to give a brief account of the ancient customary law which still obtains amongst the Mūndās and is administered by the *Panch* when that tribunal is resorted to. The joint family system of the Munda resembles the Hindu system. In the lifetime of the father, the sons do not generally separate from him in mess or property. Sons with their wives and children live under the paternal roof. They all join hands in cultivating the family fields, have their meals cooked in the same family hearth, and bring even their separate earnings, if any, to the common family fund. If a member of the joint family goes away temporarily to the labour districts or elsewhere, he does not lose his right to

[28] These rules of customary law are practically the same for the Uraons of the Ranchi District. One slight point of difference is the following. When the sons of a deceased Uraon owner are born of different mothers, all the sons by the first wife are in many villages awarded a slightly larger share than the sons by the second wife.

his proper share in the ancestral lands in the event of partition
during his absence. But as for the accumulated savings of the
family up to the date of partition, the absentee may not claim
a share in them unless he brings his own individual earnings into
the hotch potch. But no member of the family can at partition
claim a higher share in consideration of any special private earnings or for any extraordinary toil or trouble for the improvement
of the joint family property.

(i) Partition

As we have said, the members of an undivided Mūndā family
share all they have, in common, till the death of the father. But,
the father may, during his life-time, expel a disobedient son from
his house even without giving him any moveable property or a
share of the lands.[29] It is optional with the father, however, to
separate a son with such share of the family property as the father
thinks proper. The father is now-a-days regarded as having
almost absolute control over the family property during his life-
time, although any disposition of family property in contravention
of the customary rules of inheritance will not be binding on his
heirs. The sons cannot, as of right, demand a partition during the
life-time of their father. But the father may and sometimes does,
make a partition of family property amongst his sons. This is
almost always the case when the mother of the sons being dead,
the father has married a second wife. At partition, the eldest son
generally gets a slightly larger share than the other sons—the
excess being ordinarily one kāt (sala) of land, and in well-to-do
families, a yoke of plough-cattle or only one bullock or one goat,
and sometimes also one 'morā' or bundle of paddy measuring
from ten to sixteen maunds. With this difference, the sons all
get equal shares of moveable and immoveable property, and a
similar share of both real and personal property is taken by the
father. An unmarried son, however, will get, in addition to his
proper share, some cash or cattle or both by way of provision
for his marriage. The cattle, etc. which a married son received
at his marriage will be given to him at partition. Females
amongst the Mūndās are not entitled to inherit, but the father

[29]A Munda of village Mad-dih some time ago expelled his son from his house in
this way; and the son unsuccessfully sued his father in Court for a share of the
ancestral lands.

may in his life-time make presents of cash or moveables to a daughter, but *not* of lands. When, however, the father effects a partition during his life-time, an unmarried daughter usually gets some land to be held by way of maintenance till her marriage, and also a few kats of paddy for her consumption till the following harvest. Almost invariably, an unmarried daughter, after such partition lives either under the protection of her father or of one of her brothers; and the land allotted to her by way of maintenance till her marriage remains till then in the possession of her chosen guardian who supports her. The bride-price received at her marriage too will go to that guardian if he defrays the expenses of her marriage. This khōrpōsh land of the sister, however, will be re-partitioned amongst the brothers, after the sister's marriage. When a Mūndā father, after marrying a second wife, makes a division of the family property with his sons by his first wife, there cannot be a redistribution of the lands on the birth of other sons to him by the second wife. Till the father's death, such subsequently born children will be maintained out of the share of their father.

(*ii*) *Inheritance*

We now come to the customary law regarding inheritance amongst the Mūndās. After the death of the father, if the sons do not agree to live together, a *Panchāyat* is convened, and the property divided according to Mūndari rules of inheritance.

(*a*) *Widow With Sons*: When the deceased has left behind him a widow and grown-up sons and daughters, the *Panch* will first set apart some land, generally equal to a younger son's share, for the maintenance of the widow; and, if any cash has been left by the deceased, a small sum (generally not more than twenty rupees) is paid to the widow for her subsistence till the following harvest. In the land thus allotted to her, she can only have a life-interest. If, for the rest of her days, she lives separate from her sons and independently of any pecuniary assistance from any of them in particular, her maintenance land will, on her death, be equally divided amongst the sons. But, in most cases, the widow prefers to live with one or other of the sons. In such a case, her maintenance land is cultivated and practically enjoyed by that son, and if he meets all her funeral expenses, he becomes entitled to those lands.

(*b*) *Sons* : The residue of the real and personal property left by the deceased father will be divided by the Panchāyat in equal shares amongst all the sons of the deceased, except that the eldest son will, in most cases, get a little land in excess, and, in well-to-do families, also one 'mōrā' of paddy besides one or two bullocks or a goat, according to circumstances. If there had been a partition during the father's life-time, and, since then, other sons were born to the father, the entire immoveable property will on the father's death, be re-partitioned by the *Panch* amongst all the sons of the deceased on the principles indicated above. If, however, no son was born to the deceased father between the previous partition and his death, only the deceased father's share will be partitioned amongst the sons. If any of the legitimate sons of the deceased, owing to his marriage with a non-Mūndāri girl or other misbehaviour, has been outcasted and lost his tribal rights, he will not be entitled to a share at partition, unless he has been restored to caste by the *Panch* after he has given up the alien wife. Trivial moveable articles which do not yield themselves to accurate division, generally go to the eldest son, but the *Panch* may make them over to any one of the sons they think proper.

(*c*) *Widow Without Sons*: When the deceased owner leaves no son but only a childless widow or a widow with daughters only, the widow is allowed a life-interest in the property left by the husband. The widow may dispose of moveable articles and even house-materials in case of necessity, and give temporary leases such as Zurpeshgi, etc. of the real property left by her husband, but she has no authority to sell any real property left by her husband without the consent of all the 'bhāyāds' or agnates of her deceased husband. If the widow leaves her deceased husband's village for good, and goes to reside permanently with her father or brother, she forfeits her right to enjoy the usufruct of her husband's lands which then go to the nearest agnates. If the widow remarries, she at once loses all right to all moveable and immoveable properties left by her deceased husband. She is just allowed to take away with her the jewellery she has on and her wearing apparel.

(*d*) *Daughters* : Daughters among the Mūndās do not inherit. Nor are the sons of the deceased owner under any obligation to make over to a sister of theirs anything which their father, either on his death-bed or earlier, desired them to give her. The sons are, however, bound to support unmarried sisters until their marriage.   But an unmarried sister may elect to live in the house of any one of her brothers.   And on her expressing her desire to do so, the *Panch* effecting a partition of the family property may allot some additional land to the brother under whose care the girl chooses to live.   This additional land will be re-partitioned in equal shares amongst the brothers after their sister is married. But the bride-price (*gonong-tākā*) and presents of cattle (*sūk-mūr*) received at the sister's marriage will be retained by the brother or brothers who have borne the expenses of her marriage.

When a deceased Mūndā leaves an unmarried daughter or daughters and no widow or son, the unmarried daughter or daughters will be entitled to the personal property left by their father, and will remain in possession of the lands left by the deceased till their marriage.   Neither a daughter's husband nor a daughter's sons are entitled to inherit.

(*e*) *Bhayads* :   In the absence of sons, or widow, or unmarried daughters of a deceased Mūndā, his property goes to the nearest male agnate or agnates.   If the deceased's father is alive, the property passes to him.   If he is dead, the brothers of the deceased owner will inherit in equal shares.   The sons of a pre-deceased brother will take the share that would have fallen to their father if he had been living at the time.   On failure of father, brothers and brother's sons, the next nearest male agnates will inherit. Brother's sons and other agnates take *pir stirpes*.

(*f*) *Gor-Jonrea or a Son-in-law Brought up in His Father-in-law's Family* :   The '*Gōr-Jonrea*' or *ghar-dijoa* (घर-दामाद) who lived with his son-less deceased father-in-law till the death and assisted him in his cultivation and other affairs till his death, will get all the moveable property left by the deceased, and such share of the real property, if any, as, according to the circumstances, the *Panch* may think proper to give him, the rest going to the nearest male agnate or agnates.   In cases where a son-in-law of the deceased has redeemed mortgages given by his deceased father-in-law during his life-time, he is allowed to remain in possession of the land till the nearest male agnate or agnates (the heir or heirs) of the deceased can repay the money paid by the son-in-law in redeeming the mortgage.   Any land that may be given by the *Panch* to the *ghar-dijoa* may be enjoyed by him only so long as his wife (the daughter of the deceased owner) is alive, after which the inheritance passes to the nearest bhāyād, as a daughter's son does not inherit. When there are no agnates of the deceased left, the *Panch* may give the inheritance to the *ghar-damad*, but nowadays the *lāgān-pānewālā* (landlord) often successfully lays claim to and takes possession of the lands of such heirless deceased tenant.

(*g*) *Illegitimate Son* : Illegitimate sons of the deceased owner or sons of the deceased's wife by a former husband, do not get any share in the property left by the deceased. But if any such son had been living in the same house with the deceased, he is sometimes given a small plot of land for his maintenance, although he cannot claim this as a matter of right. He can have no legal right even to any lands that his father (the deceased owner)might have given him to cultivate. And on the death of the father, he is bound to give up such lands if the legitimate heirs of the deceased owner so demand. Even when the deceased leaves no legitimate son, and his widow taking a life-interest in the property allows the illegitimate son to continue to hold the lands, the latter is bound to give up the lands on the death of the widow, if the reversioners require him to do so.

(*h*) *Adopted Son* : Sometimes when a sonless Mūndā gets old he chooses one of his *bhāyāds*—a cousin, nephew or grand-nephew, to be his prospective son, and calls a Panchāyat of his *kili*. If the Panchāyat, including his other bhāyāds, think proper, the chosen relative may be adopted as a son, and take care of the old man and his property, and inherit his property on his death to the exclusion of the other agnates. If the adopted son is not a 'bhāyād',[30] he gets only his marriage expenses, a *mora* or so of paddy, some ploughs and plough-cattle such as may be thought proper by the *Panch*. If there is no 'bhāyād' left, the *Pānch* may make over the property left by the deceased to the *non-bhāyād adopted son*, but if the landlord (*lāgān-pānewālā*) objects, it is doubtful whether the *non-bhāyād* adopted son will succeed in retaining possession of the lands.

(5) Social Ceremonies And Social Customs

The social ceremonies and usages observed by the Mūndās are more numerous and elaborate tha n one would at first suppose. These ceremonies give us an insigh t into the many social virtues

[30] A non-*bhāyād* is, however, rarely adopted.

of the tribe—their genuine hospitality to their own people, their respect for age and social authority, their affection for their relatives, and, above all, their good humour and geniality. We shall here give a brief account of their principal ceremonies and observances in connection with marriage, birth, and death. It is to be understood, however, that there are certain local variations in minor details in the different parganas of the district.

Marriage and Its Connected Ceremonies

In the matter of marriage, as in several other matters, the Mūndās appear to have modified some of their ancient customs and practices in imitation of those of their Hindu neighbours of olden times. Although early marriages are not infrequent amongst well-to-do Mūndās in these days, especially in the eastern parganas of the Rānchi District, the days are still remembered when no young Mūndā could marry before he was able to construct a plough with his own hands, nor would a Mūndā girl be given away in marriage before she could, with her own hands, weave mats with palm-leaves and spin cotton. And, in earlier times, it is said, Mūndā young folk of both sexes had a freer hand than now in the choice of their partners in life from amongst members of marriageable *kilis* or septs. But, in modern days, the selection is ordinarily made for the boy as well as for the girl by the father or other guardian. The boy's approval of the guardian's selection is, however, frequently sought for, and generally obtained. The ultimate selection, however, rests not on human hands, but on certain omens known as *chenre-uri-ko* or *ere-uri-ko*.[31] We shall now proceed to describe briefly each of the principal observances and ceremonies connected with a Mūndāri marriage.

(*i*) *The Chenre-uri* : The *Chenre-uri* or omen-reading is performed in the following manner. When a Mūndā father has a suitable bride in view for his son, he sends a go-between called a 'Dūtām'[32] to the guardian of the girl. If the girl's guardian considers the proposed match desirable, he names a day for *chenre-uri*. On

---

[31] *Chenre*, in Mundari, means a 'bird'. And '*uri*' is the name of a particular species of bird. Cf. Lat. *augurium*, and Eng., augury,—from L. *avis* a bird, The word *er-e* in Mundari, means an augury or omen.

[32] Cf. Sanskrit *Dutam* (दूतम्) This functionary is also known as *agia* amongst the Mundas.

the appointed day, the Dūtām and the guardian of the proposed bridegroom with two or three relatives, and, if so requested by the girl's guardian, with the proposed bridegroom too, start for the girl's village. On the way, the party go on marking every omen, good or bad. Among omens considered good (*būgin eré-ko*) may be mentioned the following : a cow and her calf lowing in response to each other ; paddy being carried ; pitchers, filled with water, being carried ; well-cleaned and well-washed clothes being carried ; ploughs or yokes being constructed ; a fox passing in front of the party from their left to the right ; a person piling up dust ; and a tiger. Among bad omens (*etkan eré-ko*) are the following : a person carrying an axe, a spade, or a shovel ; a person carrying a *kumuni* or fishing-trap made of bamboo; a cow bellowing but not in response to, nor followed by response from, her calf ; rice being carried ; sweepings of a house being thrown away ; clothes besmeared with ashes or similar other substance to clean them ; and a tree falling down under the axe of the wood-cutter.

If the party happen to come across any bad omen on the way, they forthwith return home and the negotiations fall through. If, fortunately, no bad omen is encountered, the party proceed to the house of the intended bride. On their arrival there one or more mats are spread out on the *angan* or courtyard of the house. After the party take their seats on these mats, the boy's *Dutam* relates to the *Dutam* on the girl's side what omens were noticed on the way. If the latter declares these omens favourable or, at any rate, not unfavourable, he proceeds to take charge of the sticks and umbrellas of the boy's party. The women-folk of the girl's house now come out into the courtyard and wash the feet of the guests. One or more jars of rice-beer are next placed before the guests who do full justice to the liquor. They then have a hearty meal of boiled rice and boiled pulse. Now, the boy's guardian invites the girl's guardian and relatives to visit his house on a certain date, and, after mutual greetings or *salams* (*jōhār*), the boy's party take leave of the girl's guardian and relatives.

On the appointed day, the girl's guardian with his *Dūtām* and a small party of relatives start for the boy's house, and go on marking every omen on the way. If any bad omen is met with, the party return home—all except the Dūtām,—who carries the bad news to the boy's guardian. And the negotiations are at an end. If the omens are not unfavourable, the entire party proceed to the boy's house where they are received with the same ceremonies with which they themselves had welcomed the boy's party at their place. After the feet of the guests are washed, and before they begin to do justice to the rice-beer placed before them, a relative of the intended bride steps forth as the spokesman or *joārni*. This man first fills a leaf-cup with rice-beer and taking it in his left hand, makes his 'salāms or obeisance to everybody present, and delivers a set speech beginning,—"Now for this boy and this girl, in the presence of God (*Sing Bōngā*) in heaven and the Panch on earth, the omens have been all right", and ending as follows,—"To-day, the boy's father and the girl's father will thatch two roofs with one bundle of straw (i.e. will be united as members of one family) : May the roofs ever remain thatched like this". Then the *Jōārni* johārs (*salāms*) all present, and the guests all drink rice-beer and have a hearty meal of boiled rice, *dāl* (*pulses*), and goat's flesh-curry. Another jar of rice-beer completes the day's festivities. After mutual salutations, the would-be relatives take leave of one another.

(*ii*) *The Bala* : The next preliminary ceremony in connection with a Mūndā marriage is the *Bālā* or betrothal. On an appointed day, the bride's guardian with a number of relatives arrives at the bridegroom's house, and is accorded a hearty welcome. The feet of the guests are washed by young men called *Kātāabūngnis*, goats are ceremonially killed in their honour, and rice-beer is freely distributed. The bride-price is settled not by naming the demand, but by the bride's guardian signifying his demand by symbols, and the bridegroom's guardian signifying his acceptance by the use of the same symbols. Thus, a number of clay-marbles are sent to the bridegroom's guardian through the Dūtām to signify the number of rupees wanted. A number of sāl-leaves each rolled up and tied round with a coloured thread signify the number of '*sāris*' (women's clothes) wanted, and so forth. The bridegroom's guardian takes a certain number out of these and returns the rest to signify that he agrees to give as many of each item as he has kept and begs to be excused from satisfying the rest of the demand. When at length the terms are thus agreed upon, the bride's guardian and the bridegroom's guardian heartily embrace (*hāpārūp jōār*) each other, and the men of each party exchange salutations with the men of the other party. The final clenching of the contract is made by the Mūndā or the *Pāhān* of the bride's village clasping the hand of the Mūndā or the *Pāhān* of the bridegroom's village, and talking to each other as follows :

Q. Why do we clasp each other's hand ?
A. For such-and-such (names) boy and girl.
Q. Who made this hand ?
A. God made it.
Q. As we now clasp each other's hands, so may our hands remain clasped for ever. If you break this betrothment at the malicious gossip of others, you shall have to pay Rs. 5 (or Rs. 10 or Rs. 15, as may be agreed upon) to me. And if you do not pay this fine, I shall cut off your hand.
A. Agreed. And if you do the same, you must pay me Rs. 5 (or Rs. 10 or Rs. 15), or else I shall cut off your hand.

The concluding ceremony in the Bālā consists in the bridegroom-elect sitting on the knees of the maternal uncle of his betrothed (or, in the absence of the maternal uncle, on the knees of the Mūnda or the Pahan of the girl's village), and the girl's guardian presenting the bridegroom-elect with a new piece of cloth and a bead-necklace. Then follows the betrothal feast, after which the bridegroom's guardian and his party are anointed with oil mixed with pounded turmeric and are presented with the hind part of each of the goats killed at the feast. The *Dūtām* makes *jōhār* (*salām*) to the guests individually and delivers a set speech apologising humbly for the shortcomings in the entertainment. After a fresh exchange of hearty greetings and salutations, the guests depart.

(*iii*) *The Gonongtaka Idituka and* (*iv*) *the Logon-Tol.* : If the marriage takes place in the same year in which the betrothal takes place, the ceremonies of *Gōnōngtākā Iditūkā* (the carrying or presentation of the bride-price) and the *lōgōn-tōl* (selection of a suitable date for the marriage), take place on one and the same date. On a date fixed beforehand, the bridegroom's guardian with a few friends and relatives goes to the girl's house with the gōnōngtākā or bride-price, and all are received with the same ceremonial hospitality as before. After the feet of the guests are washed by the *kātāābūngnis*, and the guests take their seats, the boy's guardian makes over the gōnōngtākā to the *Dūtām* of the other side who hands over the money to the bride's guardian. Then the *Dutam* asks the boy's guardian whether they come for *lōgōn-tōl* as well. If the answer is in the affirmative, the girl's guardian names a suitable day for the wedding. Now, three goats are brought to the place, to be killed in celebration of the *gōnōngtākā* ceremony and one in celebration of the lōgōn-tōl. After the feast the *Dūtām* of the girl's side salutes the guests and delivers the same set speech as in the *Bālā*.

When the lōgōn-tōl is celebrated on the same day, the following additional ceremony is observed. Two *sāl pātris* (sāl-leaves stitched together in the form of a circular plate) are placed on a mat in the courtyard. On one of these the maternal uncle of the bride-groom-elect and on the other the Mūndā or the Pāhān of the bridegroom's village take their seats. The betrothed girl and a girl-friend (*lukundi*) of hers are made to sit down respectively on the knees of the boy's maternal uncle and the Mūndā or the Pāhān of the boy's village (or in their absence, the boy's father or other guardian). The bride-elect then takes up from out of a plate held before her, some rice, turmeric, and a few betel nuts, and places three handfuls of these on a piece of new cloth spread over the palm of her other hand. Then she gives *lōgōn'* by handing over this piece of cloth with the rice, etc. in it, to the maternal uncle of her betrothed. After regaling themselves once more with rice-beer, the guests take a hearty farewell and carry home with them the hind part of the goats killed.

(*v*) *The Arandi* : Last comes the *ārāndi* or marriage ceremony itself. We shall describe each attendant ceremony separately.

(*a*) 'Sāsāng-Gōsō'—A few days before the marriage a rectangular mud-pulpit called māndōā' is raised on the courtyard of the house of the bridegroom as well as of the bride. On each of the four corners of this *māndōā* a thin sāl' sapling is planted, and in the centre of the *māndōā* a *bhelōā* (M., *sōsō*)[33] sapling, a thin bamboo (M., mād) sapling, and a thin sāl' (M. *sārjom*) sapling, are planted together and all painted with rice-flour dissolved in water, and encircled with a cotton-thread. From the third day before the wedding, every evening the bride and the bridegroom sit down for a while on the *māndōā* at their respective houses, and are there

[33] This is the *semecarpus anacardium* of Botanists.

anointed with mustard oil mixed with turmeric-juice (berel-*sāsāng*) by some female relative.

(*b*) 'Cho or Chūmān'—On the evening preceding the wedding-day, a benedictory ceremony called chō or chūmān is performed at the bridegroom's as well as at the bride's house. The bridegroom puts on cloth dyed with turmeric-juice, and sits down on the *māndōā*, when his near female relatives, one after another, take up some arūā rice and young grass-blades from a plate or basket and with these in their folded hands touch the feet, thighs, shoulder-joints, and, last of all, the cheeks, of the bridegroom. Just after touching the cheeks of the bridegroom each female relative kisses (*chō*) her own hand,—and this is the chūmān completed. The *chūmān* of the bride is similarly performed at her father's house.

(*c*) 'The Bridegroom's Uli-sākhi'—Before the marriage-procession passes out of the bridegroom's village, it stops at the first mango (*uli*) tree on the way. Round the trunk of this tree, the bridegroom puts a mark of rice-flour dissolved in water, and ties up a thread. The bridegroom's mother then sits down under the tree with the bridegroom on her knees. The mother asks his son, "Where are you going ?" The son replies, "I am going to bring some one who will take care of you and give you rice and vegetables." The bridegroom then puts into his own mouth a mango-stalk and molasses. After chewing the mango-stalk a little, he gives the chewings to his mother who gulps the whole thing and blesses her boy. The bridegroom and his party including a number of female relatives then start for the bride's house. When the bridegroom can afford to go on a *chowdol* or on a palanquin, he always does so. Otherwise he is carried up to the limits of his own village on the arms of his relatives, and again similarly carried from the limits of the bride's village to the bride's house.

(*d*) 'Dāparom or Mergerai'—When the procession approaches the bride's village, the relatives of the bride come out to welcome the bridegroom's party, often with musicians and *pāiki*-dancers. Then the joint procession first walk round the boundary of the village and finally proceed to the bride's house.

(*e*) 'Dā-hirchi' and 'Chūmān'.—When the bridegroom arrives at the courtyard of the bride's house, a number of female relatives come out to meet him, each carrying a brass lōtā filled with water and a pestle (*sāmāt*). Each of these women first sprinkles water on the bridegroom with a mango-twig, and then brandishes the pestle, jestingly exclaiming—*Jumbūri-re-dom kūmbūrū-re-dōm ne-lekām*—[If you prove covetous, if you prove a thief, you will be thus (beaten with a pestle)]. Then the mother of the bride and the other female relatives, one after another, perform the benedictory ceremony of *chūmān* of the bridegroom with *āruā*-rice, grass-blades, cowdung balls, rice-flour balls, and rice-flour bread, in the manner described in v (b) *ante*. Finally, powdered turmeric is besmeared on the cheeks of the bridegroom. The bridegroom and his party are accommodated in a temporary shed called *Jālōm*.

(*f*) 'Chauli Heper'—Next morning, the bridegroom is carried on his palanquin from the *Jālōm* to the bride's house. When the palanquin arrives at the house, the bride is brought out into the courtyard on a bamboo basket, and in it she is carried three times round the bridegroom's palanquin. The bridegroom then throws three handfuls of *āruā* rice at the forehead of the bride, and the bride next throws three handfuls of rice at the forehead of the bridegroom. The palanquin and the basket are then put down on the ground, and the bride and the bridegroom conducted into the house.

(*g*) The Bride's 'Uli-Sākhi'—The bride with a number of her female relatives next proceeds on the palanquin vacated by the bridegroom, to a neighbouring mango tree (*ūli dārū*). Arriving there, the bride puts a mark on the tree with moistened rice-flour and ties up a thread around the tree. The tree is thus made a witness (sākhi) to the marriage.

(*h*) 'Sasāng-Goso' again—A number of female relatives of the bridegroom then come from their quarters (*Jālom*) to the house of the bride's father, carrying a little turmeric and oil, and with these anoint the bride. They then return to their quarters taking the bridegroom with them. And now it is the turn of the female relatives of the bride to go to the quarters of the bridegroom's party and there anoint (*gōsō*) the bridegroom with oil and turmeric (*sasāng*). Before the bridegroom is thus anointed, he is shaved, and during the shaving a little blood is scratched out of his little finger, and a small rag is tinged with the blood, Similarly before the *Sasang-goso* (anointing with turmeric) of the bride, her nails are pared, and a little blood drawn out of her left little finger to dye a small rag with. These two rags are called *sināis'*.

(*i*) Sindūri-Rākāb'—In the forenoon, the bride's female

relatives escort the bridegroom to the house of the bride's father. And the actual marriage ceremony is then performed. The bride and the bridegroom are carried on the arms of these relatives three times round the māndoā or marriage-pulpit in the courtyard. And now both the bride and the bridegroom are made to stand each upon a *Sāl-pātri* in the middle of the *māndoā*, the former with her face to the east, and the latter with his face to the west. In this position, the bridegroom presses the toes of the bride's right foot with the toes of his own left foot, and touches first his own neck with his '*sināi*' (rag tinged with the blood of his little finger) and then the bride's neck with it and repeats the process twice again. Then the bride and the bridegroom change places, and the bride similarly, three times, touches first her own neck with her *sināi* and then the neck of the bridegroom with the same *sināi*. Returning now to their former places on the *Sāl-pātris*, the bride and the bridegroom exchange garlands made of gulaichi flowers, and each puts three vermilion marks first on his or her own forehead and then on the other's forehead. Their garments are now knotted together and both enter the house walking one behind the other. Before they get admittance into the house the bridegroom has to pay a small sum (two annas or so) to the bride's elder sister or other female relative who by way of joke bars the door against them. Now the bride and the bridegroom sit down on a new mat and are treated to a dish of *chiura* (parched rice), *gur* (molasses), milk or curds (*dahi*) and other delicacies.

(*j*) 'Dā-āu' and 'Tuing Etel'—The ceremony we shall now describe is particularly interesting. Four unmarried Mūndā girls, two from the bridegroom's party and two from the bride's side, each with an earthen pitcher on her head, now proceed to a neighbouring tank, spring or river. They are accompanied by a band of Ghāsi musicians, and by two elderly Mūndā women one of whom carries an unsheathed sword in her hand and the other a bow and an arrow. Other female relatives and friends accompany the party. After the four Mūndā maidens have filled their pitchers with water and taken them up on their heads, the woman with the sword stands with her back towards them, and passes her sword over her own shoulder so as to touch the pitchers poised on the heads of the maidens standing behind her. Then the woman with the bow and arrow similarly stands with her back to the four maidens and passes her arrow over her own neck so as to touch the pitchers of water on the heads of the four maidens.   Now the party move in a procession towards the house of the bride's father, the four maidens carrying the pitchers on their heads, the woman with the sword brandishing and whirling her weapon all the way and the other women excitedly mimicking her with their hands, and the musicians playing on their drums and flutes.

(*k*) 'Dūl-dā'—When this procession reaches the house of the bride's father, the bride and the bridegroom change their garments and are led out into the courtyard and seated each on a yoke covered over with straw. These yokes are placed on one side of the courtyard where a plantain tree has been planted for the occasion. Seated there, the bride and the bridegroom anoint each other with oil and turmeric.   And then the water brought in the pitchers by the four maidens, described in the last paragraph, is poured over the young couple. While being bathed in this manner, the bride and the bridegroom each conceals a tiny earthen vessel (*chūkā*) in the ground now made muddy with the water in which they have bathed, for the other to find out. Finally, they put on their yellow clothes again, and once more daub each other's forehead with '*sindur*' (red lead).

(*l*) 'Bōr-āgiā'.—The young couple now walk back into the house, and there sit down on a mat. A goat is then brought before them. Ceremonial *āgiā* water is given to the bridegroom and a sword put into his hands. With this sword, he kills the goat of the courtyard. His feet are now washed, and he resumes his seat on the mat.

(*m*) 'Samdi-bhet'—The bride's parents and near relatives accompanied by musicians next proceed with a jar of rice-beer to the jālōm or quarters of bridegroom's party where another jar of rice-beer has been kept ready for the occasion. After ceremonial *jōhār* or salutations and profuse apologies by the bride's relatives for the poverty of the entertainment, the bride's guardian and the bridegroom's drink rice-beer from one and the same cup, and so also do the mothers of the bridegroom and of the bride drink out of one and the same cup. Then all the guests drink their fill of rice-beer. The bridegroom's guardian now takes up the bride's guardian on his arms and dances about till he gets tired. Similarly, the bride-grooms' mother (or, in her absence, other near female relative) takes up the bride's mother in her arms and dances about.

17

Then the bride's father (or other guardian) and mother (or other female relative) dance about respectively carrying on the arms— one the bridegroom's father and the other the bridegroom's mother. Finally, the bridegroom's father clasps the bride's father to the heart, and the bridegroom's mother similarly embraces the bride's mother. This is called the *hāpārup jōhār*. Then all the persons of one party individually salute the persons on other side, and the bride's relatives return to the house of the bride's father.

(*n*) 'Kātā-ābūng'—The bride and the bridegroom now wash the feet of the male as well as the female relatives of the bride. The relatives thus honoured put down on a brass-plate some presents, generally in cash (each paying from two pice to a rupee) for the wedded pair. The bride and the bridegroom finally make their obeisance to all and resume their seats.

(*o*) The Bridal-Feast—The bride's relatives are now seated on the courtyard, and rice, pulse, vegetables, and meat are served out to them on plates and cups made of *sāl-leaves*. Then the bridegroom places a small *sāl-leaf* by the side of the rice-plate of each guest and the bride puts a pinch of salt on it and on each of the sāl-leaf-cups. The bride and the bridegroom finally take their seats by the side of the Mānki or the Mūndā or the Pāhān of the village, and wash his hands and put a pinch of salt into one of the leaf-cups in which vegetable-curry or meat has been served to him. The bridegroom dines with the party. After the men have finished eating, the women sit down to dinner.

(*p*) 'Bābā-hertūkām'—Before the *bidā* or departure of the bridegroom and his party with the bride, the bride's mother sits down on the threshold of her house, and the bride is seated before her with her back to her mother. A female relative now brings her some paddy on a 'sūp' or winnower, and the bride takes up three successive handfuls of paddy in the palms of her hands joined together, and throws the paddy behind her, over her own head. Each time the bride's mother takes up the paddy thus thrown, in a portion of her own *sāri* or wearing-cloth.

(*q*) 'Jimmā'—The final ceremony of making over the bride is significant. In the presence of the assembled village elders (*Pancho-ko*), either the Mūndā or the Pāhān of the village of the bride's father makes over charge of the bride to the father or other guardian of the bridegroom.

(r) 'Gāti-bāge'—When the bride and the bridegroom are about to start for the latter's house, the bride's maiden-companions (gāti-kō) catch hold of her and do not let her go until the bridegroom makes a small cash present (varying from an anna to a rupee) to them. And now a demonstrative farewell is given. The bride and the bridegroom after making obeisance individually to the assembled relatives of the bride, get up on a chōudōl, palanquin, or other conveyance. When the bridegroom is not rich enough to afford to engage a conveyance, the bride and the bridegroom are carried on the arms of relatives up to the limits of the bride's village and again from the boundary of the bridegroom's village up to his own house.

(vi) *Ceremonies at the Bridegroom's House* : When the bride and the bridegroom arrive at the latter's house, a pestle is brandished before them and the chūmān ceremony is again performed, in the same way as was done on the bridegroom's arrival at the house of the bride's father. Then the bride and the bridegroom are carried three times round the māndōā or pulpit in the courtyard. The bridegroom is taken round the *māndōā* from the right to the left and the bride from the left to the right. Each time the woman carrying the bridegroom in her arms, meets the woman carrying the bride, the two women push against each other by way of joke. After this, the bride and the bridegroom both stand on the *māndōā*, the bridegroom treading on the toes of the bride. In this position, both touch each other's neck with the *sinai* and put vermilion on each other's forehead. Next, the *Dūldā* ceremony is again gone through ; and, finally, the bridegroom's relatives sit down to a dinner when the bride and the bridegroom distribute salt and wash the hands of the Mūndā or the Pāhān of the bridegroom's village. The next day, the father or other guardian of the bride with a few relatives pay a visit to the bridegrom's house to see the bride, and are received and entertained with the utmost honour and hospitality.

Ra-rura : A week or two, and sometimes even a month, after the wedding, the parents, or in their absence, a brother or uncle, of the bride come to take the bride and the bridegroom to their place, and are accorded a very hearty welcome. The bridegroom, on his arrival at the house of his father-in-law, will first uproot the *sāl*, the 'bhelwā', and the bamboo saplings planted in the middle of the *māndoā* or marriage-pulpit on the occasion of the wedding. This will be followed by a sumptuous feast.

Sakamchari or Divorce : When a Mūndā wife refuses to live with her husband, or the latter refuses to keep or support her, a *Panchāyat* is convened, three of the members being generally selected by the party wishing to snap the marriage-tie, and two by the party who wishes the marriage to continue. The *Bālāpanch* or the President of the council hands over a sāl-leaf to the party who is unwilling to continue the marriage-tie, and the latter tears the leaf in twain in indication of the dissolution of the marriage. This ceremony is known as the *Sākām-chāri*. In Pārganā Tāmār, a piece of turmeric (*sāsāng*) is also similarly broken in two, and this ceremony is known as the 'Sāsāng-hād.' If the wife is the unwilling party the bride-price or 'gōnōngtākā' and 'torā-tākā have to be returned.

Sangai (Sagai) or Remarriage : A widow can remarry only in the *sāgai* form in which the detailed ceremonies required for the *ārāndi* or marriage described in previous sections, are not gone through. The bridegroom goes with some of his relatives to the bride's house, the party is feasted, and the bride is taken home by the bridegroom. In some localities the bride and the bridegroom just put 'sindūr' marks on each other's forehead and in other localities this ceremony too is omitted. In parganā Tāmār, 'sindūr' marks are put on a *sāl*-leaf instead of on the forehead. But if the bride is a maiden, she will put *sindūr*-marks on the forehead of the widower-bridegroom.

Birth and Its Ceremonies

As with the Hindus, so with the Mūndās, there are certain religious ceremonies connected with child-birth. We shall now proceed to describe them.

(*i*) *Gārāsi-Bongā Festival* : The *Gārāsi Bōngā* is the deity who watches over females in the delicate state, and presides over child-birth. To ensure the future well-being of the expectant mother and of the baby in the womb, a red or grey fowl is set apart by the head of the family, and a jar of rice-beer is brewed, in honour of *Gārāsi Bōngā*, as soon as the first indications of the delicate state are observable in a female member of the family. A certain date is fixed for the worship of the *Gārāsi Bōngā*, and on that date, the father, brother, or uncle of the expectant mother comes to her house to perform the necessary worship. After offering up prayers to the *Gārāsi Bōngā* for the well-being of the expectant mother and of the child in her womb, he ceremonially kills the dedicated fowl and makes offerings of its head (bō), liver (*im*), and tail (*chālōm*), all boiled together, to the spirits of his deceased ancestors. Feasting and drinking follow.

(*ii*) *Observances During Confinement* : A Mūndā female is considered ceremonially unclean for eight days after a child is born to her. No caste-fellow will enter the confinement-room, or take his food at her house. As soon as a baby is born, its mother is given a quantity of *héré-dā* or water boiled with 'kūrthi' (*dolichos biflorus*) for a stimulating drink. Generally the services of a Loharā or Lohār woman are secured to cut the umbilical cord. For nine days following child-birth, the only restriction in the matter of food is that the mother is not allowed to eat stale rice, but must take hot rice instead.

(*iii*) *The Chati Ceremony* : On the eighth day after child-birth, the purification ceremony of the new-born baby and its mother, is performed. The baby and its mother as also the *bhāyāds* or near relatives (on the father's side) of the baby, all have their nails pared. Then the mother of the baby accompanied by a number of female relatives proceeds to a neighbouring stream or tank (but not to a spring or *dāri*) for ablutions. On their way to the stream or tank, they burn the *sered pāti* or unclean mat on which the baby slept all these days. On their return home, water is sprinkled all over the house out of a brass vessel into which a piece of copper and a few *tulsi* (or failing that, *bael*) leaves have been put in, rice-beer (or, in its absence, *rānū-dā* or water mixed with the root used in fermenting liquor) is also sprinkled all over the house. The house being thus purified, all the relatives and members of the family enter into it, and the head of the family goes inside the *āding* or sacred tabernacle and there makes offerings of *arua* rice etc. to the household deities—the spirits of deceased ancestors. After drinking rice-beer, the *bhāyāds* and relatives depart.

(*iv*) *The Sākhi* or *Name-Giving Ceremony* : On the day following the *Chatihulang* described above (*iii*), the *bhāyāds* and other relatives are again invited into the house. A name is selected for the baby by its mother in the following manner. A brass *thāri* or plate is filled with water and a grain of rice is first dropped into it.   Then another grain of rice is dropped into the water in the name of some chosen ancestor or other relative.   If the second grain meets the first grain which represents the baby, the baby is named after this ancestor or relative.   If, however, the second grain sinks to the bottom without meeting the first grain, another grain of rice is dropped in the same way in the name of some other ancestor, or relative.   This process is repeated till a grain of rice thus dropped meets the baby's grain.   The baby is then named after this relative who becomes the baby's 'Sākhi' or *mitā*.   After ceremonial blessings on the baby by the jōarni who prays that "the hair of the child may be white (with age) like the flower of the *'hel'* and 'rutā' creepers", rice-beer is freely supplied to the guests.   The final purification ceremony is performed by the mother of the baby going to the village dāri or spring and putting marks of vermilion with the fingers of her left hand on the wooden enclosure of the dāri, and finally drawing water from the spring.

(*v*) *Sūtām-tŏl* :   On the same day, a girdle of thread is tied round the waist of the baby.   This is called the 'Sūtām-tŏl' cere-mony.

(*vi*)   *Lūtūr-Tūkūi* :   The *Lūtūr-tūkūi* or ear-boring ceremony of the baby, is celebrated either in the first or in the second or in the third year of its life.   In this ceremony the *Sākhi* or mitā, after whom the baby has been named, takes the leading part.   On the day of the ear-boring ceremony, the *Sākhi* of the baby arrives with presents of rice, pulse, salt, mustard-oil, rice-beer, a goat, a new piece of cloth, and one or more bead-necklaces.   A figure in the form of a parallelogram with diagonals is drawn on the courtyard of the baby's father's house, with rice-flour-dough.   Over this figure a quantity of paddy is strewn, and over that a plank of wood is placed for the Sākhi to sit upon.   Seated there, the Sākhi rubs a little mustard oil first over his own head and then on the head of the baby.   Two men, barbers by preference, now put vermilion marks on the child's ears and then perforate the ears with a copper (occasionally silver) perforator.   A black fowl is then sacrificed on the spot marked with the figure of a parallelogram, and the blood of the fowl is spilt over the figure.   Then comes the usual feasting and drinking, after which the *Joārni* appointed for the purpose delivers a set speech invoking the blessings of the gods on the child and its family.   "May God (*Sing-bongā*) protect this boy", prays the *Joārni*, "with the joined palms of His hands."

Funeral Ceremonies

The orthodox method of disposal of a Mūndā corpse is to burn it and collect the bones which are ceremonially interred in the family 'Sasān' on the annual *Jāng-tōpā* (bone-burying) day.   In some villages, however, cremation has nowadays been altogether given up.   In these villages, after a provisional burying of the deceased, his bones are finally taken out, put into an earthen vessel, and ceremonially deposited under the family burial-stone at the village *Sasān*, on the next annual *Jāng-tōpā* day.   In a still smaller number of villages again, the corpse which is buried away from the Sasān, is not at all disturbed ; but an effigy of the deceased is prepared with earth and straw, and this is burnt on the *Jāng-tōpā* day, and a little earth from the spot where the effigy is thus burnt is put into an earthen '*chūka*' (diminutive pitcher), and deposited under the family burial-stone (*Sasān-diri*) in the village *Sasān*. We shall now describe the orthodox method of disposal of the dead and the ceremonies attending it.

(*i*)   *Rapa* :   When a Mūndā dies, the corpse is dressed in a new cloth and anointed with turmeric and oil.   Sometimes one or more coins of copper or even of silver are put into its mouth.   Then the corpse is carried on a string-bottomed *chārpoy* (*pārkom*)to the 'masān' or burning-place.   On arrival at the limits of the deceased's village, the *chārpoy* is put down on the ground and again taken up, and a handful of rice or mustard is placed on the four points over which the four legs of the *chārpoy* stood.   Then the corpse is taken on the *chārpoy* to the burning-place, and carried three times round the pile of wood already collected there for the cremation.   Over this funeral pile, the corpse is now placed with its head pointing southwards.   More wood is now piled over the corpse .   A son of the deceased, or, in the absence of a son, a nephew or a brother puts a burning charcoal fixed at one end of a *bāel* twig into the mouth of the corpse.   After the corpse is burnt, some female relatives of the deceased pour water over the ashes, and then the bones of the deceased are collected, washed with water, and tied up in a piece of cloth.   Now a small effigy of the deceased is constructed with tender grass-shoots (*dūbi-tāsād*), and a figure is drawn on the ground with parched rice (*bābā-ātā*) to represent the deceased. Over this figure is then placed the grass-effigy with its head pointing south (*bō-kāndrū*). The grass-effigy and the parched rice are then taken up and put into the cloth containing the bones. The relative who constructed the grass-effigy next takes up two *pipar* (*Ficus religiosa*) leaves with a little *khichri* (rice and pulse boiled together) over each, and sways the leaves backwards and forwards three times. Finally, the grass-effigy, the parched rice, and the bones are all put inside a small earthen pitcher (*chūkā*) which is covered up at the top with the piece of cloth. This earthen pitcher is then carried in procession to the village, and there hung up on a tree close to the house of the deceased. The party now bathe themselves, and then a member of the family of the deceased sprinkles on his own person and on the head and limbs of other members of the family, water sanctified by dipping *tulsi* leaves and copper into it.

(*ii*) *Umbūl-ader* : Either on the third, or on the fifth, or on the seventh, or on the ninth day from the death,[34] the *bhāyāds* of the deceased assemble at the latter's house, and have their beards shaved and their nails pared. After the shaving or *hōyō*, they all go to a neighbouring tank or stream for ablutions. After having bathed, one of the *bhāyāds* brings four *tiril* (Hindi, *keond*) saplings (*ōpād*) or branches (*kōtō*). Three or five of the bhāyāds now take these *tiril* saplings to the spot on the boundary of the village where the 'chārpoy' of the deceased was put down on its way to the *masān*. Two of the saplings are planted there in the form of a cross and a third sapling is planted vertically so as to intersect the other two at their point of junction, thus making the figure of a six-pointed star.

A thorn (*jānum*) is tied up at the point of junction of the three saplings. A small earthen vessel (*dibi*) is placed over this tripod of *keond* (*Diospyros melanoxylon*) saplings, and the whole thing is covered over with straw so as to appear like a *Kūmbā* with a small opening on the north. A *bhāyād* of the deceased sits down before this opening, with his face to the south, and presents offerings of rice mixed with pounded turmeric to the shade of the deceased. Finally, the *kūmbā* is set fire to, and the earthen *dibi* placed over the tripod is smashed into pieces by striking it with the remaining (fourth) 'keond' sapling. While the *kūmbā* is on fire, the assembled

[34] When a religious festival intervenes, then on such festival day.

kinsmen of the deceased thrice call out the name of the deceased
and exclaim, "Come,—thy house burns !" Then the whole
party start for the deceased's house, one of them striking two
ploughshares one against the other (or against a sickle), and
another *bhāyād* carrying a low stool (*māchiā*) in his hands. In
the meanwhile, the female members of the deceased's family have
placed just inside the door of the house a few leaf-cups filled
respectively with boiled rice, boiled vegetables cooked pulse, and
chicken-curry,—all covered over with a 'sūp' or winnowing fan.
They also strew ashes on the floor of the house. The door of the
house is fastened from inside, and the inmates maintain a dead
silence from the moment they catch the first sound of the plough-
shares striking against each other. On their arrival at the house,
one of the party knocks at the door. On being questioned by the
inmates of the house from within as to who they are, they all reply
in one voice,—"We take away sorrow and bring happiness."
Then the door is opened, and the party enter the house. The
man carrying a stool in his hands, goes with it to the āding and
leaves it there. He then comes out of the *āding* and scrutinises the
ashes and the leaf-cups to discover if the ashes have been disturbed
and any portion of the rice has been taken by the spirit of the deceased. For, the Mūndās believe that the spirit of a dead man will
come and take a portion of the rice thus laid out for it, and as a
sign of its having partaken of the offering leave a grain or two of
rice on the ground and leave the mark of its footsteps on the ashes.
If no such marks of the return of the shade to its former house are
discovered, the *ūmbul-āder* ceremony is repeated. Last of all, a
member of the family enters the āding, offers libations of rice-beer
to the spirits of departed ancestors and prays to them that the
deceased may enter into "your fraternity, your caste, and your *kili*
(sept.)" A feast to the assembled relatives concludes the day's
functions.

(*iii*)   *Jang-tōpa* : After the winter rice is harvested, a date
for the Jāng-tōpā or bone-burial ceremony is fixed in every Mūndā
village in which one or more Mūndā residents have died during
the preceding twelve months. On that day, in the month of
Pūs or *Māgh* (January-February), the bones of the deceased are
ceremonially deposited in the family *Sasān*. Invitation is sent
out to all relatives of the deceased a few days beforehand. On
the appointed day, the invited relatives arrive at the house of the

deceased with presents of rice-beer, rice, pulse, salt, tobacco, and similar other things. If the deceased's family is poor, or if the deceased was a mere child, and if there is already a stone-slab under which the bones of the father or other predeceased member or members of the family have been buried, the earthen vessel containing the bones of the deceased is deposited underneath the old stone-slab. Otherwise, a new stone-slab is placed in the *sasan* for the deceased. When this has to be done, the relatives of the deceased go with two country-carts ((*sagars*) to some hill or rocky place where a suitable stone-slab is available. Thence a large stone-slab is carried to the burial-ground ('*Sāsān*') on the two *Sāgars* fastened side by side. A grave is dug at a selected spot in the '*Sasān*', and in it the earthen vessel containing the bones of the deceased is interred. Along with the bones, a little rice, oil mixed with turmeric, and a few copper coins (pice) are put into the vessel. After the excavation is filled up, the large stone-slab is placed over it supported on four small pieces of stone at the four corners. Rice-flour (*bābā-hōlŏng*) is sprinkled on this stone-slab and then over the older stones in the 'sasān'. A few pieces of bread are thrown towards the new stone by the widow of the deceased, and then other pieces of bread are thrown towards the other stones. The stones are also anointed with oil. Last of all, three, five, or seven marks are made with vermilion on the new stone, and one or three vermilion-marks are put on each of the older stones. Then the relatives bathe and go to the house of the deceased, where they sit down to a banquet.

(6) RELIGION

The Munda Faith

The Mūndās are sometimes represented as worshippers of malevolent deities whose business it is to bring drought, disease, and death. And the sole object of Mūndā worship is generally believed to be to avert disasters with which their deities delight in afflicting mankind. A careful inquiry will prove such views to be erroneous. The designation of 'Animism' now commonly applied to their religion appears to us to be inaccurate, if not actually a misnomer. A careful study of their religious beliefs and ceremonies will show that the Mūndās believe in a Supreme Deity whom they call *Sing Bōngā*, and whose blessings they invoke before every important religious ceremony. Besides Sing Bōngā, the Mūndā ordinarily worships the spirits of his deceased ancestors and the presiding deities of his village. *Sing Bōngā* or the Supreme Deity has indeed no specific worship, but is reverentially remembered by the Mūndā when, before every meal, he puts down on the ground a few grains of rice from his plate. In serious general calamities, however, Sing Bōngā is specially invoked and a white fowl is sacrificed to Him. The second class of gods are the presiding deities of the village—the *Hātū Bōngāko* (village-gods) such as the *Desāuli Bōngā*, the *Jāher Būri*, and the *Chāndi Bōngā*. These gods aid the Mūndās in their agricultural operations and hunting excursions, and guide them in every concern of life, and order every human event. They are worshipped by the Pāhān or village-priest at stated times in the sacred groves of each village. The third class of gods are the gods of the household—the *Orā Bōngāko* (house-gods)—who are the spirits of the deceased ancestors of each Mūndā family. The head of every Mūndā family worships these house-hold deities in the 'āding' or sacred tabernacle of his house. Their blessings are invoked at every social ceremony and religious festival. The last two classes of deities—the village-gods and the household-gods are the *mānāting bōngās* of the Mūndās,—the gods who have to be *worshipped*. The idea that the Mūndās are worshippers of malevolent spirits appears to have arisen from confounding these two classes of deities who are the *Mānitā bōngās* or gods to be *worshipped* with a third class of spirits known as the *bānitā bōngās* or spirits who require to be *appeased* or *propitiated*. This latter class are indeed no gods at all, nor are they believed by the Mūndās to be such. These malevolent entities—among whom may be mentioned the Churins, the *Mūas*, the *Apsāns*, the *Hānkār Bōngās*, and the *Nāsān Bōngā*—are believed ro be the earth-bound spirits of persons who died a violent or unnatural death. The propitiation of this class of spirits is the duty—not of the Mūndā householder nor of the Mūndā village-priest or Pāhān—but of the ghost-finders—the Nājōs, Mātis, and Deonrās, who are not infrequently non-Mūndāris by race. Occasionally, indeed, the earth-bound spirit of some deceased member of a family haunts his old fields and may do some mischief, and has, in such a case, to be propitiated by sacrifices. But such a spirit forms no part of the regular Mūndā pantheon. There is still a fourth class of spiritual entities recognised by the

Mūndās. These are the elemental spirits or Nature-gods—such, for example, as the *Būrū Bōngā*[35], the *Ikir Bōngā*, and the Nāge Erā. These stand midway between the beneficent deities (the '*Mānitā Bōngās*) and the malevolent spirits (the *Banita Bōngās*)[36] and are powerful for good and for evil alike. Their ordinary function, indeed, is to do good,—but when an individual Mūndā or a family or a village offends them, these spirits are roused to mischievous activity, and have then to be propitiated by a Nājŏ or Deonrā and sometimes by the village-Pāhān. Nor should we omit to mention a fifth class of Mūndāri deities, whose function again is one of beneficence. These are the protecting deities— the guardian angels —of particular families and classes. Such is the *Achrael Bōngā*, who presides over the interests of married women; but should any such woman surreptitiously carry away any article from the house of her parents, the *Achrael Bōngā* would mark his displeasure by bringing sickness to the house where the stolen goods are taken. Such, then, are the various classes of inferior *Bōngās* of the Mūndās—the ministers of Divine Will— who may not inappropriately be compared to the '*Devas*' of the Hindus, the 'Angels' of the Christians, the 'Ferishtās' of the Mahomedans, the 'Ameshaspentas' of the ancient Iranians, and the '*Malakhs*' of the ancient Jews. As there are good angels and bad angels in other religions so are there good *bōngās* and bad *bōngās* in the Mūndā's Theology. Over these various classes of inferior deities and spirits rules the great *Sing-Bōngā*—the ever beneficent God of gods, by Whose appointment the inferior deities hold their places and perform their functions—and Who is, in fact, the Author of the whole universe including the whole host of these *bōngās* themselves. According to the good or bad life led by a man during his present life, he will be sent back to the world by *Sing Bōngā* either as a man or as a beast, as a bird or

[35] The original signification of the word '*Buru*' was 'God' and in that sense the name would apply to *Sing Bonga* (who was perhaps the original Marang *Buru* or the great God). But that sense of the word is now obsolete. And the name *Buru Bonga* is applied to a 'spirit who resides in the hills'.

[36] We leave out of account a few local gods such as the *Pangrua Bonga* in a portion of the Khunti thana and the Marang *Buru Bonga* who is worshipped in different parts of the District on the nearest hill in the locality—and in some locality where there is no hill at an easy distance, the *Buru Bonga* is worshipped on some *danr* land.

as an insect. On death, the rōā or soul is carried away by the *Jŏm Rājā* (the 'devouring' king), the god of death to his abode in the south (*kātā-jambar*). Such is the Mūndā's idea of re-birth which is yet in a rudimentary stage, and not half so elaborately worked out as by his Hindu neighbours.

Hinduised Mundas

There are at present a large number of Hindūised Mūndās, mostly in the Pānch Parganās, who no longer join in their old national worship. In most cases, however, they have not yet dispensed with the office of the village Pāhān who still offers the customary sacrifices to the village gods. For, the influence of the village gods—the *Hātū Bŏngāko* or *Gaon Deotās*—over the well-being of the village is never questioned. Mahādeō is a favourite god with these Hinduised Mūndās and, curiously enough, animal sacrifices are offered by these Hinduised Mūndās to this 'Lord of Ascetics'. Devi Māi (*Sakti*) also receives homage and worship.

The Birsa Dharam

The closing years of the Nineteenth Century saw the rise of an eclectic religion amongst the Mūndās. Birsa Mundā of Chālkād was the founder and prophet of this religion which is a mixture of Hinduism and Christianity. The central doctrines of this 'Birsa Dharam' are that there is only one God, that Birsa is His incarnation on earth, and that purity of character and habits are the essential things demanded of man by God. A Birsaite must wear the sacred thread (*janeu*), abstain from animal food, shall not sit down to dinner in the same row with non-Birsaites, must not work on Thursdays (the day of Birsa's birth), nor cut down *sāl* trees on Tuesdays. The number of Mūndās professing this faith is comparatively small.

Religious Festivals

We shall now proceed to give a brief account of the different general religious festivals observed by the Mūndās who still retain their ancient faith.[37]

---

[37]There are slight variations in the ceremonies observed at these festivals in different parts of the Ranchi District. In the account here given, we have described the festivals as they are observed in the Siri Pargana.

(i) THE MAGE POROB

This festival is celebrated on the day of the full moon (*Purnima*) in the month of *Pous* (January). The Mūndās call the month of *Pous* by the name of *Māgé* and the month of 'Māgh' by the name of *Gōlā Māge*. The spirits of deceased ancestors—the household gods of the Mūndās—are the main objects of worship at this festival. Now that the Mūndā householder has garnered his winter hārvest and is happy in an abundance of grain and liquor, he turns with gratitude to his gods, and after having fasted the previous day and performed ablutions, he offers up prayers to his household deities (*orabongāko*) at the 'āding' or sacred tabernacle of his house as follows :

"May we all, young and old, keep well in mind and in body. May our cattle thrive. May neither tigers attack us, nor stubs and stumps of trees nor thorns hurt us when we enter the jungles to gather wood for fuel. May we not fall down into pits in the jungles. May we go about our work in health. May we have plenty to eat and drink. May we have enough to entertain our relatives and friends with, and to pay our dues (rents and taxes) to landlords and to rulers."

After the worship at the '*āding*' all the members of the family as well as the servants sit together and have a hearty meal of rice-flour bread, fried rice (*chiura*), molasses (*gūr*), and, in well-to-do families, curds and even milk. Servants are released from their yearly engagement, and, for a few days after the festival, go about visiting their families and relatives who entertain them with more than ordinary warmth and liberality. About a fortnight after the Māgé festival, servants are engaged afresh by the Mūndās for the ensuing year. The contract of service and employment is made both in the case of old servants and of new servants in the follow-ing manner : Either the master or the mistress of the house drops a little oil on the ground, and then pours a little oil on the head of the intending servants (*dhāngar*) and finally puts down the oil-cup with oil in it on the ground. The *dhāngar* then takes up the oil-cup and anoints his own person with the oil. Along with the oil either one *anna* in cash, and, in some villages, one *paila* of rice, or, in other villages, two bamboo hair-combs, are given to the *dhāngar* And the contract is now complete. This ceremony in engaging servants is observed even by non-Mūndāri masters in the Mūndā country.

The next festival is the *Phā-gū*. This festival corresponds to the Hōli festival of the Hindus. On the evening preceding the full moon in the month of *Fālgūn* (March-April), the young Mūndās of the village plant a small *erendi* tree (*Palma-Christi* or *Ricinus communis*), on the road leading to the village-dāri (spring). This *erendi* or castor-oil plant (*M., jārā dārū*) is covered over from top to bottom with straw, and finally set fire to. When it is all ablaze, a number of young Mūndās run towards the castor-oil plant and, with shouts of merriment, cut it down with their axes. The next day, most Mūndā ·young men of the village go out to the forest singing *Jāpi* songs and playing on their drums and tomtoms. In the forest, they cut down a *semar* (*Bombax malabaricum*) tree and go back with it to the village, singing the well-known song beginning '*Madkām Jāer dō senderāi-senōjānā*'[38] When they approach the village, the remaining young men and maidens of the village go out to meet them. And then all return to the village singing *Jāpi* songs, and dancing the *Jāpi* dance. They at once proceed to the spot where the castor-oil plant had been burnt and there plant a branch of the cotton or *semar* tree (M., *edel dārū*) and cover it over with straw. Then the Pāhān or village priest is called to the place. And to all the *Bōngās* or deities presiding over the woods, the hills, the streams, the fields, and the groves—to the *Jāer Būriā*, the *Pāprā Chāndi*, the *Būrū Bōngā*, the *Ikir Bōngā*, the *Mārā* (ng) Buru, the Desauli, *Chōwrāni*, *Nāge Erā*, *Bindi Erā*—etc., the Pāhān makes joint offerings of three pieces of .rice-flour-bread, one pot of rice-beer and a black hen, and prays for success in hunting. Then the *semar* tree is set fire to and cut down with an axe. Different pieces of the tree are thrown away in the four directions of the compass. Now, the whole party go singing and dancing to the house of the village Pāhān, who provides plenty of rice-beer for them to drink. On their return home, the head of each family worships the spirits of his departed ancestors with offerings of bread and rice-beer inside the āding of his house.

---

[38] See sub-section (12), *post.*

Next day, all the young men of the village go out into the jungles on a hunting excursion.

(iii) THE BA-PAROB (FLOWER FEAST)

This festival, also known as *sarhūl*, is celebrated in the month of *Chait*, when the *Sāl* trees are in flower. On the fifth day of the moon in *Chait*, *Sāl* flowers are gathered and taken to the *Sarnā* or sacred grove, and placed at the foot of the *Jāher Sarnā* tree. There, the Pāhān, who has been fasting since the previous day, worships all the gods of the Mūndā pantheon in general, and the *Chāndi Bōngā* in particular, and, in the presence of the assembled Mūndās, sacrifices a number of fowls. Food is cooked in new earthen pots at the *sarnā*. The worship at the *Sarnā* over, the villagers return home singing, dancing, beating their drums and tom-toms, and carrying *Sāl* blossoms in their hands. The head of each family also worships his household gods—the spirits of departed ancestors—in the *ading* of his own house. Garlands of *sal* flowers are hung about the house, and *sāl* blossoms are worn on the head by every Mūndā. At their meals that day the Mūndā use only *sāl* leaves as plates, as cups, and even as seats. Plenty of cooked *urid* pulse, rice and rice- beer is consumed in each Mūndā family that day. The following morning, the village Pāhān (priest) with a number of 'sāl' flowers used at the pūjā or worship on the previous day visits each house in the village, inserts a bunch of sāl blossoms into the door or roof of each house and receives a small perquisite (from half an anna to two-annas) from each family. In the afternoon, one female member of each Mūndā family in the village goes to the Pāhān's house with a jug of water and a little oil. Each woman on her arrival washes the Pāhān's feet, anoints him with oil, and washes his feet again. The Pāhān makes a present of two jars of rice-beer to the Mūndā women of the village. On the day of the *Bā-Parōb* or the *Sarhūl* as well as on the day preceding it, no Mūndā will handle his plough or do other work in his fields.

(iv) THE HON-BA-PAROB

This festival is celebrated in the month of *Baisak* or *Jeth* (April-May), on the day preceding that on which the villagers commence sowing paddy in their fields. There is no public worship on this occasion, but the head of each family worships the household gods—the spirits of deceased ancestors —as well as other deities, at his own *āding*.

(v) THE BATAULI OR RADLETA

This sacrificial feast is celebrated in the beginning of *Asārh* (June) just before the transplantation (*rōpa* or *rōa*) of paddy seedlings commences in each village. The Pāhān, who has been fasting since the day preceding, sacrifices fowls at the *Jāher Sarnā* of his village, and with offerings of rice-beer, leaves of the '*marūā*' plant (*marūā-sāg*), *gāndhāri-sāg*, and the sacrificed fowls, worships all the bōngās or deities of the Mūndās. The fowls are cooked and other food (boiled rice, *sāg* etc.) is prepared at the Sarna, where all the Mūndā men of the village have a sumptuous feast. Finally, the Pāhān is taken home in state. Such of the villagers as go with the procession up to the Pahan's house are there given rice-beer to drink.

(vi) THE KARAM

This festival is celebrated only in certain Mūndā families, and has evidently been borrowed from their Hindū neighbours. The Pāhān or village priest has nothing to do with it. On the eleventh day of the moon in the month of Bhādo (August-September), the head of the family celebrating the festival brings two branches of the *Karam* (Nauclea-parvifolia) tree and, in the evening, plants them side by side in the courtyard (*rāchā*) of his house. He then makes offerings of milk, *ghee* (clarified butter), and bread made of rice-flour to the gods. On his courtyard or close by his house, singing, dancing and uproarious drumming go on all the night through. Next morning, the *Karam* branches are carried in procession by a number of young men with songs and music, and thrown into a tank or a stream.

(vii) DASAI

This festival, like the *Karam*, has been borrowed from the Hindus. On the *Dasahara* (*Bijoyā Dasami*) day (which comes on generally

18

in the month of *Aswin* and sometimes in *Kartik*), the Mūndās celebrate this festival not by any public worship, but by singing and dancing only. It is only in a few Mūndā families that goats are sacrificed and the *orā bōngākō* and other deities are worshipped by the head of the family on this occasion.

(viii) KOLOM SING BONGA

This festival, also known as the 'Kharihān Puja' festival, is celebrated in the month of Aghān (November), after the transplanted (ropā) paddy has been harvested. No villager will thresh his paddy before this festival is celebrated at the Pāhān's Kharihān or thresh-ing-floor. The *bongas* are worshipped with sacrifices of fowls supplied by the villagers and with offerings of rice-beer. All the villagers eat and drink to their hearts' content. Dancing and singing go on at the Pahan's house and at the village *ākhrā* the whole night.

(ix) JOM NAWA

This is, strictly speaking, not a religious festival, nor is it observed by the Mundas in general. It is only in some localities that the Mūndās have adopted the Hindu custom of celebrating with certain ceremonies the eating of the new rice in the month of Bhādo or *Aswin* (September) or, sometimes, even later. *Chiura* made of new rice is eaten with milk or curds and molasses. Rice-beer is, of course, freely drunk. The Pāhān and some villagers sacrifice each a fowl in his own house.

(x) THE IND PAROB

The *Ind* festival is celebrated by the Mūndās in a few villages only, generally in villages of which the landlord is a Nāgbansi. Two poles of sālwood are posted on the ground, and a cross-pole, also of salwood, passes horizontally through two holes in the two per-pendicular poles. Through a hole in the middle of the cross-pole, again, the *Ind*-pole, which is a very long sal-post is made to stand upright on the ground, parallel to the other two perpendicular poles. On the top of this central *Ind*-pole a huge cage-like thing like the tājiā of a Maharrum is put up. This is covered up with a white cloth, supplied by the landlord of the village. The *Ind*-pole is taken down on the seventh day after it is planted. On the first day, the Pāhān sacrifices a goat and on the last day offers rice-beer to the gods. This festival is celebrated in memory of the first Nāgbansi Chief.

(xi) THE SOHORAI

This festival is celebrated in the month of *Kartik* (October-November). On day of the new moon in *Kartik* (*Kārtik-amāwas*), Mūndā owners of buffaloes remain fasting the whole day. In the evening, the buffaloes and other cattle are brought home and lamps lighted near them. The mistress of the house takes up a handful of 'arua' rice from a plate and throws the rice on the back of the buffaloes and other cattle by way of *chūmān* (benedictory kissing). At the door of the buffalo-shed, a black fowl is sacrificed, and this fowl and rice-beer are offered up to the *Goreā Bōngā*, the deity presiding over cattle.

A lamp is kept burning the whole night in the buffalo-shed. Next morning the hoofs of the buffaloes, oxen, cows and calves are washed by the mistress of the house with water ; and rice-beer is then sprinkled over their hoofs. Now, the master of the house sacrifices a fowl at the door of the buffalo-shed. This time it is a red cock that is offered up to the deity. The buffaloes are then anointed with *ghee* (clarified butter), and the oxen, cows and calves are anointed with oil. Plenty of rice and *urid* pulse boiled together is now given to the buffaloes and other cattle to eat. Finally, the buffaloes, the oxen, the cows, and the calves are all bedecked with yellow flowers of the marigold (*calendula*) species, and sent out to the pasturage.

(xii) THE SOSO BONGA FESTIVAL

Last of all, we come to the only festival in which the ghost-finder—the *Māti* or Deonrā—officiates as the priest. This Deōnra or *Māti* may be, and often is, a non-Mundari by birth. The *Sōsō-bōngā* festival is not a public one, but is celebrated in such Mūndā families only as choose to do so. On a certain day in the month of Bhādo, the *Māti* or *Deonrā* sits down on the courtyard of the house, and with coal-dust, red earth, and rice-flour draws a figure on the ground.

The egg of a fowl is placed in the centre of the figure, and to this egg is attached a sōsō slip split at one end. The Deonra then takes up a winnowing-fan (*sūp*) containing a quantity of *āruā* rice, and chants a long-winded Mundari song in which the story of *Sing Bōngā* and the twelve *Asūr* brothers and thirteen Deota brothers[39] is related. After offering up prayers to the *Sōsō Bōngā*, the Deōnā (or *Deonrā*) salutes (*jōhār*) every one present. Then all present drink rice-beer, and the Deonā eats up the yolk of the egg along with a cup of *ili* (rice-beer). On the following morning, the master of the house plants the branch of the Sōsō or *bhelwā* tree (*semicarpus anacardium*) and a branch of the *keond* tree, in the middle of each of his paddy fields.

(7) DANCES

All the distinctively Mūndāri religious festivals, with the single exception of the *kadleta*, have each its appropriate dance and songs. And music invariably accompanies this dancing and singing. The principal classes of Mundari songs and dances are the *Māgé* or *Jārgā*, the Jadurā, the *Jāpi*, and the Lahsuā or *Karam*.—The *Māgé* dances and songs begin from after the Sōhorāi festival in *Kartik* (October,-November) and continue right up to the *Kolom Sing Bōngā* and the *Māge* festivals in *Aghān* or *Pūs* (December). The songs and dances of the last fortnight or so are specially known as the *Jārgā*. From after this the Jādur and Genā songs and dances are taken up and continued up to the *Sarhūl* or *Bāparob* festival in *Chait* (March-April). One *Gena* is sung after every two 'Jadurā' songs. After the *Sarhūl* festival, the '*Jāpi*' or hunting songs and dances are taken up and continued for two or three weeks, during which period the Mūndā youth have their principal hunting excursions. Then follow the *Lahsūa* or *karam* dances and songs which go on right up to the Sohorāi festival in *Kartik* (October-November). Thus, the Mūndās have a regular round of still-returning dances all the year through. These dances are classified by the Mūndās, according to the different postures of the body in dancing, into two classes, namely, the *Tingu Sūsūn-ko*, or the standing-dances and the *Ungūd Sūsūnko* of the stooping dances. The *Tingū Sūsūn* again is sub-divided into the Nir-Sūsūn or running dance, and the *Tingū Sūsūn* proper. Thus, the *Jadūr* dances, in which

[39] Given in *Appendix II*.

the dancers stand upright and run in a circle from right to left, are *nir susūnko* or 'running dances',—whereas the Genā and the *Jāpi* dances in which the dancers move at a more moderate speed—in a circle in the former, and in a straight line in the latter, are 'standing dances' (*tingū-susunko*) proper. The *Lāhsuā* or *Karam* songs are 'stooping dances', (*ungud-sūsūn-ko*), in which the dancers join hands, stoop forward, and form themselves into an arc of a circle. Towards the centre of the circle they advance with graceful steps and retire backwards in the same bending posture, all the time the dancers slightly moving towards the left so as to complete the circle in some time. Two sub-divisions of the *Karam* dance are the *Khemta* in which the movements are very slow and graceful, and the *Bin-sāri* which is played from cock-crow to sunrise and in which the posture is more erect than in the other *Karam* dances. In some of the dances, we have pantomimic representations of agricultural operations such as reaping. It is not religious exultation or the pleasure of the performance alone that prompts these dances. Social joy and merriment also finds rythmic expression in the steps of the dance. There are special dances for marriage festivals. One of these marriage dances (*arandi-sūsūnko*) is the *Dām-kach.*

(8) 'SUPERSTITIOUS' BELIEFS AND PRACTICES

Banita Bongas

The religious festivals described above are connected with the worship of the beneficent deities, the *mānitabōngās*, of the Mūndā pantheon. There is, as we have seen, a second class of spiritual beings who are sometimes roused to mischievous activity, and are therefore called the *banita bongas*, spirits who require to be appeased. The proper persons to appease these spirits are the *Deonrās*, *Najos* and *Mātis* to whom we referred in connection with the *Sōsō Bōngā* festival. These ghost-finders employ many occult methods to ascertain which spirit has been offended in any particular case. One principal method is the following : When a person fancies himself to be the victim of the wrath of some such offended spirit, he goes with some *ārūā* rice and a small quantity of oil to one of these ghost-finders. The latter takes the oil and the rice, lights a small earthen-lamp with this oil, and places the rice on a winnower (*sūp*). He now concentrates his gaze on the light of the lamp.

After watching the flame intently for a few minutes, the ghost-finder chants his *mantras* or incantations in which all the spirits are named, and at each name a few grains of rice from the winnower are thrown into the flame. As soon as the flame flares up to more than its accustomed height at the name of a spirit, that particular spirit is declared to have caused the affliction. And the appropriate sacrifices for propitiating the offended spirit are named by the ghost-finder.

Witchcraft

The Mūndās are great believers in the power of the evil eye. And in cases of repeated sickness in a family or among the cattle of a family, a witch-finder—the *Sōkhā*, *Māti*, or *Bhagat*—is appealed to for detecting the witch. The afflicted person accompanied by a few neighbours arrives at his house with some *arua* rice and a few pice. The *Bhagat* or *Māti* lights a fire, and when the smoke rolls up and curls around him, he begins by slowly chanting his *mantras* and quietly swaying his body, till at length he works himself up to a state of frenzy and declares he has seen the witch who has roused up a particular spirit to afflict his client. The spirit, too, is named, as also the sacrifices required to appease him. The party now return to their village, hold a panchayat—before whom the offender is summoned, and he is required to pay as a fine the cost, often estimated liberally, of the sacrifices necessary to appease the infuriated spirit. In case of denial of guilt and refusal to pay the fine demanded, the suspected witch is not un-often severely thrashed, dispossessed of his lands and in some cases driven out of the village. In times within living memory, people accused of witchcraft but denying the charge have sometimes been beaten to death. Since the establishment of the British Government, however, matters have improved immensely, and instances of such extreme violence have become much less frequent.

Superstitious Beliefs about Diseases

Generally, *Nāsan Bōngas* and some other evil spirits are believed by the Mundas to bring on deseases. Diseases of the skin, particularly leprosy which is of three kinds—namely, 'Berel-sūd', 'Ror-sūd', and 'Pundi-sūd'—are believed to be caused by the *Nāge-erās*. When a man bathes in, or otherwise uses the water of, a tank, a stream or a spring haunted by a *Nāge-Erā*, he is sure to

contract the disease. Madness or lunacy (M., *bālu*) is believed
to be caused by one's own '*bhūt*' (*ayegā bōngā*), when the latter has
been somehow offended. Cholera and diarrhoea (*lāi-dūl*) are
caused by the *Rōg-Bōngā* or *Deb-imāi*, who has to be propitiated
with sacrifices and offerings made to her, outside the village limits.
It is not, however, evil spirits alone who bring on diseases. Wicked men, too, can cause them by magic. Thus rheumatism
(*Tānārom*) of the lower limbs may be caused by an enemy getting
hold of a little dust of one's feet (*jāngā-durā*) and uttering some
magical incantations over it and sacrificing a fowl or making offerings of *arūā* rice over the dust. The origin of certain diseases,
however, is ascribed to physical causes, occasionally quite fanciful.
Thus epilepsy (*Hānāb gōnoi*) is said to be caused by two insects
(*tijū*) inside the brain-matter : When the two insects fight with
each other, the man falls down in a swoon. Head ache (*Bō-hāsū*)
is attributed to a poison (*bishi*) from the liver or rather bile (*rinri*)
ascending the head.

Ondoka

Mūndās of ancient times, it is said, were addicted to the terrible
practice of *Ondoka* or human sacrifice. And even to this day,
it is said, the practice, though rare, has not altogether died out.
When an extraordinary calamity visits a family (and sometimes
a village or a *pārhā*), and the *māti* or *deōnrā* declares that a human
sacrifice is required to appease the offended '*bhūt*' or evil spirit
who has brought on the disease or other calamity, an *ōndōkā*
is performed with the strictest possible secrecy. It is believed that
the victim is decoyed at night into the house of the sacrificer by the
offended *bhūt* himself. And, at dead of night, the victim is
conducted into a deep jungle or to the secluded bed of a hill-
stream or to some secret place, by the sacrificer and a few
friends. The friends seize the victim by his hands and legs,
and the sacrificer (also called *ōndōkā*) invokes the blessings
of the gods and especially of the offended spirit, sprinkles a
little '*arūā*' rice on the victim, and dashes his axe against the victim's
neck. As blood gushes out of the severed head, a little of this
blood is taken in a vessel, and a second finger of the victim is also
taken off. After the corpse is carefully hidden away, the sacrificer goes home with the blood and the finger of the '*ōndōkā*' (which
name is also applied to the sacrificed man or boy), and takes it to

the *āding* of his house, where prayers are offered.   The blood and
the finger, it is said, are finally buried under the floor of the *ading*.

Eclipse

An eclipse of the Sun or the Moon, so the Mundas believe, is
caused when the emissaries of *Sing Bonga* (God) surround the Sun
or the Moon for the debts of the *Mundas*.   During an eclipse, the
Mundas bring out of their houses any implements or other things
in which there is any metal.   These implements (such as plough-
shares, brass utensils, arrows with iron points) are exposed outside
the houses so long as the eclipse lasts.

(9) GAMES

A large variety of games have been always popular with Munda
boys and girls.   Conversion to Christianity, now on the increase,
does not impair the Munda's love of sport.   On the other hand,
under the excellent guidance of European missionaries, Christian
Munda boys have formed excellent hockey teams, and are further
developing their other national games and sports.   The Munda's
games may be roughly divided into three classes, namely (1)
Athletic Sports, (2) Popular Juvenile Pastimes, and (3) Dramatic
Games.   We shall here describe one or more instances of each
class.

(A) ATHLETIC SPORTS

(i) Phodi

A principal indigenous athletic game of the Mūndās is the
'*Phodi*', which is a kind of Hockey.   This is generally played in the
day-time in winter.   The ball is picked up by a player on one side.
A player from the other side comes and confronts him.   The first
player throws the ball into the air, and both players strike at it.
Thus they go on till the ball is driven to one or other of the fixed
boundaries.   '*Phōdi*' matches are now played between two villages.

(ii) Khati

The game of *Khāti*, too, is played in the day-time.   Often on a
summer noon, you meet with a group of Mūndā boys playing this
game in some shady spot.   Against a peg fixed at some distance,

the player propels a small flat piece of wood by holding a short stick upright behind it and striking against this sharply with a third stick.

Among other indigenous athletic sports may be mentioned the *gobar-hot-ko-khel* the *chengahāl*, and the *hārdāng*.

(B) JUVENILE GAMES

Among the popular pastimes of the Mūndā cowherds and other lads are several games of touch, marbles, knuckle-bones, and back gammon. Some of these are described below :

(i) Chhur

The most popular game of touch is the Chhūr. The players divide themselves into two parties of equal number. Parallel lines are scratched on the ground. One party guard the lines and the other seek to enter the furthest portion within the lines which is designated the *non-gharā* or the salt-house. When the latter party succeed in reaching the *non-gharā* without being touched by a member of the opposite party guarding the lines, the parties change places.

(ii) Til-guti

The *Til-guti* is a sort of back-gammon. Seven holes are made in each of two parallel lines on the ground. And five mallstones (*gūti-ko*) are shifted about in these holes by two opposing players.

(iii) Kouri-Inu

In the *Kouri-Inu* game, two boys stand face to face, joining their hands and repeatedly clapping them. Two other boys, with their hands similarly joined, run underneath the joined hands of the former pair from one side to the other.

(iv) Dundu-Khel

The *Dūndū-Khel* is a variety of the blind man's buff. A boy's eyes are blindfolded and his play-mates slap him one after another. When he can recognise a boy slapping him, his eyes are uncovered, and the boy who has just slapped him and has been recognised takes his place and is blindfolded.

(v) Bhoura-Inu

The *Bhourā-Inū* is played with the top which is made to spin on its point by drawing a string round its stem.

(vi) Uku-Inu

The *Ukū-Inū* is a game of hide-and-seek.

(vii) Hunt the Slipper

'Hunt the Slipper' is one of the European games introduced by Christian missionaries amongst Mūndā and Urāon boys. In this game, a large number of boys sit down in a row with their legs extended in front, and a piece of rag is adroitly passed on under the legs of the boys, one boy passing it on to another unobserved. One or more boys move about trying to find out the rag.

(c) DRAMATIC GAMES

These form the most interesting class of Mūndāri games. They are meant to combine amusement with instruction and are generally played in the evening. The Mūndās have a large number of games of this class. We shall describe one which may be taken as typical of the whole class.

(1) Kantara-Inu

In the *Kāntārā inū* or the jack-fruit game, one boy represents a jack tree, a number of boys and girls represent its fruits, one boy personates the owner of the tree, and another boy a dog, and a third boy a thief. The boys and girls representing the jack-fruits hold on to the boy representing the tree, and shout— *Hété téré bāndā hūkā, hété téré bāndā hūkā.* The thief comes to the tree when the owner is asleep. The dog gets scent and barks at him. The barking awakens the owner from sleep. On seeing the thief stealing his jack-fruits, he raises a hue and cry. Thereupon the thief takes to his heels. carrying away with him the fruits he has just plucked. In the morning, the thief comes to the owner of the tree and requests the loan of a knife. The latter asks, "What do you want a knife for ?" The thief replies, "I have killed a goat. I require a knife to dress the slain animal with". The owner of the tree unsuspectingly lends his knife. Giggling with mirth, the thief runs home with the knife, rips open the jack-fruit, and eats his fill. When he takes back the knife to its owner, the latter smells it and asks "Why does it smell of jack-fruit, eh ?" Before the words are spoken, the thief runs away. The following night, jack-fruits are again stolen. The dog barks again; its master gets up and raises a hue and cry; and the thief bolts away with the stolen fruits as before. In the morning the owner of the tree exclaims, "No more jack-fruits will I leave on the tree. The thieves are taking them all away". Just when he is saying this, the thief, looking the very picture of innocence, once more appears, asks the loan of a knife to kill a fowl with, and goes away with the same knife he had borrowed the day before. In the night, the thief cuts down the jack tree with this knife. And early next morning he takes the knife back to its befooled owner. The owner comes out of the house to see his jack-tree lying down full length on the ground. He then seeks out a *sōkhā* or ghost-finder to ascertain what evil spirit may have caused the mischief. The selected sōkhā, however, is none other than the thief himself ! And in a mock-solemn tone, this pretended *sōkhā* directs the owner of the tree to bring "one white hen, one black goat, one buffalo", besides rice and other customary offerings to propitiate the offended *bhūt* (evil spirit). The offerings are duly brought forth, and a mimickry of a *pūjā* ceremony is gone through. The sham puja over, one of the boys seizes hold of the legs of the boy representing the fallen jack tree, and another seizes him by the two hands—all shouting in chorus :

> *Sim darom joma chi* ?
> *Merom darom joma chi* ?
> *Kera darom joma chi* ?[40]

The tree will now stand up again. And all the other players will join hands and dance round the tree.

Other Dramatic Games

Among other dramatic games may be mentioned the *Didi-inu* or 'vulture-play' played by two boys on all-fours and a third boy representing a dog; and the *Tūyū oro sim lun*, or the 'game of the fox and the hen' in which one boy or girl represents a hen, and a number of children represent so may chickens, one boy represents the keeper of the fowls and another a fox who makes many unsuccessful attempts to catch the chickens.

[40] These lines may be literally translated as follows : 'Will you eat fowl-sacrifice ?' 'Will you eat goat-sacrifice?' 'Will you eat buffalo-sacrifice?'

(10) LANGUAGE[41]

(*i*) *Geneology* : So far as its geneological or historical relationship is concerned, the Mūndāri language forms a branch of the Kolarian or Mūndā family of languages.[42]

The careful investigation of Father W. Schmidt of Germany has now conclusively established the connexion between this Mūndā family and the Mon-Khmēr family of languages.

(*ii*) *Phonology* : As regards its phonetical system, the Mūndāri language has almost complete sets of vowels, semi-vowels or checked vowels, hard and soft consonants, and a set of semi-consonants ('k', 'ch', 't', 'p'). The 'f', 'x' and 'z' sounds are absent.

(*iii*) *Morphology* : As regards the structure of words, Mundari has outgrown the monosyllabic or isolating stage in which roots are used as words without any prefixes or suffixes or other change of form, but has not advanced beyond the agglutinative stage in which words are formed by joining together two or more unaltered roots, one of which is the primary or governing root to which the others are subordinated. These subordinate or secondary roots are pronominal ones which are either suffixed to the primary root or infixed in the compound.

(*iv*) *Etymology* : The Mūndāri language has a fairly large stock of relational or demonstrative roots indicating position or relation to time, space etc. As for predicative or notional roots, indicating acts, things, and attributes of things, the rudimentary civilisation of the tribe is accountable for the comparative scantiness of such roots as compared with those of peoples of better culture. Roots denoting specific abstract qualities are rare, only a few general abstract terms doing duty for all. A large number of Hindi and even Sanskrit words appear to have been incorporated in the Mūndāri vocabulary.

---

[41] The Mundari language has been exceptionally fortunate in having an eminently scholarly Grammar of it written in English by the Rev. Father J. Hoffmann, S. J. and published by the Bengal Government. For further information the inquisitive reader is referred to that book. See also Dr. Grierson's *Linguistic Survey of India*, Vol. IV.

[42] Vide, pp. 18—21, *ante*.

(v) *Accidence* : The evolution of separate parts of speech has hardly begun in the Mūndāri language. The same root may be used as a noun, a verb, an adjective, an adverb, and so forth, without any change of form. The particular function the root performs in the sentence can only be understood from its position in the sentence and from the context. The relations denoted by cases of nouns or tenses of verbs in the organic or inflexional languages, are indicated in the agglutinative Mūndāri language by compounds in which the secondary roots correspond to the case-suffixes and tense-suffixes of organic languages. Among the peculiarities of Mūndāri accidence may be mentioned the dual form of nouns and pronouns and the double form of the dual of personal pronouns of the first person, one excluding and the other including the party addressed. No different forms or suffixes are employed to denote gender of nouns and pronouns. The natural gender is indicated by the use of different words or by prefixing some word meaning 'male' and 'female' respectively. There are three numbers, the singular, the dual and the plural. Real cases do not exist, but postpositions are employed to denote the locative and the ablative. The genitive is formed by suffixing *ra* or—*a* to the noun or pronoun. Adjectives undergo no change to express gender, number, or case. As for numerals, the Mūndās count in twenties and not in tens, and have only two ordinal numbers, viz.,—'sidā', the first, and *etā* the other.

(vi) *Syntax* : In sentences in which the predicate denotes the substance of the subject, the predicate is connected with the subject by the copula *tān*. In sentences in which the predicate denotes some accidence of the subject, the link word used is—'a'. In sentences in which the predicate denotes the relation in which the subject stands to some other being, thing, place, or time—the ideas of existence, presence, possession, etc., are expressed by *menā* and the reverse by the suffix *bānoā Kā* and *ālō* are the negative particles. The absence of the indirect speech is a peculiar feature of the language.

(11) FOLK-TALES, RIDDLES AND PROVERBS

We have seen that in every typical Mūndā village, there is a common dormitory or *giti-ōrā* for all the bachelors, and another for all the maidens of the village. This *giti-ōrā* is at once a sleeping-house, a club, and an educational seminary, for the young folk. But the Mūndā is an unalphabet, and up till recently instruction through books was altogether unknown to the non-Christian Munda. Even to this day, it is only a microscopic minority of the unconverted Mūndās who have learnt the Hindi alphabet. The only vehicle for instruction and culture known to the ordinary Mūndā is folklore or *kāhāni*, consisting of narratives or folk-tales, riddles, and proverbs. These are recited and learnt in the evening by young bachelors and maidens assembled in their respective *giti-ōrās*, after the day's work is over.

(*i*) *Kaji-Ka-ani* : The commoner class of folk-tales is called *kāji-kāhānis*, and is in prose. As an instance, we give below the story of the Tiger and the Thief—*Kūlā ād kūmbūrūā-kā-āni* :

A thief used to lurk about a king's stable night after night, seeking an opportunity to steal a horse. For the first few nights, no suitable opportunity presented itself. But at length the opportunity came, and on one dark night the thief entered the unguarded stable, unperceived. A tiger, however, had already noticed the thief lurking about the stable. And anticipating that the thief would enter the stable, and promising himself a meal of human flesh, the tiger forestalled him and lay crouching at one end of the stable. The thief on entering the dark stable began to scrutinise each animal by feeling its back with his hands. When at length he felt the back of the tiger, he adjudged this to be the best horse in the whole stable. Accordingly he put a bridle into this selected animal's mouth, and forthwith got up on its back. Unused to such treatment, the tiger got frightened out of his wits and thought within himself that the man who thus succeeded in mounting his back was undoubtedly stronger and more powerful than himself. In a mortal fright, the tiger began to run with all possible speed. And thus with the thief on his back, on and on he ran through jungles and over rocks, the whole night through. The thief too was no less frightened than the animal on whose back he rode. And at frequent intervals, the thief would call out to the animal in the most coaxing tones he could command,' 'Slowly, slowly, O royal horse," "Wait a little, O king's horse !". At these words, however, the tiger would get more frightened than ever, and would double his speed. When, at length, day dawned, the thief was horrified at discovering that he was riding a veritable tiger. His first consternation, however, did not get the better of the thief's accustomed presence of mind. At the very first opportunity he caught hold of the overhanging branches of a tree. And, in the twinkling of an eye, he scrambled up the tree and heaved a sigh of relief. The tiger too was overjoyed at finding his human rider mysteriously vanished. And in great glee the animal ran away with all possible speed. When the tiger was at a safe distance, the thief got down from the tree but felt so exhausted that he lay down on the ridge of a field and fell fast asleep. A wolf now came that way, saw the sleeping thief, and took him for a corpse. The wolf looked about for a coadjutor to help him in carrying the supposed corpse to his den. At some distance, he met the very same tiger whom the man had ridden the previous night. "Friend, I have found out excellent food for you," said the wolf to the tiger. The tiger, whose recent experience made him extremely suspicious, replied, "Who knows you may be playing me a trick ?" The wolf assured him that he was in earnest and described the appearance of the intended victim. The tiger said, "Who knows but that it may be the same being that made me run for life the whole night !" The wolf assured him that it was a lifeless object when he had seen it. The tiger, grown more cautious from the incidents of the previous night, replied, "I am afraid still, my friend. If I must go with you, fasten your body to mine, so that in case things do not turn out to our expectation, you may not run away leaving me in the lurch." To this the wolf agreed, and the two, tied to each other with a cord, approached the field where the thief was still lying asleep. When the tiger saw the sleeping man, he began to move backwards, and importuned the wolf to unfasten the rope. The wolf remonstrated. Their words awakened the thief, who at this extreme peril desperately shouted out at the top of his voice, "What ! you come again, tiger !" In a mortal fright, the tiger ran away, dragging the wolf along the stony ground. This was too much for the poor wolf who was soon done to death. The thief, now a sadder and a wiser man, returned home, and was cured of his thievish propensities.

(*ii*) *Durang Ka-ani* : A second variety of the folk-tale is the *Dūrāng Kā-āni*, in which bits of song are interspersed. A boy in the boys' *giti-orā* or a girl in the girls' *giti-orā* tells the prose part of

the story, and when a song comes in, all the assembled boys or
girls, as the case may be, sing it in chorus.   Here is an example
of this class of folk-tales.

Once upon a time there lived seven brothers and an unmarried
sister of theirs.   Of the brothers, six were married and the youngest
was a bachelor.   The unmarried brother and the unmarried
sister occupied one hut, and the other brothers lived in other huts
with their wives.   One day, these wives and the unmarried sister
of their husbands all went together to the village-jungles to gather
green herb (*sāg*) for food.   In the jungle, they discovered the egg
of a serpent.   The six women told their husbands' maiden sister,
"Take this egg home, and boil it for yourself and your (unmarried)
brother.   The unsuspecting maiden took it home and told his brother to boil and eat the egg.   The brother quite unsuspectingly
boiled the egg and ate it up.   In the evening the sister, as usual,
went to the maidens' dormitory (giti-ōrā) leaving her brother
alone in the hut.   In the course of the night, her brother was
metamorphosed into a snake.   At cock-crow, this human snake
began to sing aloud—

CHORUS

Ko-ko-re cho.
Baum-do-na mai,—
Buru-bing janae chi,
Sangsuri jana ?[43]

At the sound, the matron of the giti-ōrā told the girl, "Listen !
a cock is crowing at your house !"   "Probably," replied the girl,
"my brother has seized some neighbour's fowl."   On her return
home in the morning, the girl opened the doors of the hut to find a
huge snake occupying it.   She stood spellbound at the threshold
when the snake called her out by name and said, "Fear not, sister.
I am your brother.   The egg you gave me to eat is responsible for

---

[43] This and the following bits of song are sung by all the boys or girls of the
giti-ora   The song may be translated as follows:

> At cock-crow,—
> Thy brother, O girl,—
> Has he become a hill-snake,
> Or has he become a female snake?

this transformation.   Sweep the dust off half the room and prepare it for your own use, and I shall occupy the other half."   The girl obeyed, and swept the floor of half the room with her broom. Then her snake-brother told her to get ready one basketful of parched rice (*chiura* and *murhi*) for him.   When the basket was placed before him, he directed his sister to bring together as many knives as she could procure from the village.   When she had done this, her snake-brother told her to place all the knives within the heap of parched rice in the basket.   The knives having been thus arranged to his satisfaction, he directed his sister to take up the basket on her head and follow him.   And thus off they went into the forest, and finally stopped at the spot where the fateful egg had been found.   Arrived there, the man-snake told his sister to get up on a tree and hide herself.   He himself remained under the tree and began to sing aloud :—

CHORUS

> *Hesel juru juru,*
> *Kareketa lidi lidi;*
> *Neado neado,*
> *Burubing king ora,*
> *Chi sangsuri king rosom ?*[44]

At this song, the 'būrūbing' and *sāngsūri* (the male hill-snake and his consort) came out of their hole.   The human snake offered them the basket of fried rice, which the pair eagerly fell to eating. The knives concealed within the basket soon split their tongues. Then the hill-snake told the human snake, "If you can smooth the surface of a bamboo with your tongue, we shall admit you into the serpent race."   The human snake did what was required of him and was accordingly admitted into the tribe of the 'būrūbing'. Now the human-snake entered a neighbouring hill-stream and

---

[44] This song, sung by all the assembled young folk in chorus, may be translated as follows :

The *dhouta* (*hesel*) tree stands with widespreading branches,
The *kerketa* tree towers high;
Is this the house of the male-snake,
Or is this the house of the female-snake?

19

stopped the current by interposing his own huge body as an embankment. At his desire, the girl invited all her sisters-in-law to come and fish in the stream whose flow had been arrested. The girl herself stood on the bank, as directed, but her sisters-in-law eagerly rushed into the water and began to catch fish. When they were in the height of excitement, the man snake suddenly slipped away, and the released current swept away all his malicious sisters-in-law. The man-snake remained in the stream, and his forlorn sister returned home alone with a heavy heart.

(iii) *Nutum Ka-ani* : The third class of *Kā-ānis* or *Kāhinis* are not stories but riddles which put to test the powers of observation of the Mūndā youth. When the young folks are assembled in the evening, at their *giti-ōrās*, these riddles give them pleasant intellectual exercise. There are hundreds and hundreds of these riddles out of which we cite only half a dozen examples:

(1) *Riddle* : *Mōyōd māchire mōnré hāgākō dūbākānāko, jūpūtid kāko jupitid tānā.*

[On one chair, sit five brethren, although touching, they do not touch one another.]

Answer: The two ears (*lūtūr*), the two eyes (*med*), and the nose (*mū*), all sitting on one chair, namely the head (*bō*).

(2) *Riddle* : *Mōyod hōrō dō senōtānre hāpé hāpéte senoa; birte tebākiāté kāklāe.*

[A certain individual keeps quiet while going along; but makes noise while he reaches the wood.]

Answer : '*Kōndé*' (the axe) which makes noise while cutting wood.

(3) *Riddle* : *Ritipité sākāmteā, gāgāralekā jō-teā.*
[It has small leaves, and fruits like small ankle-bells.]
Answer : '*But*' (gram).

(4) *Riddle* : Moyod horo *deā-sāre dātāākāna.*
[Someone has his teeth on his back.]
Answer : *Pāti* (leaf-palm-mat).

(5) *Riddle* : *Pūndi lōyōngre karāni bābā kō herjedā.*
[On white field grows *karhāni* paddy (which is black.)]
Answer : *Pūndi kagach* (white paper, which is written upon with black ink.)

(6) *Riddle* : *Atōm atōmtē dāé jāng-gea, tālāre dāe jilūgia.*

[On the sides are the bones, and in the middle is the flesh.]

Answer : *Pārkōmre gititān hōrō* [the man (flesh) sleeping on the string-bottom (middle) of the *charpoy* or bedstead which has wooden frames at the sides].[45]

Kajira Jukutu

The fourth division of Mūndāri folklore is the Proverb or *kājirā Jūkūtū*. From riddles to proverbs we see the advance from simple observation to reflection. In the *Kājirā Jūkūtū*, the Mūndās embody their worldly wisdom and experience. We give below a few samples of Mūndrāi proverbial lore :

(1) *Chāulim ōmāia, ini māndim āsiā.*

[Ask for boiled rice from the person to whom you have given your rice. That is to say, do not expect benefits or favours from a person to whom you yourself have done no good turn. This saying is, however, sometimes applied to criticise the action of a creditor who harasses a third person instead of seeking his remedy against the original debtor.]

(2) *Lūpū menere isū sūkūri-kō nāmoā.*

[Pigs will come in herds when you have plenty of pumpkins.—That is to say, when you are rich, many people will seek your acquaintance and friendship.]

(3) *Lād bitar-rā rāmbārā okoe leleā* ?

[Who can see the *urid* pulse inside a bread?—That is to say, do not be deceived by a fair exterior only.]

(4) *Toāte lō-jāni, ūdāsioē bōrōā.*

[A man who has got burnt with (hot) milk will stand in dread of curds or *dahi* as well. That is to say, a man who has been injured or has suffered losses from any object or transaction will ever afterwards seek to shun other allied objects or similar other transactions.]

(5) *Bārāngsā ūltālerē enāng lād isinōā.*

[A bread is duly baked only by turning it on the oven and presenting both sides to the heat of the oven. This is used in

---

[45] For a number of such riddles, vide an article by the Rev. Paul Wagner in the *Journal of the Asiatic Society of Bengal*, Vol. LXXIII, Part I, Extra no, 1904.

connection with the sale and purchase of goods. It means that both the buyer and seller must state their terms and offers before a transaction can be completed.]

(6) *Lūtūrem chāpua, chi kāūām hārā* ?

[Should you examine your ears (to see if they are all right) or pursue a crow (who, you are told, has lopped off your ears)? That is to say, do not act unthinkingly at the instance of others, but examine the real state of things for yourself and then move in the matter, if necessary.]

(12) SONGS

Impulsive to a degree, strong in love as in hatred, with a keen sense of self-respect and an eye for the beautiful in Nature, truthful and honest so long as the evil surroundings of law courts do not contaminate him[46], hospitable to his own tribesmen but suspicious of aliens, industrious and lazy by turns, a keen hunter, inordinately fond of drink, and improvident in the extreme —such is the Mūndā of Chōtā Nāgpūr. It is in his songs that the good traits of his character are seen at their best. Though the higher flights of Pegasus are beyond the reach of the unlettered Mūndā singer, his poetry, such as it is, is remarkably true to nature. His songs graphically represent the inner emotions that move him and portray the outer world that surrounds him.

To speak of a semi-barbarous people like the Mūndās as having anything like poetry may appear to many of our readers as a misuse of language. And we must admit that poetry in the sense of finished literary productions, the Mūndās certainly do not possess. But what race or tribe is there that is altogether devoid of the 'faculty divine' of Poesy? The savage and the semi-savage, as much as the civilised man, glows with the inward flame, whose wider halo wreathes the poet's name.

In the case of the Mūndā, this inward flame of emotion, in its endeavours to exhibit itself in rhythmic language, has unusually great obstacles to overcome. And the Mūndā poet is driven to

---

[46] The Munda in the village is altogether a different being from the Munda in the law-courts. To form a just estimate of the Munda's character, you must see him in his home and his village. In many cases the Munda is driven by injustice and oppression to use the methods of his adversaries against them.

various expedients to contend against the deficiencies of his
language and his own want of culture. Repetition of the same
idea[47] to mark intensity of feeling, the invention of onomatopo-
etic words and expressions,[48] piling up synonym upon synonym,
the use of expletives,[49] the employment of such appropriate Hindi
words as he may have picked up from his Hindu neighbours—
these are some of the devices by which the Mūndā poet sup-
plements his own imperfect vocabulary to give adequate rythmic
utterance to the surging feelings of his heart and the imaginings
of his brain. And thus through the mist of his halting and imperfect speech and crude imagery, there shine out in many of his
songs surprising gleams of genuine poetry.

Of all the sentiments that inspire the Muse of Poetry, the sentiment of Love is perhaps the strongest as it is certainly the oldest.
In fact, this sentiment is as old as the human species. And naturally the poetical activity of the Mūndā mind is primarily,
though not solely, taken up with the delineation of this primal
passion of the human heart. A whole volume might be filled
with the impassioned songs in which the Mūndā poet, with ex-
quisite tenderness and simple pathos, expresses the ever-varying
joys and sorrows of the lover. We shall content ourselves with
citing only a few out of a large stock of Mūndāri love songs. The

---

[47]These repetitions, however, are seldom made in identical words, but synonyms
are freely used and occasionally coined. These synonymous repetitions form a
marked feature of the poetic diction of the Mundas.

[48]These expressive and sonorous phrases greatly add to the effect of the Munda's
songs. Among these sound-pictures may be mentioned the following : *ari-ari*
ata-mata, *biana-bokona*, *barang-barang*, *bijir-balang*, *biring-biring*, *bojor-bojor*, *bojo-*
bojo, *bangad-bungud*, *binga-banga*, *chere-bere*, *chom-chom*, *doed-doed*, *dugu-mugu*, *dugur-*
dugur, *gasa-gasa*, *gaja-baja*, *gule-gule*, *jaram-jaram*, *jenged-jenged*, *jilib-jilib*, *jolob-*
iolob, *jipir-jipir*, *keleng-beleng*, *kandang-kundung*, *kere-bore*, *kidar-kodora*, *lange-change*,
lindu-lindu, *lese-lese*, *loso-loso*, *lenge-lenge*, *leon-leon* *limang-lomonga*, *lada-ludu*, *mondol-*
mondol, *nalai-balai*, *nambar-dumbar*, *pisir-pisir*, *rarae-barae*, *rarang-rarang*, *riring-riring*,
rolo-rolo, *rese-pese*, *ribi-ribi*, *ribir-ribir*, *saigo-maigo*, *seke-seke*, *tapu-tupu*, *tiri-riri*.

A masterly treatment of the formal part of Mundari poetry as also its distinctive
characteristics, appeared in the *Memoirs* of the *Asiatic Society of Bengal*, Vol. II.,
No. 5, pp. 86—12, from the pen of the Rev. Fr. J. Hoffmann, S. J. A few Mundari
songs with English translations, by Maulavi Abdul Wali appeared in the *Calcutta*
Review, for January, 1907.

[49] Among these other devices may be mentioned the free use of certain expletives such as *ge, go, ho, re, do*, etc., the arbitrary lengthening of vowel-sounds
for the sake of euphony or emphasis, and the insertion of short vowels in the middle
of words or suffixing such vowels at the ends of words for purposes of melody.

Mūndā lover, like lovers all the world over, sees "Helen's beauty in a brow of Egypt''. And hear how he describes the charms of his beloved :

Lahsua[50]

Bo tama risa risa,
Supid kedam ranga nacha,
Nida singi, ba-gem gututana.
Nama nagen jige lotana!
Andutadam sakomtadam,
Hotore do hisir mena,
Polatamdo chilka saritana,
Nama nagen jige lotana.

Translation

How lovely thy head with wealth of waving hair,
Its locks with red twine tied in round knot fair !
O ! day and night, thou wreathes of flowers dost weave,
For thee my heart doth burn and bosom heave !
How bracelets and armlets those fair arms bedeck !
And necklace bright adorns thy beauteous neck !
Sweet sounds the jingling pola[51] on thy feet,
For thee my heart doth burn and anxious beat.

The unaffected simplicity and artlessness of the following appeal to his beloved is just like the simple-hearted Mūndā :

Lahsua

Alom maire kakapajia,
Nama nagen lotana hia,
Namo dinda naio dinda,
Da chatu jeson binda,
Alom maire kakapajia,
Nama nagen lotana hia.

[50] In our translations of Mundari songs, we have endeavoured to keep to the spirit of the songs, although the translations are generally free renderings of the text.
[51] *Pola* is the Mundari name for a toe-ring.

TRANSLATION

O ! Speak no cruel words, dear girl, to me,—
Ah ! How my heart is burning, dear, for thee—
A maiden thou, and here in verity,
Know—that for thee a maiden heart beats free.
A pitcher upon its stand doth firmly sit,
E'en so shall we each other meetly fit,
O ! Speak no cruel words dear girl, to me,
Ah ! how my heart is burning, sweet, for thee !

The homely illustration of the earthen pitcher and its birā (straw-cushion), though it may jar on over-refined ears, has yet a natural freshness about it which is charming in its naivete. If it be said that the simile of the earthen pitcher smells of the earth and savours of the stench of the Mūndā's mud-hut, the Mūndā may as well retort that he smells the breath of cattle and the stench of the stable in the forcible simile with which Tennyson's blue-eyed prince describes his friend Florian :

> My other heart
> And almost my half-self, for still we moved
> Together, *twinn'd as horses, ear and eye.*

The Mūndā poet is not, however, content with a mere subjective delineation of the workings of the human heart under the influence of the tender passion. As the poet's heart glows at the sight of the blossoming of new love in others, he contemplates it objectively and expresses in song the overflowing sympathy of his own heart. Thus, hear how in the following song the Mūndā poet gives expression to his own joyous sympathy with the first demonstrations of dawning love :

LAHSUA

Bhati ora piti piri, honortanaking juri juri,
Niral sobha nelotanaking, kulgeaking bano hiating,
Nawa hiriti piritiking, bano hiating, re-gating.
Samrom rupa munga mala, sasang sari katare pola
Fiure do rajijanaking, bano hiating, re-gating.
Nawa hiriti piritiking, bano hiating, re-gating.

TRANSLATION

By grog-shop thus through market-place,
    As arm in arm yon couple go,
Sweet Beauty doth their motions grace,
    No saddening thought the couple know.
Young Love admits no fears, in troth,
    Nor cares their new-found bliss to blight.
With *polas*[52] and corlas and yellow cloth,
    With gold and silver see them dight.
When heart with heart in unison beats,
    Away flies care that glooms the brow ;
When Love young hearts in union knits,
    No cares, no fears, the lovers know.

Here we have the same sentiment, the same human sympathy
that inspired the well-known exclamation of the peasant poet of the
Cotter's Saturday Night :

O happy love ! where love like this is found !
O heart-felt raptures ! bliss beyond compare !
I've paced this weary mortal round,
And sage experience bids me this declare,—
If Heav'n a draught of heavenly pleasure spare,
One cordial in this melancholy vale,
'Tis when a youthful loving modest pair,
In other's arms breathe out the tender tale,
Beneath the milk-white thorn that scents the vale.

In the poet's eyes, youth is never so lovely as when Love casts
its golden halo around it. And to the poet, as to every feeling
heart, there is perhaps no picture more attractive than that of two
young lovers in the fine intoxication of first love.

But with the Mūndā, as with other people, the course of true
love does not always run smoothly. At times it is the social restriction that forbids marriages within the *kili* or clan, and at others it
is the inability of the bridegroom to meet the pecuniary demands of
the bride's guardians that stands in the way of the fulfilment of the
delightful promises of the heart. The Mūndā is, if anything,

---

[52] *Pola* is the Mundari name for a metal ring worn on the toe.

intensely conservative. And the Munda lover, in such a predicament, generally bows down to the immemorial social laws of his tribe. But the more impatient spirits among the Mūndā youth sometimes rebel against society and cut themselves off from its moorings.

Hear with what passionate love the Mūndā lover clings to the maiden of his choice and for her sake is ready to give up the rest of the world. :

JARGA

Kucha mucha kunduru,
Kucha kotong tadinga kundurum.
Kucha kotong tadinga nairi.
Narin narin palandum narin,
Kotong tadinga palandum narin,
Kotong tadinga nairi.
Fibare sukujanre do dolang senoa,
Kunduru,—do dolang senoa, nairi,
Kurambare rerajanre,
Mare dolang birida, palandu,
Mare dolang birida, nairi.

TRANSLATION

Like *kunduru*[53] winding round the tree, thou girl,
    Infold'st me in thy loving coils,
Like *kunduru* clasping round the tree, my girl,
    Thou hold'st me close in thy tender toils.
As *p'landu* creeper round the tree, my love,
    Around my heart so dost thou twine,
As *p'landu* twists around the tree, my love,
    So hast thou bound my heart in thine.
My heart feels warm, O come along, my love,
    O come with me my *Kunduru*, dear,

[53] *Kunduru* and *palandu* are names of creepers. It is only natural that the Munda should borrow his metaphors and similes mostly from the *fauna* and *flora* as also from the beasts and birds of his native woods and hills.

O come with me, and thus through life,
 We both will move together here.

In thee my heart in bliss doth rest[54]
 Together will we run life's race,

O come, *Palandu*, come together thus,
 We'll stride across life's narrow pace.

In songs like this we have the same sentiment, though indeed
not as eloquently expressed, as in the Irish song of Francis Fahy :

Maid of all maidens, my life is entwined in thine,
 Turning to thee, like the flower to the sun,

Tell me, oh ! tell me, thy heart is enshrined in mine—
 Tell me, asthore, we had better be one.

Come with me, roam with me, over the foam with me,
 Come to my home with me near Carring rock.

Light of my life to be, sweet-heart and wife to be,
 Free from all strife to be, flower of the flock !

To such a pair the rest of the world has no significance. They
ask for nothing in the universe save each other's company. Fear
and anxiety these young lovers have none. The slightest attempt
to check the natural bent of their affections they forthwith resent.
And hear with what obstinacy one of these unruly Mūndā youths
bids defiance to all social restrictions :

Jadur

Kerketa dutamo kainga, Demchua darara kainga.
Aingego salajoma, aingego pit joma.
Dugumugu chaurol kainga, gajabaja bajuria
        [kainga.

Aingego salajoma, aingego pit joma,
Ulisakam hirichiu kainga, molongreo tika
        [sinduri-o kainga.
Aingego salajoma, aingego pit joma.

---

[54] Literally, the original would be translated thus—As the heart becomes cool
(i.e., filled with calm delight and joy).

TRANSLATION

O ! none of your ugly matchmakers I need !
    Do send them away your *kerketa* and crow[55]
For a bride I shall look where affection will bid,
    My wishes alone the sole mentor I know.
O ! none of your gaudy *chaudols*[56] will I need,
    No clanking musicians behind me will go !
For a bride I shall seek where affection will lead,
    My wishes alone the sole guide that I know.
No sprinkling of water with mango-twigs I'll need,
    Nor mark of vermilion over my brow[57]
For a bride I shall look where affection will bid,
    My wishes alone the sole mentor I know.

In this way the more unruly amongst the Mūndā youth defy all social restrictions. Away they go from their native village and hide themselves with their sweet-hearts in the distant tea gardens of Assam, or in the bleak swamps of the Sūnderbans, and, like the hero of Tennyson's Locksley Hall, curse, to their heart's content, the social laws that constrain them to adopt such a course.

Cursed be the social rules that sin against the
                [strength of youth,
Cursed be the social laws that warp us from the
                [living truth.
Cursed be the sickly forms that err from honest
                [Nature's rule,—
Cursed be the gold that gilds the straitened forehead
                [of the fool !

[55] The birds *kerketa* and crow were the messengers of *Singbonga* (God) in the Asur Legend (vide *Appendix*), and are here contemptuously applied to match-makers.

[56] *Chaudol* is a corruption of *Chaturdola*, a sort of gaudy conveyance—an open *palanquin*—used by well-to-do people in carrying the bridegroom to the bride's house.

[57] The sprinkling of water with twigs of the mango tree over the body of the bride and of the bridegroom and the besmearing by each other of their foreheads with vermilion are necessary parts of a marriage ceremony of the Mundas.

The average Mūndā youth, however, takes his disappointment rather soberly, and in time outlives his sorrow and gets married to some socially eligible girl. For a time, however, when the wound in the heart is still green, he naturally wears out his broken heart with bootless grief. And hear how the Mūndā poet commiserates with him in his sorrow :

JADUR

Juri juri sen baraea, jota jota honor baraea
Juri re gatimdo ka hom namia, jota re sangam
                     [do kahom chimaea.
Modekia[58] *sindurite harating jana do,*
Bare tari[59] *sasangte jirating jana.*
Chakating monaia, harating janado,
Chakating monaia, jirating janado;
Neating reo ho kahom namia,
Chakating reo ho, kahom chimaia.

TRANSLATION

Then, side by side, you walked about, a youthful
                     [loving pair;
With woven arms you moved about,—unknown to
                     [Fear and Care
But *now* no more will she be here to grace thy side,
                     [I ween !
Oh ! arm in arm, no more with thee will she be roving
                     [seen !
One scarlet mark of *Sindur* made her mated, Oh !
                     [for aye;
Her limbs with turmeric twice besmeared, she's tied
                     [in nuptial tie.
One *Sindur* mark on that dear brow, has left thee
                     [quite forlorn !
Oh ! twice with turmeric daubed, is she from thee
                     [for ever torn !

---

[58] *Kia* in Mundari means a small receptacle for holding vermilion or such other things.

[59] *Tari*, in Mundari, means a plate.

It pains me sore, that she no more, will bear thee
                                   [company,
It rends my heart to think that she for aye is lost
                                   [to thee;
Oh ! vain thy grief ! no longer she can grace thy
                                 [side, I trow.
Ah ! though thou mourn, no more will she to thee her
                                 [love avow !

More pitiable is the condition of the girl, whose lover proves faithless to her. The 'hapless doom of woman happy in betrothing' is thus expressed in song by the Mūndā :

JADUR

[*Kuri*]   *Ata mata birko talare*
              Aloho nirja baginga
              Ramecha marechare
              Alohome nojor rarainga
              Kachiho me leledinga,
              Sengel lekaing juletanre,
              Kachihome china leledinga
              Da leka-ing lingitanre.
[*Kora*]   *Kage choaing lelejadme*
              Disumdo dudugarjana
              Kage choaing chinajadme,
              Gamaya do koansi jan.

TRANSLATION

[Maiden]   Amid this forest dense and dark,
              Oh ! let me not deserted pine !
              On this wide waste of Ramecha,
              Forsake me not— for ever thine !
        Didst thou not know me when in youth,
              My beauty bright as fire did beam ?
        Didst thou not then my motions mark,
              As graceful as yon flowing stream ?

[(Heartless)

    youth]   I did not—could not—mark thee then,—

            For all around with mist was dim !

        I did not—could not—mark thee true,—

            Black fog the village did bedim !

This naturally recalls to mind the opening lines of Francis Sempell's "Auld Lang Syne" the Seventeenth-century original of Burns' famous poem on the same theme:

        Should auld lang acquaintance be forgot,

           And never thought upon ?

        The flames of love extinguished,

          · And freely past and gone ?

        Is thy kind heart now grown sae cauld,

           In that loving breast of thine,

        That thou canst never ance reflect

           On auld lang syne ?

Thus, we find that among the Mūndās, as amongst better races, there are some heartless people, whose 'Love will fly the fallen leaf, and not be overtaken'. When the roses in their sweet-hearts' cheeks are gone, the love of such people, too, is 'lost in loathing'.

Love, though the chief, is not, however, the sole inspirer of the Mūndā's Muse. Nor could it very well have been so. For, whatever moves the human heart, whatever kindles the emotions and fires the imagination of man—in fact, every object of human interest and affection, is the proper domain of the poet. We all beam with happiness, smile with joy, glow with hope, tremble with fear, sigh in despair and weep in sorrow. It is the poet alone who from an intense imaginative realisation of the emotion can "summon back the original glow," and reproduce it in an embodiment of rhythmic and musical language, instinct with the warm breath of life. The poet alone can clothe in words of flame the emotions felt by all. As the American poet James Russel Lowell expresses it :

        In his wide brain the feeling deep,

        That struggled on the many's tongue,

        Swells to a tide of thought, whose surges leap,

        O'er the weak thrones of wrong.

As for the unlettered Mūndā poet, the Lyric form of poetry is naturally his proper sphere. The Epic and Dramatic forms with their essential elements of character, action, plot and catastrophe, require a degree of intellectual culture to which the rude Mūndā can as yet lay no claim. Some external object, scenery, character, or incident stirs his imagination and moves his feelings, and out he comes with a song. And in this the lyric department of poetry, the teeming creativeness of the Mūndā Muse is well-nigh bewildering. The Mūndā has songs without number about every possible theme that interests him. In the infancy of civilisation, keen-eyed wonder sways the human mind more completely than in an enlightened state of society. For the rude Mūndā the hand of science has not yet drawn aside the thick veil between appearances and realities. And naturally, imaginative faith reigns supreme. To him, things are but what they seem. The poetic temperament is consequently strong in such a primitive people. For, as Wordsworth himself has defined the function of the poet:

The appropriate business of poetry (which, nevertheless, if genuine, is as permanent as pure science), her appropriate employment, her privilege and her *duty*, is to treat of things not as they *are*, but as they *appear*, not as they exist in themselves but as a they seem to exist to the *senses*, and to the *passions*.[60]

Again, while referring to the primitive stage of human society the great Lake Poet expresses the same idea in verse :

O Fancy ! what an age was that for song !

That age, when not by *laws* immaculate,
As men believed, the waters were impelled,
The air controlled, the stars their courses held,
But element and orb on *acts* did wait,
Of *powers*, endowed with visible form, instinct
With will, and to their work by passion linked !

It is but natural, therefore, that the uncivilised Mūndā should have a variety of other objects and ideas besides the sentiment of Love to stimulate his poetical sensibilities.

[60] Essay, Supplementary to the preface of Wordsworth's Poetical Works.

As may be expected, the Mūndā enjoys life with a keen zest and relish which many of his more civilized fellowmen may very well envy.   The keen excitement of the chase, the hilarious pleasures of his village dances, the ravishing strains of his weird music— these are to him sources of intense delight, and many are the songs in which he proclaims that delight.   Hear how in the following song, the Mūndā poet describes a hunt.

JAPI

Chetan kutire, gosain,
  Terea tereako, gosain
Latar kutire gosain,
  Marea, mareako,
    Sari japi sari. [61]

Rutaba saili do, gosain,
  Rukuken rukuken, gosain.
Saidaba sukuri, gosain,
  Chotabaken, chotabaken
    Sari japi sari.

Tuiu mendo gore, gosain
  Rukuken rukuken, gosain.
Terangi mendo, gosain,
  Chotabaken chotabaken,
    Sari japi sari.

Torahoe togejan, gosain
  Chutima kanasul, gosain.
Torahoe togejan gosain,
  Subama serom gosain,
    Sari japi sari.

Torahoe senojan, gosain
  Singeko birite gosain,
    Sari japi sari.

Torahoe senojan, gosain
  Madeko landirite, gosain,
    Sari japi sari.

[61] *Sari japi sari* is an expression often used at the end of each stanza of the Munda's hunting songs.   But the Mundas cannot explain this expression.

TRANSLATION

Up there ! now the hunters in excitement and glee,
"Look ! Look !" do they cry as yon game there they see.
Down there ! other hunters in enthusiasm high,
"On ! on !" do they cry as yon game there they spy.
Now, lo ! the poor sahil[62] like rutaba[63] grey,
Doth tremble and quake at the noise and the fray;
And there the wild boar like a saidaba[2] white,
Doth grunt and squeak in sheer terror and fright.
Now huntsman's fell arrow doth tremble and shake,
As bends the big bow and his aim he doth take.
Now 'smack' sounds the arrow as it pierces the breeze,
And flies the keen shaft with a whirr and a whizz.
Oh ! slight is the wound that yon game doth receive,
Alas ! just the skin the keen arrow doth cleave !
Lo ! there flies the game,—for but slight is the hurt,
Below the boar's neck has but grazed the keen dart.
Away runs the game where the forest of Sing,
Affords but poor refuge to the doomed dear thing.
Ah ! there flies the game where the bamboo so high,
In serried long phalanx doth brave the blue sky.

Songs like these remind us of the old Border Ballads like that
of the Chevy Chase which describes how :

> To drive the deer with hound and horn
>   Earl Percy took his way,
> The child may rue that is unborn,
>   The hunting of that day.
> The hounds ran swiftly through the woods
>   The nimble deer to take,
> And with their cries the hills and dales
>   An echo shrill did make.

And we may say of the Mūndā's hunting-songs what Sir Philip
Sidney in his 'Defence of Poesy' says of the old Border Song of
Percy and Douglas :

[62] Sahil is the Mundari name for the wild buffalo.
[63] These are names of jungle-flowers.

"Certainly I must confess to my own barbarousness : I never heard the old song of Percy and Douglas, that I found not my heart moved more than with a trumpet; and yet it is sung by some blind crowder, with no rougher voice than rude style, which being so evil-apparelled in the dirt and cobweb of that uncivil age, what would it be trimmed in the gorgeous eloquence of Pindar?"

Hear again the Mūndā poet describing in the following song how a young deer grazing on *mohua* flowers on a moonlit night is silently tracked and suddenly surprised by the huntsman. While you listen to a Mūndā singing the following song with its reverberating refrains you almost fancy you see the huntsman moving bodily before you with a stooping gait and stealthy steps. Now he reaches a point within bow-shot of the unsuspecting game, and all on a sudden up he springs and sends forth his arrow. Down falls his prey, as if before your very eyes, and the huntsman's triumphant shout of joy echoing through hill and valley seems to ring in your ears.

JAPI

Madukam subare jiluhon atingtanae,
Ho ! atingtanae.
Hora   horate   pardia   sesentanae,
Ho ! sesentanae.
Madukam nagenge jilu hon atingtanae,
Ho ! atingtanae.
Jiluhon   nagenge   pardia   biridtanae,
Ho ! biridtanae.
Madukam   subare   jiluhon   raure   jana,
Ho ! raure jana.
Jiluhon   raurejan   pardia   rasikatanae
Ho ! rasikatanae.

TRANSLATION

Underneath yon *mowa* tree,—grazes, lo ! a fawn—
Grazes on !
Crouching down yon path see huntsman moving slow,—
Stooping low !

Meals of *madkam* sweet have hither lured the deer,—
Roves it here !
Quick to shoot the fawn doth huntsman upright stand,—
Bow in hand !
Down beneath the *madkam's* shade, lo ! falls the fawn,—
Falls adown !
Glad the huntsman, hark ! with merry voice,—
Doth rejoice !

The vivid realism of this description needs no comment.

The Munda, in the plenitude of his faith, believes that it is the gods presiding over his sacred groves that assist him in the chase as they assist him in securing a good harvest. And in songs like the following we hear the Mūndā poet expressing his simple faith :

JAPI

Madukam Jaiar do senderai senojana,—
Bhai, senderae senojana,

Papra Chandi do karingae biridjana,—
Bhai, karingae biridjana.

Madukam jaer do tuing jilutana,—
Bhai, tuing jilvan.

Papra Chandi do da-babatana,—
Bhai, da babatan.

Madukam jaer do, kutungan kulai,—
Bhai, kutungan kulai.

Papra Chandi do, bhai, jatarang mara,—
Bhai, jatarang mara.

TRANSLATION

The god in Madkam Sarna reigns,
To join our chase that deity deigns,
And out he goes a-chasing.
The God of Papra Chandi grove,
With village huntsmen doth he rove,
The hunters' party gracing.

> For us the Madkam Deity high,
> At beasts doth let his arrows fly.
> 　　　　And down he shoots the game.
> The Papra Chandi brings us rain,
> That helps the growth of paddy grain
> 　　　　His bounty the rains proclaim.
> And there behold the Madkam Jaer
> Shoots down and bags a nimble hare,
> 　　　　And carries in joy his prey.
> And there the Papra Chandi good,
> Down shoots the peacock in the wood,
> 　　　　And shoulders his game full gay.

A faith like this reminds us of the numerous invocations of the Vedic Rishis to Indra and Varuna, the Pushan and the Aswins to help them to subdue the black aborigines or to bring down rain to fertilise their fields.

If the Mūndā is passionately fond of the chase, his passion for dancing is, if possible, still greater. Visit a Mūndā village any moonlit night, and you will find the young folk of the village assembled at the village *Akhra* or dancing meet merrily dancing to the *dumang's* sound till a very late hour of the night. And on occasions of their tribal festivals, you see them sing and dance the whole night through. Nor is even the day-time excepted. All work is practically suspended for a few days. And the Mūndā gives himself up wholeheartedly to dancing and drinking, music and song. Mark how the heart of the Mūndā bounds with joy at the sound of the music that heralds a dance :

Jadur

> *Kote Karambu dumang sari,*
> *Jige ho litib litiba,*
> 　　　　*Ho ! lilib litiba !*
> *Barigara karetal saritana*
> *Kuram ho dopol dopola,*
> 　　　　*Ho ! dopol dopola !*
> *Kote Karambu dumang sari,*
> *Senoge sanaia,*
> 　　　　*Ho ! senoge sanaia !*

Bairgara   karetal   saritanae,
Biridge monea,
   Ho ! biridge monea !

TRANSLATION

The *dumang* sounds at *Kot' Karambu*
My heart leaps up at the sound,
   At the sound.
The *kartal* rings at *Barigara,*[64]
My heart with glee doth bound,
   At the sound.
The *dumang* sounds at *Kot' karambu*[64a]
O ! Haste, my dear, to the dance,
   To the dance.
The *kartal* clanks at *Barigara*
O ! Rise, my dear, from thy trance,
   To the dance.

If the Mūndā gives himself up wholeheartedly to dancing and singing, music and merry-making in his festive seasons, he is no less whole-hearted in his devotion to his duties when the season for work arrives. We notice in the following song with what joyful alacrity his womenfolk go out to the fields in the rains and transplant the paddy seedlings all the day long, and in the evening merrily return home with their wages in paddy.

LAHSUA

Asar chandu tebalena—
Dola maire roa nalate.
Haturen horoko do oronglena
Sobenko senotanako.
Midtarebu kamiabu panti pantige.—
Singido dubuilena,
Dola maire nalatalate.
Nalabutelakeda
Rurungiabu—mandiabu,
Honhopon tenda nuiabu.

[64] Names of villages.   [64a] Names of Villages.

Translation

Now Asarh is here
O come, my dear,
Transplant the paddy seedlings green,

The   village   all,
Obey   the   call,
Out streaming from their houses seen.

Together   we
Will work in glee,
O, side by side in rows so gay.

When sets the sun
We will be gone
And take our wages for the day.

Our wages ta'en,
We'll husk the grain.
Prepare and boil sweet rice for food

Our children dear,
Will share the cheer,
With us will quaff the gruel good.

Paddy is to the pastoral Mūndā the chief food stuff that sustains life, and the source of all his wealth. And naturally the Mūndā invests it with a personality and regards it with an affectionate veneration. To his imagination, the biting cold of the winter seems to afflict and the warmth of a snug cottage to cheer up the paddy-grains. And thus he sings as follows :

Mage

Lorbo sokora Laki-rajam rabangtana,
Lakirajan   rabangtana.
Lorbo sokora Lakirajam rearatana,
Lakirajam   rearatana.
Ela Raja bolome, tantaraing baisaititad.
Ela Raja sorome, koaluing, bailaruitad.
Sartia chim labara koaling baisaititad,
Sartia chim labara, koaling baibaruitad.

TRANSLATION

Thou Paddy on yon field &t the head of the river,
O ! how with the winter's sharp cold dost thou shiver !
         O how thou dost shiver !

Thou Paddy this *Lorbo Sokora*[65] bedecking,
O ! how with the winter's keen blast art thou quaking.
         O how thou art quaking !

Now, *hail*! thou king *Paddy*, come inside my hovel,
For thee I have raised a *nice tantara* novel !
         A *tantara* novel ![66]

Oh, hail ! thou king Paddy do enter my cot,
For thee a nice seat made of wood I have got,—
         Nice seat I have got.

Rice and rice-beer are the principal food and drink that nourish
the Mūndā's body and cheer his spirits.   In the following song,
we hear a Mūndā couple bewailing their lot on being prevented
by the rising flood of a hill-stream from carrying home rice and
rice-beer for their children.

JADUR

> *Marang gara do kaubautana,*
> *Hela re gatinglang kesedjana*
> *Huring garado ebetebetana,*
> *Helare sangainglang darabarajana.*
> *Helare gatinglang kesedjana,*
> *Tungkiri chaulido kesedjana,*
> *Helare sangainglang drararana,*
> *Chature ili do dararajana.*
> *Tungkiri chaulido kesedjana,*
> *Chire gating chenalang menea ?*
> *Chature ilido dararajana.*
> *Chire sangaing chenalangmena ?*

[65] The name of a paddy-field. All paddy-fields in the Ranchi District have
got specific names.
[66] A *tantara* is a platform made of wood.

TRANSLATION

There roll and surge, the sounding waves,
    On yon broad river high;
Alas ! my dear, thus stranded here,
    On river's bank we sigh.
E'en tiny stream, now filled to brim,
    Flows rippling on with speed,
And now, alas ! We cannot pass,
    The streams our course impede.
Alas ! my dear ! Thus stranded here,
    With basket full of rice,
The stream, alas ! We cannot cross,
    Here rots our rice-beer nice !

If the sudden floods of his native hillstreams are a source of occasional inconvenience and insecurity to the Mūndā, more frightful is the danger on land and water from the wild beasts and venomous serpents that infest his native forests. Listen to the Mūndā mother, in the following song, warning her child against these terrors of her native woods and streams :

JADUR

Birko norante, maina, nalom sesena, maina.
Garako paromtea, maina, nalom nonora.
Biriko noranre do, maina, kula dubakanae maina,
Garako noranre do, maina, binge menaia.
Kula jomekemredo, maina, disum disum-meing [maina.
Darabaramereo, maina, kaing nam-me-a,
Bingko huakemredo, maina, gamai gamai, maina,
Niame nojora, maina, kaing nam-me-a.

TRANSLATION

O ! do not tread yon forest road, my dove,
Nor wend thy way across yon river, love.
A tiger on jungle's path doth sit astride,
And snakes infest the ford across yon tide.

O ! should that tiger thee, my child, devour,
Oh ! vainly shall I seek thee far and near.
If serpent fell, my love, should swallow thee,
Where'er I go, thy face no more I'll see.

Nor are the horrors of drought and famine unknown to the
Mūndā. Like all agriculturists in India, the Mūndā depends on the
annual rainfall for the crops that sustain his life.   And dearth of
rain conjures up before him the spectre of an impending famine.
We have in the following song a realistic description by the Mūndā
poet of the effects of drought :

KARAM

Note ho dudugar,
Sirma ho koasi.
Nimindin da-ge banoa.
Ghimente kage gamaia ?
Asar Saon moyod rati ho banoa,
Bhadorge dharti nore-jana.
Chimente kage gamaia ?
Sirmare Singbonga,
Otere Marangdeota;
Chimente kage, gamaia ?
Lai-renge da-tetan.
Jige senotana.

TRANSLATION

Dry dust is blowing,
The earth o'erflowing,
Grey mist doth cover
The sky all over,
No rains on earth we get.

In Ashar and Saon
Not a drop of rain,
Comes Bhado forth
Heat rends the earth,
O ! Why, no rains as yet ?

> There up in heav'n,
> Doth Sun-God reign;
> And down below,
> The Marang-Deo;[67]
> Yet why no more it rain'th ?
> The pangs of hunger.
> Bring death-like langour,
> With thirst severe,
> In drought so drear,,
> We stand on th' brink of death !

In spite of the many dangers on land and water that beset his path, and the scourge of drought and famine that occasionally afflicts him, the Munda is by no means impervious to the lively excitements of the senses. A lovely landscape, the sight of beautiful flowers, the green and yellow crops on his fields, these and other beauties of Nature thrill the Mūndā, as we have seen, with unspeakable delight.

Love of flowers is a marked characteristic of the Mūndā. In the following song we hear him comparing the common flowers of his fields to the brightest and loveliest objects within his ken— the magnificent morning sun and the peerless orb of night.

Gena

Singiturorea ho dada ! Singituro gulaichi !
Chandu-mulurea, ho, dada ! Chandu-mulu natal-ba !
Singiturtanleka, ho, dada ! Singituro gulaichi !
Chandu-mulutan leka, hoa dada ! Chandu-mulu [natal-ba !

Translation

> Ah ! There in the east, my brother dear,
> In the east sweet blooms the *gulaichi* bright !
> The west where the moon doth first appear,
> The west is fragrant with th' *atal* white !
> Like the rising Sun, my brother dear,
> In the east bright glistens the *gulaichi* wild !
> Like the rising Moon, my brother dear,
> In the west sweet blooms the *atal* mild !

[67] Literally, the great God.

The rare sight of the gaudy retinue of big people, the less imposing but not less curious sight of the Hindu or Mahomedan pedlar with his pack-bullocks carrying novel merchandise, the strange appearance of a Hindu sādhū or ascetic—make the average Mūndā gape with amazement, and the Mūndā poet expresses his wonder and his amusement in songs like the following :

Jadur

> Siri pargana hesa subare,
> Sodomdoe susuntanae;
> Pokar pind Rajabandare,
> Paiki doe khelouditanae
> Sadomdoe susuntanae
> Litige loponge;
> Pciki doe khelouditana
> Notange kuare

Translation

In Sitr'neath a spreading *pipar* tree,
   Behold a pony prancing quick !

Beside yon lovely tank of Raja-band,
   Behold a *paiki*[68] whirls his stick !

How nice that pony there doth prance about
   And pulverise the earth below !

And look how quick that *paiki* whirls his stick,
   Thick curls of dust about him blow !

Although the Munda is not over-pleased at the sight of strangers and foreigners, he is extremely hospitable to his own tribesmen, relatives, and friends. When a welcome guest is expected, the Munda gets his choicest viands in readiness, and the pleasurable trepidation of the Munda's heart may be perceived in all his movements. Thus in the following song, we have a description of the affectionate care with which a Munda girl is trying to get up a dinner to welcome a young friend of the family to whom she is attached :

---

[68] A retainer (*lathial*) of some Raja or big Zamindar.

Jadur

Okoe hijutan, chaulim chapitan ?
Chimae setertan rambaram salatan ?
Gatim hijutan chaulim chapitan,
Sangam setertan, rambaram salatan.
Chitem aiumli chaulim chapitan ?
Meratem atenli rambaran salatan ?
Kataperedo richi gugura,
Naiang peredo besera dambarkom;
Richi gugura riringkenado,
Besera dambarkomrarangkenado :
Enatege-ho chaulim chapitanado,
Enatege ho rambaram salatanado.

Translation

For whom, my girl, that rice thou wash'st with care ?
For whom dost clean those peas with hands so fair ?
Thy lover comes, I ween, for him so nice,
That pulse dost cleanse, for him dost wash that rice.
How know'st thou thy lover comes this e'en,
That thou dost wash that rice, those peas dost clean ?
About his legs such bells as falcons wear,
Around his waist big bells as *besras* bear :
Small *richi* bells, they jingle sweet and boon,
Big *bisra*-bells they clink in merry tune ![69]

The Mūndā is brimful of good humour and delight when he meets his friends and relatives. And in the exuberance of his heart, the Mūndā tries to be witty and humorous in his own way. Many of his songs give us a glimpse of the social virtues of the Mūndā. In the following song, we are introduced to some welcome guests arriving at a Munda's hut. The master of the house asks his wife to bring out a mat of palm leaves for the guests to sit upon. The genial wife, with her eyes twinkling with mirth, jestingly replies that there is no mat nor any other seat in the house nor a single grain of rice to make up a meal. The husband joy-

[69] Munda young men adorn themselves, especially on festive occasions, with small brass bells on the waist.

fully takes up the jest and with a roguish smile lighting up his eyes and playing at the corners of his mouth informs his guests that they will have a sumptuous dinner with Duke Humphrey and will have mother earth for a bed that night.

LAHSUA

Singido   dubuijan,
Kupulko hijujan,
Saonarige, pati bilakom.
—Ganduo banojan
Patio banojan
Marea olereko dubarikakom.
Kochakochaing
Honorkedaing
Besao kageing namojan.—
—Helaia kupulko,
Patio banojan,
Besao banojan, samagekogitika.—

TRANSLATION

[Host]   The sun is set,
              Good friends, well met.[70]
              Spread out the mat for them, my dear.

[Hostess]   We mats have none,
              Nor *gandus*[71] own
              O, let them sit on th'bare earth here.
              Each cranny and nook,
              For grains I did look,
              Not a grain of rice for them I found.

[Host]   Dear friends, how nice !
              No mat, nor rice !
              Lie down to sleep on this bare ground !

The reader may picture to himself the merry peals of hearty laughter that follow such simple banter.

---

[70] Literally, relatives are arrived.
[71] *Gandus* are wooden seats.

If the Mūndā is all benevolence and complacence when he meets friends and relatives, he boils with fierce indignation and unutterable hatred at the sight of his oppressors and enemies. The Hindu and Mahomedan merchant and moneylender, and the alien *thikadar*, *jagirdar*, or *nilamdar* of his village, are often the greatest eyesores to the Mūndā. The merchant and the money-lender, year in year out, fleecing him to their heart's content, and the alien *diku* often bent on reducing the Mūndā from his former position of a village landlord to that of a mere hewer of wood and drawer of water, are, as we have seen, indignantly compared by the Mūndā poet to the blood-sucking kite and the greedy vulture, the ominous crow, the sullen owl, and the vain-glorious peacock.

In the following song we hear how a troop of outlandish pedlars who enter a Mūndā village with cheap trinkets which they want to palm off on the unsuspecting Mundas as valuable articles, are refused admittance into the village-*basti*.

MAGE

Naku nakuja daromda
Kurid ko lapaluriaga
Naku nakuja agamariko
Geon geona.
Udubakope jojoko jumbulae
Udubakopega.
Chundulakope uliko ambarain
Chundulakopega.
Kako sukujan
Jojoko jumbulai,
Kako sukujanga.

TRANSLATION

These kites have hither wing'd their way,
    A-thirst for water clear;
These greedy geese with graceful swing,
    Thus wend their way up here.
Oh ! take them where yon tam'rind tope
    Doth stand,—do take them there;

Point out to them yon mango grove,
    O, let them there repair.
The tam'rind tope they do not like.
    It does not please them so.
Yon mango grove these geese mislike,
    Ill-pleas'd are they, I trow.

It is against the alien *diku* or landlord that the Mūndā's feelings are most bitter. In the song cited on another page which is one of the most spirited Mūndāri songs we have come across, the Mūndā poet bewails the condition of his country over which, to use the words of the Hon'ble Mr. (now Sir Francis) Slacke in his speech in the Bengal Council on the 18th July, 1903, "a horde of middlemen were let loose by the then Maharajah of Chota Nagpur" towards the beginning of the last century.

This state of things naturally called for redress. And the Almighty in His Providence brought the mighty British Lion to the rescue of these people. Naturally, however, it took the British Government some time to realise the true position and legitimate rights of the Mūndās. And by the time our benign Government sought to protect the Mūndās by enacting the Bengal Act V of 1903 and Act VI of 1908, incalculable mischief had already been done to the majority of the Mūndās, and much of that mischief was past all remedy. The arrival, in 1834, of Captain Wilkinson, the first Governor-General's Agent stationed at Ranchi, was, however, hailed at the time with a sigh of relief by the Mūndā. And hear how in his songs he cherishes the memory of the day which saw upliftment in his land :

'The fair streamer of England which floats o'er the brave,
The fairest unfurled o'er the land or the wave,
The brightest in story and matchless in fight,
The herald of mercy as well as of might :

JADUR

Kalikata telengako rakablena,
Nokore najinako derakeda ?
Sarghati sahebko uparlena,
Chimaere najinako basakeda ?

Mena menado Ranchipiri,
Ranchi pirire derakeda.
Mena menado Durundabadi,
Durunda badireko baasa-keda.
Ranchi-pirireko dera-keda,
Ranchi-piri kare nekelajana.
Durunda-badireko baasa-keda,
Durunda-badi chiru taiurtana.

TRANSLATION

Soldiers from Calcutta hither came,
Say, where, grandmother did they stay ?
The Sarghati Sahebs high in fame,
Where they encamped, grandmother say.
Uplands of Ranchi tower high,
On Ranchi uplands did they stay.
Bleak *badi* lands in Dornda lie,
There their encampments gleaming lay.
Pitched their pavilions on Ranchi waste,
The grass in the fields did quake anon.
They fixed their tents where Durn'da rests,
Trembled the tall grass they trod upon.

Such are a few gleanings from the vast storehouse of simple songs which cheer the toil-worn sons and daughters of the Mūndā at the close of a laborious day. Songs like these mirror forth the better side of the life and manners, the thoughts and passions, of these people. And if we care to study them with a broad-minded sympathy, we cannot fail to observe that even behind the rudest and shabbiest exterior there may exist a warm heart and a strong will, an eye for the beautiful in nature and in man, and an ear for melody of sound. Deny these songs the name of poetry, if you choose, you cannot ignore the occasional presence in them of some of the qualities that we admire in all good poetry. Melting passion, burning indignation, generous sympathy, realistic imagination—these are here—and are expressed in rhythmical language with an unexpected vividness, directness and force. And, it is to be hoped, the most fastidious critic will allow that even the heart of the rude Mūndā has caught some stray 'melodies of the ever-lasting chime', and that the Mūndās too, to use the words of John of Keble,

> Carry music in their heart,
> Through dusty lane and wrangling mart,
> Plying their daily toil with busier feet,
> Because their secret souls a holy strain repeat.

In what we have said above, we must not, however, be taken to imply that the Mūndās are free from serious defects of character. There can be no denying the fact that morally, almost as much as intellectually, they are at a much lower stage of evolution than the races in the vanguard of civilisation. To use the terminology applied in the Hindu books, one may say that the 'tāmasic' element predominates in the character of the average Mūndā. It is in his domestic affections, and social virtues, in his appreciation of the beauties of Nature, and his sense of reverential awe for the Supreme Intelligent Power pervading and governing the universe, that we have glimpses of the higher or 'sāttwic' element otherwise almost entirely enveloped in the mist of the grosser 'tāmasic' in the Mūndā's character. Many of his songs, as we have seen, reflect the gleams of that higher nature.

Sexual Morality

The most prominent vices of the racial character are a love of drink, and the sexual liberty permitted to the unmarried of both sexes. This licence, however, is confined within the tribe, and—thanks chiefly to the refining influences of Education, Christianity and Hinduism—is now on the wane. But in villages where the people have not been Hinduised nor has the voice of the Christian missionary been heard, traces of premarital communism may still be met with. It no longer exists, however, as a regular thing nor indeed as what has been called 'group-communism'. True, bachelors and maidens often find their way to each other's dormitories ; but a Mūndā girl nowadays, it is said, would perferably confine her favours to some bachelor of her own choice. Theoretically, liaisons between boys and girls of the same *kili* or sept are not permissible, and it is asserted that formerly such liaisons, when detected, would be punished with the expulsion of the offending boy and girl from the village. But in these days, so long as inconvenient consequences do not follow, such liaisons appear to be often condoned. When, however, a Mūndā maiden is found to have become pregnant through a lover of her own *kili,* the girl's family and her lover have to be excommunicated. This rule, too, no longer seems to be always strictly enforced : a fine to the *Panch* and a feast to relatives often satisfy the offended conscience of the community. And although no formal marriage is allowed, the offending pair sometimes live as man and wife for the rest of their lives.[1] It is on occasions of certain religious festivals and tribal dances that great laxity prevails. The practice which still obtains of the young folk of one village joining the seasonal dances of another village would appear to be the relic of the days when the prohibition against sexual connection between men and women of the same village was still more rigidly enforced than now.

When a Mūndā maiden becomes pregnant through a Mūndā youth of the same village but of a *kili* different from her father's, a formal marriage is generally arranged. But a Mūndā father is always averse to marrying his son or daughter to a girl or a boy of his own village ; and, before a scandal leaks out, the girl's father generally marries his girl to a suitable bridegroom from a different village. The horrible practice of abortion is known, though not extensively practised.

However lenient a Mūndā may be in dealing with such informal unions within the tribe, he is scrupulously strict in punishing similar offences when the lover happens to belong to a different tribe. When a Mūndā female, married or unmarried, is found to have gone astray with a man of a different caste or tribe, the latter is summoned before a

1 Although this is considered improper, we have heard of some instances in which such informal unions have been tacitly permitted.

Panchayat, and a heavy fine (generally up to fifty or sixty rupees in the case of a maiden, and one hundred rupees in the case of a married woman) is exacted from the lover. The fine, when realised, is paid as compensation to the parents of the seduced maiden or the husband of the married female, and the seducer is compelled to take the girl or woman as a wife or a mistress. In case of refusal (which is rare) to submit to the orders of the Panchāyat, a criminal prosecution follows. The family of the seduced female remains outcastes until a purificatory ceremony is performed in which the head of the *Pārhā* sacrifices a white fowl and each member of the family (after he has fasted the whole day) drinks a little of the blood of the fowl and a little turmeric juice mixed with water, and eats *sasāng māndi* (rice and turmeric boiled together by the head of the *Pārhā* in a new earthen vessel). Thus restored to caste, the members of the family cook rice and pulse (*dāl*) and themselves distribute the food to the assembled relatives.

If a widow is found going wrong with a Mūndā of a different *kili*, a marriage is generally arranged. In married life, however, the Mūndās generally maintain a high standard of conjugal fidelity.

As for the unholy custom of pre-marital sexual liberty, the more thoughtful amongst the Mūndās already appear to have realised the immorality of the custom. And we hear the Mūndā poet lamenting—

> *Natagota bano uru, nutanaking puru puru*
> *Fiu redo raji-janaking, banohiating, re-gatim.*

TRANSLATION

> When drinking hard from leaf-cups, friend,
>   They reck not who is who,
> When heart meets heart, they care for naught,
>   To Reason they bid adieu.

Thus the poet sounds the first note of warning to his fellow-tribesmen. After this it may be reasonably expected that the beneficent rays of education and civilisation will before long go far to dispel the mist of the *tamasic* and bring about a better state of things. Truly did the German poet Schiller sing—

> So Song—like Fate itself—is given,
> To scare the idle thoughts away,
> To raise the Human to the Holy,
> To wake the Spirit from the Clay.

APPENDIX I

MUNDA COSMOGONY AND
LEGENDARY HISTORY

An ardent desire to unlock the mystery of creation and un-ravel his own past history is inborn in man. The problem of the origin of Man and the world around him appears to have haunted the human mind in every time and in all ages. Like the riddle or the Sphinx, the question 'Whence' has insistently presented itself to the mind of man from the earliest times to the present day. It has perplexed the primitive barbarian no less than the civilised man—The rude savage, wont to—

'Whistle back the parrot's call and leap the rainbows of the brooks',

has exercised his mind over the problem of the origin of things with as much eagerness and curiosity as those most glorious products of the highest civilization—the scientist and the metaphysician

"On Man, on Nature, and on Human Life
Musing in solitude."

And each has attempted to read the riddle in his own way. But the world has not yet seen an Œdipus to propose a final solution of this most difficult of all riddles.

The various endeavours of the human mind to travel back to the 'sources of Time,' and solve the eternal mystery of creation, have originated the many crude cosmogonic myths of the savage tribes of India, Australia, Africa, America, and other countries on the one hand, and, on the other, the sublime metaphysical conceptions of the Greek and the Hindu philosoph-ers of old and the more matter-of-fact scientific theory of Evolu-tion of modern times. From the Vedic conception of the *Purusha*[1] out of whose body worlds and animals and men were

---

[1] The *Purusha* of the famous *Purusha-Sukta,* the 90th hymn of the Eighth Chapter (*ashtaka*) of the Rig-Veda, is figuratively represented as having a thousand heads and thousand eyes and a thousand feet.

evolved, down to the Kolarian legend of the first pair evolved by Sing Bōngā out of the egg of a bird,—from the Greek conception of the Earth "couched in love with heaven" and begetting the gods,[1] and the Olympian gods in their turn, ordering the quintuple succession[2] of earthly races, down to the conception of the Pundjel or Bird-Creator of Australian Savage Mythology,— all cosmogonic legends are the outcome of man's ambitious attempts at a solution of the insoluble mystery of creation.

Whatever be the historical value of the cosmogonic mythus of primitive man,—whether they are mere moral allegories, as Aristotle taught us, or embody systems of physical philosophy as Theagenes and his school believed, or whether they are but imaginative renderings of actual history, as another school of ancient thinkers concluded, or whether, indeed, an ancient *mythus* is almost wholly, as Max Muller told us, "a disease of language," traceable to the loss of the original signification of the primitive names of elemental phenomena,—certain it is that the creative fancy of man has had a hand, more or less exclusive, in weaving these legends into shape. And the warp of fact in them, if any, is so closely intertwined with the woof of fiction, that it is well-nigh impossible to disentangle the one from the other.

Not so, however, with the various traditions regarding the prehistoric migrations of primitive tribes. These in the main are based on actual events of the past. Amid the monotonous round of savage life, nothing is calculated to impress the primitive mind more forcibly than change and movement. And impressions of this nature are the longest to endure. Primitive tribes are likely to retain the memory of their successive changes of abode long after the recollection of. other events of their prehistoric existence has faded away from the tribal memory. Not that the aid of fiction to embellish their scanty traditions is altogether neglected by savage tribes. But the

[1] *Vide* Hesiod, Theogon., 45.

[2] The poet of the Hesiodic "Works and Day" describes how the gods made first the golden race and next the silver race, thirdly zeus made the brazen race and next the race of Heroes and, last of all, the Iron race.

main facts stand out in such bold relief from their setting of fiction as to be obvious to the merest tyro.

The real difficulty, however, lies in another direction. It is in separating the narratives of actual events of the past, handed down by ancient tradition, from surmises and theories foisted in by more enlightened later generations as real facts and since passing current as integral portions of the original traditions, that the historical inquirer experiences the greatest difficulty. In this debatable borderland between fact and theory, the historical inquirer has to seek the guidance of the beacon-light of philology, archæology, geology and other handmaids of history.

The Mūndās, though not rich in traditions regarding their prehistoric migrations, still recount a few legends which may serve as landmarks in the wide ocean of their past history. The student of Mūndā antiquities may find in such legends golden keys to unlock the invaluable secrets of the past.

We have attempted in the earlier chapters of this book to separate fact from fiction in the following legends and to discuss their historical import. We here reproduce them as we heard them narrated by some simple Mūndās. Adapting the words of the poet of the "Song of Hiawatha," we may tell our readers,—

> Should you ask me, whence these stories ?
> Whence these legends and traditions ?
>
> ★   ★   ★
>
> I should answer, I should tell you,
> I repeat them as I heard them
> From the lips of many a Munda.
> Ye who love a nation's legends,
> Like the ballads of a people—
> That like voices from afar off
> Call to us to pause and listen,
> Speak in tones so plain and child-like
> Scarcely can the ear distinguish
> Whether they are sung or spoken,
> Listen to these Indian legends.

The most valuable of Mūndāri mythical legends opens with the creation of the Earth, and runs as follows :

In the beginning of Time, the face of the Earth was covered over with water. *Sing-Bŏngā*, the Sun-God, brooded over the waters and the first beings that were born were a *Kachua* or tortoise, a *Karakom* or crab, and a *Lendad* or leech. *Sing-Bŏngā* commanded these first-born of all animals to bring Him a lump of clay (*hasa*) from out of the depths of the primeval Ocean. The tortoise and the crab by turns tried their skill, but in vain. The persistent leech, however, met with better success. It succeeded in fishing out a bit of clay from underneath the deep. And with this clay, *Sing-Bŏngā* made this *Ote-Disum*, this beautiful earth of ours. And, at His bidding, the Earth brought forth trees and plants, herbs and creepers, of manifold varieties. *Sing-Bŏngā* next filled the earth with birds and beasts of all sorts and sizes. And now happened the most memorable incident of all. The bird *Hur*[1] or swan laid an egg. And out of this egg came forth a boy and a girl, the first human beings. These were the progenitors of the *Horo Honko*—the sons of men, as the Mūndās still style themselves.

This first human pair, however, were innocent of the relation of the sexes. So, *Sing-Bŏngā* pointed out to them certain vegetable roots and taught them the secret of making *ili* or rice-beer therewith. And the first pair, since remembered as *Tota Haram* and *Tota Buri* (the *naked* male ancestor and the *naked* female ancestor) brewed *ili* as directed, and drank their fill. And the *ili* tasted very sweet and it inflamed their passions. And in due course they were blessed with offspring. Three sons were born to them, one after another. And these were named respectively Mūndā, Nānkā, and Rora.[2] All this

---

[1] This bird is said to lay its egg secretly in a *fir* or *fovi* (marshy ground). And the common belief among the Mundas is that a *hur* will not lay more than one egg in its life time. The most solemn oath of the Mundas of old was, it is said, by *Hur farom*, the egg of the *hur* or swan.

[2] According to another account the three sons were named Munda, Nanka, and Tenha. From the youngest Tenha, it is said, the Matis or Soothsayers of the Mundas are descended.

happened at a place named Ajam-Garh.[1] On their parent's death, the sons wandered about over the face of the earth—over hills and dales, through forests untrodden by the feet of man and over fields unworn by the plough.

From Ajam-Garh, the descendants of Tōtā Hārām went successively to Kālangjar-Garh, Garh-Chitr, Garh Nagarwar, Garh Daharwar, Garh Pāli, Garh Pipar, Māndār Pāhār, Bignagarh, Hardinagar, Laknaurgarh, Nandangarh, Rijgarh, and Ruidāsgarh. While living at Ruidāsgarh, the Mūndās incurred the ill-will of a Khārwar chief of the name of Mādhō Singh. Afraid of meeting the Mūndās in fair field, Mādhō Singh surprised the unsuspecting Mūndās with a huge force at dead of night. The Mūndās had no course open to them but to retreat southwards. And southwards they went till they crossed Būrmūghat on to Omedānda in Jhārkhand, the modern Division of Chōtā-Nāgpūr. Finally, on the arrival of the Urāons the Mūndās—always averse to living among strangers—made for the Central Plateau of Chōtā Nāgpūr. It was the famous patriarch Risā Mūndā who led his tribesmen in this eastward march. And Risā's followers numbered full twenty-one thousand. On they moved till at length the present site of village Mūrūma, not far from the modern town of Rānchi, took their fancy and here they came to a halt.

From their encampment at Mūrūma, the Mūndās scrutinised the forests all around them. Not a trace of human habitation or pasturage for cattle could they discern. And at this the Mūndās were not displeased. Their _Panch_—the Council of the Elders of the tribe—laid their hoary heads together. And they decided on resorting to the ordeal of fire. For the length of seven painful days and nights, a hen was made to walk over a huge fire. And at the close of this dreadful week, the hen came out quite unscathed. This augured well for the future safety and peace of the tribe in their proposed new home. As

[1] Curiously enough, we heard a non-Christian and illiterate Munda living among Christian neighbours, explaining this name as "_Adam-garh_ or _Adambakri_", the Garden of Adam.

the hen emerged unharmed from the ordeal, no harm could possibly befall the Mūndās if they dwelt in this region. Thus argued these hoary-headed patriarchs. And so they settled in the country all around. On their way to Mūrūma, it is said, one of the Mūndā patriarchs, Kōrūmbā by name, went to the site of the present village Kōrāmbe which he founded and named after himself. And from Mūrūmā, another patriarch, Sūtiā by name, established the village since called Sūtiāmbé after its founder. And the majority of the present generation of Mūndās, who have now forgotten the earlier vicissitudes of fortune of their valiant forefathers, still name Sūtiāmbé Korāmbé' as the original cradle of the Kōmpāt or Kōnkpāt Mūndās, as they sometimes call themselves. A third patriarch, Chūtū or Chūtiā Hārām, the head of the Chūtū Pūrthi Kili, established the village Chūtia, now a suburb of Rānchi. And to this once Mūndā village the present Division of Chūtu-Nāgpūr is sometimes said to owe its name.

A second version of the above legend is given by some old Mūndās of Pargana Sōnepur as follows :

Mankind (*Horo honko*, the sons of man) threw off their allegiance to Sing-Bōngā. Sing-Bōngā thereupon sent a warning to men on Earth through His servant-bird 'Kāuā Bhāndāri' (crow, the steward) and *Lipi Susari* (Lipi, the cook). But men refused to obey Sing-Bōngā. Enraged at the impious contumacy of man, Sing-Bōngā showered down on the Earth below a terrible rain of fire to destroy mankind. And the race of man ('Hōrōkō') would have been altogether extinct but for the saving pity of the sister of Sing-Bōngā (*Sing Bonga Misi*). The compassionate goddess carried off a man and a woman, related as brother and sister to each another, and kept them hidden underneath a *jovi* or marsh full twelve *koses* in length and of equal breadth. And to reach this hiding-place, one would have to pass successively through ten massive door-ways. The wary Sing-Bōngā had his suspicions. And he despatched 'Kāuā-Bhāndāri' and *Lipi Susari* to look out for any human being that might have escaped the general conflagration. Long and patiently did the sagacious birds search for some trail of the existence of man. They had well-nigh despaired of success when at length the crow (*kaua*) alighted on a leaf-cup (*eana*) such as men use. It lay on the *jovi* and betokened the presence of man. But no human being could anywhere be seen. Straightway the crow picked up the leaf-cup with his beak and carried it to Sing-Bōngā.

Thereupon Sing-Bōngā Himself went down to the *jovi*. Here he was met by Nāge Erā, the presiding spirit of the *jovi*. And of her, Singa-Bōngā demanded to know if she had any human beings in her custody. Nāge Erā promptly replied : "All men hast Thou struck down with fire and brimstone. Where shall I get one, now ?" But Sing-Bōngā was not convinced. At length, however, He won the Nāge Erā's confidence by promising not to destroy mankind again. And He further added : "Henceforth you shall have two parts of the sons of men and I shall take only a third part to myself." At this the Nāge-Erā brought out the surviving human pair from inside the *jovi*, And Sing-Bōngā placed them once more on the green earth. And this man and this woman were called Lūtkūm Hārām and Lūtkūm Būria respectively. They lived together as man and wife at *Ajamgarh*. And the world was peopled by their progeny. Since then as a mark of the Nāge-Erā's power over them, most men have some wart or other mark on their skin. From Ajamgarh their progeny went to various places, to Kālāngjar, to Garh Piprā, to Garh Nagarwar, to Garh Daharwar, to Garh Pāli, to Bignāgarh, to Laknaur, to Hardinagar, to Rijgarh, and to Ruidas. [The rest of the story is almost the same as the preceding legend and need not be repeated here].

More ambitious though obviously less authentic is the following legend which was communicated to us by a Mūndā convert to Christianity. We give below a translation as literal as possible of the narrative recounted to us. The influence of a knowledge of Bible History and of the early European accounts of the Kolarian tribes is patent on the face of the legend. But the genuine portions of the legend can be easily told off from the excrescences put upon it. Thus runs this modernised version of ancient Mūndā History :

Lūtkūm Hārām was the first ancestor of the *Horoko*. Lūtkūm's son was Hembo. Hembo begot Kūs, Kūs begot Mōrih. From Mōrih descended the Kōrkū, the Mārki, the Sāntāl, the Hō or Lārkā, the Bhūmij, the Kōnkō, the Kōrwa, the Pinji and many other tribes who composed the Mūndā race.

Mōrih migrated from his native land in Central Asia[1] with his whole family and his fowls. Mōrih passed through Tibbat-*nagar* and crossing the north-eastern 'ghāts' (hill-passes) entered Jhār-Khand Hindusthan (the forest-covered India), and spread over the whole of northern India—over Behar, Bundelkhand, Jabbalpur, Hosengābād, up to the very banks of the Narbada. They worshipped *Sirma-sing* (the Sun god of Heaven) and established powerful kingdoms in which they erected big *maths* (temples) and *garhs* (forts) and small *thilas* (mounds).

On the death of Mōrih, they elected Seto Mūndā as their leader. Later on, they built a big fort in Behar which they called Raj-Nagar.

One Sisirim,[2] king of Missour (Egypt), led his forces against the Mundas, but the powerful Chief Seto, at the head of his terrible troops, repulsed them.

Hundreds of years later, the Hindus, Gonds, Urāons, Kherwārs, and other tribes entered the Mūndāwar country by the north-western *ghats* (passes). And in time war broke out between the Hindus and the Mūndās. Some bloody

---

[1] The mention of Central Asia as the ancient home of the Mundas, and the North-Eastern passes of the Himalayas as the route by which they entered India, is evidently an echo of the opinions of Hodgson, Colonel Dalton, Sir William Hunter, and others of the old school. Later researches, however, throw great doubts on this theory.

[2] The earliest foreign invasion of India that classical Tradition records is that of Bacchus. The second expedition into India is said to have been led by Semiramis, the celebrated queen of Assyria. We also hear of a fabulous invasion by the Egyptian Sesostris. But neither History nor classic Tradition records any invasion of India by Sisirim.

battles were fought in the Punjab. The mighty warriors of the ancient Mūndā race, with their bows and arrows, their stones and slings, their drums and tom-toms, fell upon the new-comers like tigers on a flock of sheep. But after long years of warfare, the Mūndās began to make peace with the Hindus, Gonds, Urāons and other races. The Mūndās by degrees went even so far as to adopt from the Urāons the worship of the *bhuts* and choose *Urain* wives for themselves. And the offspring of such intermarriages formed a new tribe which came to be called Khāntias or Khārias.

Years afterwards, the son of a Kherwār Chief, named Mādhō Dās, became enamoured of a Mūndā girl. When his parents wanted to marry the young man to some Kherwār girl he declared that he would marry none other than the Mūndā girl of his choice. His parents did all they could to dissuade him, but to no purpose. At length, the doting father sought the parents of the Mūndā girl and proposed the marriage of his son with their daughter. The Mūndās assembled in a Panchāyat and discussed what they should do. And in the end, they unanimously declined to enter into such marital relations with other races. "For," said they, "if once we begin to do so our race will gradually degenerate and at length die out altogether."

The baffled Mādhō Dās was not long in wreaking his vengeance on the haughty Mūndās. Under cover of night, the Kherwār Chief with three hundred followers came down upon the Mūndās, burnt down their houses, and put them to flight. And the Mūndās retreated to the Binji (Vindhya) hills. And there they had a very bad time of it. They constructed leaf-huts to shelter themselves against the rain and the wind, and had to live solely on roots and fruits of jungle growth. And now Sirmā-Sing made Risā Mūndā the leader of the tribe. One night Risā had a vision of Sirmā-Sing in a dream. He dreamt he heard Sirmā-Sing addressing him : "Your sufferings shall soon be at an end. Awake ! Arise ! And go to the extensive and elevated country to the south where the Asūrs lived in the days before the Deluge. There, you shall make for yourselves a permanent home." Risā Mūndā guided by Heavenly light led the Mūndās southwards into an immense forest tract. There he raised an altar (*pinda*) and burnt incense in honour of Sirmā-Sing and made clearances in the forest and settled down for good.

Risā Mūndā with a few followers got up on their *Pankhraj* ponies and in a short while (one *ghari*) went round, and fixed the boundaries of the country. The country was infested with large and venomous 'Nāg' (cobra) serpents. And so they called it Nag-disūm or the land of serpents.

Risā prayed to Sirmā-Sing to rid the country of the serpents. And Sirma-Sing destroyed the big Nag serpents and made the country an agreeable home for the Mūndās. The King Risā under instructions from Sirmā-Sing appointed the Pāhān, Sūtiā, as the head (*pradhan*) of the Mūndās. And Sūtiā Pāhān named the elevated forest tract 'Sūtia Nāg Khand' after him.

Sūtiā the Pāhān next divided the country into seven *garhs* after the seven original 'pūrthis' or ancestors. And as the Mūndās originally belonged to 21 clans or *kilis*, the seven *garhs* were sub-divided into 21 Pārhās or Parganas. The seven *garhs* were named Lohrā-garh, Hazāri-garh, Pālūm-garh, Mānu-garh, Singhā-garh, Kesal-garh and Sūrgūs-garh. And the 21 Parganās were : Omedāndā, Doisa, Khūkhrā, Sirgūja, Jāshpūr, Gāngūāpūr, Porhāt, Girgā, Bisūa, Lāchra, Birūa, Sōnepūr, Belkhādu, Belsing, Tāmār, Sohārdih, Khārsāng, Udaipūr, Bōnai, Kōrea, and Chāngbhāngkar. These originally consisted of 151 villages and counted 21,000 inhabitants.

Sūtiā was the 'Sardār' or chief of all the seven *garhs*. And as an insignia of his chieftainship of the seven *garhs* he wore a *janeu*[1] with seven threads. Sūtia appointed 21 Pārhā Mūndās to manage the affairs of the 21 Pārhās or Parganās.

Once upon a day Sūtiā Pāhān lay down underneath an overspreading *Bar* tree not far off from his house. After he

---

[1] *Janeu* is the sacred thread worn by the Brahmans and other 'twice-born' Hindu castes.

had fallen asleep, a huge Nāg serpent at the bidding
of Sirmā-Sing proceeded to the spot and spread out
his hood like an umbrella over him to protect the
sleeping patriarch from the rays of the Sun. When Sūtiā
awoke he saw the serpent, and was mightily amazed. At
length he thanked Sirmā-Sing and got up and went his
way.

Not long afterwards Sūtia wanted a bride for his son.
But no girl of a different clan or *gotra* from his own was to
be had. And Sūtia would not marry his son to a girl of the
same Mūndā *gotra*, for, such a marriage he considered as
incestuous as the union of two offsprings of the same parents.
So Sūtiā collected various birds and beasts and took them inside
the seven gates of the Sūtiāmbe-Garh. And the 'Pradhāns' or
heads of the 21 Pārhās were also called in. Each of the 21 chiefs
was asked to choose the animal or plant he would have for
his totem. And in this way the 21 Pārhās were divided into 21
kilis or septs for purposes of marriage. Sūtia Pāhān became
the founder of the Bārla *kili*, Dūka Mūndā of the 'Hōrō' *kili*,
Kūra Mūndā of the *Kerketa kili*, Belā Mūndā of the *Kaua
kili*, Dūkhnā Mūndā of the *Hau* *kili*, Gāngū Mūndā of the
Dhechua kili, Lākhō Mūndā of the *Baba kili*, Laimbō Mūndā
of the *Dung dung kili*, Jit Rāi Mūndā of the *Jojobar kili*, Birsā
Mūndā of the *Barwa kili*, Chāmpa Mūndā of the *Sanga kili*,
Karmā Mūndā of the *Tiru kili*, Gomea Munda of the *Lugun
kili*, Somrā Munda of the Būdū *kili*, Ledā Mūndā of the
Herenj kili, Udoy Mūndā of the *Nag kili*, Mangtā Munda of
the *Ore Kandir kili*, Rāiā Mūndā of the *Tuti kili*, Sāmū
Mūndā of the *Bagsuria kili*, Porhā Mūndā of the *Hemrom kili*
and Sānikā Mūndā of the *Dahang kili*. And thenceforward no
Mūndā can lawfully marry within his own sept or *kili*. In
course of time these original *kilis* were sub-divided, and other
kilis branched off out of them. All the heads of the *kilis* were
subordinate to Sūtiā, the *Rajya-Pahan* or Pāhān of the kingdom
as he alone could receive instructions direct from Sirmā-Sing,
and he, like Longfellow's Hiawatha,

—Prayed and fasted in the forest,
Not for greater skill in hunting,
Not for greater craft in fishing,
Not for triumphs in the battle,
And renown among the warriors,
But for profit of the people,
For advantage of the nation.

Such are some of the legends that the Mūndās still treasure up in their memory as invaluable bequests left them by their forefathers. And the curious foreigner often tries in vain to induce the Mūndā to open his lips about the traditions of the past. But once you succeed in breaking the ice, it will make your heart glad to witness the enthusiastic volubility of the ordinarily taciturn Mūndā. Once "the pictures that hang on his Memory's walls" set his imagination on fire, he will cast all reserve to the winds. And with his face, all aglow with conscious pride and emotion, he will recount the traditionary legends of old, though with little skill of story-telling, with

—Homely phrases, but each letter
Full of hope and yet of heart-break.

From the gleam of tender pathos that shines in his eyes when he tells his legends, one fancies him telling his hearers as Schiller's Poet addressed his friends :

"Friends, fairer times have been
(Who can deny ?   ) than we ourselves have seen,
And an old race of more majestic worth,
Were History silent on the Past in sooth,
A thousand stones would witness of the truth
Which men disbury from the womb of Earth."

THE LEGEND OF LUTKUM HARAM
AND LUTKUM BURIA

ALL ancient history shades off into the mists of the legendary.
If this is true of the early history of civilised races, it is much
more so of the history of an unlettered semi-barbarous tribe
like the Mūndās. The past history of this people is shrouded
in an obscurity on which modern researches have yet to shed but
a dim uncertain light. In fact, Mūndāri history, anterior to
the British occupation of the country, has hardly yet been
extricated from the "mists of fabling Time."

The historical memory of such a savage people as the
Mūndās is necessarily short and faulty. And even such
traditionary legends as have been handed down to them by
their ancestors are apt to get more or less transfigured in the
very process of transmission from one generation to another.
They get hopelessly intermixed, at times with figments of some
individual brain, and, at others, with embellishments borrowed
from alien races with whom they may have come in intimate
contact at some period or other of their chequered tribal
existence. Not infrequently perhaps both these causes combine
to transform the original tradition into a strange shape past all
recognition. And such indeed may have been the fate of not
a few of the scanty traditions and legends that have come
down to the present generation of the Mūndās.

It is none too early then to attempt to bring together the
few comparatively genuine traditions and legends still current
among the Mūndās of the Chōtā-Nāgpūr Plateaux. Such traditions and legends may perhaps cast some glimmer of light on
the past history of the race. And by focussing the stray rays
of light thus obtained, we may possibly expect to catch a
glimpse of some of the realities of the dim dark ages of Mūndā
antiquity.

First and foremost in point of sanctity and popularity,

though not indeed of historical luminosity, stands the Mūndā *mythus* of Lūtkūm Hārām and Lūtkūm Būriā, otherwise known as the Asūr Legend.

Thus runs this curious legend of Mūndā mythology :

It was long—long—before the dawn of human history. The earth was yet in its infancy. Sing Bōngā,[1] "the dreaded lord of Time," was seated on his throne of gold, engaged in happy converse with his heavenly consort,

Wiling with love the morning calm.

But the heavenly pair had not long been thus agreeably occupied, when they were disturbed in their dalliance by an intolerable heat which suddenly surcharged the thin atmosphere of haven. And just at that moment, there went up from the beasts that roamed the earth below piteous complaints to Sing Bōngā's throne on high. "The heat emanating from the furnaces of the Asūrs," so ran the complaints, "this unearthly heat is drying up the streams, the tanks and the pools, and scorching up all vegetations. We are dying of hunger and of thirst. Neither do the birds of the air nor the worms that crawl on the earth find any food to eat or water to drink".

At this, the enraged Sing Bōngā armed himself with his sword and his shield and fiercely exclaimed, These *Asūrs*[2] I *will* slay and hack them into pieces." But his wife protested. "Alone", said she, "thou art no match for the whole host of the Asūrs. Rather employ state-craft and artifice." This appeared to Sing Bōngā a wise counsel. And to this He agreed, and acted accordingly.

The energetic bird Dingchūā (Dhechūā) and the watchful Kerketā were selected as messengers to convey Sing Bōngā's

---

[1] Sing Bonga is the beneficent Sun-God, the Supreme Deity of Munda Mythology. A mutilated version of this legend has been adopted by the Uraons of Chota-Nagpur.

[2] There is a Kolarian tribe of this name dwelling mostly in the more jungly places in the western parts of the Ranchi district. Iron-smelting is the tribal profession of the Asurs of Chota-Nagpur.

high behests to the Asūrs. And, forthwith, the Dingchūā and the Kerketā--

O'er the wide expanse of ether stray'd,

and carried their message to the human Vulcans. In the name of Sing Bōngā, they commanded the Asūrs to stop all work at their furnaces in the day-time if they should work at night and to stop all work at night if they worked in the day-time. But the Asūrs laughed at them and declared they owned no allegiance to Sing Bōngā, and insulted His messengers by besmearing the Dingchūā with coal-dust and the Kerketā with the dust of iron-ore. The unfortunate messengers flew back to Sing Bōngā and in great grief exclaimed : "Alas alas ! what shall we do ? Now will our kith and kin undoubtedly excommunicate us."—Sing Bōngā, thereupon, consoled them, saying : "Return you both to your own places. Like you, all Dingchūās shall henceforth turn black and all Kerketās shall from this day be grey in colour." And since then Dingchūās have become black and Kerketās grey.

Now, Sing Bōngā selected the golden vulture (*Sonadidi*[1]) and the silvery vulture (Rupādidi) for the same errand. And forthwith the vultures 'plied their pinions bold,' and sought the Asūr village. But no sooner had they delivered their massage than the Asūrs struck them with a hammer and coked them with iron pincers. And thus were they both driven away.

Fresh messengers were now dispatched. And this time Sing Bōngā's choice fell upon the *Lipi*[2] and the Kāūā.[3] Their nimble wings wafted them "fleetly through the air." But at the Asūra village, the same fate awaited them as had attended the Dingchūā and the Kerketā. The Asūrs cast coal-dust on the crow and iron-dust on the lark, and expelled them from their presence.

[1] *Didi* is the Mundari name for a vulture.
[2] *Lipi* is the Mundari name for the lark.
[3] *Kaua* is the common crow.

Last of all, the little birds Lang[1] and Bōchō[2] proceeded on the same errand. Lightly they "skimmed through regions rare" and alighted where the grim Asūrs were smelting iron at their furnaces. But these messengers too did not fare any better. The wicked Asūrs bathed the Bōchō in saffron-water and lengthened the Lang's tail by pulling hard at it. And the Lang and the Bōchō were driven away.

Now at length Sing Bōṅgā Himself had to stoop down from His ærial heights, and had to resort to artifice and cunning. Down He descended from His throne on high and alighted on *Ekasipiri Terasbadi*—the land of eighty-one uplands and eighty-three elevated rice-fields. There He met a labourer working in one of the fields. And Sing Bōṅgā raised up the itch all over this labourer's skin. Then He requested the man to allow Himself to try His spade. But the man would not, out of respect for the noble-looking stranger, listen to such a proposal. Thereupon Sing Bōṅgā seized him by the hair and gave him such a vigorous shaking as served to peel off the servant's skin. And now Sing Bōṅgā put on the servant's cast-off itch-covered skin, and, personating a boy affected with the itch, went about in search of the Asūrs.

Arrived at the place where the Asūrs lived, He moved about from door to door, offering His services as a servant-boy. "I shall guard your grains against the ravages of the fowls," He went about saying, "food and shelter only do I want for my services." But the Asūrs dreaded the contagion of His loathsome itch and would not have Him for a servant. To the next village then He went. There too at first none would have His services. But some kind people of this place directed Him to a miserable hut at one end of the village where lived an

---

[1] The *Lang* is a small bird with a beautiful long tail, Munda girls sometimes stick feathers of the *Lang's* tail into their hair as an ornament on festive occasions.

[2] The *bocho* is a small bird of a deep yellow colour. It is considered by the Mundas to be a propitious bird. And its whistling notes if heard in the course of a journey augur well for the success fo the fortunate traveller.

aged Mūndā couple called Lūtkŭm Hārām and Lūtkŭm Būriā.[1]

Arrived before the Lūtkŭms' hut, Sing Bōngā called out, "Grandfather and grandmother,—are you in? I am Tōrō Kōrā,[2] the itch-afflicted boy." And the old couple took pity on the poor Boy and took Him under their protection. And day after day, the Tōrō Kōrā, as He was called, dutifully kept off the fowls from the grain spread out by the Lūtkŭms to dry.

Thus, His days passed smoothly along. After a time, the Tōrō Kōrā requested the Lūtkŭms to get some eggs of hen for Him,—as His sores, said He, produced a strong craving for such delicacies. And the old couple procured Him a few eggs and prepared a few rice-cakes for Him.

Not long afterwards, the Boy, taking advantage of the Lūtkŭms' absence from home, went to the Asūr boys and drew them on to play a game of *guli*[3] and *kati*[4] with Him. Twelve Asūr boys (and thirteen Deōtā[5] boys) accepted His challenge and entered the lists against Him. They had their *gulis* and *katis* all made of iron. But the Toro Kora had only a few

---

[1] Lutkum Haram is, literally,—Lutkum the old man, Lutkum Buria is, literally,—Lutkum the old woman.

[2] *Kasra* or *Toro* in Mundari means the *itch*, and *Kora* means a boy.

[3] *Guli* is a marble ordinarily made of clay. And the game of *guli* resembles a game at marbles.

[4] *Kati* is a small wicket more broad than long, which is planted on the ground and the players aim at these pickets from some distance with other *katis* in their hands, which are shot like balls in a game of cricket. The players have each a stick in his hand which serves as a bat to drive the *katis*.

[5] There is really no mention of the Deota boys in any portion of the legend except in the song given below. Evidently this song is of a later date than the original legend; and the introduction of the Deotas or Gods is an embellishment borrowed much later from Hindu legends. It is significant that in the version of this legend as related by the Uraons (who appear to have adopted many religious practices and part of their mythology from the Mundas) we hear of thirteen brothers Lodhas and twelve brothers Asurs. In the Uraon version we also hear of Ansraj Pankraj—God's horse—another invention of Hindu folklore.

eggs for His *gulis* and rice-cakes for His *katis*. And with these He engaged in an apparently unequal contest with His better-equipped opponents.

[Here the impulsive Munda narrator breaks out into something like a *durang*, or song. We give the Dūrāng below and append a free metrical translation of it.]

Mare honko[1] guli inungtana' do
Mare honko kati inungtana' do.
Toro Kora gulikedae,
—Baro bhai hasurkoa mered guli rapud-jana
Kasra Kora katikedae,
—Terobhai deotakoa mered kati rapud-jana
"Auri hale Toro Kora
Auri hale Kasra Kora
Ama jiangking,
Ama tatang king,
Buru bichatanaking,
Tondang kuila tanaking,
Babaking tasitukadmeaking,
Simko jomchaba rikaked koam."
"Hela-a jiangking !
Hela-a tatangking !
Burubicha janaben,
Tondangkuila janaben.
Toro Kora do, Kasra Kora do,
Mod pati baba do,
Bar pati baba do,
Tasitukaiaben.
Toro Kora do, Kasra Kora do
Nekasipirire Tesasibadire
Aleloge guli inungjana' do
Simko sukuriko jom chabakeda
Naeke daia tatangkin,
Chinape loloa ?
Chinape basana ?"
"Hela-a Toro Kora,
Hela-a Kasra Kora,
Mod pati baba do,
Bar pati baba do.

---

[1] *Hoko* is sometimes used.

Simko sukuriko jomchabarikakedkoam.
Chinabu loloa : chinabu basana ?"
            "Ka-a jiang king !
            Ka-a tatangking !
            Ka-aing jomrikaledkoa
            Sehelre ing rurungakada
            Sehelre mena
            Enabu mandia,
            Enabu basana.

                [Translation]

    Now see them play, th' *gulis* go bang
    The *katis* clash in merry twang.
    There lo ! the itch-afflicted boy
        Now deals his master-stroke ;
    And straight, like glass, are th' iron *gulis*
        Of the Asura brothers broke.
    At *kati* next, his hand he tries,
        With all his might and main—
    The Deota brothers' iron *katis*,
        Alas ! they break in twain.
  [Ill could defeat the Asuras brook,
        With spite and ire their bodies shook
    Grieved to find themselves thus foil'd,
        In rage the Deota brothers boil'd.
    Addressing the boy whom they'gan despise,
        The Deotas and Asuras exclaimed this wise:]
  "Hold ! Hold ! thou boy with th' itch on thy skin
  We'll teach thee a lesson a short while within,
  Thy granny and grandpa' well hast thou obey'd,
  Who left thee in charge of all and sped
  To yon blue hill for iron ore,
  Or to the woods for charcoal more.
  The paddy they had left in the sun to dry,
  The fowls have devour'd and all their fry.
    [Soon as the approaching Lutkums they spied,
      The Asuras and the Deotas the old pair hied,
        Still smarting under their ill success
      The Lutkums did they thus address :]
  "O ! listen, grandfather, and O ! grandmother dear,
  A fine account of your boy from us you'll hear !
  Away in the woods for charcoal and iron ore,
  Whilst you did roam deeming your home secure,

A mat or two of rice spread out to dry
In charge of your *protege* that scabby boy,
O ! what guess ye, your boy the whiles was after ?
A jolly time he had of play and laughter !
With us at *guli* and at *kati* he play'd, in troth !
At Nekasipiri Terasibadi, forsooth !
And th' fowls and th' pigs as jolly a time had they,
Who ate their fill of the rice on the mats that lay.
Say, what will you for your daily meal have now ?
Not a grain is left to cook or boil, we trow,"
          [At this their boy the Lutkums seek,
            And thus in angry accents speak :]
"Look here ! thus scabby boy, what hast thou done !
The rice we left on the mats to dry in the sun,
The pigs and the fowls you've made it all devour,
Whilst away we went for charcoal and iron ore.
What shall we for our daily meal have now ?
Not a grain is left to cook and boil, we trow !"
     [Unmov'd was the boy :—To his cheeks not a blush did arise
But softly the angry Lutkums he address't this wise :]
"A pretty tale from prating imps you hear !
Heed them not, grandfather and grandmother dear.
Not a grain is lost, not a grain did the fowls devour,
With the thrashel I husk'd them, in th'husking pit they are,
All winnow'd is the paddy. Go, your accustom'd meal prepare
Oh, fret not grandmother. Go, cook a delicious fare."[1]

The incredulous old couple thereupon examined the husking-pit. And what was their astonishment and delight when they found it full of husked rice ! And so too were the basket and the mat found full of paddy. But theirs was only a momentary happiness. The good old couple soon had their misgivings. Had the boy stolen the paddy of others ? Were they going to partake of the fruits of crime ? They felt quite ill at ease. And they entreated the boy to speak out the truth. "Be not uneasy, my grandsires. It is all your own. Sing Bōngā gives it to you in plenty". With these words, at length, the virtuous old couple were reassured.

---

[1] A few more lines of song precede the stanzas given above. Those introductory lines of the song are as follows :

Once, again, during the Lūtkūms' absence from home, the
Tōrō Kōrā matched his egg-*gulis* and his cake-*katis* against the
iron-*gulis* and iron-*katis* of the Deōtās and the Asūrs. And once again
the iron-*gūlis* and iron-*katis* of the Deōtās and the Asūrs smashed
into pieces at a stroke of the egg-*gulis* and cake-*katis* of the Tōrō
Kōra. And once more the envious complaint of the Deōta boys
and the Asūr boys were falsified by the discovery of plenty of rice
in the husking-pit and in the basket and on the bamboo-mats.
And not unnaturally the itch-covered Boy came to be regarded
as endowed with supernatural powers.

Now, it so happened that the outturn of the Asūrs' furnaces
began habitually to run short. And the Asūrs were mightily dis-
tressed. They searched about for a sooth-sayer, but none could
be had. And, at their wit's end, they had recourse to the magic
Sūp'[1] or winnowing-fan. The Sūp pointed them to the Tōrō
Kōra. And to Him accordingly the Asūrs applied for a remedy
for their difficulties. They carried rice-grains to Him and requested
Him to examine them and divine the means they should adopt
to ensure the desired supply of iron. Toro Kora examined the
rice-grains and directed the Asūrs to offer up a white fowl in
sacrifice to Sing Bōngā. And this the Asūrs did. And then their

> Nekasipirire Terasibadire,
> Toro Kora do Kasra Kora do
> Simjarom gulite : lapulad katite
> > Barobhai hasur kolo ;
> > Terobhai Deota kolo.
> > Guli inungtana do,
> > Kati inung tano do.
> Hasur honko idikeda mered guli do,
> Deota honko idikeda mered kati do.
> Toro Kara idikeda simjarom guli,
> Kasra Kora idikeda lupulad kati do.

[1] The 'sup' or winnowing-fan test is the orthodox method employed by
the Mundas and Uraons to ascertain the will of the gods. This test is
ordinarily applied when by reason of the extinction of the original hereditary
Pahan family of the village or for other sufficient reason, a new Pahan has to
be elected.

furnaces again worked fairly well. Not long after, however, the
Asūrs' supply of iron again ran short. And again they applied to
the Tōrō Kōrā. This time a white goat was pronounced to
be the proper sacrifice. And a white goat was accordingly
sacrificed,—and it came about all right as predicted. And
at this the Asūrs rejoiced. But their rejoicings were not to
last long. Again, their furnaces fell in. The Tōrō Kōrā was
again appealed to. The sacrifice of a young sheep was now
recommended. The Asūrs hastened to comply. And, again,
great was their rejoicing, for again their furnaces worked all
right.

Before long, however, the old troubles with their furnaces
recurred. And once more the Asūrs had recourse to the young
prophet. But this time nothing less than a human sacrifice was
indicated by the rice-grains examined by the Tōrō Kōrā. And
so the Tōrō-Kōrā revealed the Divine will. At this startling
revelation, the Asūrs were dumb-founded and knew not what to
do. In vain they searched for an available human being for the
dread purpose. They went among the Mūndās[1] and offered to
buy for any price a child for the intended sacrifice. But the
haughty Mūndā parents spurned such an offer, and would have
killed the heartless men who dared make such an unfeeling
proposal had not the Asūrs straightway fled for dear life. And
so the Asūrs returned to the Tōro Korā and again besought His
advice. Now, the itch-afflicted Boy thus proposed to solve their
difficulty. Said he, "Life has become unbearable to me by reason
of the constant pain all over my body. Do, for pity's sake, offer
me up as a sacrifice to Sing Bongā." But the Lūtkūms would
hear of no such thing. "Who will guard our house," they
exclaimed, "who will support us now in our old age ?" And the

---

[1] Some versions of the legend mention the Doisa Pargana and the Khukra
Pargana in the district of Ranchi as the localities where the Asurs searched
for a Munda child for the sacrifice. This, however, appears to be one of the
subsequent embellishments with which later generations of Mundas sought
to improve upon the original legend—"to adorn the tale," if not "to point a
moral."

Tōrō Kōrā had much ado to persuade the old pair to give their consent. And, at length, by way of consoling them for their prospective loss, He made an important revelation to them. "I will establish the Pahan's son under a tree in the middle of the village. And he shall offer up sacrifices for you, once at the *Baha* or Flower Feast, once at the Bātāuli Festival, and once again at the Māgé Feast." And thus were the Lūtkums consoled.

And now the Asūrs led the Tōrō Kōrā towards their furnaces to offer Him up as a sacrifice to appease Sing Bōngā. The Tōrō Kōrā had already given directions as to the proper mode of the sacrifice. "Two virgins," he had said, "who will have fasted for three days and nights shall work the furnaces with bellows newly made of white goatskin and furnished with new bellow-handles and a new bellow-noozle. By day and by night must the bellows be worked without any respite. And at the end of three days, let them sprinkle water on the furnaces with mango twigs, and then put out the fire. And the water shall be carried on new earthen pitchers on head-cushions made of cotton thread." And all this was done just as the Tōrō Kōrā had directed.

At the end of three long days and nights, the huge fire was put out, and the furnace opened up. And now lo ! and behold ! out cometh the erstwhile Tōrō Kōrā, effulgent as the morning sun, bedecked with gold and silver, and with a precious plate and a costly bowl in His hands. And the avaricious Asūrs eagerly inquire : "Is there more of such treasures left in the furnace ?" "Ah, yes, plenty and to spare," replies the now glorious Boy. "you are many in number, and you will thus succeed in bringing out a lot of such things. Men alone and not women should go in for them. Leave not a single man behind, lest you should fall out among yourselves and rob each other. Inside there, you will find a golden vulture and a silver vulture hovering about under the roof of the furnace. Ransack them underneath their wings and in between their feathers where their treasures are hid." And now, when all the Asūrā men have taken in the bait and entered the furnace, Sing Bongā orders the women to plaster up the furnace and kindle the fire and work the bellows. And right away the women work the bellows hard.

But, hark ! What betokens that faint murmuring sound the women fancy issuing out of the furnace ? Can those be the groans of their husbands, sons and brothers ? The women start in fear and horror at the very idea. But, now, the confused inaudible sounds gradually develop into distinct howls. A cold shiver runs through the Asur women from head to foot. And the women now vehemently accuse Sing Bongā of having played them false. "Ah, no ! affrighted ones," says He, "no harm to your men. Everyone of them perchance has not yet had enough, and so they are all quarrelling over the division of the spoils. Work the bellows faster still." And faster still the women worked away.

But, horror of horrors ! What is this, again ? This horrid sight is enough to curdle weak woman's blood. Appalled at the sight of the stream of bloody liquid that now begins to ooze out through the air passage of the bellows and through the outlet for molten dross, the women wax still more clamorous in their accusations against the mysterious Boy. "A murrain on thy eyes !" they exclaim, "dost not see how blood streams out of the furnace ?" "Deluded women," replies Sing Bongā, "they are chewing *pan*[1] and *kasaili*[2], and that is why they are spitting red saliva. Quick ! Quick ! Blow away, my girls, and ere long you will have cause to rejoice." And with misgivings at heart, and cold sweat covering their limbs in clammy drops, the timid women obeyed. A little while later, Sing Bōngā perceiving that His fell purpose has been accomplished, orders the furnace to be opened up. This done, what do the unhappy women discover ? They stand aghast at the sight of the charred bones, and ashes of their unfortunate husbands, sons and brothers. Long and piteously do the poor women weep. And they tear their hair and they beat their breast and curse the Toro Kora. "Alas ! alas !" at length they cry out, "who could have suspected this of thee ? Thou hast made us put our men to death with our own hands."

1 Betel leaves.
2 Betel nuts.

At this, Sing Bonga thunders out—"Well ! well ! messenger after messenger I had sent to you. But you heeded them not. Will you henceforward obey me in all my behests ?" "Yes, yes, we will," answer the Asūr women all in one voice, "who else will support us now ?" "Well have you spoken," says Sing Bōngā, "I will now reveal to you the way in which you shall support yourselves. I will establish two sooth-sayers, the Patgūrū and his disciple Tūrā. They shall always appeal to you for guidance through half-husked rice grains and through lamp-light and through torch-light,[1] and you shall give them proper directions. Ever do you reveal to the 'Pātgūrū' and the 'Tūra chelā, the hidden causes of human ills and the proper sacrifices requisite to avert them. Under a tree in the middle of the village, shall henceforth dwell a Mūndā as sacrificer,, and he shall be called the Pāhān and shall make offerings to you."

Now, when Sing Bōngā is ready to ascend to His seat in heaven, the Asūr women will not let Him go. Thereupon Sing Bōngā seizes them by the hair and hurls them in different directions. Some are flung on high mountains, some on rocks, some in deep waters, some on *piris* or uplands, others again fall on wooded spots by the side of delightful springs, and yet others are assigned pleasant meadows and groves for their future abode. And in caves and woods, on hills and trees, on meadows and groves, in streams and springs, their disembodied spirits are to dwell for ever and ever as presiding deities. And thenceforward for the Munda every fountain and mountain, every rill and gill, has its Naiyad and its Dryad. To him there are sacred "Presences in Nature," invisible spirits everywhere. And this Pagan "suckled in a creed outworn" is in his own way, in closer touch with Nature than many a votary of what we term "higher faiths."

Such is the origin of the minor deities—the*Bhuts*—of Mūndā Mythology—the *Buru Bonga,* the presiding spirit of the hills, the *Ikir Bonga* whose seat is in the deep waters, the *Nage Bonga* who

---

[1] This is a reference to the various processes of divination in vogue among the sooth-sayers of the Mundas.

resides in the uplands and in the ravines, the *Desauli Bonga* whose dwelling is in beautiful wood-lands, the *Chondor Ikir Bonga*, who haunts romantic wooded spots by the side of crystal springs, and the *Chandi Bonga* whose altar is in shady groves, in the open fields or on the heights.

These, however, are but the "lesser gods" of the Mūndā faith. Over this goodly band of spirits reigns supreme, the great Sing Bōngā,—

> Father of All, in every Age,
> In every Clime ador'd
> By Saint, by Savage, and by Sage,
> Jehovah, Jove, or Lord.

THE LAND TENURES OF THE
RANCHI DISTRICT

Estates : The present area of the Rānchi District is 7,103·6 square miles ; of this, 7,052·28 square miles constitute one revenue-paying estate now owned by the Mahārājā of Chōtā-nāgpūr ; 21·5 square miles constitute a second revenue-paying estate now owned by the Rājā of Pachete in the Mānbhūm District, to some ancestor of whose this area was originally granted as a marriage present by a former Rājā of Chōtānāgpūr ; and 30·27 square miles appertain to the revenue-paying estate of the Rājā of Padmā (formerly of Rāmgarh) in the District of Hāzāri-bāgh but included within the limits of the Rānchi District, as this tract, too, is said to have passed to the Rāmgarh estate as a marriage present from a former Mahārājā of Chōtānāgpūr.

In very few parts of India can the various stages of evolution of successive village systems and forms of landholding be found existing side by side to this day as we find them here. We have seen how originally the country formed a congeries of independent village communities, and each village community was the proprietory body owning all the land inside the village boundary. Then we have seen these village communities forming themselves into groups or Pārhās for purposes of mutual support and each group acknowledging a leader styled the Mānki. We next saw how, in course of time, a Rājā arose amongst them, and got all the village communities under his domination. This Nāgbansi Rājā who was originally perhaps of the same race as the primitive settlers, and was no more than the chosen leader of the people, gradually became Hindūized, and then commenced a serious change which gradually evolved the various land tenures existing at the present day.

Khas Bhandar : The Rajā first gradually managed to take actual '(khās)' possession of some villages as his special demesne (khās bhāndār). The area in the *khas* possession of the Mahārājā as his private demesne now measures 631·93 square miles within the Rānchi District.

Khorposh Tenures : The Rājā next granted a number of villages to his brothers and other near relatives the—Thakurs, Lals, etc,—for their maintenance (*khorposh*). At first, it would appear, these grants meant nothing more than assignments of the tributes or supplies which the Rājā used to get from the village communities. The *khorposh* tenures created by the Mahārājā or his predecessors within the Rānchi District measure 1,050·93 square miles. These include the Deori Mahals or villages granted to the Mahārānis by way of dower or maintenance.

Feudal Jagir Tenures : But, as the Rājā grew more and more ambitious, and began to surround himself with a court composed of Hindū adventurers from Bihār and the Central Provinces, these Hindū courtiers and āmlāhs came to be remunerated for their services with grants (*jagirs*) of villages. Unlike the Rājā and his kinsmen, these alien adventurers could not rest satisfied with such nominal rights over the villages as the Rājā himself owned, or, was in a position to grant. And these alien Jāgirdārs gradually attempted to assert and acquire real rights to lands and villages comprised within their *Jagirs*. The Rājā and his khōrpōshdārs would appear to have given more or less support to such attempts. The original settlers naturally showed fight. And the Rājā and his Jāgirdārs thereupon called in the aid of more war-like foreigners to overawe the aboriginal peasant-proprietors into submission. These newly-arrived military adventurers, too,—the Chatris, the Bārāiks, the Rāutias, etc.,— were similarly remunerated with *jagir* grants of villages and the grantees undertook to render military service whenever required.

Service Jagirs : As the Rājā's power thus gradually increased and he assumed all the pomp and pageant of Hindū royalty, he came to entertain a large retinue of political and domestic favourites and servants, and each of them had to be provided for.

Similar grants were also made to certain persons by way of reward for particularly meritorious services, or for remarkable feats of strength or intellectual skill. And thus a number of service tenures came into existence, some of which were held rent-free and others on quit-rents.

Incidents of Jagir Tenures : The Jāgir Tenures of all sorts (except life-grants) are held on what is locally known as *Putra Patradik* tenure. These are by custom resumable by the Mahārāja on the extinction of the direct legitimate male descendants of the original grantees. Old records show that these tenures were in former times neither partible nor alienable. On resumption, the widow of the last holder is by custom entitled to a suitable maintenance. Judicial decisions originally based on a mistaken analogy with similar tenures in Bihār and Lower Bengal would appear to have made these tenures partible as well as transferable. Originally, it would appear no rents used to be paid by the holders of Jāgir tenures. When, however, these feudal and other services gradually became obsolete, small cash rents came to be assessed. The rents payable by most of these *Jagirdars*, though formerly enhancible from time to time with the increase of the cultivated area, have ceased to be enhancible at all by operation of judicial decisions. In some forms of such grants, however, such as the "Hindu Hārāmi" and the "Bhāndowa," it was distinctly stipulated from the beginning that no increase of rent could ever be demanded. It is curious that the incident of resumability applies in the District even to religious grants. Impartibility and primogeniture would seem to have at one time been the *lex loci* of the District, but since comparatively recent times, most jāgirdār families have been following the ordinary rules of inheritance under the Mitakshara School of Hindu Law. The *Jagir* tenures in the Rānchi District under the Mahārājā, together with the dominions of the dependent zamindars of Tāmār, Silli, Būndū and Bārāndā (which do not properly fall into this class) measure as much as 4,475·36 square miles.

Dependent Rajas : As for the dependent chiefs of the Five Parganās. they were not, it would seem, creations of the Chōtānāgpūr Mahārājā, but in former times appear to have sometimes allied themselves to the Chōtānāgpūr Rājā and acknowledged his suzerainty and at other times assumed independence. It was not till the last quarter of the Eighteenth Century that the chiefs of the Five Parganās had to definitely acknowledge the Chōtānāgpūr Mahārājā as their superior landlord and pay their quota of the revenue into the hands of the Mahārājā as rent. But these estates, it would seem, were not resumable by the Mahārājā for default of direct heirs. Rāhe has been resumed, but the grounds on which resumption was granted in 1845 have been declared unsound by subsequent judicial decisions.[1] Tāmār has been judicially declared to be non-resumable. As for the Borway chief, his ancestors appear to have been originally dependent on the Rājā of Sūrgūjā. He appears later on to have transferred his allegiance to the Rājā of Chōtānāgpūr, but the Sūrgūjā chief would seem to have effected a reconquest. The troops of the Sūrgūjā chief who 'kept possession of Borway for several years', retreated only when a British detachment under Colonel Jones appeared in the Parganā. Walter Hamilton writes : "Conceiving this a favourable opportunity, the Rājā of Chotānāgpūr determined to attempt its reconquest, but he stood not the least chance of success had not the British Commander, and the Magistrate of Rāmghar, advised the Burwe chief to submit on the assurance of personal safety."

Religious Brit Tenure : The parapharnalia of a Hindū Rājā's court could not be complete without a posse of Brāhmans. And consequently a number of Brāhman priests were invited from outside, temples of Hindū deities were erected in the country, and 'bramhōttar,' 'debōttar' 'kusāhā' and other *brit* grants of lands and villages were made to these Brāhman priests for their maintenance, and for the upkeep of the temples, and the worship of the deities. The number of such grants is, however, rather small, and the majority of those that exist appear to be of comparatively recent origin. The *brit* tenures granted to Brahmans and others measure 134·89 square miles, other service tenures measure 0·15 square miles and miscellaneous tenures measure 12·29 square miles within the Mahārājā's estate in the Rānchi District.

---

[1] *Vide* Judgment of Major Hannyngton passed on August 1, 1851, in appeal in the Tamar resumption suit

Thikas and Other Leases : In the first quarter of the Nineteenth Century, a different class of adventurers appeared in the country. These were North Indian traders—Mahomedans, Sikhs and other Hindūs—who swarmed into the country with various merchandise and sold them at exorbitant prices to the Nāgbansi Rājā and his big jāgirdārs and khōrpōshdārs. Still later, the growing luxurious habits and general improvidence of some of the Rājās and Jāgirdārs made them incur similar other liabilities to the Sāhūs or moneylenders and others. Unable to pay their creditors in cash, the Rājā and his Jāgirdārs and Khōrpōshdārs, from time to time, granted permanent (*doami*) or temporary (*miadi*) leases (thikās), perpetual leases at fixed rentals (*makarari*) and usufructuary leases (*zarpeshgi* and *bhugut*) to these several classes of creditors, over the heads of the aboriginal proprietors. The ignorant Mūndāri Khuntkāttidars themselves were sometimes gulled by the sāhūs into transferring their villages to them generally for inadequate consideration. Determined to make the best of their bargain, these various classes of grantees, lessees, and purchasers spared no pains to break down the original village system of the Mūndās and Urāons. And the various classes of existing land tenures in the villages of the Rānchi District mark the varying degrees of success achieved in this attempt in the different parts of the country.

Such, in brief, is the history of the growth of the different intermediate tenures under the Rājā (now Mahārāja) of Chōtānāgpūr. At present as much as 659·15 square miles within the Rānchi District are held under the Mahārājā in leases, temporary or permanent. The respective areas of the different classes of these leases are : *Mokarrari* tenures, 22·55 square miles ; permanent (*doami*) absolute grants, 493·34 square miles ; temporary leases *(thika* proper), 111·94 square miles ; permanent leases *(doami thika)*, 6·44 square miles ; rent-free *(khairat)* tenures, 12.11 square miles ; and usufructuary mortgages (*zarpeshgi*, etc.). 2·77 square miles.

Percentages : Thus, of the total area of the Rānchi District a little less than 9 per cent. is now in the direct *(khas)* possession of the Mahārājā of Chōtānāgpūr and 9 per cent. has been given away by him in leases, temporary or permanent. Nearly 63 per cent of the area of the District is held by the Mahārājā's Jāgirdārs and 14·8 per cent by his khōrpōshdārs, 1·8 per cent by his *brit*-holders, 0·1 per cent by other service-holders and 0·2 per cent by his Lākhirājdārs or rather *khairatdars* (rent-free tenure-holders).

Mundari Khuntkatti Tenancies Held Directly under the Maharaja : Of the 7,652·28 square miles of the Chōtānāgpūr (Mahārāja's) estate only 96·94 square miles are held directly under the Mahārājā as *Mundari Khuntkatti* lands (included within "Intact" as well as "Broken" Khuntkatti villages) by the descendants of the original Mūndā settlers [1] and includes some lands held by the Parjās in 'intact' Mūndāri Khūntkātti villages. The total area represents not more than 1·4 per cent. of the total area of the District. Other Khūntkatti lands, or lands originally reclaimed by non-Mūndāri aboriginals or semi-aboriginals and still held by their descendants as privileged tenancies altogether measure only 21·12 square miles within the Ranchi District, but only 12·16 square miles are within the Chōtānāgpūr (Mahārāja's) estate. Besides these, there are, as we shall see later on, other Mūndāri Khūntkātti villages and lands held by Mūndās under the Jāgirdārs and others.

Having thus taken a general view of the infeudations of the first degree directly under the Mahārājā of Chōtānāgpūr, we shall attempt a general survey of the remnants of the original communal villages and the various cultivating tenancies which have sprung up on the ruins of the original communal system.

Intact Mundari Khuntkatti Villages : Only 156 villages in the Ranchi District have successfully withstood the aggressions of Jāgirdārs and Thikādārs and retained their "Khūntkātti" character

---

[1] Of this, 93·68 square miles are within and 3·26 square miles outside the *Manki Pattis*. Within the estate of the Raja of Pachete there are 3·3 square miles of *Mundari Khuntkatti* lands and 9 square miles of other *Khuntkatti* lands (within the Ranchi District). So also within the estate of the Raja of Padma, there are (within the limits of the Ranchi District) 12·7 square miles of Mundari Khuntkatti lands appertaining to the Manki Pattis, besides 0·5 square miles of other Khuntkatti lands.

"intact" to this day. The village community is theoretically the joint owner of all village lands, and actually joint owners of all unoccupied and waste lands and of all rights to these villages. Of these "intact" villages, 87 are within the Khūnti Thānā, 59 in Thānā Tāmār, 9 in Thānā Būndū and 1 in Thānā Rāhe. The total area of these villages is 153·7 square miles. The greater portion of this area is held under the Jāgirdārs or other tenure-holders. In these "Intact Khūntkātti" villages, the original village community, or the Khūntkāttidārs as a body, still retain full proprietary rights, subject to the payment of a permanently fixed quit-rent to the superior landlord. Each khūntkāttidar pays his share (*chanda*) fixed originally irrespective of the quantity of land he held ; this quit-rent is paid to the secular headman (Mūnda) of the village who, in his turn, pays it, in a Mānki-patti, to the Mānki, and, outside the Mānki-pattis, to the superior landlord himself or his agent. Originally, it appears there used to be a periodical redistribution of the cultivable lands of such a village amongst the Khūntkātti brotherhood. But in course of time the first step in the change from absolutely communal property to qualified individual property was taken when in-dividual Khūntkāttidārs came to hold specific portions of these cultivable village lands and called such lands their own and left them on their death to their own heirs. But even then, when the necessity arose, the community could take away a portion of the lands of one member who had too many plots and hand it over to another who had too little for his increasing requirements. Neither the Mānki nor the Mūndā nor the Pāhān has any superior right of property. The Mānki gets a small remuneration for his trouble in collecting the contributions (*chandas*, often misnamed "rent") from the different villages of the *patti* and taking them to the superior landlord. This remuneration is derived from the *chandas* payable by one of the villages of the *patti*. Such a village is called the *chaputa* village and the other villages of the *patti* are called *thakur* villages in the Sonepūr Paraganā, because it is out of the *chandas* collected from such villages that the dues of the superior landlord—the Thākur—are paid. Every Khūntkāttidar of an *Intact Khuntkatti* village has the right to reclaim any waste land within the village limits or take any jungle produce or timber he requires from the village jungles. Underground rights belong to the Khūntkātti community as a whole. Khūntkātti tenancies are inalienable except for certain purposes and under certain conditions and restrictions now laid down by law, and are heritable. The rent or *chanda* of old Mūndāri Khūntkātti tenancies can never be increased.

Broken Mundari Khuntkatti Villages : The first stage in the disintegration of the "Intact Khūntkātti" system may be seen in some villages of Pārganā Tāmār, where although the "Rājā" or superior landlord receives at the hands of the village Mūndā the quit-rent payable by the Khūntkātti village community, the "Rāja" has succeeded in getting hold of a few acres of land as his own share (*Raj-angs*) and named such land as the *Raj-has*. He has since either been in cultivating possession of the land or settled his own tenants on such land. When the "Rājā" or l'ikait of Tāmār began to lease out such villages, these "Raj-has" lands came to be excluded from the intermediate tenure, and the *parjas* settled by the Rājā on such lands began to pay rent direct to the "Rājā." In this respect, the history of Rāj-hās lands in Tāmār appears to differ somewhat from the villages in Nāgpūr *proper*.

Other Broken Mundari Khuntkatti Villages : The next stage in the breakdown of the original communal village system may be seen in those villages—also called *broken khuntkatti* villages— in which either an alien (Dikū) landlord or the village headman (Mūndā) himself, prompted by avarice has gradually arrogated to himself the proprietary rights in the village and thereby broken its communal nature. Either the superior landlord himself, or the Mūndā or a Zarpeshgidār (mortgagee) or a Nilāmdār (auction-purchaser) from him, began first by himself collecting the chāndās from the *parjas* ('etahoroko'), proceeded next to enhance the chāndās payable by the Khūntkāttidars, and lastly reduced most of the Khūntkāttidārs to the position of ordinary rayats. The Pahān's office was indispensable and his

Khūntkātti status could not, therefore, be interfered with. The near relatives of the Mūndā were reduced to the position of Bābūs, *i.e.*, Khorposhdārs or maintenance-holders. The rest of the fraternity gradually sank to the position of rāyats. Finally, the Mūndā assumed the control of the village jungles and waste lands.[1] The Khūntkātti brotherhood has lost its joint ownership of the entire village area, but each Khūntkāttidār only retains his proprietary rights over the old lands he cultivates. These lands form his individual "Mūndāri Khūntkātti" tenancy, for which he must pay his fixed *chāndā* (now practically "rent") direct to his new "landlord." Khūntkātti tenancies are heritable, and their rents can never be increased unless where a new tenancy has been created within twenty years prior to the date of the landlord's application for enhancement. Although the rights to jungle produce and jungle trees become more restricted than when the village was "intact," a Khūntkattidār of a "broken" village may reclaim any waste land he chooses. In the Parganā of Tāmār, we find a third class of "broken Khūntkātti" villages, which take us one step further in the disintegration of Khūntkātti system. In this class of "broken" villages, the "Rājā" or superior landlord, has introduced an intermediate landlord, probably originally called *Manjhi*.[2] The "Rājā" of Tamar remained the master of the block of lands he had first secured for himself as his "Rājhas" and his new lessee or intermediate landlord began to collect the *chandas* direct from each individual Khūntkāttidār, just as his lessor—the "Rājā"—used to do before he leased out the village.

---

[1] During the recent Settlement operations, where the descent of a tenant from the original founder of a Khuntkatti village could be traced, his Khuntkatti *status* was recorded and thus saved from future attacks. For an account of the breakdown of the Khuntkatti system *vide* the special memorandum prepared by the Rev, Father J. Hoffman, S.J., and Mr. E. Lister, I.C.S., and appended to Mr. Justice Carnduff's and also to Mr. J. Reid's editions of the Chota Nagpur Tenancy Act.

[2] It seems probable that some men of the Sarwak caste (known as Manjhis in the Ranchi District) were such original intermediate landlords and from them the name "Manjihas" or "Majihas" originated.

This intermediate landlord or "Mānjhi", too, soon began to cast
covetous eyes on the village lands and before long possessed
himself of some of these lands, probably held originally by some
of the *eta-haturenko* or *parjas* who used to hold them under one
or more of the Khūntkattidārs. These lands came to be called
the "Mānjihas" or "Māji-has" and became the privileged lands
of the lessee of the village. In this last class of "Broken Khūntkātti" villages we are landed almost on the threshold of the next
kind of Rānchi villages. The total area of "Broken Khūntkātti"
tenancies in the Rānchi District measures about 35 square miles.

Bhuinhari Villages : In the villages now known as the
Bhuinhari villages, the *Khuntkatti* system or even the very names
of "Khūntkātti" and "Khūntkāttidar" have been obliterated.
Only a few miserable fragments of the old *Khuntkatti* lands of
the original clearers of the soil have been left to their descendants
as privileged tenures, and these are called their "Bhūinhāri" lands.

The rest of the village lands have been absorbed mostly within
the "Rāj-has" and partly within the "Māji-has." The names
Rāj-has" and "Māji-has" no longer connote the same meaning
which we have seen them bear in the last class of "Broken Khūntkātti" villages in Tāmār. What is called *"Rāj-has" in the
Bhūinhari* and Zamindari villages are *known as prajāli lands in
Tāmār.* The "Raj-has" lands in the Bhūinhāri and purely
Zamindari villages have no longer, as in Tāmār, any concern
with the "Raja" or superior landlord, where there is an intermediate landlord over the village. But the rents collected from "Rajhas" lands in these villages are supposed to make up the superior
landlord's dues which, however, are generally satisfied with a
fraction only of the profits derived by the intermediate landlord
from these Raj-has lands. "Maji-has" lands, though originally
created only in villages in which the superior landlord introduced
a lessee under him, have since arisen even in villages in the direct
possession of the superior landlord. "Maji-has" lands in such
villages have been created by the latter for his own benefit partly
out of the "Raj-has" and partly out of old "Chūntkātti" or
Bhūinhari" lands of the descendants of the original settlers. The

"Raj-has" lands in most Bhūinhāri villages now cover the largest area of cultivable lands and are generally cultivated both by holders of Bhūinhāri lands and by other cultivators as ordinary rayats on cash rent or produce rent or both. The greater the disintegration of the ancient system in such a village, the larger has been the number of sub-divisions or classes of "Raj-has" lands in them. Thus, in the Mūndā country—the southern and eastern pārganās of the Rānchi District—the names "Raj-has," called 'pārjāli' or 'rayatāli' in parts of the Panch Pārganās, and "Kōrkar" (land reclaimed by the individual exertions of a tenant and held on privileged terms) only are known, and the name "Chhatisā" has just found its way in but a few villages, The various sub-divisions of the 'Rāj-has' named "Chhalisā," "Murli Chhatisa," Utakār," "Māswār," etc., with their varieties of incidents and liabilities, are widely used only in the purely Zamindāri villages and in such Bhūinhāri villages as are nearer the Mahārāja's seat, as for example, in thānās Mandār, Lāhārdāgā, etc. We shall describe these different sub-divisions of "Rajhas" lands when we come to the last class of villages.

Bhuinhari Tenures : Let us return now to the *Bhuinhari* tenures. These mark the final change from joint or communal ownership to individual ownership. When the old Khūntkātti or communal system was thoroughly broken down by the "Rājā" or the jāgirdār or the thikādār (lessee) or the auction purchaser or the Zarpeshgedār, and even the name of Khūntkātti was lost, portions of their ancestral lands were, either by way of compromise or owing to the new landlord's inability to grab them, left in the possession of the members of the original village community and named their "Bhūinhāri" lands. Originally, an aboriginal village community in the Rānchi District was divided into two khūnts or stirpes, as they are still so divided in the intact *khuntkatti* villages. These were the khūnt of the Pāhān or village priest called Naiga or Baiga in some parts and the khūnt of the Mūndā or secular headman of the village. In some villages, particularly in the western parganās, a sub-division of the Pāhān khūnt, known as she Pujār khūnt, has come into existence, probably from the real Pāhān having delegated his priestly duties to a junior branch of the family. An addition to the number of khūnts or stirpes in the Bhūinhāri and purely Zamindāri villages was in course of time made by the landlords themselves to safeguard their interests in the villages. This is the Mahāto khūnt which has in most villages been probably created out of the Mūndā khūnt.

In a Bhūinhāri village, these village officials have each been allotted specific lands for his services. But it is the *Mahatoi* land alone which is, properly speaking, a service land. The Mūndāi and Pāhānāi lands are generally practically hereditary as the offices of a Mūndā and a Pāhān too are ordinarily hereditary. It is only in a few Mūndā vlllages near the Urāon country and in a number of Urāon villages that the Pāhān's office is not hereditary. In such villages an election of a Pāhān and his assistants is made every three years from amongst the members of the Pāhān khūnt and in some villages even from amongst the Bhūinhārs in general, by certain well-recognised supposed supernatural processes.[1] We shall now describe each class of these privileged tenures in a Bhūinhāri village separately. The total area of *Bhuinhari* lands in the Rānchi District is now only 203 square miles.

(*1*) *Khunt Bhuinhari Lands*—These are the Bhūinhāri lands *proper*. Up till the recent survey and settlement of the District, the holders of such lands were generally required to render certain specified services called *bet-begar*. These services have now been commuted into cash payment. Besides services, quit-rents are also payable in most villages for such lands. These rents and services can never be enhanced on any account what-soever. The Khūnt Bhūinhāri lands are heritable. Up till the passing of the Bengal Act VI of 1908, these lands used to be trans-ferred, although it would seem that up till a recent period, in places where the older custom appertaining to communal lands had not died away, a transfer of such lands could not be made by an individual Bhūinhār without the consent of all the members of his *khunt*. As late as in November, 1880, in the Final Report of

---

[1] They are principally the *Sup* process and the *lorha* process.

the Bhūinhāri operations, published in the *Calcutta Gazette*, we are told : "Where the land of the Khūnt are held jointly or at least under the control of a single Head Bhūinhār, such right of transfer cannot be exercised unless the members of the Khūnt choose jointly to do so." But even this trace of the older communal character of the tenure finally disappeared and the share of an individual Bhūinhār, even in undivided Bhūinhāri lands, came to be freely transferred. Since November, 1908, only usufructuary mortgages and leases, not exceeding seven years, if in the *bhugut banda* form, and not exceeding five years in other cases, are permitted. Formerly, when a Bhūinhār died heirless or abandoned his Bhūinhāri lands, such lands were regarded as still the lands of his *khunt* or stirp, and the headman of the khūnt generally distributed the lands amongst such members ās had not enough lands with them. But it is now many years that the zamindārs, in a large number of Bhūinhāri villages, have been taking possession of such lands. In the same Government Report of 1880 we find the senior Bhūinhāri Commissioner, Mr. R. D. Hāldār, writing : "We find instances of lands held by subordinate Bhūinhārs who have left the country for good, retained within the *khunt*, another member taking the place of the one who is absent. But this occurs where the Bhūinhārs muster strong. In the majority of cases, however, where the Bhūinhār leaves his village, the zamindār takes forcible possession of his lands, and does not allow a Buūinhār about to leave his home to sell or mortgage his lands for his own benefit. This is regarded as a great hardship. . . The tenures registered at so much public cost should be made as secure as possible, and the greatest obstacles should be placed by rules in the way of assessing them as rāj.has."

(2) *Bhutkheta Lands.* These constitute the second class of Bhūinhāri lands and are of three kinds :

(*a*) The *Bhuinhari Bhutkheta* or private *Bhutkheta* lands. These are included within the Bhūinhāri lands of a particular khūnt. Each khūnt may have its separate Bhūinhāri Bhūtkhetā. The members of one khūnt can have no rights to the Bhūinhāri Buūtkhetā of another khūnt. No rent or begāri is due for such lands. As a former Commissioner of Chotanagpur, Colonel Dalton, ruled,—"such lands are like the Debottar . . . lands of the Hindus, and cannot be alienated." The reason the aborigines assign for the non-saleability of such lands is that in the event of the land passing into the hands of an alien, the *bhut* will not be worshipped and calamity will befall the khūnt. Since November, 1908, non-alienability except under specified restrictions and conditions is an incident of all Bhuinhari tenures.

(*b*)   *The Gaoro or Mardana Bhutkheta*. This class of Bhūtkhetā is found only in some Urāon villages. The land is considered to be the property of the aboriginal village community and is settled periodically by the village headmen with different rāyats who each pay a small rent with which the expenses of the periodical pūjās and feasting are met. The landlord receives no rent for such lands. The name *gaoro* indicates the communal character of such lands and the name *mardana* (male) is applied because only men and no women can take part in the pūjā or the feast.

(*c*)   *The Deswali or Public Bhutkheta*. This land is cultivated either by the Pāhān or village priest himself or by rāyats who have to pay him rent for it. The income derived from this class of Bhūtkhetā land is spent on a grand triennial festival in honour of Desāuli Bōngā. The village landlord receives no rent for such lands.

(*d*)   *The Andher Bhutkheta*. This is found only in a few Urāon villages. The fields are devoted to certain spirits mysteriously imported there by the *ojha* or ghost-finder when a village is visited by some calamity.

(3)   *The Pahanai Lands*. These are the lands held by the Pāhān or village priest, called Baigā in some villages, and include also the service lands of the Pāhān's assistants. These latter bear different names in different villages. We give below the principal divisions of 'Pāhānāi' lands.

(*a*)   *The Dalikatari* : This is the Pāhānāi land proper, enjoyed by the Pāhān himself for his priestly services to the village community. No alienation of such land by the Pāhān beyond the term of his Pāhānship is binding on his successors. The land is said to be so named from the branch (*dali*) of a *karam* tree *cut* and planted on the occasion of the Karam festival.

(b) The Panbhara Land : This is the service land of the Pānbhara (called *tahalu* in some Urāon villages) whose duty it is to supply water for the *pujas*. Other service lands allied to the Pānbhara lands are found in certain Urāon villages. Such are the *Susari-khet, the Sup-kheta*, and the *Murgipakowa* lands.

(4) *The Mundai* : The Mūndāi lands of a village are held rent-free by the village-Mūndā. The landlord, it appears, has no right to take possession of such lands—at least so long as there is a member of the Mūndā Khūnt alive in the village. Ordinarily, the office of the Mūndā is hereditary.

(5) *The Mahatoi* : This is the service land of the Māhtō. It is held rent-free. The landlord, in some instances, has been known to dismiss a Māhtō for absolute neglect of duty. But when there is a Māhtō Khūnt in the village, the new Māhtō must, according to custom, be appointed from among the members of the Māhtō Khūnt, and the Māhtōi land will go to such newly-appointed Māhtō.

Maji-has Lands : In most of the villages of Rānchi District in which *Bhuinhari* lands were demarcated and registered under the Bengal Act II of 1869, the landlords were found to have been in possession of privileged private lands called *Manji-has* or *Maji-has*. In such lands a rāyat cannot now acquire a right of occupancy even though they are settled with him on cash rent and for an indefinite term. The total area of *Maji-has* lands within the district including Betkhetā lands described below is 89 square miles or 56,904 acres. In many villages where "landlords' privileged lands" were not demarcated under the Bengal Act II of 1869 the landlords have somehow managed to get hold of some lands as their private demesne. The landlords hold 65 square miles of such undemarcated 'Zirat' lands within the District. And the total area of non-privileged *Nij-jote* or *khas* lands of the Rānchi zamindars is 251 square miles.

Betkheta Lands : These lands are now considered as privileged lands of the landlords. Unlike Rāj-has lands, no right of occupancy can accrue to such lands. They are given to rāyats free of rent on condition of their performing certain services to the landlord. The principal services required is the cultivation of the landlord's *maji-has* land for him. The landlord can resume such lands whenever he chooses to dispense with the customary services in the future. In some villages, however, where we find a very large area of *Betkheta* lands with a very small area of *Manji-has* lands, the so-called "Betkheta" lands would appear to have been originally granted in lieu of services rendered in the past and not on condition of rendering services in the future. This second class of *Betkheta* lands should be properly classed as *Raj-has* lands, as by local custom all the incidents of 'rāj-has' lands attach to such lands, although the law appears to have ignored the distinction.

Purely Zamindari Villages : We now come to the last class of Rānchi villages in which either by reason of their recent establishment the old communal system of land-holding never existed, or the old khūntkātti community died away or were long ago obliged to abandon the village leaving no trace behind except their time-worn tombstones. In these villages, not many in number, the landlord is the absolute master, subject only to such rights in others and liabilities on his own part as have been created by contract, custom or law. In most of such villages we find all the various sub-divisions of the *Raj-has,* some or others of which we meet with in the several Bhūinhāri villages in the Urāon country and in the portion of the Munda country adjoining the Urāon. These "Pure Zamindari" villages are to be met with mostly in the western and north-western parts of the district. Except 'the lands in the *khas* possession of the landlord and those given by him to servants, and lands given as *betkheta* to tenants in consideration of *bet-begari,* all lands of such villages are rent-paying. Of these rent-paying lands the whole with the negligible exception of 14 square miles [1] of non-

─────────

[1] Of these only 5 square miles are within the Chotanagpur Estate and 4 square miles within the Pachete Zamindari.

Mūndāri Khūntkātti tenancies is in the whole District, is known as *Raj-has* (the same as the *Parjai* or *Parjali* of Tāmār Pārganā) and are mainly divided into the following classes :

(i) *Chhatisa* : This is the principal class of Rāj-has lands and, originally, it would seem, the only class of such lands besides *Korkar*. A quantity of *don* or wet rice field with a proportionate area of complementary (*lagan*) upland or *danr* make up each *chhatisa* holding. In the more jungly parts of the District the area of *langan-danr* or complementary upland was up till the recent survey and settlement operations altogether indefinite. In some villages two *poas* of *don* and in a very few three *poas* go to make up one *poa chhatisa*. The chief *poa* is called the *matha* or the head, the second the *latha* or the feet, and the third the *majhia* or the middle. *Chhatisa don* lands pay higher rent than other sub-divisions of "Rāj-has" lands and generally also pay certain produce rents called *rakumats*, because no separate rent is assessed on *danr* lands that go along with *chhatisa don* lands. The name is said to have been derived from the word (*chhatis*) *thirty-six*, as, it is said, the *chhatisa* tenant had formerly to obey "thirty-six" (*i.e.*, numerous, and not literally *thirty-six*), orders of the landlord.

(ii) *Korkar Lands*—Amongst Rāj-has lands, this class carries the greatest privileges. As *khuntkatti* lands were originally prepared in the jungles by the exertions of a *khunt* or village family, so *korkar* lands are prepared in beds of streams or out of waste lands by the exertions of an individual cultivator in villages other than 'Intāct Khūntkātti' ones. A right of occupancy accrues to such lands as soon as they are prepared. No rent is payable for the first few years (varying in different villages generally from three to five years), after which half *chhatisa* rates are imposed. In the Pānch Pārganās these lands are called "Bahbāla" lands.

(iii) *Murli Chhatisa*—These are *don* lands without any appendage of *lagan* (complementary) *danrs*. One *poa* of *murli chhatisa* contains nothing more than one *poa* of *don* land alone. No *rakumats* or payments in kind are realisable for such lands. This class of lands would seem to have arisen when, in course of time, some zamindars grew zealous of the large area of complimentary 'tānrs' held by tenants. In the struggle that ensued, some of the best 'dōn' lands which could afford to spare their complimentary 'tānr' lands were disvested of their appendage of *lāgān dānr* lands, came to be called *murli chhatisa*.

(iv) *Uttakar* or *Balkat* : Originally these lands, it is sometimes said, were of the nature of *utbandi* tenures of Lower Bengal, the tenant paying rent (*kar*) for it for the year in which he raised (*uthao*) any crops (*bal*) on it and no rent for the year in which it was left fallow. In the beginning these *lands* would seem to have been complimentary *tanr* lands for which grasping landlords succeeded in realising rent (*kar*) in years in which they were under cultivation. Finally, when these lands were converted into rice fields they were permanently assessed to rent. Nowadays these lands are generally in continuous cultivation, but, even if left fallow in any particular year, no remission of any sort is any longer made for that year. *Uttakar* lands are now *don* lands inferior in quality to *Chhatisa don* lands and have no complement of *lagan danr* or attached uplands. These are assessed to rent at much lower rates than *chhatisa* lands (generally at half and some-times two-thirds the *chhatisa* rates). The fact that in some villages we now meet with *Uttakar* but no *Korkar* lands, and that the *Uttakar* lands are almost always the worst class of *don* lands would seem to show that they were originally *tānr* lands which were converted into *don* (korkar) lands by the tenants holding them. *Uttakar* lands, like *murli chhatisa* lands, are the results of a similar struggle, and, as such, are met with in some villages only.

(v) *Maswan Danr Lands* : These are uplands held in excess of the complementary *lagan-danr* lands of the tenant. This class, it appears, arose even later than *Murli chhatisa* and *uttakar* lands ; and in some parts of the District, the name is yet unknown. For such *danr* lands, rent in kind equal to the quantity of seed-grains sown has to be paid. In parts of the Pānch Pārganās these lands are called "Khor" lands. When money rent is payable for such excess *danr* lands, they come to be called *damgat danr* lands.

Such is a rough outline of the history, and the present condition of the Land Tenures of the Rānchi District. The

different degrees of success attained by the Rājā and his Jāgirdārs
and Thikādārs in various parts of the district in their endeavours
to break down the old communal system are marked by the
different classes of villages and their various land tenures
described above. How great has been the success the Rājā
(now Mahārājā) and his Jāgirdārs and Thikādārs achieved in
revolutionising the old land system of the country may be judged
from the fact that out of a total area of 3,614 square miles of
cultivated lands in the Rānchi District only 188 square miles are
now held by Mundas as Khūntkātti lands, 14 square miles as other
Khūntkātti lands, and as little as 203 square miles as Bhūinhāri
lands. These 405 square miles are the only remnants of the
original form of landholding in the District. Of the rest, by a
curious coincidence, just the same area—namely, 405 square
miles—are in the direct possession of the Rājā and his Jāgirdārs
and Thikādārs, or their transferees, as their *Majhi-has, nijjote*
and "landlords' privileged lands." The remainder (2,804 square
miles) forming the bulk (about $\frac{7}{9}$ths) of the total cultivable lands
of the District now constitute *Raj-has* lands. Out of this, 2,469
square miles are held by settled rāyats and occupancy rāyats,
223 square miles by non-occupancy rāyats, 56 square miles by
rāyats holding rent-free lands and 56 square miles by rāyats
paying only produce rents.

Thus, from the communal system of "Intact Khūntkātti"
villages in which the village community is the exclusive proprietor
of all lands inside its limits, subject only to the payment of a quit
rent to the Rājā or other landlord, down to the purely zamindāri
village in which the landlord has now the actual proprietary
right subject to the maintenance of all existing subordinate
interests in land, we have in the Rānchi District every successive
grade of rights in land arising out of the disintegration of the
primitive aboriginal village communes. The record of existing
rights for every village in the District recently prepared by the
Government at a great expense will, it is fervently hoped,
effectively arrest further disintegration, and bring about more
friendly relations between landlord and tenant in the district.

It is to be hoped that both the landlord and the tenant will henceforth ungrudgingly give each other his just dues, and each respect the other's recorded rights. And, finally, we appeal to both that they should cease any longer to fritter away their energies and substance in useless quarrels and ruinous litigation, and henceforth co-operate to improve the material condition of their country, ever remembering that :

> The interest of the rich man and the poor,
> Are one and the same, inseparable evermore.

APPENDIX IV

EPOCHS AND DATES, OR A CHRONOLO-GICAL SUMMARY OF THE HISTORY OF THE RANCHI DISTRICT

I.—PRE-BRITISH ERA

(i) Hindu Period

Circa **6th Century B.C.** : The Mūndās settle in Chotānāgpūr.

4th Century A.D. : Emperor Samudra Gupta of Magadha marches through the country in his southern expedition.

Circa **5th Century A.D.** : The advent of the first Nāgbansi Rājā.

(ii) Mahomedan Period

Circa **1510 A.D.** : Sher Shah sends an expedition against the Rājā of Jhārkhand (Chotānāgpūr ?) to secure the possession of an elephant named 'Syam Chandra.'*

1585 : An expedition sent by Akbar's general Shāhābaz Khān reduces the Raja to the position of a tributary of the Emperor of Delhi.

Circa **1616** : Jehāngir sends Ibrāhim Khān to invade (Chotā) Nāgpūr. The Rāja is defeated, captured, and incarcerated in the Gwalior fort.

1628 : The Rājā returns to his country with the title of Shāh or Shāhi and thenceforward styles himself Mahārājā.

1632 : Shājāhān grants Pālāmaū including (Chōtā) Nāgpūr as a Jāgir to the Subādār of Pātnā on an annual rental of Rs. 1,36,000.

Circa **1686.** : This revenue is raised to Rs 1,61,000, "Koira Orissa or Nāgpūr with Karanpur or Badaun being rated at Rs. 40,505."

* This is said to be mentioned in a manuscript chronicle attributed to Ahmad Yadgar. We are indebted for this information to **T. S. Macpherson,** Esq., M A., I.C.S.

1724 : The Sūbādār of Pātnā marches against the Rājā of (Chotā) Nāgpūr, and returns with a large *nazarana* in cash and diamonds.

1731 : The Sūbādār of Pātnā marches against the Nāgpūr Rājā again, and compromises his claims by receiving Rs. 12,000 from the Ghātwāl (Rājā) of Rāmgarh on account of the Nāgpūr Rājā. And thus from this time until 1771, the Chōtānāgpūr Rājā had to pay his tribute through the Rājā of Rāmgarh (now, of Padmā) who had before been his vassal.

II. BRITISH ERA

(i) Mokhareji Period

[1765—1770]

1765 : Chōtānāgpūr passes to the East India Company as part of the Diwāni of Behār of which it is shown as a 'mokhareji' (dismembered) *mechal* in the *jamabandi* (Revenue return) prepared by Mahomed Rezā Khān on behalf of the Company.

1770 : Captain John Camac, the first British Agent enters Chōtānāgpūr.

(ii) Period of Military Collectorship

[1771—1779]

1771 : First settlement of revenue is made direct with the Rājā of Chōtānāgpūr for a term of 3 years by Captain Camac who is stationed at Chātrā as the 'Military Collector of district Ramgarh' directly under the Governor at Fort William.

1774 : The Military Collector is placed under the Governor *and his Council*, and not under any of the six Provincial Revenue Councils.

1777 : From 1777 to 1788, yearly settlements are made with the Rājā of Nāgpūr.

[**Social condition.** With frequent incursions of the Marhattas, repeated risings of the aboriginal population, occasional raids by the Larka Kols of Singbhum, and incessant hostilities between rival jagirdars, the country was in a most distracted condition during this and the preceding period ; and a more effective form of administration was deemed necessary]

(iii) Ramgarh Regulation District Period
[1779—1833]

1779, June 7 : A Munsiff is first appointed and stationed at Chātrā. [The first Munsiff was Kazi Golam Moiuddin]

1780 : The District of Rāmgarh or Chātrā (which included Chotānāgpūr proper) is placed as a regular *Zilla* under a Judge-Magistrate-Collector.

[As *Judge* this officer remains under the appellate jurisdiction of the Governor-General up till 1793, and after that under the Provincial Court of Civil Appeal at Patna. As *Magistrate,* he is subordinate to the Patna Court of Circuit and to the Nizamat Adalat at Calcutta. As *Collector,* he is placed under the Committee (styled 'Board' since 1786) of Revenue at Calcutta.]

1781, April 6, and July 5 : Regulations for the administration of justice are passed for the regular *zillas* including zillā Chittrā or Rāmgarh.

1789 : The settlement of revenue with the Rājā of (Chōtā) Nāgpūr is extended for a term of ten years, after which (in 1799) it is held to be permanent.

1793 : Major Farmer compels the Rājās of Būndū and Rāhe to give *kabuliats* to the Nāgpūr Rājā.

1793 : A junior covenanted civil servant is appointed Register (Registrar) of the Judge-Magistrate-Collector to assist him in his judicial work ; a Hindu Law Officer is appointed to expound the *Shastras* and a Mahomedan Law Officer to expound the *Koran*.

1794 : Regulation IV of 1794 exempts the Behār portion of zillā Rāmgarh from the operation of the rules regarding 'pātwāris' and delivery of pāttās.

1799, April : The post of Collector is separated from that of Judge-Magistrate in Rāmgarh.

1800, April : The post of Collector of Rāmgarh is abolished, and the Collector of Behār (Gaya) is placed in charge of the Revenue Administration of zillā Rāmgarh as well.

1808 : Captain Roughsedge marches into (Chotā) Nāgpūr to reduce the Rājā to a proper state of subjection. The Rājā's evil genius, Déwan Dindayal, flies to Calcutta where he is arrested. The Rājā submits and his disputes with his brothers are settled.

1809, June 4 : Six (Zamindari) Police Thānās are for the first time established in (Chotā) Nāgpur.

1809 : Mr. Richard Walpole is deputed to Chātrā as the first Assistant Collector of Behar at Rāmgarh.

1816, June : The Assistant Collector at Rāmgarh is directed to correspond directly with the Board of Revenue instead of through the Collector of Behār.

1817 : The Collectorate of Rāmgarh is removed from the jurisdiction of the Calcutta Board of Revenue and placed under the Behar-Benares Board of Commissioners (styled, since 1822 the Board of Revenue, Central Provinces).

1819, January : Major Roughsedge is appointed "Political Agent to the Government in South Behar, &c."

1819, April : The Rājā of Chotānāgpūr is divested of the charge of the police pending the enquiry into the case of the murder of a suspected witch (Adhur Dye) and her family.

1819, May : The Chotā (Nāgpūr) police is temporarily placed under a new officer (Mahomed Uzeem) styled the Superintendent of Police.

1823 : The Rājā is deprived of excise collections which Collector Nathaniel Smith now farms out for Rs. 6,500.

1824 : A tax on *hanria* (rice-beer) is imposed, and begins to cause discontent.

1825 : Two other Munsiffs are appointed in the district, one for Lohārdāgā and another for Lesliegunj.

1826 : A Pandit Adālat and a Moulvi Adālat are established in the District. [These two Courts had concurrent jurisdiction : they tried civil suits, heard appeals from the decisions of the Munsiffs and were subject, like the Register, to the appellate jurisdiction of the Judge.]

1826, September 26 : The Vice-President in Council passes a resolution prohibiting the collection of tax on *hānriā* prepared for private consumption.

1828 : A fourth Munsiff is appointed in the District and stationed at Būndū.

1831 : Insurrection of the Kols breaks out. Captain Wilkinson (Officiating Political Agent at Hāzaribagh) and Mr. Cuthbert (Judge-Magistrate of Rāmgarh) are appointed "Joint Commissioners for the affairs of Parganā Chotanāgpūr."

1833 : The tax on *hanria* is entirely abolished.

1833 : Zilla Rāmgarh is broken up, the South Western Frontier Agency is established under Regulation No. XIII of 1833, and the ordinary Regulations are withdrawn. (Five short rules are passed in December, 1833, for the guidance of the Agent and his subordinates).

[**Social Condition :** The country was never so full of turmoil as during this period. With frequent inroads of the Marhāttās (at times fearfully devastating such as in 1798 and 1803), bitter hostilities between rival Jāgirdārs (as in Parganā Udaipūr, 1806-8, in Parganā Nawāgarh, 1812-18), and invasions from without (such as those of Parganā Borway by the Rājā of Surguja in 1793, 1795, 1798, and 1801), the country was in a most distracted condition. The worst of all evils were, however, the ceaseless aggressions against the ancient landed rights of the aboriginal population which led to repeated insurrections, the most serious of which were—the rising of the Mūndās of Parganā Tāmār (June and July, 1789) who repulsed the troops led against them by Captain Hagan but were finally put down by Captain Cooper ; the rising of the Tāmar Mūndas under Bishun Manki in 1797 ; the rising, in 1807, of 5,000 Mūndas of the same Pargana under Dakhin or Dukan Shahi Manki (who was with difficulty captured by Captain Roughsedge in March, 1808) ; the Mūnda revolts in Parganas Rahe and Silli from 1796 to 1798 which could only be quelled by Lieutenant Welsh after several difficult engagements ; fresh disturbances in Rahe in 1812, the more formidable disturbances under Rudu and Konta Mūnda (1819-1820), quelled by Lieutenant Billu ; and the most formidable of all insurrections—that of the Sōnepūr Mūndas in

1831·32. These led to a thorough administrative change, and the S. W. F. Agency with its headquarters in the heart of (Chōta) Nagpūr was established.]

(iv) The South-Western Frontier Agency Period
[1834 -- 1854]

1834, Jan. 15 : Captain Wilkinson assumes charge as the first Governor-General's Agent for the South-West Frontier Agency, with his civil headquarters at Kishenpur (Ranchi) and a military cantonment at Dōranda. Lieutenant Ouseley is appointed Principal Assistant to the Agent, for Lohardaga, two Mūnsiffs are appointed—one for Lohardaga and another for Kishenpur.

1834, Feb. : Government approves of the arrangements proposed by Captain Wilkinson regarding the respective jurisdictions of officers, and sanctions a set of rules for criminal justice.

1837, May : The Agent issues to his Assistants 31 'Rules' for administration of civil justice. [Although the general Regulations were withdrawn from the Agency, the Courts ordinarily acted up to the spirit of the Regulations except where the Agent by any circular or special orders directed any particular Regulation to be disregarded. Such were the orders directing the enforcement of the customary law of *primogeniture* in place of the Bātwārā Regulations, the orders of September 26, 1842, discontinuing enforcement of *interest* on loans under certain conditions, and the rules prohibiting *sales of lands* in execution of decrees and allowing 'equitable adjustment of debts' by official management of "attached estates."]

1837, June 6 : Government by its letter No. 615, approves of the 31 rules.

1842, Sept. 27 : Government orders the removal of the headquarters of the Principal Assistant from Lohārdāgā to Kishenpur (actually removed in 1843).

1843, Nov. 13 : The post of Deputy Commissioner (corresponding to the present post of Judicial Commissioner) is created with jurisdiction to try all Sessions Cases, hear criminal appeals and civil appeals and ciril appeals and try original civil suits.

1843, Nov. : The German Lutheran Mission is established at Ranchi.

1845, Nov. : A principal Sadar Amin is appointed for Hāzāribāgh and Lohārdāgā Divisions, and is stationed at Hāzāri-bāgh. [This officer is given concurrent jurisdiction with the principal Assistants.]

1853. The principal Sadar Amin's Court is removed to Gola.

1853. The Parganā of Palāmau is constituted as a sub-division with headquarters at Korndā, under an Assistant to the Agent. [Of the 7 Government Police Thanas in the Lohardāgā district, and 10 Zamindari thānās, four of the former and one oi the latter go to the Korndā sub-division.

[**Social Condition.** Although on the establishment of courts of justice and a Military Cantonment in their midst, the jagirdars and thikadars became less openly turbulent than before and generally referred their mutual disputes to the British tribu-nals, they continued their campaign against their aboriginal peasant-proprietors steadily though silently. As Colonel Dalton wrote in 1871, "it was then that the greatest disturbance of peasant proprietary tenure occurred."]

(V) The Period of Commissionership
[1854-1912]

1854 : By Act XX of 1854, the districts of the Agency are formed into a Non-Regulation Division under a Commissioner. [The Agent becomes the Commissioner, the Principal Assistant Agents become Principal Assistant Commissioners. Other Assistant Agents become Senior Assistant Commissioners]. The 31 rules approved by the Government in its No. 615 of 6th June, 1837, remain the law of the Division till they are gradually limited by the operation of legislative enactments.

1857 : The Sepoy Mutiny breaks out.

1858 : The Commissioner issues a set of rules and a calendar for the use of the Zamindāri police.

1859, June 15 : The Civil Procedure Code (Act VIII of 1859) is extended to Chōtānāgpūr with a proviso that "no sale of immovable property shall take place without the sanction of the Commissioner." [The same proviso is also contained in the notification of June 27,1878, which extended the C. P. C. Code (Act X) of 1877].

1859, Aug. 28 : The Board of Revenue decline to recommend the introduction of Act X of 1859 as proposed by the Commissioner, but suggest the modification of the existing procedure in accordance with the spirit of the Act. [Accordingly the old Regulations are dropped in favour of Act X, but the provisions of Act X (Ss. 112-145) as to 'distraint' are not acted upon in the Lohardaga District, and the provisions (Ss. 105-111) as to the sale of lands in execution of rent decrees are exercised with the previous sanction of the Commissioner in each case.

1861, May 1 : The designation of 'Deputy Commissioner' is changed into 'Judicial Commissioner' and of 'Principal Assistants' into 'Deputy Commissioners,' and of 'Sub-Assistant Commissioners' into 'Extra Assistant Commissioners.'

1862, Dec. 26 : The Criminal Procedure Code (Act XXV of 1861) is extended to Chotanagpūr.

1863 : All the Zamindari Thanas are entirely occupied by the new constabulary under Act V of 1861.

1868 : All Deputy Commissioners in Chotānagpūr are vested with the powers of Subordinate Judges, as also all Assistant or Extra Assistant Commissioners who passed the first standard of examination ; all Assistant and Extra Assistant Commissoners who passed the second standard are vested with the powers of Munsiffs.

1869, April : The Anglican Mission is established at Rānchi. The Rānchi Municipality is constituted.

1872, July 26 : The Chotānagpūr Tenures Act is passed.

1875 : The Government of India formally recognises the title of Mahārājā as hereditary in the Chōtānāgpur Rāj family.

1875 : The posts of Extra Assistant Commissioners are amalgamated with Deputy Magistracies.

1876 : The Chōtānāgpūr Encumbered Estates Act is passed. [This Act is the natural successor of the old systems of "Attachēd

Estates" and "Equitable Adjustment of Debts." It has been amended by Bengal Act III of 1900, but there seems to be hardly any justification for its existence now].

1879 : Bengal Act I of 1879 is passed as the Rent Law for the district.

1881 : The Secretary of State sanctions the substitution of Assistant Commissioners by Assistant Magistrates and Joint Magistrates. The Government issues notifications under Section 3 of the Scheduled Districts Act, extending a large number of enactments of the Supreme Council and of the Bengal Council to the Lōhārdāgā District.

1882, June 3 : The restriction on sale of lands in execution of decrees under the Civil Procedure Code is modified by allowing the Commissioner of the Division merely the right to for bid the sale of any estate or part of an estate. [Even this power of vetoing sales has been withdrawn by the C.P.C. Code of 1908].

1888, Nov. 7 : Free home-brewing of 'Pachwāi' to the extent of 4 seers is granted to the aboriginal tribes of the District. [This restriction as to quantity is withdrawn by the Board on April 18, 1889.]

1888 : A Municipality is constituted in the town of Lōhārdāgā.

1889-1890 : Agrarian disturbances occur in the western parganās of the district.

1891 : A special Subordinate Judge is appointed for the districts of Hazaribāgh and Lōhārdāgā, with his headquarters at Rānchi.

1892 : The sub-division of Palāmau together with Pargana Tori is formed into a separate District.

1897 : The Chotānāgpur Commutation Act is passed.

1899, Jan. : The name of the district is changed from 'Lōhardaga' to 'Ranchi.'

1899-1900 : The Birsaite revolt.

1900, April, 1 : The Ranchi District Board is constituted to supersede the old Road Cess Committee.

1902 : The Gumla Sub-division is opened. Survey and Settlement operations commence.

1903 : Act I of 1879 and Act IV of 1897 are amended by Bengal Act V of 1903.

1905 : The Mūnda Sub-division with its headquarters at Khūnti is opened.

1908 : Act VI (B. C.) of 1908 (Law of Landlord and Tenant) is passed.

1911 : All Mūnsiffs in Chotanagpūr are vested with the powers of Deputy Collectors under Act VI (B. C. of 1908.)

1912, Dec. 12 : A Royal Proclamation at Delhi announces that a new Lieutenant-Governorship-in-Council will be formed to administer the areas of Bihar, Orissa and Chōtanagpur.

[**Social Condition** : From the beginning of this epoch the struggle between the aborigines and their superior landlords became more marked than in the preceding period. Violent manifestations of discontent culminating in the Birsaite revolt of 1899-1900 brought into prominence the many crying grievances of the people. And the Government, ever ready to uphold the just rights of all classes of its subjects, adopted several measures with a view to settling long-standing disputes and bringing abiding peace to the district].

INDEX

Agriculture, 214, 215, 219, 224-228, 230 ; agrarian disturbanes of 189-90, 187 ; agricultural implements, 214,215,227; crops, 223-25, operations involved in, 226-28, harvesting, 227, 228, threshing, 228, watching, 229, weeding, 227

Ahir Kanee, 137

Ain-Akbari, 102

Aitareya Brahmana, 15, 16 ; reference to Dasyu tribes in, 15

Ali, Golam, 137

Allen, W. J., 130

Anglican Mission, 152

Aryans, 13-15, 17, 20n, 30, 31 ; conflict with the aborigines of India, 13-15, 17 ; immigration into India, 13, 20n, 30, 31, controversy over period of Aryan immigration, 13, 20n, 30, 31

Asura (tribe), 14n, 21, 24, 32, 33, 59, 78, 79, 228 ; reference in ancient Hindu scriptures, 14n

Azamgarh, 5, 24, 31-33, 331 ; also Azimgarh ; early abode of Mundas at, 31 ; in Munda legends, 24

Baker, Edward, 201

Ball, discovery of ancient sites of human settlements in India, 10

Baraiks, 91

Batsch, F., 132, 144, 145

Batsch, H, 144, 145

Bayley, Steuart, 171-73 ; on the antagonism between landlords and ryots, 173

Beechang, Captain, discovery of

ancient sites of human settlements in India, 10

Begari, 122, 143, 366 ; system of *bets-begāri*, 143

Beglar, 56

Bengal Act of 1869, 94, 95, 365 ; Bhuinhari settlement under, 94, 95 ; Act V of 1903, 197, 319 ; Act VI of 1908, 319

Bengal Government Resolution, of 25th November 1880, 113, 114

Bengal Regulations, 105

Bengal Rent Act, 1859, 167

Bhaivas (Jagirdars), 91

Bhar (tribe), 47-49

Bhāyād, 261, 264, 265

Bhils, 31, 36n, 40, 47n

Bhimcoran, Raja, 90n

Bhūnihāri land tenure, 92, 94, 95, 156, 165-67, 360-64 ; Under Bengal Act II of 1869, 156

Bhuinyas (tribe), 31

Bhumijes, 31, 228, 230, 231

Binrai, 114, 118

Biree family, 90n

Birjias (tribe), 59

Birsa Munda, 188-95 ; arrest of, 191 ; propagation of new faith by, 188-90 ; revolt by the Birsaites, 192-96 ; rise to popularity, 188-91

Birsaite Rebellion, 192-96

Bjornstjema, Count, on the date of Aryan immigration into India, 20n

Blochmann, 83

Blunt, on the causes of the insurrection of 1832, 120, 121

381

Hazaribagh and Lohardugga Rural
Police Act, 167

Heeren, 33

Hindu, impact on Munda land
system, 97 ; settler in Munda
country, 96, 143

Hinduism, cosmogonic legend in
Hindu scriptures, 4 ; impact on
Munda culture, 3, 4, 85, 86, 97-
100, 203, 212, 218, 219, 238, 243,
249, 260, 269, 271, 273, 274, 341 ;
Vaishnavite influence. 97, 98 ;
reference to Asur tribes in ancient
scriptures of, 14n. to black
aborigines, 14-18, 21, 23, 24,
27-29 ; 36-28, 44

Hiuen Tsang, 19, 57

Hoffmann, J. Father, 169n, 183-85,
191, 196, 167, 284 ; establishment
of Chotanagpur Catholic Coopera
tive Credit Society, 184 ; Mundari
grammar of, 169n

Hos, 31, 70, 115, 230 ; role in the
insurrection of 1832, 114

Hunter, William, 55n, 138

Hwen Thsang, 48n

Hyde, H. B., Venerable, on Catholic
Missions in India, 186

Impey Captain, 116

India,
    institution of individual marriage
    among Mundas, 29 ; Kolarian
    aborigines of, 1, 2 ; Munda popu-
    lation in, 205, 206 ; physical
    features of Kolarian tribes, 2, 209,
    210 ; sites of ancient human settle-
    ments in, 10, 12, 27 ; weapons of
    the aborigines, 29

Insurrections (Munda) Insurrection of 1794 in Tamar, 106, rising
of 1811, 106 ; insurrection of 1832,

114-21, causes of, 113-15, 120, 121,
description in Munda literature,
117, leaders of the insurrection of
1832, 114

Irish Christian Brothers, 187

Jacobi, on the date of Aryan immigration into India, 20n

Jagirdars, 77, 91, 94, 96, 107, 112,
131, 156, 368 ; denominations of,
91 ; general resentment against,
113 ; oppression of, 131, 156 ; rise
in the powers of, 91, 92, 94,
95, 107

Janke, H., 132

Jelinghans, Herr, on Kolarian
tribes, 17n

Jones, William, 33n 354

Juangs (tribe), 13, 26n, 31 ; habitat
of, 13

Judiciary, 143, 144 Sudder Court 144

Kalang ancient Munda patriarch, 36

Kalinjar, 35, 36, 38, ancient history
of 35

Kambu Shabaz Khan, 83

Karma puja 98, 99

Kate Sarder 114, 118

Kean R, on Munda insurgency of
1832, 116

Khan, Aliverdi, 88

Khan, Amir Ali, 137

Khan, Jafar Ali, 115

Khan Kale, 115

Khan Saifullah, 115

Khanda Pator, 118

Khangars, 35, 228

Kharia, 70, 146, 169, 228, 230 ;
conversion to christianity, 169

Kharwars (tribe) 11, 59

Khasis (tribe) 9, 13

Khorposhdars, 107, 359